AHMANSON · MURPHY
FINE ARTS IMPRINT

THE AHMANSON FOUNDATION
has endowed this imprint
to honor the memory of
FRANKLIN D. MURPHY
who for half a century
served arts and letters,
beauty and learning, in
equal measure by shaping
with a brilliant devotion
those institutions upon
which they rely.

The publisher gratefully acknowledges
the generous contribution to this book provided
by the Art Endowment Fund of the University of
California Press Associates, which is supported by
a major gift from the Ahmanson Foundation.

Postmodernism and the Postsocialist Condition

Postmodernism and the Postsocialist Condition

Politicized Art under Late Socialism

Edited by Aleš Erjavec

WITH A FOREWORD BY Martin Jay

AND CONTRIBUTIONS BY

Boris Groys

Miško Šuvaković

Aleš Erjavec

Péter György

Gerardo Mosquera

Gao Minglu

UNIVERSITY OF CALIFORNIA PRESS

BERKELEY / LOS ANGELES / LONDON

University of California Press
Berkeley and Los Angeles, California

University of California Press, Ltd.
London, England

Library of Congress Cataloging-in-Publication Data

Erjavec, Aleš, 1951–.
Postmodernism and the postsocialist condition : politicized art under late socialism / edited by Aleš Erjavec ; with a foreword by Martin Jay and contributions by Boris Groys . . . [et al.].
p. cm.
Includes bibliographical references and index.
ISBN 0-520-23334-4 (alk. paper)
1. Postmodernism. 2. Socialism and art. 3. Art—Political aspects. I. Erjavec, Aleš. II. Grois, Boris.

N6494.P66 P684 2003
709'.171'709049—dc21 2002027173

Manufactured in Canada
12 11 10 09 08 07 06 05 04 03
10 9 8 7 6 5 4 3 2 1

The paper used in this publicaton meets the minimum requirements of ANSI/NISO Z39.48-1992 (R1997) *(Permanence of Paper)*⊗

Contents

Illustrations

PLATES *(following page 58)*

FIGURES

Acknowledgments

Numerous people helped in getting this book off the ground, supplied information, publications, contacts, names, ideas, and criticism. Let me acknowledge with gratitude at least some of those without whom it could not have come into being: Lars-Olof Åhlberg, Gábor Bachman, Imre Bak, Geremie Barmé, László Beke, Ákos Birkás, Tony Cascardi, Paul Crowther, Dubravka Djurić, Grzegorz Dziamski, Andrzej Ekwinski, Cola Franzen, Bora Gabor, Marina Gržinić, Lóránd Hegyi, Ludvik Hlaváček, Maria Hlávajova, Hanru Hou, Martin Jay, Anna Kiss, Noémi Kiss, Želimir Koščević, Attila Kovács, Lev Kreft, Ada Krnačová-Gutleber, Eva Kit Wah Man, Raffaele Milani, Miran Mohar, Stefan Morawski, Suzanne Mőszely, Katalin Néray, Heinz Paetzold, Darko Pokorn, the editors of *Poliester*, Paul Reitter, Judith Sárodsy, Margarita Schultz, Marketta Seppälä, Jiři Ševčík, Roman Uranjek, Mark Valentine, Rachel Weiss, Ernest Ženko, and Paula Zupanc-Ecimovic. Substantial help and support were offered by the Scientific Research Center of the Slovenian Academy of Sciences and Arts and its director, Oto Luthar. A part of the research for this book was carried out with the support of the Higher Education Support Scheme, which is hereby gratefully acknowledged. I also feel indebted to Deborah Kirshman, the editor for fine arts at the University of California Press, and her assistant, Jennie Sutton, to Stephanie Fay, and to copyeditor Bud Bynack.

ALEŠ ERJAVEC
Ljubljana, August 25, 2000

Foreword

As early as the 1820s and the French Saint-Simonians, the vivid metaphor of an "avant-garde" was taken from its military origins to denote the self-conscious vanguard of a political movement fancying itself to be the cutting edge in the struggle for human emancipation.[1] By the 1870s, the metaphor had drifted from politics into the world of art, where it came to mean an embattled and courageous elite of writers and artists who spurn conventional taste and challenge the power of reigning art institutions, following instead the imperatives of aesthetic innovation wherever they might lead. The story of the two avant-gardes and their ambivalent relationship to each other—often mutually reinforcing, at other times mortally opposed—is an oft-told tale.[2] Both shared a faith in the future, rather than a reverence for the past. Both reveled in their roles as beleaguered minorities whose sacrifices in the present would be honored by a grateful posterity. And both often fantasized about the future in redemptive terms, whether envisaged as a political and social utopia or as the realization of a dream of artistic purification, absolute beauty, and autotelic self-sufficiency.

By the 1960s, it has often been observed, both avant-garde projects were in serious disarray. Ironically, it was their relative successes that helped undermine faith in their redemptive potential. A vanguard party had, after all, gained control over what became known as the "Second World" of "actually existing socialism" and over a large part of the "Third World," as well. But the harsh realities of their rule and their increasingly evident failure to fulfill the promises they had made during their ascendancy to power left widespread disillusionment in their wake. And when the traditional art institutions of the First World opened their doors wide to the no-longer-scorned martyrs of early modernism and their increasingly market-savvy successors, it was clear that the future had arrived, but without the expected redemptive payoff. Or rather, the payoff turned out to be more commercial than aesthetic as modernism became the easy handmaiden of late-capitalist economics, even at times a tool in the Cold War struggle with the political vanguard in its reigning form.[3] Although it took a while for the full implications of this twin decline to manifest themselves, by the end of the twentieth century, it was no longer possible to wring much hope out of either avant-garde project. Even the most intransigent defenders of their promise, such as the distinguished art historian T. J. Clark, ruefully conceded that it was time to bid "farewell to an idea."[4]

Much of this now-familiar story has been told in terms of the weak, posthumous afterlives of Marxism and modernism, producing leading exemplars of the ubiquitous "post" mode of conceptualizing our current cultural and political situation. In this telling, the teleological impulse in both radical politics and radical art has withered away, providing little resistance to the assumption that we live in an era of *posthistoire* in which history itself seems to have ended.[5] In its bleakest version, postmodernist art is understood to be a cynical surrender to the bourgeois marketplace, a servant of globalized capitalism.[6]

But what if there were other narratives that could resist being subsumed under this grandiose story of rising and falling expectations, other models of the intersection of art and politics that are only now becoming visible as the shadow of Marxism recedes? What if, amid the ruins of the avant-gardes, both political and aesthetic, some artists were finding ways to avoid both the discredited rhetoric of redemption and the nihilism of despair and surrender? What if, for a brief moment, the familiar music stopped, and the seats in the orchestra were occupied by players who insisted on making their own tunes, producing a new and unprecedented combination of aesthetic creativity and political activism?

The opportunity for such an alternative, in fact, arose in those societies undergoing arguably the most significant political transformation of the second half of the twentieth century: the transition from failed Communism to an amorphous and still-unsettled something else.[7] From the point of view of those who yet clung to the older redemptive narratives—and at least in countries like Cuba and China, it remains part of the official rhetoric to this day—the work of artists anticipating the transition might be damned by that time-honored epithet "counterrevolutionary." These were figures deeply disillusioned with both traditional vanguards, which they treated with relentless irony, if not outright contempt. But such a predictable label patently fails to do justice to the complexities of their situations and the creativity of their responses to it. Although at times they did revisit and reappropriate older cultural values and symbols, some nationalist, others religious, they did so without any naive belief in the desirability of their resurrection. Even the icons of high modernism, so often denounced as decadent by Socialist Realist dogmatists, were fair game for citational repositioning, but never for simple restoration. Keenly aware of developments on the international cultural scene—Pop Art, Conceptualism, punk, performance art, and the like—these artists were fully cognizant of the dangers of populist parochialism.

What most powerfully motivated them was a desire to register the exhaustion and to hasten the end of the "actually existing socialist" societies in which they were living, not to return to an imagined state of bliss before the Fall. Absent, however, was the apocalyptic intensity of the classical avant-garde, which often sought the cleansing power of violence, both symbolic and literal, as a means to bring about the New Jerusalem. Anticipating the relatively bloodless revolutions at the end of the 1980s, the art that preceded them had little of the savage power—or grandiose pretensions—of its early-twentieth-century predecessors. Having absorbed the lessons of postmodernist antihistoricism, with its distrust of metanarratives of any kind, these artists knew better than to expect a clean break with the past and an absolutely fresh beginning. And yet once the political transition was over, as it was by 1990 in most of the cases explored in this collection, so, too, was the unusual combination of political and aesthetic impulses that nurtured their work. As in the case of the classical avant-gardes, once their subversive moment was at an end, something intangible was gone, and they, too, passed into history—or sometimes were absorbed into the international art market.

A remarkable moment it certainly was, although until now, after its irrevocable passing, not fully appreciated in a comparative sense. It is perhaps fitting that the angle of vision that allowed that comparison to take place found its vertex in Slovenia, a new country that emerged only with the collapse of the Yugoslavian Communist federation in 1991. A province relatively remote from the centers of Communist power, less a Balkan nation than a remnant of the Hapsburg Empire, and open to the winds blowing from neighbors to the west such as Italy and Austria, Slovenia was a hotbed of artistic-cum-political creativity in the 1980s. The story of its ferment has already been told in *Ljubljana, Ljubljana,* coauthored by Aleš Erjavec, a philosopher and aesthetician, and Marina Gržinič, a video artist and aesthetic theorist. Over the years, Erjavec has assumed an increasingly visible role on the international scene, culminating in his presidency of the International Association for Aesthetics and organization of the Fourteenth International Congress of Aesthetics in Ljubljana in 1998.[8] Through his extensive travels and contacts, he came to understand that the Slovenian situation was by no means unique. Something roughly akin to what he had experienced in Ljubljana had transpired in Budapest and Belgrade, in Moscow and Leningrad, perhaps even in Beijing and Havana.

Despite the concrete differences making each case irreducible to a single norm, all of the artists had responded to the example of Western postmodernism, with its effacement of high/low distinctions, intertextual citational practices, and appropriation of the symbolic resources of consumer culture. But unlike postmodernism in the West, postsocialist postmodernism had a genuinely transgressive charge that allowed it to play a role in the transition that occurred in the 1980s. Despite all the homogenizing power of globalization at its most totalizing, here was an instance of an import from the West that was refunctioned in local contexts to produce unforeseen results. Built into that reception, however, was a realism, which at times verged on cynicism, about the long-term effects of those changes. And so it is no surprise the narratives told by the expert witnesses amassed by Erjavec avoid triumphalist conclusions. To be postsocialist, they imply, is not yet to be free. The mandate of art to protest against that condition of unfreedom has not yet expired.

MARTIN JAY
History Department
University of California, Berkeley

Notes

1. Perhaps the first self-conscious use of the term "avant-garde" came in Olinde Rodrigues's dialogue "L'artiste, le savant et l'industriel" of 1825. See the discussion in Matei Calinescu, *Five Faces of Modernity: Modernism, Avant-Garde, Decadence, Kitsch, Postmodernism* (Durham, N.C.: Duke University Press, 1987), p. 101. He

notes an even earlier example in the French writer Étienne Pasquier (1529–1615), who made casual use of the metaphor to describe certain poets engaged in a war against ignorance.

2. See especially Eugene Lunn, *Marxism and Modernism: An Historical Study of Lukács, Brecht, Benjamin and Adorno* (Berkeley: University of California Press, 1982).

3. The now-classic account of this process is Serge Guilbaut, *How New York Stole the Idea of Modern Art: Abstract Expressionism, Freedom, and the Cold War,* trans. Arthur Goldhammer (Chicago: University of Chicago Press, 1984).

4. T. J. Clark, *Farewell to an Idea: Episodes from a History of Modernism* (New Haven: Yale University Press, 1999).

5. For an analysis of this discourse, see Lutz Niethammer, *Posthistoire: Has History Come to an End?* trans. Patrick Camiller (London: Verso, 1994).

6. See Fredric Jameson, *Postmodernism, or, The Cultural Logic of Late Capitalism* (Durham, N.C.: Duke University Press, 1991).

7. The other candidate for most significant transformation would be the collapse of the European imperial order. It would be enormously fruitful, if dauntingly difficult, to compare the art produced by decolonization with the art discussed in this collection.

8. The congress proceedings in English, French, and German are available in the journal he helps edit, *Filozofski Vestnik* 2 (1999) and its supplement.

Introduction

Aleš Erjavec

On December 31, 1990, Marina Gržinić and I wrote the following:

> The numerous events of the 1980s . . . prepared and foretold the current social and political conditions in Slovenia and in Ljubljana as its capital and major urban center. What we call the "Slovenian political spring," with our first postwar free elections, with parliamentary democracy and all its consequences, has evolved, both materially and symbolically, from the processes, events, and actions of the past decade. Art—or more broadly, culture—was the key component, yet endowed with a reality of its own.[1]

Six months later, Slovenia proclaimed its independence, left Yugoslavia, and started on its own way down the road to an uncertain future by way of what is now usually called a period of "transition," a stage of the journey that was also traveled by most of the countries in what was once popularly known in the West as the Communist bloc. As Leslie Holmes has put it, "In the span of approximately two years between late 1989 and the end of 1991, all of the former Communist states of Eastern Europe (Albania, Bulgaria, Czechoslovakia, the GDR, Hungary, Poland, Romania, and—with some reservations—Yugoslavia) moved to post-communism. . . . This move can be called the *first* transition, away from communism; moves towards new destinations . . . constitute the *second* transition."[2] The Soviet Union was also among the countries that moved away from communism in that same period, and although China and Cuba still remain officially communist or socialist, it is generally agreed that China, in particular, started down the road to capitalism quite some time ago.[3]

Art and culture, during that same decade—a few exceptions notwithstanding—followed the same path. Now, a decade later, similar political and social events from the former (and, in some instances, the present) socialist countries, most of them from the late 1980s, have become a thing of the past.

Consequently, it is difficult today to evoke the creative impulses and imagination of that time. The creative outbursts, especially in Slovenia, Hungary, Cuba, and to some extent in parts of the Soviet Union, in many respects resembled those at the time of the October Revolution and the First World War in Europe or during the 1960s in Europe and the United States, when social tensions and historical upheavals also engendered rearticulations of the symbolic space and reconfigurations of the social one forcefully carried out by art and culture. In the countries under discussion—Russia, China, the former Soviet bloc countries of Europe, plus Yugoslavia, and Cuba—the political impact of that art varied, especially during the 1980s. Nevertheless, this epoch signified a pivotal *artistic* break with their Socialist Realist past and partly with their modernist past. A new art was emerging, in many respects similar to its contemporaries in the First World, but at the same time vastly different from them. Although we may disagree about the real political influence or role of such art, it is justified to say—as I hope this book will prove—that from the early 1970s until, broadly speaking, the late 1980s, an artistic revolution occurred in many former or present socialist countries.

As the successor to revolutionary avant-garde art of the early twentieth century, however, art created in the seventies and eighties had distinctive characteristics. It was as if, by some comic sense of historical perversity, Marx's famous Hegelian dictum about historical events appearing twice, first as tragedy and then as farce, was materializing before our very eyes. The initial political unity of socialism between the two world wars, with the attempt to implement the progressive promise historically held out by socialist ideas, was followed, after the post–World War II diffusion of communist ideas, by splits among the socialist countries and the visible dissolution of socialism. The old system was officially gone, but its mental frame of mind and institutional essence were still dominant. At that point, the very time when socialism thus was disappearing as a unified political force, a unity of art developed in these same countries, a unity that expressed this historical change, a change that the political sciences and social theory were not yet able to articulate discursively. The early period of late socialism thus is highly reminiscent of the notion of postmodernism as suggested by Zygmunt Bauman: "the only solid and indubitable accomplishment of the post-modernist debate has been thus far the proclamation of the end of modernism. . . . What has happened in recent years could be articulated as the appearance of a vantage point which allows the view of modernity itself as an enclosed object, an essentially complete product, an episode of history, with an end as much as a beginning."[4] Late socialism is in this sense "postsocialism"—the proclamation of the end of socialism from within socialism itself. It is thus that the historical promise and failure of socialism were repeated by a moment of comic unity that reflected on that promise and failure and then itself passed away.

When many of the the socialist countries split with the USSR—Yugoslavia in 1948, China around 1960, Albania in the 1960s, Romania in the early 1960s, under Gheorghiu-Dej, and, again in 1965, under Nicolae Ceauşescu, and Cuba in the Gorbachev years—some of them then started promoting the idea of "socialism as a world process" as a late and more benign variant of the idea of "world revolution." Despite scarcity and economic and social crises, no tangible alternative to socialism existed in these countries, for the only option at hand was the restoration of the previous capitalist society—a possibility that for the majority of intellectuals, especially in countries with a more independent brand of socialism, such as Cuba, China, and Yugoslavia, was no better than the extant socialism.

What happened then was a slow and initially almost imperceptible crack in the social and political fabric of these societies. In the vast, and centrally controlled Soviet Union, it began in the 1970s and continued in the 1980s with Gorbachev, who, like the intellectuals just mentioned, still believed socialism could be reformed. It ended in the late 1980s, when social changes were not only experienced in everyday life, but also officially and politically sanctioned. Such a process, although much accelerated, occurred in countries ranging from Czechoslovakia to Poland, Hungary, and Bulgaria, with the few exceptions—Cuba, China, and, with reservations, the remnant of the former Yugoslavia—more or less unsatisfactorily tackling the problem of "leaving socialism behind without really leaving it behind."

Today, these countries share very similar problems, such as rising unemployment, a crisis of values, a loss of identity, commercialization, nationalistic ideas, and a resurgence of sympathy for the former political system, but they also share something else. At the historical point that marks the beginning of their transition to capitalism, these countries also possessed a similar cultural and ideological legacy. From this legacy there emerged similar kinds of artistic endeavors. These were not limited to the officially imposed and often officially sanctioned Socialist Realism, although they were frequently strongly related to it. During the late socialist period, such endeavors emanated spontaneously, and often with no visible connection.

At an early stage, a whole series of small incidents made people conscious that the ruling ideas were becoming obsolete, that the link between the ideological signifier and the social referent was irreparably destroyed, and that the gap between the two was becoming an abyss, serving as an argument for the view that socialist countries had actually entered the "hyperreal" postmodern world before their Western counterparts: "Long before Western video technology began to produce an overabundance of authentic images about an absent reality, this problem was already being solved by our ideology, press, and statistics, which would calculate crops that would never be harvested to the hundredths of a percentage point."[5] The optimism of early socialism had vanished long ago, and the ideas of communism or Socialist Realism, even among the most devout Party officials, no longer provoked enthusiasm. Instead, the period of postsocialism was an era of social and political cynicism in which irony was the dominant trope.

Among the few still-visible signs of their common aspirations toward a classless society, the socialist countries undergoing the initial transition away from socialism began to display not only similar kinds of social and economic stagnation or crisis, but also a specific kind of art and culture. Postsocialist or late socialist art and culture exhibited a number of common, often interrelated, traits: Conceptualism, the conscious or spontaneous use of what are today considered to be postmodernist techniques and procedures, profuse employment of socialist and Communist imagery, the use of national heritages and of folk, traditional, and mass culture, and frequent use of what I term a "binary" artistic approach, which results in works in which two realities (the aesthetic and the ideological, or the literal and the metaphorical) retain their mutual incompatibility.

For example, in the work of Sándor Pinczehelyi (Figure 1; see also Plate 11) and that of the Cuban artist Flavio Garciandía (Figure 2; see also Figures 59 and 60), numerous hammers and sickles appear, equaling in their abundance consumer products in the West. The Czech émigré artist Milan Kunc goes a step further. Kunc's "Embarrassing Realism," also called Ost Pop—paintings, installations, and collages that overtly mock the ideological symbols of Communism—consciously juxtaposes the two ruling world ideologies, communism and consumerism (Figure 3).[6] These juxtapositions are similar to those made by the team of Vitaly Komar and Alexander Melamid and other Russian artists. In works such as these, elements of what originally appeared in the art of the Communist era reappears, but in significantly altered form.

Although in practically all the socialist countries at least some measure

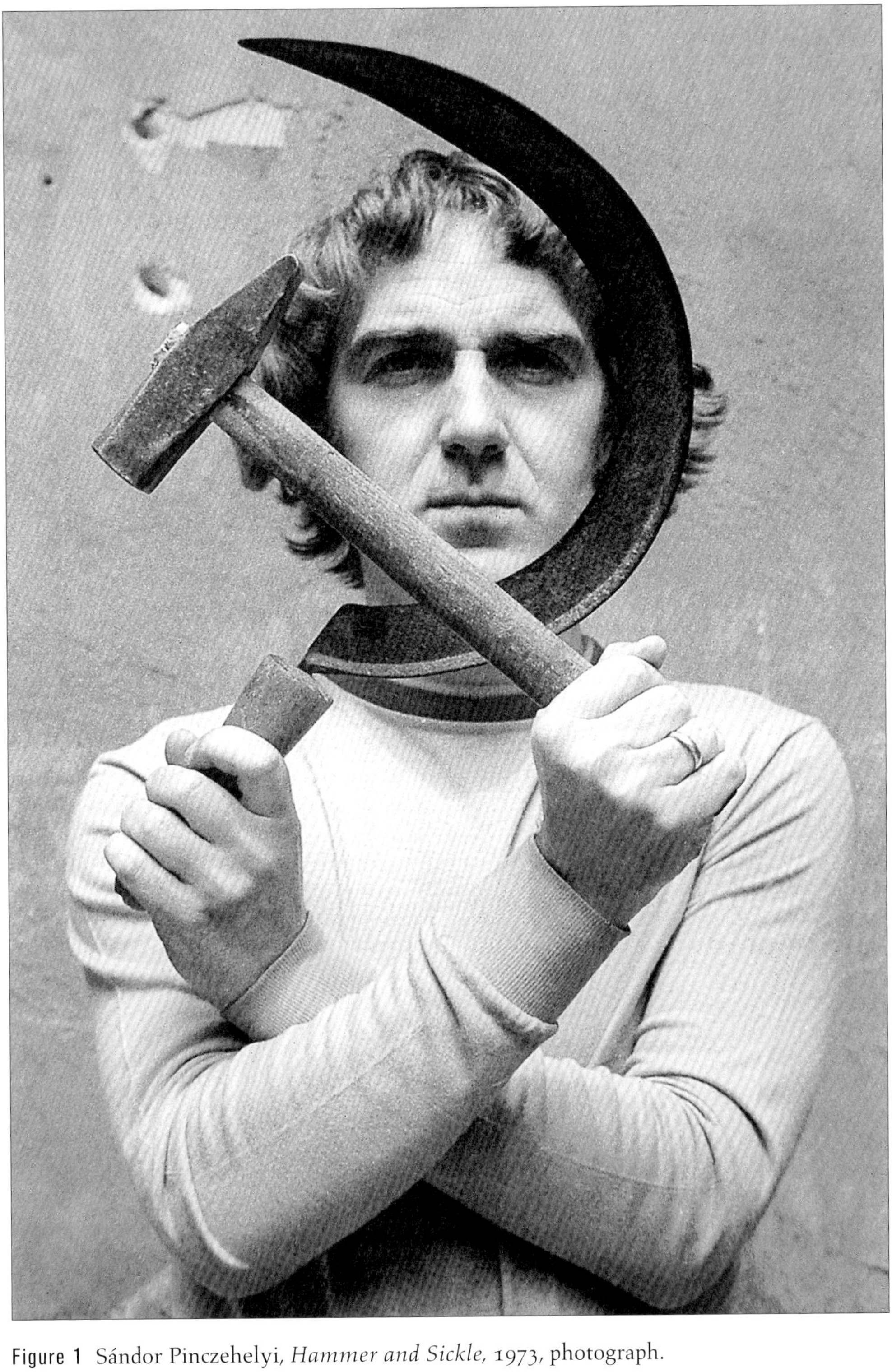

Figure 1 Sándor Pinczehelyi, *Hammer and Sickle,* 1973, photograph.

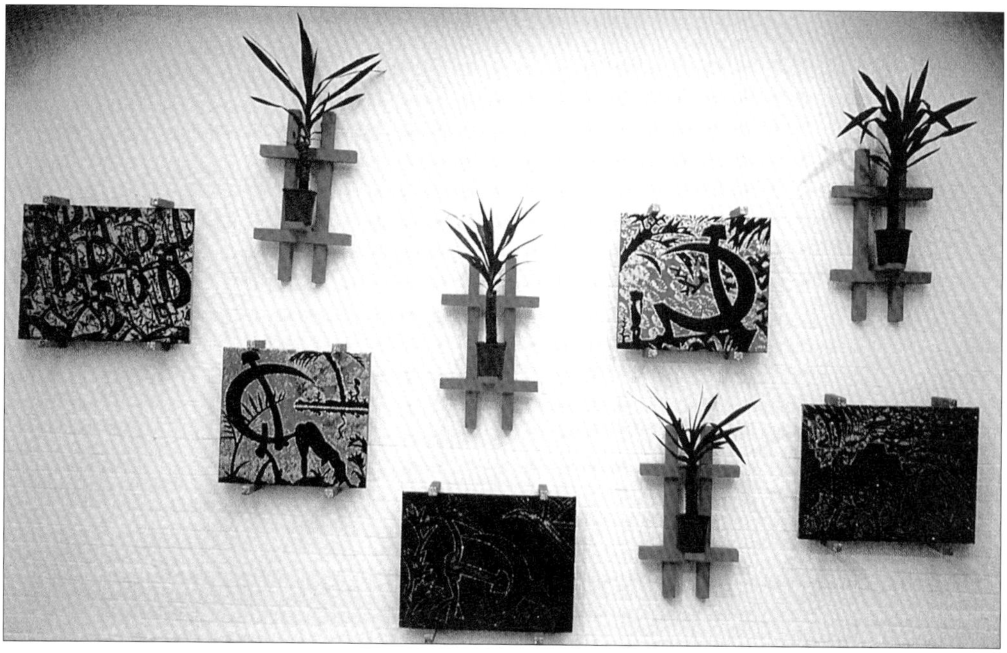

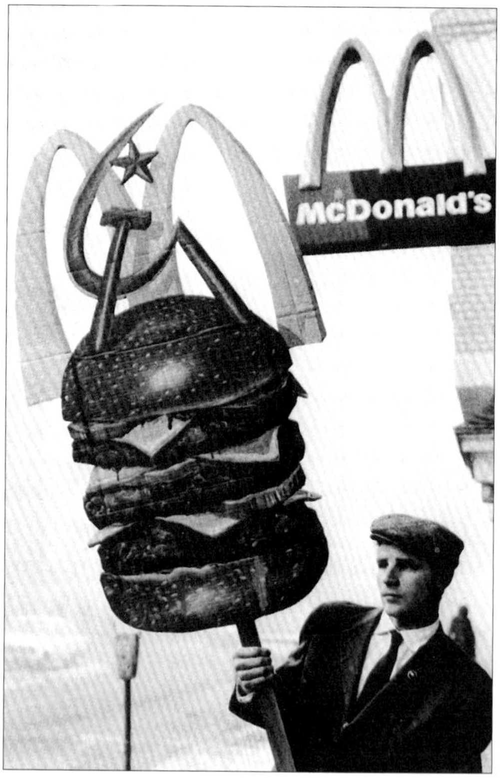

Figure 2 Flavio Garciandía, *Untitled,* 1989, installation; acrylic and glitter on canvas, wood, plants.

Figure 3 Milan Kunc, *Consumerists of the World, Unite!* 1978.

of the legacy of Socialist Realism remained, and although the postsocialist art and culture they produced have traits in common, we cannot designate these traits as purposefully shared. Although they were somewhat similar, in the late 1980s, Cuba and China, or Slovenia and Romania, certainly didn't "share" artistic ideas in any conscious way, nor were artists in one country often aware of what artists in another were doing, despite the frequently startling similarities between their works. Instead, at a certain point in their individual histories, these countries—or should I say cultures?—engendered art that possessed strikingly similar features. Its shared traits, which simultaneously distinguish it from the art of the same period from Western Europe, the United Sates, and elsewhere in the First World, thus arise from specific conditions of possibility, the framework conditioned by the disintegration of various forms of socialism. Phrased differently, the common conditions of late socialism or postsocialism from which such art emerged also engendered its common traits. In some cases, such art appeared as early as the early 1970s, in others in the early or late 1980s, and in a few, it appeared only in the early 1990s. In any event, art and culture expressed and mirrored historical processes at the same time that they were contributing to them, and they often carried this out in new and startling ways. Art was not only visibly expressing the ongoing events that led to what Holmes has called "the *first* transition," but also finding a unique way to articulate a historical, social, and political situation while the political sciences and social theory were still in that "unstable state and instant of language wherein something which must be able to be put into phrases cannot yet be."[7]

That situation was an evanescent one. When the artists and authors that it produced and that had a hand in producing it executed the works with which this book is concerned, the political and social context was unstable and transitional. The unique artistic, cultural, and political effects of these works thus proved as evanescent as the social and political conditions under which they came into existence. When the cultural context changed from that of late socialism or postsocialism to that of an overt and clearly visible transition to capitalism, very little of the previous interest in such art and culture remained, for they carried little potential for the social promotion of the new elites. The artists and authors of this transitional moment sometimes were marginal, marginalized, and known only to friends and a few other individuals. Others were publicly praised only for a short period and then drifted back into obscurity. A few became the acclaimed artists of their national cultures, and some have retained this status until today. I thus by no means want to claim that the works, artists, or authors presented in this book were or are necessarily central in their own countries.

Sometimes what we present here is no more than an episode in the career of some artists; sometimes it is their whole career. It is also the art and culture of a period of recent history—politicized art and culture created within the confines of the postsocialist condition. It is well worthwhile to ask why and how such art should come into existence at all.

Socialism

In his writings, mostly those from the 1970s, the French historian and political philosopher Claude Lefort offered a persuasive theory of totalitarian societies, be they fascist or communist: In his view, the difference between political and ideological discourse and power is annihilated in both. Various modern forms of democratic bourgeois society allow for this difference and thus permit dissent without its endangering their existence. In totalitarian societies, however, the totalitarian discourse must identify itself completely with power and with those who possess it. Totalitarian discourse doesn't allow the subject any distance from the discourse and "demands his identification with power and with the person or persons who retain it at the top of the State."[8] Thus, while in traditional democratic bourgeois societies the locus of power and the locus of enunciation of ideology are separated and disseminated, in a totalitarian society, they coalesce or conflate in a single location—the Party, for example—preventing dissent. This coalescence is carried out in an attempt to encompass everything within a homogeneous and controlled social field in which all differences and social antagonisms have collapsed.

What distinguishes a totalitarian ideology from a democratic one is that totalitarian ideology "implies the aim of a certain *center* . . . which moves from one sector of the civil society to another, but which in the heart of the State apparatus retains power and knowledge."[9] The totalitarian society thus gives a semblance of being completely homogeneous and unified, with social divisions completely masked, and with the border between the state and civil society concealed, if not eliminated, the former annihilating the latter, along with the difference between the public and private spheres. This complete politicization almost entirely interiorizes political ideology. It is the elimination of any distinction between the public and the private spheres that impedes the ability of the subject to achieve any critical distance from that ideology or to retain that distance if it is achieved.

Within this framework, art and culture historically possessed a central role, for the promulgators of socialist and communist ideas considered themselves the descendants of the Enlightenment and Romanticism and therefore viewed art and culture and their development as essential for any authentic socialist or communist society.[10] We should also not forget that for Karl Marx, in his early writings, art was the highest form of creativity, and its flowering was one of the essential attainments in the utopian classless society.

In most socialist countries during the period of late socialism, art retained and even strengthened its special political and social position. Artists were allowed to mix with Party dignitaries, had special privileges, and so on. In 1983, the dissident Hungarian writer Miklós Haraszti described this peculiar "master-slave relationship" in the following way:

> Censorship is no longer a matter of simple state intervention. A new aesthetic culture has emerged in which censors and artists alike are entangled in a mutual embrace. . . . If I still speak of censorship, what I refer to is not merely certain bureaucratic procedures, but the whole context of culture, not just state intervention, but all the circumstances that conspire to destroy the basis of autonomous or authentic artistic activity, not just political *diktat*, but the individual's *Weltanschauung* within an all-embracing and unified society, not only "legal" and "illegal" restrictions, but also the secret psychological sources that sustain the state's reach, even in the last cell of culture. Hence I will refer not only to punishment, but also to reward and sustenance, privilege and ambition.[11]

Or, as the same phenomenon was described by a Polish author: "No doubt it was a prison[;] still, for those who accepted its rules and regulations, the cells were very comfortable. Generally speaking, the artist was free of the pressure of the market. Fulfilling a number of conditions, he or she could live safely and comfortably, enjoy high prestige, respect, and appanage."[12]

Artists and writers often used a "secondary" discourse that enabled the articulation of a critique. The traditional procedures of this kind are the famous Communist jokes and the use of political "Aesopian language," a form of political and ideological criticism often employed by traditional dissidents in the countries under discussion,[13] although, historically, this maneuver is by no means limited to them.

Because special rules applied in this peculiar "natural reserve," as Claude Lévi-Strauss once called culture, in the socialist countries, its inhabitants possessed a political role unfathomable in a great majority of Western countries, where political views can be enunciated in a variety of venues.

As "the pressures for change in Eastern Europe built up over the years because of the communist regimes' inability to solve the central problem of legitimation" (and to a large extent this is true not only of Eastern Europe), "these pressures found multivarious outlets—in culture, in religious organizations, even in rock music."[14]

In the socialist countries, however, yet another, probably more sophisticated or at least more novel, approach to political critique emerged, an approach typical of late socialism, which was no longer equally totalitarian and therefore less repressive than in the past. This was to articulate a secondary discourse in the form of the primary ideological discourse.

This procedure was employed by many of the artists discussed in this book and in fact constitutes one of the characteristics of their art. It consisted of the use of mimicry, of conscious and complete identification of the secondary discourse with the ideological discourse, thus paradoxically revealing the inconsistencies of the latter, the voids in its purportedly impregnable discursive armor, and especially its ideological nature. The Slovenian rock group Laibach, for instance, proclaimed: "Politics is the highest and all-embracing art, and we, who create contemporary Slovenian art, consider ourselves to be politicians."[15] How could Communist political ideology respond to or counter such a statement without contradicting its credo of an all-embracing politicization of society?

Although it was becoming increasingly clear that the result of totalitarianism in socialist countries was economic and social stagnation, the majority of these countries were unable to change their petrified social and economic relations effectively without accepting the social consequences, including class antagonisms and actual unemployment. Consequently, almost all of them made various attempts at overcoming this inertia and petrification within the existing socialist framework by implementing diverse economic reforms or developing their own brands of socialism—"socialism with a human face," for example, championed especially in the second half of the 1960s in Czechoslovakia and Poland, "self-management," promoted especially in the 1970s in Yugoslavia,[16] or "socialism with Chinese characteristics." They thus produced what in effect became a variety of what could be called "national" socialisms.

The allusion in the term "'national' socialisms" is deliberate. Another of Lefort's tenets is that *all* totalitarian societies are in fact a stray variant of bourgeois society—bourgeois societies with a twist. More recently a similar conjecture has been advanced by Slavoj Žižek: "Is not Fascism a kind of inherent self-negation of capitalism, an attempt to 'change something so that nothing really changes' by means of an ideology which subordinates the economy to the ideological-political domain? Is not the Leninist 'actually existing socialism' a kind of 'socialist Jacobinism,' an attempt to subordinate the whole of socioeconomic life to the immediate political regulation of the socialist state?"[17] In other words, aren't fascism and communism nothing but (unsuccessful) attempts to accomplish the aims of capitalism by discarding its negative effects, such as social antagonisms, social and economic crises, and unemployment? "The 'socialist bloc' was the true 'third way,'" Žižek argues, "a desperate attempt at modernization outside the constraints of capitalism."[18]

In Western Europe, and especially in the United States, the socialist countries were usually referred to as "communist." While I don't dispute the benefits of this widely accepted usage, I will nonetheless employ the term "socialist"—hence the terms "postsocialist" and "late socialist." The political system was called "actually (or "really") existing socialism" (Realsozialismus). Just as often, it was called "state socialism." The term "Communist" was primarily applied to the political parties and their members. Yugoslavia is a special case, because beginning in the early 1970s, the League of Communists implemented a more decentralized political system of self-management within which the notions of the "state" and of a centralized power center lost much of their previous meaning, making an idea such as "state socialism" inappropriate. The smallest common denominator of all these countries in terms of their political system was therefore one-party (mostly state) socialism, with the period under discussion primarily the period preceding its demise.

According to Marx and his early followers, communism was a "movement" leading the working masses via revolution from capitalism through a transitional period of socialism into communist society. Since the main traits of communism pertain not only to a classless society, but also to the distribution of wealth "according to one's needs," it was patently clear that the Soviet Union of the 1950s, 1960s, and 1970s could not be designated as already de facto "communist." In fact, the Soviet ideologists themselves didn't think so, for if they had, Khrushchev would not have proclaimed in 1961 that the Soviet Union would enter an early stage of communism in the 1980s. In the cases of some other countries, the term "communism" is equally problematic. Castro did not declare himself a Marxist-Leninist until three years after taking power in Havana, with a real Marxist-Leninist party emerging only in 1965. "Castro was above all a Cuban nationalist, who was increasingly attracted to communism because of its alleged commitment to greater equality and justice, and because it was total anathema to the Americans."[19]

There is but a single socialist nation that has so far remained an exception to the economic and social stagnation of late socialism—China: "There can be little doubt that Deng's approach to and successes with economic policy was a major reason why the Chinese communist system did not collapse when so many others did. In the aftermath of the Cultural Revolution, the new Chinese leadership sought to move away from coercion and towards a more stable system in which eudaemonism would be a—perhaps the—salient mode of legitimation."[20] As Jean Baudrillard puts it, "the communist systems did not succumb to an external enemy, or even to an internal one (had that been the case, they would have resisted), but to their own inertia, taking advantage of the opportunity, as it were, to disappear (perhaps they were weary of existing)."[21]

Socialist Culture and National Culture

It is not only socialism, be it state socialism, actually existing socialism, or self-management socialism, that the countries under discussion have in common. With the partial exception of China and Cuba, they all possess two other interrelated features that they shared even before the advent of socialism: the importance of national sentiments and the significance ascribed to culture, especially to national culture. "In Eastern Europe . . . the national principle already existed in the consciousness of a small group, long before the state itself came into being." However, "a characteristic of the 'Third World' today is that the state has been established first—as occurred in Latin America as well." As a result, "the nation and the sense of nationality follows afterwards, under the influence of the newly established state itself."[22] That this is true is testified to by Luis Camnitzer's observation that Latin Americans "felt the absurdity of the nation-state concept,"[23] while the Eastern and Central Europeans found it of seminal importance. In Europe, Russia included, the national principle is rooted in national culture, resulting in

"Hegel's notion of 'nation-as-culture,' [and] the over-use of culture as a 'replacement for politics.'"[24] There, more inclusive notions such as Eastern and Central Europe, Mitteleuropa, and so on, are permanently questioned and disputed:

> Perhaps, as the Czech writer Milan Kundera has observed, if East Central Europe exists at all it is only in the imagination of those who have never experienced it. With geographical boundaries wholly dependent on ethnicity, politics, or personal bias, this *other* Europe is consistently described as if it is a negative space—that is, in terms of what it isn't rather than what it is. East Central Europe remains, after the curtain has been drawn aside, an empty screen on which almost anything can be projected.[25]

In this environment, nation and culture are inextricably linked. It is politics that links them and that has caused art and culture to play such a significant role in the 1980s and early 1990s, enabling writers to become heads of state; painters and poets, ambassadors; and sociology professors, city mayors and foreign ministers, just as in 1918–20 or in the years following 1945. Within this context, culture denotes "'high culture'—that is, what artists, writers, musicians, and scholars produce, sometimes for fairly narrow specialist audiences and sometimes for broader publics."[26] It is in this sense that the notion of culture is employed in this book, because in this transitional period of late socialism, culture still possessed this particular role and position.

At the same time, culture also often can possess a peculiar existential function. Culture is designed "to liberate a person from the very society in which he is doomed to live. Culture is not a product of society, but a challenge and alternative to society."[27] In the former Soviet bloc countries, culture and art represented one of the rare venues for expressing political dissent and, just as important, for expressing personal and private views aimed at having an existential and a social impact. In this respect, socialism signified a continuation (and perhaps a petrification) of the role that art, culture, and the intelligentsia had played in the Central and Eastern European countries for a hundred years or more.

One of the most widely accepted observations in the late 1980s and early 1990s was that in the former socialist countries, nationalism was replacing socialism as the ideological cement holding these societies together. While I do not intend to dispute this observation, it is equally true that such a process has been taking place for quite some time. It would therefore be possible to view the breaks between Mao Zedong and Stalin, or Tito and

Stalin, and even Ceauşescu and Khrushchev as early signs of the disintegration of the global communist movement, this being so despite the Soviet Union's firm control over its European satellites, where any real dissent, such as in Budapest in 1956 or in Prague in 1968, was soon neutralized. And, it should be added, nationalism was frequently used to complement socialism. As we have seen, "national" paths to socialism and arguments supporting them could at various times be encountered in many former socialist countries. Romanian scholars under Ceauşescu, for example, arguing for their own brand of socialism and nationalism, claimed that "the idea of an integral national essence could actually make sense *only* in socialism, for in capitalism, the social psychology of nations is divided by classes, whereas in socialism, the national culture becomes fully integrated and can at last constitute a progressive force."[28]

A persuasive argument supporting the thesis that nationalism had already played a pivotal role under socialism is offered by Slavoj Žižek:

> It is . . . wrong to conceive this rise of nationalism as a kind of a "reaction" to the alleged Communist betrayal of national roots: the common idea that because Communist power ripped out the entire traditional fabric of society, the only remaining point on which to base resistance is national identity. It was already Communist power which *produced* the compulsive attachment to the national Cause, an attachment that became more exclusive the more totalitarian the power structure. The most extreme cases are to be found in Ceauşescu's Romania, in Cambodia under the Khmer Rouge, in North Korea and in Albania.[29]

The artists that we are discussing in this book, however, almost never succumbed to the imaginary outlet supplied by nationalism. In this respect, their art strongly resembles that of the international wing of the classical avant-gardes as exemplified by the cosmopolitan and urban Vladimir Mayakovsky rather than that of the nationalist and anti-Western Velimir Khlebnikov. Similar, although more polarized, cases are the Futurism of Marinetti, who, in spite of supporting fascism, remained cosmopolitan and opposed to the officially promoted and nationalist culture of Strapaese, which attempted to combine patriotism with the provincial and pastoral idyll,[30] and, in the German case, the art derisively called Entartete Kunst, degenerate art, as opposed to Nazi Kunst.

Something like this polarization between nationalist and internationalist orientations occurred in many countries at the time of the demise of socialism. The dividing line ran between politicized postmodernism, on the one hand, and politicized or "dissident" modernism, on the other, with the latter often becoming the promoter of national sentiments. In some of the former socialist countries of Central and Eastern Europe, the modernist "dissident" writers and artists were those who most strongly defended "national identity," and the mythic notion of Mitteleuropa, which purportedly constitutes a unique historical and regional cultural entity, transcending individual national cultures yet retaining their specific features, prompting the Austrian writer Peter Handke to remark that for him, on the contrary, Mitteleuropa is but a meteorological notion.

In Cuba, however, because no real sense of national identity preceded the founding of the state, no such division over nationalism occurred. In Cuba, as well as in other countries in Latin America, and even in China, where postmodernism was partly appropriated by the state and consequently carried a slightly suspect meaning, the opposition between modernism and postmodernism likewise never emerged on a scale found in the First or the Second World, although sometimes the label of postmodernism carried an ambivalent significance. Instead, the arts, and especially the visual arts, came to be seen as a means for articulating widespread popular concerns.

> The decade of the 1980's brought about a turning point in social consciousness . . . its most advanced expression has not been linked to the trade unions, the popular assemblies, the student movement or the press: it has manifested itself in none other than in the visual arts. That the visual arts find themselves playing such an active social or ideological role is truly surprising, I'd say unique. Spokespeople of popular opinion, they are in Cuba today the most daring current being voiced. They are almost the only space where analyses much needed by Cuban society are being communicated, as well as shedding light on the problems of contemporary socialism. All of this is being done without the slightest loss in artistic complexity.[31]

Some of the artists discussed here were marginal or marginalized in their own countries. Sometimes, in Slovenia and a few other places in the former Yugoslavia, for example, the art under discussion here mostly belonged to a "subculture" or "alternative culture." For the most part, it was not supported by state cultural institutions, but took place in clubs, the suburbs, and places where one would not otherwise encounter "art" in these countries. It frequently consisted of rock music concerts and took place in underground discotheques, where exhibitions of paintings, posters, or graffiti would be staged, and was also, in this respect, much removed from the high art and culture of the intellectual elites. It was not altogether the underground culture of the West, nor was it the "unofficial" or "prohibited" art of the more stringent socialist regimes.

The repressive regimes in Romania postponed any such development of an expressive popular culture there. "The nation" (and the Party) asserted their identity with every element of the social field. According to Călin Dan, a member of this younger generation and of the group subREAL, "Alternative culture had but two options: suicide or survival in the underground culture. The second option was more reasonable and so the idea of subREAL appeared."[32] But in Romania, these events took place late:

> The late '80s brought a new oppression of dictatorship that has ruined the last attempts of Romanian art to assume modernity. Projects like *The Sibiu Installations Workshop* (Sibiu, 1986), *The Space of the Mirror* (Bucharest, 1987) and *Alternatives* (Bucharest, 1987) have been brutally disrupted by the activists of the Communist Party and by the Securitate. The goal of these half-private initiatives (which had the support of the Artists' Union) was in no way spectacular: They were supposed to prove, by means of diverse stylistic and media options, the development of Romanian art in connection with other cultural areas in and outside Europe. Conceptualism, Expressionism, video, performance, Mail-Art are not subversive in themselves. But in a system dominated by suspicion, every step beyond conventions meant treason, both in relation to the Party and the Nation.[33]

Under such conditions, it was only in 1990 that the subREAL group came into existence—as compared with similar events occurring in the other socialist countries at least since the early 1980s.

In China, because of its earlier historical and cultural circumstances and its colonial past, along with its own path toward a classless society (not to mention the period of the Cultural Revolution, which effectively prevented any external influence and also represented a clear break with previous tradition), the situation was again different from that of Central and Eastern Europe. As in the Soviet Union, the emerging late socialist art in China did not relate to national issues but to political and ideological ones.

In China, politicized postmodern art never had the effect it enjoyed in Central and Eastern Europe or Cuba. As in the Soviet Union, its influence was limited to fellow artists and their foreign buyers. After the political changes implemented by Deng, which brought about economic changes effectively making China partially a market economy, the role of art diminished further. It started in this respect to resemble that held by art in the contemporary European countries in transition:

> It is both a cruel and happy fate to be an artist in Reformist China.
>
> Cruel because chances of exhibiting one's work are slight, recognition rare and distorting and there is little or no chance of having an impact on society at any level. . . . An erratic toleration has replaced pervasive totalitarianism; a laissez-faire *realpolitik* has been instituted for the rebellious who act within reason. Dissident and diverse art thus became another jewel in the crown of Chinese socialism.[34]

China in many respects resembles the Soviet Union. "Maoist art, then called revolutionary realism, was influenced by Soviet art and Chinese folk art, and it developed during the fifties, sixties and seventies into a style that was dubbed 'great,' 'important,' 'omnipotent,' 'red,' 'brilliant,' and 'light.'"[35] In 1993, Lao Li observed in retrospect: "Chinese art rests on three legs. One is traditional brush and ink painting. One is realism, a concept imported from the West at the beginning of this century. One is the international language of contemporary Western art."[36]

Between 1979 (the *Stars* exhibition) and 1989 (the *China / Avant-Garde* exhibition) art developed in China that strongly resembles that of other countries under discussion: "A truly innovative art movement of unparalleled dimensions had swept China throughout the 1980s."[37] In the late 1980s and early 1990s, there appeared a more playful kind of art, such as that by Yu Youhan (born in 1943): "His paintings are less a message than a portrayal of the reception and mechanics of Chinese propaganda art and its trivial side-products. Even his colours correspond more to the smooth coldness of the consumer aesthetic. Yu Youhan's art reflects with ironical insight the changes in the cultural environment of China today—to a certain extent it is a Chinese variant of pop art"[38] (Figure 4).

Postsocialism and Postmodernism

Although the countries dealt with here exist on three different continents and exhibit different histories, cultures, and mutual relations (or, rather, in the period of late socialism, exhibited an increasing lack of mutual relations), they all embraced versions of "postmodernism." In the words of Charles Jencks: "All the avant-gardes of the past believed that humanity was going

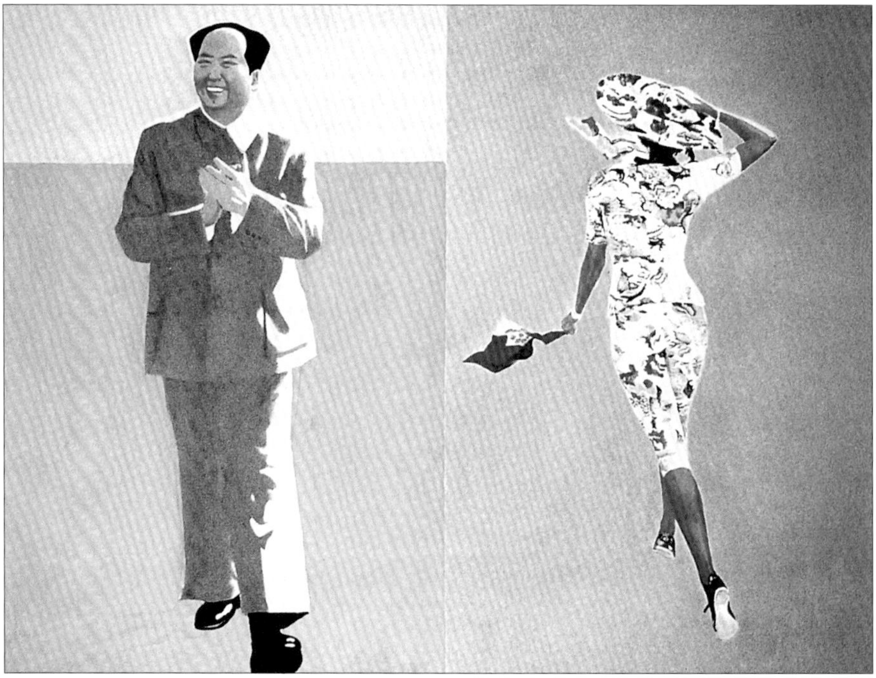

Figure 4 Yu Youhan, *Girl,* 1988, oil on canvas, 59 × 76 cm.

somewhere, and it was their joy and duty to discover this new land and see that people arrived there on time." In contrast to this progressivist orientation toward a utopian future, however, "the Post-Avant-Garde [a strand of postmodernism] believes that humanity is going in several different directions at once, some of them more valid than the others, and it is their duty to be guides and critics."[39]

In socialist countries, postmodernism often came into existence as a simple transposition and appropriation of Western or First World postmodernism. However, as we will see, because of specific conditions such as cultural appropriation and frequent eclecticism that existed in the different countries even before they became socialist, there was already a fertile ground of orientations, techniques, and procedures that ensured its growth. A further ingredient was offered by differing political circumstances: "We have to do with what must now be called Second World culture, an emergent socialist culture whose development, in its Eastern or Slavic form, has been cut short" and "whose originality was defined in part by its distance from commodity fetishism."[40] The label "postmodern" therefore designated both something coming from the desirable West and an oblique entity that could become a vessel for almost any artistic endeavor growing from native stocks.

> The surprise experienced by Western observers upon viewing Cuban art during the decade of the 1980s—its lack of Soviet socialist realism and its apparent formal closeness to the products of the capitalist mainstream—was glossed over by labeling the art as postmodern. This label, often used by Cuban artists themselves, seems to facilitate an easy connection between two cultures. It provides an easy cataloguing from the outside and a sense of a validating context from the inside. As with much of the art on the periphery, superficial viewing of the work seems to confirm the classification, since in many cases there is a conscious appropriation and use of borrowed art solutions.[41]

This "postmodern" eclecticism has long been characteristic of the larger cultural situation of many socialist countries. In Camnitzer's view, societies on the periphery "have developed what could be called an *eclecticism of despair* in which elements are merged through appropriation. Subservient and fragmentary mimesis blends with a defensive syncretic use of resources and with recontextualization. The result is an aesthetic that long predates postmodernism but that often matches it in visual terms."[42] "In the case of Cuba (as in the rest of Latin America), this appropriation is not focused on an abstracted research around the topics of historicism and recycling as it is in the West; instead, it is connected with the long tradition of attempts to syncretize unstoppable imported influences with the surrounding reality."[43] The same observation is directly applicable to many Central and Eastern European countries[44] and can explain the ease with which these cultures, too, appropriated postmodernism. For them, postmodernism was yet another instance, albeit more pronounced, of a long and continuous process of appropriation of cultural and artistic trends and influences emanating from the larger cultures and cultural centers. Their continuous fate since the nineteenth century has been to appropriate various artistic influences and graft them onto their own already acquired and assimilated linguistic, artistic, and cultural traditions. They thus have created local versions of larger cultural developments while often also "losing" their greatest artists to the hegemonic cultures and large urban and cultural centers. With the advent of postmodernism, such appropriations became legitimate and even desirable, although hindered by the very limited means of promotion and distribution.

Postsocialist postmodernism thus possessed different traits than postmodernism in the West because the cultures and societies in which it sprang up were different. And for the same reason, when artists in the different socialist countries embraced some version of postmodernism, they did so with different ends in mind. Postsocialist postmodernism differed in some ways not only from Western postmodernism, but from country to country.

In his analysis of contemporary Russian culture, Mikhail N. Epstein observes that the "'communist future' has become a thing of the past, while the feudal and bourgeois 'past' approaches us from the direction where we had expected to meet the future."[45] One would discard such an idea with the claim that, of course, nothing of the past returns to the present in its original state, for it is always decontextualized, then recontextualized. Nonetheless, Epstein's view frequently is expressed by contemporary Russian authors and artists. This reversal of the past and present is also a relatively common feature of past Russian thinking, as Iurii Lotman and Boris Uspenskii claim: "The idea that forward movement is a return to a lost truth (movement into the future is movement into the past) became so common that it took hold of diametrically opposed social groups." Thus, for example, the sect of Old Believers from the seventeenth century placed "paganism *after* Christianity instead of *before*. This ordering undoubtedly derived from the general eschatological nature of their thought, which was oriented toward the end, rather than the beginning, of history."[46]

The interpretation of historical temporality in this characteristically Russian way provided Russian art and culture with a crucial link with postmodernism. As Epstein puts it:

> Postmodernism is essentially a reaction to utopianism, the intellectual disease of obsession with the future that infected the latter half of the nineteenth century and the first half of the twentieth. The future was thought to be definite, attainable, and realizable; in other words, it was given the attributes of the past. Postmodernism, with its aversion to utopias, inverted the signs and reached for the past, but in so doing, gave it the attributes of the future: indeterminateness, incomprehensibility, polysemy, and the ironic play of possibilities.[47]

In Boris Groys's view, "beginning with the Stalin years, at least, official Soviet culture, Soviet art, and Soviet ideology became eclectic, citational, 'postmodern.'"[48]

In other socialist countries under discussion, the rise of postmodern art and culture had less to do with the demise of Socialist Realism than with the development of local versions of the postmodern. First and foremost, in many of these countries, artists, critics, and the public commonly referred to works or artists as "postmodern" or "postmodernist." The reasons for such a designation varied, and the term itself often carried different connotations. Just as different cultural and political contexts produced a variety of different socialisms, they produced a variety of different postmodernisms, as well.

With significant exceptions, Socialist Realism had been the "official" art of many of the socialist countries. By the mid-1970s, however, an opposition had developed in both the Soviet Union itself and in Central and Eastern Europe that initially pitted official art, together with the "unofficial" modernists, who defended abstract painting and believed that there could be a "neutral zone" in which art could exist autonomously, against the proponents of the more recent art under consideration in this book.[49] This disjunction between official and unofficial art persisted. Although unofficial art was not banned in the Soviet Union, the extant conditions hindered its development. And as Igor Golomshtok has explained of Russian unofficial art in the 1950s, "while not being forbidden in the strict sense of the word and not hiding deep underground (as art of that kind had to in Nazi Germany), it . . . is indeed subjected to all sorts of persecutions and repressions."[50] Since no art market, no private galleries, no independent curators, and no revues existed that were not state funded, it was impossible to enter the usual channels of promotion.

The opposition between official and unofficial art also developed in China: "After 1979, the art world began to split into official and unofficial camps. The officially acknowledged artists concentrated on traditional Chinese painting, wood-engraving and oil-painting as developed under the influence of Soviet Socialist Realism. The unofficial camp worked on experimental forms, partly derived from modern Western art."[51] The main difference between China and the European socialist countries was that in China, modernist influences were hindered by the Cultural Revolution and therefore never were developed sufficiently enough to exert a strong influence on contemporary Chinese art.

Although in the Soviet Union, Socialist Realism had become an official doctrine in the early 1930s, in most of the other socialist countries, it became that only in the late 1940s. As a consequence of that shorter epoch of socialist art, the earlier art and culture of the European socialist countries and China had a stronger presence and thus Socialist Realist aesthetics, less influence.

Very often, earlier art and culture were reinterpreted to conform to the new ruling ideology and aesthetics.

There was a considerable amount of resistance within the Soviet bloc to the hegemony of Soviet-style Socialist Realism. In the Soviet bloc countries, artists and writers were for the most part increasingly opposed to closer contacts with the official Russian culture and, in the period of late socialism, to the promotion of Socialist Realism. "One could find no trace of 'Socialist Realism' in Hungary at the beginning of the new era of the 1980s. Granted, 'official' artists were still awarded many important contracts for monuments, but by about 1985 even this kind of cultural/political activity had all but disappeared."[52] An uneasy truce existed between the Polish, Czech, and Hungarian art worlds and that of the Soviet Union. In certain quarters, the aversion toward Russian culture was very strong; the Hungarian artist Attila Kovács, for example, explicitly stated that he would never consider using Russian Constructivist or Suprematist elements in his works.[53] An absence of this influence and others from Russian or early Soviet art, for reasons similar to those expressed by Kovács, is also evident in recent Polish and Czech art.

In the work of other artists, such as Gábor Bachman, also from Hungary, elements of early Russian avant-garde art reemerged in a different form, as a dehistoricized political application. Bachman mixes Constructivism, Futurism, and deconstruction as promoted by Derrida and practiced in architecture by Bernard Tschumi. Bachman explains: "I chose as a foundation a segment of the past, the so-called fantastic Russian architecture of the 1920s. . . . German expressionism and Russian futurism mingle with the philosophy of chaos and thus, together, lead to a deconstructionist trend that I consider specific because of its political context. . . . I work with the kind of allegories that make use of pathos, heroism, utopia and humour."[54]

In countries such as the former Yugoslavia and Cuba, Socialist Realism was either short-lived or never existed. In Yugoslavia, the ideals of the October Revolution were perceived as being relinquished by both Stalinism and Socialist Realism—a view also accepted by many Western art critics and writers. Beginning with the second half of the 1950s in Yugoslavia, because of the break with Stalin in 1948, the Socialist Realist doctrine (although not necessarily also its practice) was regarded as a Stalinist invention and hence politically inappropriate. From the early 1960s on, it was modernism that was considered politically correct. In Cuba, unlike the European Soviet bloc countries, socialism was not imposed from the outside, and as in the former

Yugoslavia and in "contrast to Eastern Europe, critical art in Cuba did not develop underground."[55] In Cuba, "from the very beginning of the Revolution, a majority of the Cuban artists distrusted Socialist Realism, a distrust shared by many political leaders."[56] Instead, Constructivist or Suprematist influences abound in the works created there, as they do in works from Yugoslavia.

Unlike Russia, the majority of the socialist countries in Europe had experienced the Enlightenment and for the most part perceived themselves as a part of the West, accepting its belief in historical progress and the possibility of infinite development, often identified with modernity: "In the vision of modernity, only the starting-point was more or less firmly fixed. The rest, precisely because of its undetermined character, appeared as a field of design, action and struggle."[57]

This vision of modernity also prevailed in Cuba, in spite of its obviously different history, providing an openness to art that went beyond the limits of Socialist Realism. This is testified to by the reception and artistic influence there of the works of one of the key figures of Russian art of this century, Kazimir Malevich, which were interpreted along the same abstract lines as in the West and were seen as devoid of their originally intended spiritual and mystical content. Malevich, and especially Russian Constructivism, with its openness to a wide range of materials, played a pivotal role in some of the artistic events discussed in this book. In some instances, non-Russian artists took into consideration Malevich's own intent, but most of his Suprematist works, which he believed emphasized abstraction as a way of making pure feeling triumph over mere objectivity, like the works of El Lissitzky and Vladimir Tatlin, were perceived primarily as aestheticized geometric forms or, more recently, as sacred objects to be taken from the repository of modern art history and appropriated freely by postmodernism—this appropriation being carried out not as a continuation of Russian mystical tradition, but as a recontextualization of their purported political intent.

It should be added that the reason for such a reception of Russian artistic and cultural trends in the socialist world was not only the predominantly nonmystical cultural tradition of these non-Russian countries, but also the fact that in much of the Soviet bloc, knowledge of Malevich was perhaps even more meager than that about Western art. Thus, for example, Hungarian artists such as Gábor Bachman and László Rajk had a firsthand encounter with Malevich's works for the first time during an exhibition in 1987 and were appropriately impressed.[58]

Conversely, however, during this period, the barriers to the exchange of information between the socialist countries and the West started to break down. It was therefore increasingly difficult to preserve the information blackout that existed in the 1960s or 1970s (in some countries, even in the 1980s). According to the Czech artist Milan Knížák, when he first encountered magazines on modern art in 1964, "I was very happy that I could see [the art of modern artists from abroad] and see there were people in the world who were similar to me."[59]

As in the Soviet Union, Socialist Realism was, of course, accepted as the official style in most of these countries, but in Europe, its historical connections were often interpreted or perceived as related to nineteenth-century realism or to local traditions of social realism in the 1920s and 1930s. In this way, Socialist Realism was mediated by local concerns and hence more easily assimilated. Still, this assimilation was mostly confined to official circles and varied in extent from country to country and from one period to another. The politicized art of the 1970s, 1980s, and 1990s appropriated primarily the most visible and most ideologically fraught symbols.

Unlike Socialist Realism, in practically all instances, postmodernism in the former and present socialist countries was apprehended as a positive phenomenon. In Central and Eastern Europe—especially in Hungary, Czechoslovakia, the former Yugoslavia, and Poland—it signified the most recent trend emanating from the West and its cultural capitals. Also, it initially allowed the proponents of the more recent art, that of the 1980s (often called marginal, alternative, subcultural, etc.), to draw a provisional line between that work and the overtly modernist and high-modernist art and literature of the 1960s and 1970s. Moreover, it permitted an artist to articulate and legitimize a different political stance toward ideology. The modernist artists and authors may have made use of the Aesopian language and, in the fine arts, retained the avant-gardist or high-modernist detached position toward politics and ideology, but the radical members of the younger generation viewed their activity very differently: Attila Kovács (born in 1951), one of the members of "the strange and new manifestation of Hungarian post-modern or alternative interior architecture and scenic design,"[60] thus claimed—in contradistinction to his older colleagues—that for him, "art is not a mission."[61] It is for this reason that these younger artists in Hungary and Slovenia, as well as the Czech émigré painter Milan Kunc, for example, were able to transgress the confines of the fine arts and become intensively involved in stage design, posters, architecture, or even chinaware.

Despite the generally favorable attitude toward postmodernism, however, a division existed within "socialist" postmodernism. One branch followed or imitated the somewhat fashionable trends imported from the West, such as the Trans-Avantgarde or the new classicism, while the other used postmodernist techniques and procedures but carried them out in more original ways, although these sometimes are still reminiscent of certain kinds of postmodernist—or even modernist—works of the First World. It is only this second kind that concerns us in this book.

In the former socialist countries, the dividing line between uncritical postmodernism and politicized postmodernism, the postmodernism that revealed the need for a new social "cognitive mapping," was much more pronounced than in most of the highly developed countries. This reenacts to a certain extent the division that existed at the time of the First World War between modernist nonpoliticized art and literature such as Kafka's and politicized Futurism, Vorticism, Constructivism, and Suprematism. Furthermore, Terry Eagleton's observation that "much postmodernist culture is both radical and conservative, iconoclastic and incorporated, in the same breath"[62] holds true not only for First World postmodernism, but frequently for its Second World counterpart, as well, and at least partly for that of China.

There were, of course, exceptions to the emergence of postmodern and postsocialist art in the socialist countries. In East Germany, political repression was so strong that the only artists who succeeded in developing postmodern art were those who emigrated to West Germany. It is for this reason that art of the German Democratic Republic is not discussed in this book. In Poland, the political and economic crises in the 1980s were so severe that postmodernism was only a vague idea, more potent among philosophers and writers than among visual artists. The result was that there, the legacy of the nonpoliticized Conceptual Art from the 1960s remained almost intact well into the late 1980s and even into the early 1990s. In Czechoslovakia after the Prague Spring of 1968, the regime was so oppressive that very few visual artists dared to invest their works with overt political views. Milan Knížák was jailed almost three hundred times, while the other prime exception, Milan Kunc, has lived in the West since 1969. It was instead up to the writers and playwrights to criticize old political ideas and promote new ones.

There also have been countries where the transition away from socialism has been arrested, and where the sociopolitical context, art, and culture have not moved beyond this first stage of late socialism. In the remnant of the former Yugoslavia and in Croatia, the transition from socialism was complicated, hindered, or even halted by the war in Bosnia and its vicinity, the consequence of such events being that the few international artists who remained there continued to practice an art strikingly similar to postsocialist postmodernism.

The Postsocialist Condition: The Age of Empty Signifiers

An essential part of the "postsocialist condition" was the ideological, political, and social vacuity of the ruling utopian political doctrine, a doctrine that exceeded plain political ideology, for it held in its grasp the whole of the social field and hence spontaneously affected all social realms. The situation that prevailed after fall of the Berlin Wall in November 1989 and after the subsequent fall of the regimes of various state-socialist countries and their Communist parties, is aptly summed up by Žižek with regard to what happened in Romania after the fall of Communism there:

> The most sublime image that emerged in the political upheavals of the last years—and the term "sublime" is to be conceived here in the strictest Kantian sense—was undoubtedly the unique picture from the time of the violent overthrow of Ceaușescu in Romania: the rebels waving the national flag with the red star, the Communist symbol, cut out, so that instead of the symbol standing for the organizing principle of the national life, there was nothing but a hole in its center. It is difficult to imagine a more salient index of the "open" character of a historical situation "in its becoming," as Kierkegaard would have put it, of that intermediate phase when the former Master-Signifier, although it has already lost its hegemonical power, has not yet been replaced by the new one. . . . The masses who poured into the streets of Bucharest "experienced" the situation as "open" . . . they participated in the unique intermediate state of passage from one discourse (social link) to another, when, for a brief, passing moment, the hole in the big Other, the symbolic order, became visible. The enthusiasm which carried them was literally the enthusiasm over this hole, not yet hegemonized by any positive ideological project; all ideological appropriations (from the nationalistic to the liberal-democratic) entered the stage afterwards and endeavored to "kidnap" the process which originally was not their own.[63]

Accompanying this enthusiasm was a sense of openness, a sense that the future is not just more of the same late-socialist present, but a different temporal realm, the beginning of which is incarnated in the present sense of anticipation of what is to come in post-utopian times. This postsocialist period produced a "post-utopian" art, as opposed to the prime example of utopian art, the art of the classical or historical avant-gardes.

A mundane description of such events in China can serve as an example of this sense of anticipation: "In the frightened and grey Beijing world of the late seventies . . . a small number of intellectuals and artists contributed to the strange atmosphere of unrest and expectation by using the narrow scope created by the cautious economic reforms to articulate an individual language."[64] One of the results of this new "atmosphere of unrest and expectation" was the foundation of the Beijing group Stars in 1979, a group that was at the root of post-Maoist art in China. Similar events, although taking place at different times during the period from the early 1970s to the early 1990s and in the other countries under discussion, offered the possibility that the long social stagnation and economic decline could finally be transformed into something different, that the quantitative accrual of economic failures, shortages of consumer goods, and unsuccessful economic and social reforms would bring about a qualitative change, to use a vintage formula of dialectical materialism. In this way, the vicious circle consisting of only two seasons—a political spring producing a "thaw," and another winter that always followed it—would be broken.

This openness was characterized foremost by indeterminacy, marking "the unique intermediate state of passage from one discourse (social link) to another," as Slavoj Žižek defines this Foucauldian break from the previous symbolic order and the onset of a new one. In the intermediate period of the first transition away from socialism, what Žižek calls the "vanishing mediator," borrowing the term from Fredric Jameson, enabled the change from one political system to another to take place, but was itself dialectically lost, transmogrified and marginalized in the process. "The 'vanishing mediator' . . . emerges because of the way, in a dialectical process, form stays behind content: first, the crucial shift occurs within the limits of the old form, even taking on the appearance of its renewed assertion . . . then, once the 'silent weaving of the spirit' finishes its work, the old form can fall off."[65] In Eastern Europe, as in Russia under Gorbachev, the vanishing mediator appeared as the "new social movements" that emerged during the last years of "actually existing socialism":

> groups of passionate intellectuals who "took socialism seriously" and were prepared to stake everything in order to destroy the compromised system

and replace it with the utopian "third way" beyond capitalism and "actually existing" socialism. Their sincere belief and insistence that they were not working for the restoration of Western capitalism of course proved to be nothing but an insubstantial illusion. . . . once their job is done, they are "overrun by history."[66]

A similar fate was destined for many artists under discussion here. It was also destined for much of the art they created during this intermediate period. Whether we are talking of Apt-Art of the 1982–84 period in the Soviet Union, the works from 1980 to 1982 by the Slovenian music group Laibach, the early projects of the subREAL group, or Milan Knížák's Conceptual work from the early 1960s in Czechoslovakia, none was ever capable of reinstituting the aura of its original appearance as a unique event. This loss came about even though such works and their authors had an enormous and later often undisputed influence upon subsequent art and culture.

Another facet of the enthusiasm for an indeterminate "third way" was skepticism concerning capitalism and the West. This predilection was discernible throughout the period on the three continents. Thus, within the Cuban "generation of the eighties," there were many who emigrated to Mexico during that decade and in the early 1990s but who nonetheless retained the belief in a brighter future for a truly socialist Cuba and "continue[d] to be, in however eclectic fashion, people of the Left."[67]

A step beyond such beliefs represents the disappointed reconciliation with the existential inappropriateness and vacuity of both "actually existing socialism" and capitalism. Erik Bulatov, one of the most important artists of the late socialist and postsocialist period in Russia, is just as critical of Western capitalism as he is of the Soviet system, and, unlike Vitaly Komar and Alexander Melamid and a series of others, he has not left the Soviet Union. "When they say that in contemporary America the dollar has devoured art, I always want to add that it devoured that art which itself tried to devour the dollar. Any society devours art that places itself in a common space with the society. It doesn't matter how this is done, whether through the dollar or through ideology. Every society simply uses the means at its disposal."[68] In this view, an equivalence thus emerges between the two countries that are the prime examples of capitalist and communist political systems. The role of commodity in one equals the role of ideology in the other. Each permeates all pores of the respective society. In the former, the billboards promote consumer products, while in the latter, they display ideological slogans and promote political ideology.

Also, for Bulatov, communist symbols never were an object of an artistic "unrestrained manipulation of meaningless ideologies. Bulatov's objective is to show that such ideologies are not dead but very much alive, and because they are so entrenched in the hidden depths of individual awareness they cannot be circumvented."[69] Bulatov's paintings reveal the belief that we all belong to a certain social reality and cannot pull ourselves out by our own hair.

Many of the artists who were critical of both the Soviet system and capitalism a decade or more ago have not changed their views much recently, although they have, of course, admitted the demise of the former and the successes of the latter. This stance has resulted in ambivalent or plainly critical positions concerning the West. On the one hand, in 1992, Mladen Stilinović from Croatia exhibited a plaque with an inscription "An Artist Who Cannot Speak English Is No Artist," while on the other, the group Laibach pronounced in one of its many statements that their performances in Western Europe represent an irritating "foreign body in the disintegrating entrails of a voracious beast."[70]

With the transition out of postsocialism and toward capitalism, the majority of the artists under discussion were forced to adapt to the emergent world of capitalist aspirations in their own countries or be marginalized. In this respect, the position of these artists was, of course, not much different from that of other intellectuals of the period or of ordinary people who were also forced to reinvent new lives and learn to live without the meager, but still-extant, socialist safety net.

The new, emergent conditions are more favorably inclined toward the globalized cultural artifacts than toward elitist, politically provocative, and socially subversive art and culture. What currently remains of this art is mostly its lighter or commercialized versions, such as "cynical realism" in China,[71] the continuation or imitations of the Russian Sots Art, and the commercialized and politically explicit art produced by the Cuban expatriate artists in Florida and sold to the "yuccas," the "young, upward-climbing Cuban Americans."

Late Socialist Postmodernism

I have so far referred almost exclusively simply to "art," without being too explicit about the artistic genres with which we are dealing. Most of the art discussed in the contributions that follow involves the visual arts in the broadest sense of the word—painting, installations, photography, design, and video. In the case of painting, very often images are supplemented by words, but postsocialist art can also be found in poetry, fiction, and music—in Russia, with the group Pop Mekhanika, which imitated the behavior of official brass bands, for example, and in Slovenia, in the music of the group Laibach, which forms the core of the Neue Slowenische Kunst organization, segments of which also work in theater and the cinema.

It often exists as Conceptual Art—art that is concerned more with exploring ideas than with exploring the materials it employs. In the countries under discussion, Conceptualism has persisted from the late 1960s or early 1970s up to the present.

Both the reasons for employing the term "Conceptualist" in describing some of the art under discussion and the difficulties encountered in attempting to delimit it are offered by Mikhail Epstein:

> [Russian] Conceptualists readily elaborate such general themes as "the communist conquers his inner hesitations and boldly leads his comrades to increased labor productivity." Since no self-respecting Soviet writer would limit himself or herself to such truisms, he or she would try very hard to describe this communist and his comrades as real people, with many plausible details, including their foibles and personal weaknesses. Nevertheless, this character essentially remains only a vehicle for some predetermined idea or ideological tenet. Conceptualists grasped and unmasked the artificial nature, not only of Soviet literature, but of Soviet reality itself. Their works cannot be *reduced* to concepts, only because they are willfully and fundamentally *deduced* from them. . . . They create excellent works of bad art that purposely and often masterfully imitate the typical Soviet range of ideas.[72]

Conceptualism was an "avant-garde" notion, designating both politicized art and the nonpoliticized art that was closely related to the avant-garde of the West. From its inception, Conceptualism in the socialist countries was an unofficial art form, possessing at the same time the aura of elite art. As we have seen, postmodernism entered these cultural spaces as a similarly positive and therefore desirable designation. In these cultural contexts, "Conceptualism" and "postmodernism" often have been used interchangeably: "The designation, Russian Conceptualism, is a highly contingent one and ultimately should be considered under the rubric of the postmodern, a term that in the West marks the end or at least conditional end of modernism."[73] However, the postmodern Conceptualism of the socialist countries developed differently from Conceptualism in the United States or Western Europe.

Unlike most Western Conceptual Art, Conceptual Art in the socialist countries was frequently politicized. This was so first and foremost because of the enforced homogeneity of political ideology in all facets of daily life. In the Soviet bloc countries, *everything* was by definition political. But frequently, in these countries, Conceptual Art consciously and overtly expressed political statements. Such was the case with Pinczehelyi and with certain Chinese and Cuban artists of the 1980s, with some of the early performances by Milan Knížák in the 1960s, with Balint Szombathy from the Yugoslav town of Subotica and Mladen Stilinović from Zagreb, and especially with a series of Russian artists ranging from the poet and visual artist Dmitrii Prigov to Ilya Kabakov.

Especially in smaller countries such as Slovenia, Hungary, and Cuba, the art under discussion had a significant political effect and was not, politically speaking, only a marginal social phenomenon: "1980s art ended up conversing with official institutions. The state was snubbed, courted, feared, defended, denounced, and mocked. Its modernizing project was thus dismantled."[74] In Slovenia, discussions about Laibach (which could not really be called Conceptual) took place not only among its fans, but also in the municipal and local governments, veterans' and youth organizations, and the Central Committee of the Slovenian League of Communists, while in Hungary, the postmodern architects Gábor Bachman and László Rajk staged the official commemoration for the victims of the 1956 revolution (see Figure 58).

These characteristics are reflected in the traits shared by postsocialist art: its Conceptualism and its specific use of the secondary discourse, ironically distanced from the official ideology that it employed; its conscious or spontaneous use of what are today considered to be postmodernist techniques and procedures; its use of socialist and communist imagery, national symbols, and folk, traditional, and mass culture; and its "binary" artistic approach, which results in works in which two realities retain their mutual incompatibility.

Postsocialist Conceptualism

Historically speaking, the majority of artists under consideration started as Conceptual artists, and many have remained that until today—Sándor Pinczehelyi (born in 1939) and Mladen Stilinović (born in 1947), from Zagreb, for example. Others, such as the Slovenian group Irwin and the Romanian group subREAL, may have exhibited works and put on performances that could legitimately be called "Conceptual" or " Neoconceptual," but they hardly ever refer to these notions when discussing their politicized works. The same holds true of those Chinese artists whose works could easily be designated as Neoconceptual. However, in Russia, because the notion of "unofficial art" even at its inception designated very little and has meant even less since the demise of the Soviet Union, the term "Conceptual Art," sometimes related to or used interchangeably and synonymously with notions such as Sots Art (Socialist Realism + Pop Art) and deconstructive postmodern or post-utopian art, has started to be employed, especially for the art created in the 1980s.

Much of the art from the other countries under consideration—especially the work from Hungary and China—is still or until very recently has been called "avant-garde." While this term is valid as long as it is used in a technical manner, it loses credibility when employed in a broader historical framework. A specific case is that of China, where some contemporary Chinese artists explicitly showed modernist avant-garde aspirations.

What is typical for many of the groups, individuals, and works discussed here, regardless of the country of origin, is the simulation of socialist imagery and ideological discourse, the invocation of socialist symbols "which become all signifier and no signified."[75] Again, a good example is the photograph *Hammer and Sickle* (1973), by the Hungarian Sándor Pinczehelyi (see Figure 1), of which a black-and-white and a red version exist. As Lóránd Hegyi says of this work:

> the artist keeps real objects, a real hammer and a real sickle, in his hands, and strains the known political symbols to his body. His two hands are strictly crossed in front of his chest, as in Egyptian representations; his face is framed by the sickle and the hammer. . . . Pinczehelyi abolishes the symbol—by means of tautology—as he makes the abstract concept a concrete object. However, by this, he creates a new symbol as well, which acquires a new content by the radical reinterpretation.
>
> Tautology completes the process of defetishization: the sickle is nothing else than an ordinary sickle, the hammer is nothing else than an ordinary hammer. . . .
>
> Pinczehelyi with this piece of art joins with the conceptualism of the sixties. In Joseph Kosuth's work *One and Three Chairs,* dating from 1965, tautology appears in the same form . . . as a means of identification of abstract concept and concrete object, or that of the documentation of the object.[76]

The Hungarian artist "shows the object itself," revealing the meaningless materiality of the two objects, which in the 1970s still functioned representationally only in their symbolic emanation. By doing this, Pinczehelyi engendered one of the early postmodern works. Postmodernism

> consists not in demonstrating that the game works without an object, that the play is set in motion by a central absence, but rather in displaying the object directly, allowing it to make visible its own indifferent and arbitrary character. The same object can function successively as a disgusting reject and as a sublime, charismatic apparition: the difference, strictly structural, does not pertain to the "effective properties" of the object, but only to its place in the symbolic order.[77]

Exactly the same procedure is employed by Dmitrii Prigov in his *Signature Can* from 1977–78, a metal can covered with signatures, with a little sign on top reading: "A can of signatures for the complete and unconditional disarmament of America." It is again a political gesture that is revealed in its materiality: The can of signatures is but a harmless and pitiful can, which in its artistic emanation reveals its total ideological finality.

Desymbolizing the otherwise potentially political signification of such an object by exhibiting it in its materiality and by showing its arbitrary character is just the opposite of the procedure elaborated theoretically six decades earlier by Victor Shklovski and the Russian Formalists. Their intent (and that of the Russian Futurists) was to show the poetic nature of everyday words, sounds, and objects, to make us conscious of the originary, poetic nature of words, a gesture similar to that elaborated by Heidegger and Merleau-Ponty in their existential phenomenology. In the case of the art under discussion, the intent is to reveal the sheer material nature of objects that have been devoured by ideological symbolization.

Prigov's work displays the signatures, written in various alphabets and by different hands and with pens of different colors, on the outer surface of the can. Although this is "a can of signatures," the signatures do not exist materially—on slips of paper, for example. They appear instead on the two-dimensional surface of a three-dimensional object—a rudimentary form of the procedure that would be developed in all its potential by Erik Bulatov (born in 1933) and Ivan Chuikov (born in 1935). Bulatov's paintings from 1971 on represent a continuous and successful attempt to combine the material two-dimensionality of the painted surface with the three-dimensionality of the depicted perspectival space of the picture (see Figures 15, 16, and 17).

Within Bulatov's pictures of serene landscapes and scenes from quotidian city life, everyday signs appear, usually signifying an interdiction: "Do

Not Lean On," or "Dangerous." In what is probably his earliest work of this sort, *The Horizon* (1971–72), Bulatov depicts a group of people on a beach, gingerly walking toward the water. Superimposed on the horizon is a red ribbon that "turns out to be the ribbon of the Order of Lenin."[78] The picture, which also resembles Malevich's *Red Cavalry at Full Gallop* (1928–32), combines "the illusionary three-dimensional realistic picture and suprematist flatness. . . . By symbolizing the victory of social space, the Order of Lenin, so to speak, concretizes Malevich's 'abstract' geometric forms."[79]

In Bulatov's work, the social space always intrudes upon the pictorial space of art, for "Culture [= art] is not a product of society, but a challenge and alternative to society."[80] Art and society exist in two different spaces. As Bulatov himself put it: "Our task and the task of our generation is to show that this world depicted as unshakeable, immutable, eternal is not everything. This apparently immutable world is in fact false, ephemeral and untrue. Real existence is to be found on the other side of the boundary. This explains why that space beyond the picture is so important to me too. For me it is the true existence." That is "the difference between us [Bulatov and Ilya Kabakov] and all the other artists who oppose Soviet power, such as Komar and Melamid or our émigré writers":

> their subconscious is so conditioned that an entire world can be described using their system of symbols (i.e. those of communism and socialism). They don't ask themselves: Is this the whole world? To them it really is, they merely reverse symbols; the world is not good, but bad, there are holes in it. The communist consciousness remains intact, and only the symbols are exchanged. This differs fundamentally from our consciousness . . . we don't believe that it is necessary to change the entire world, only that it is important to regard it as totally false.[81]

Art such as Bulatov's, although Conceptual, thus is far removed from its counterparts from the West: It serves a transcendent function. And although it employs signs and, like the work of other Russian artists such as Ilya Kabakov, uses an abundance of slogans and other narratives, it is patently different from the work of Jenny Holzer or Barbara Kruger.

In the series of paintings also entitled *Hammer and Sickle* from 1986 (see Plate 11) Pinczehelyi carries out the same procedure, making the arbitrary character of the symbolic objects visible, but now serializes the motif of the hammer and sickle in a Warholian fashion. This gesture, however, deprives his 1973 *Hammer and Sickle* of none of its premonitional value. In this earlier work by the artist from the provincial town of Pécs, we sense the same gesture exhibited by Andy Warhol in his series of prints from the early 1960s on as described by Fredric Jameson:

> Andy Warhol's work in fact turns centrally around commodification, and the great billboard images of the Coca-Cola bottle or the Campbell's soup can, which explicitly highlight the commodity fetishism of a transition to late capital, *ought* to be powerful and critical political statements. If they are not that, then one would surely want to know why, and one would want to begin to wonder a little more seriously about the possibilities of political and critical art in the postmodern period of late capital.[82]

British Pop Art from the 1960s also carried a critical and antiauthoritarian potential, but was later transformed into traditional gallery art, so Jameson's question may be pertinent to more than Warhol's work alone. Within the former socialist countries, however, the tradition of Pop Art and related trends offered a venue for the artistic expression of social and political reality and retained this potential well into the period of postsocialism. It introduced the possibility of a simultaneously critical and unauthoritarian treatment of political ideology.

In the paintings of Carlos Rodríguez Cárdenas (born in 1960), who belongs to the "second," or postmodern, generation of Cuban artists, we can discern a procedure very similar to that employed by Pinczehelyi. In his *Building the Sky* (Figure 5), we see exactly what its title denotes: a wall of blue bricks rising above the green rolling hills, thus visually depicting the ideological slogan used for the title. We are confronted with a materialization of the enunciated words. Metaphor, often so dear to creators of ideological imagery, here is taken seriously—literally—as in the case of Pinczehelyi's hammer and sickle. As Gerardo Mosquera observes, the artist "concentrates on appropriating the stereotyped slogans that inundate Cuban life . . . placing them in new semantic settings by means of a process of ironic deconstruction."[83] Again we encounter explicit links with Conceptualism. The generation of the teachers of Carlos Rodríguez Cárdenas organized the *Volumen I* exhibition in 1981, which represented their break with the traditionalist past. In its time, it was "described as 'a challenge' and 'formalist,' and it was said to 'have given up identification with values that define our national identity.'" However, "after this the way was clear for the overthrow of traditional values in art. Certain features of conceptual art and affiliated trends became the focus of attention."[84]

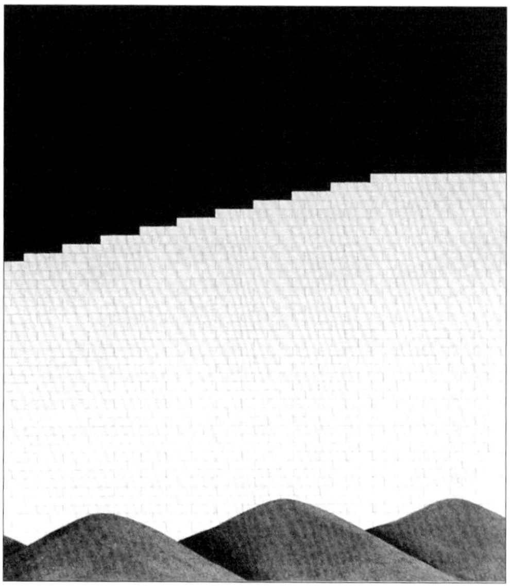

Figure 5 Carlos Rodríguez Cárdenas, *Building the Sky*, 1989, acrylic on paper, 19.3 × 16 cm.

As these examples show, a central feature of Conceptual Art from socialist countries is its preoccupation with words, captions, and slogans:

> The emergence of Soviet Conceptualism in the early 1970s can be linked to [the] sudden intrusion of speech into visual art . . . the use of text in the works of Kabakov, Bulatov and Komar and Melamid stressed the "infection with speech practices" that pervaded the Soviet sociocultural atmosphere. Second, their use of generic language or other elements from "low" culture transformed the attitude of alternative practitioners toward the mass media, which was still regarded primarily as a vehicle of official propaganda. And, finally, as a result of these new attitudes toward text and Soviet mass culture, these artists redirected alternative art away from Western sources and closer to the local ones.[85]

Words become real material objects in the paintings of Erik Bulatov (see Figures 16 and 17), Aleksandr Kosolapov, Ilya Kabakov, and Komar and Melamid, in accordance with the political slogan that ideas are a material force. In this respect, this art differs from its modernist predecessors, as well: "In the formal respect, the Soviet post-utopian art of the 1970s is characterized above all by a renewed narrativity that runs counter to the avant-garde rejection of literariness and instead continues the narrativity of socialist realism."[86]

In Bulatov's case, slogans intrude upon the inner subjective reality that, in the artist's view, is the authentic reality. They represent instead the unavoidable reality of political ideology that permeates all socialist existence.

Just as Lenin claims in his essay "What Is to Be Done?" that there is no space without ideology, that ideology is either socialist or bourgeois, Kabakov's paintings and those of Wang Guangyi and Milan Kunc, for example, imply that the symbolic universes of capitalism and socialism function according to a similar economy.

However, let us compare the slogans and images. Pinczehelyi's hammer and sickle are no less eloquent than a painting that contains Communist political slogans. The hammer and sickle have lost their original meaning as mere tools and have been completely appropriated by the symbolic universe of political ideology. It is now up to the artist to revert them to their nonsymbolic, quotidian reality, producing by this procedure an artistic effect. It could therefore be said that the political symbols, as well as consumerist Western symbols, are equal in the signification they possess to the narrative structures included in some of the paintings. The narrative and visual symbols are interchangeable: The whole realm of the social, the whole lived world, is nothing but a symbolic universe that, in the socialist case, is completely subjugated to political ideology. To be more precise, this social space is almost completely permeated with ideology, and no difference or distance exists between the two. Art is one of the few venues open for revealing this consubstantiality, for it enables us, as Louis Althusser remarked, "to see the reality of the existing ideology"—although art is at the same time part of that ideology.[87]

Postmodern Applications

As we have already seen, the politicized art of the postsocialist era employed many of the characteristic techniques of postmodernism. Although the term "postmodernism" has acquired different meanings in various socialist and nonsocialist countries and in the works of various authors,[88] and although the eclecticism of peripheral cultures may only appear to be "postmodern," as Camnitzer has argued, too many common features link recent Western and Eastern art to make us abandon this common designation.

By making such a claim I am but rephrasing the argument advanced by various authors (and especially artists) from the former socialist countries that the consumer ideology of the West has paralleled the political ideology of the East. In late socialism and postsocialism, the situation became more complex. This complexity mirrors the demise of the master narratives of the twentieth century, socialist ideology among them.

One of the better-known tenets of Marxism was the belief that capitalism produces commodity fetishism. The aim of socialism was said to be just the opposite. In place of the consumerism with which Western capitalism purportedly "bought" workers, persuading them that new cars, refrigerators, washing machines, and TV sets were "better value" than world revolution, socialism promised a classless society devoid of alienation, reified intersubjective relations, social insecurity, and so on. Socialism attempted to persuade its people to accept such a view by means of ideology understood as class consciousness, a notion already developed by Lenin in his essay "What Is to Be Done?" of 1902. There, Lenin distinguished between bourgeois and socialist ideology: "The working class spontaneously gravitates towards Socialism, but the more widespread (and continuously revived in the most diverse forms) bourgeois ideology nevertheless imposes itself upon the working class still more."[89]

This parallel between the ideological universe of the socialist world and the consumerist universe of the capitalist one was most forcibly developed in the Soviet Union: "The most banal language in the Soviet Union is the ideological one. In the West there are the commercials, television, the giant flood of images. There, too, it is a question of a language of banalities. This language of Western truisms can describe the social space equally well as the language of ideology in the Soviet Union."[90]

However, the antithesis between ideology and consumerism, East and West, becomes less valid when applied to countries such as Hungary, not to mention the former Yugoslavia, on the one hand, and Western European social democracies, on the other. It would therefore be a great oversimplification to claim that we can transpose the place of the USSR vis-à-vis the United States to all the former or present socialist countries. The Western and Eastern symbols—the Coca-Cola, McDonald's, and Marlboro logos and the red stars, hammers and sickles, Lenins, and Marxes—were much more abundant and publicly visible in both superpowers than elsewhere. Only when they became common currency were they also employed in China.

The artists from Yugoslavia never applied these Western trademarks (or the Eastern ones, for that matter), for their use would appear too banal. There, Western consumer products were a part of everyday life and possessed no symbolic political significance. The same was true of the socialist ideological icons. The first time that the Irwin group began to use socialist paraphernalia extensively was after the demise of socialism in the early 1990s, when it started to include party publications and party signs in its installations. In Cuba, the major part of the "generation of the eighties" viewed a Sots Art approach as too irreverent for serious art, the exception being some émigré artists in Florida, while Pinczehelyi's art remained unique in Hungary.

One of the most salient features that postsocialist Conceptualism had in common with Western art, however, was its use of the techniques characteristic of postmodernism—eclecticism, pastiche, quotation, intertextuality, reevaluation of the past and of traditional art, frequent use of figurality, and so on. Although terms such as "intertextuality" and "remake" are mostly applied to fiction, they are also useful in the realm of visual arts and other artistic genres. In the major part of the art under discussion, works from various periods are profusely employed, and in certain cases, whole works are remade. The Belgrade artist Goran Djordjević (and his anonymous counterpart), for example, copied not only individual works, but a whole series of them, and whole exhibitions. In this way, he carried out an aim similar to that of certain New York artists from the late 1970s who also copied the works of others and questioned the notion of authorship. In this early period, the early 1980s, he also promulgated the art of Malevich and his contemporaries.

Djordjević also strongly influenced the Slovenian music group Laibach, which was in the habit of adapting not only songs by other musicians, but whole albums, including *Let It Be*, by the Beatles.[91]

Copying the works of other artists was a common practice in many countries. Not only Goran Djordjević, but also the Slovenian group of painters called Irwin, which was founded in 1984, practiced this procedure. Irwin not only used works by Marcel Duchamp, René Magritte, and Slovenian artists, copying them and introducing them as motifs in their own paintings and installations, but also consciously revealed the problematic relationship between the original and the copy and between art and its broader political context or background. The group of designers called the New Collectivism, another member group of the Neue Slowenische Kunst organization, produced remakes of posters, the best known among them being the one to honor the 1987 Youth Festival in Belgrade. When it had already been selected by the federal jury as the official poster of this all-Yugoslav celebration of Tito's birthday, it was discovered that the chosen work was a remake of a painting by Richard Klein entitled *The Third Reich* (Figure 6).

In China, at *A Modern Exhibition of Five Artists* in 1983, the painting *The Haystack*, by Huang Yongping (born in 1954), "triggered a scandal.

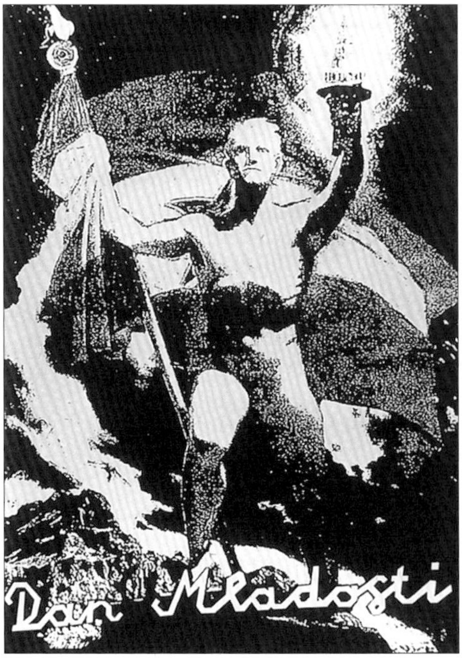

Figure 6 New Collectivism, a draft for the "Day of Youth" poster, 1987, 100 × 70 cm.

It was a new version of a copy of a painting which had been made in 1978 by one of his teachers at the Academy, itself a copy of *Les Foins*, a work by the French painter Jules Bastien-Lepage (1848–1884)."[92]

Yet another series of postmodern remakes consists of some works produced by Milan Kunc from 1974 to 1979 in a genre that he calls "Embarrassing" or "Painful" Realism, which employs everything from the old masters to Pop Art and Communist imagery.

These are only some of the most obvious cases of postmodern appropriation visible in the works of the late socialist artists. Many other works employ a Pop Art or a Conceptualist approach, which fortuitously juxtaposes or mixes everyday objects, political paraphernalia, and narrative elements borrowed from socialist political propaganda slogans and metaphors. In this respect, they strongly resemble postmodern works from the First World, except that political ideology and its signs take the place of everyday objects and commodities.

In early and late works of many of the artists under discussion, the influence of Pop Art is obvious. In addition to its influence on the Russian Sots Art movement, Sándor Pinczehelyi's works from the 1970s and 1980s, and Milan Kunc's Ost Pop, it is immediately recognizable in the Chinese "Political Pop," which started with Yu Youhan's *Mao* series in 1989 and became most widely known with Wang Guangyi's *Great Castigation* series (see Figure 75). In it, as in Aleksandr Kosolapov's, Milan Kunc's and Komar and Melamid's works, capitalist and Communist imagery are placed side by side or, rather, layered: Marlboro, Cadbury's, and Kodak signs are superimposed on political propaganda images from the time of the Cultural Revolution, creating a two-dimensional space in which two symbolic realities meet: the East represented by petrified and desubjectivized figures of socialist workers depicted in the style of revolutionary realism and the East "where the taste of Coca-Cola and McDonald's was nearly unknown [and where] such signs assumed a purely abstract ideological role as signs of the West."[93]

Socialist and Communist Imagery

Thus, the most obvious feature of socialist postmodernism is its exuberant use of Communist and socialist imagery. In the frequent division of art into official and unofficial or dissident spheres during the era of modernism, ideological symbols or slogans appeared only in a satirical context, or their presence was perceived as proof that the artist who employed them had succumbed to political propaganda. Imre Bak (born in 1939), one of the leading Hungarian modernist painters, considered since the early 1980s to be a "postmodern eclectic," explained that "art, if it is to remain art, should never have a political function."[94] Postsocialist postmodern art, however, uses political slogans and statements and their visual depiction, plus official portraits, symbols, and icons, in an infinite number of ways and eclectically mixes them. Aleksandr Kosolapov, for example, in his painting *A Malevich Page* (1986), created a copy of the well-known Socialist Realist picture *Stalin and Voroshilov in the Kremlin* (1938), by Aleksandr Gerasimov, with the word "Malevich," executed in the manner of the Marlboro cigarette logo, superimposed on the three-dimensional painting. The same device is employed in numerous Chinese works from the early 1990s on and in those of the group Irwin, for example in its 1987 painting *The Red Districts* (see Plate 4). The work is a remake of one of the few Slovenian works of Socialist Realism. Although it was made by the Irwin group, afterward, it was signed by the original work's creator, the painter Janez Knez.

What is at stake in *The Red Districts* is a relation to the past, not just the issue of an original and its copy. In the paintings and installations by Kosolapov, in many works by Komar and Melamid, in certain works by Sándor Pinczehelyi, in those of Cuban artists such as Flavio Garciandía, René Francisco, and Ponjuán, and in Chinese Political Pop and Rogue Cynicism,[95] however, the aim is more playful. Russian Sots Art especially, inaugurated by Komar and Melamid in 1972 and overtly related to Pop Art, aims mainly at amusing, not at spiritually heightening our awareness, as Erik Bulatov, Ilya Kabakov, and Oleg Vasilev do.

The prime Communist symbol, the hammer and sickle, is to be found in the works of many late socialist artists. In the work of Flavio Garciandía (see Figures 2, 59, and 60), "the phallic anthropologization of the hammer and sickle, aside from being an allusion to *perestroika* as a revitalization of the USSR, also represents a 'third world' appropriation of a communist emblem."[96] In some of these cases, the hammer and the sickle are the works themselves: Leonid Sokov in 1988 created his own pair made out of fur, while in 1979, Milan Kunc made loaves of bread in their shape and titled them *The Food of Tomorrow*. In 1989, Andrei Filippov exhibited them on a table as eating utensils.

Innumerable Lenins, Stalins, and red stars employed in installations, paintings, and sculptures are used in the same manner as the Pop Art icons and objects of mass consumption in the West. The abundance of works with these motifs can also be explained by commercial aspirations and expectations, although this predominantly applies to art of the two biggest countries under discussion, the Soviet Union and China. The demand for such art, some of it executed by émigré artists, was greater there than in the Central and Eastern European countries, where only a few foreign collectors visited and where art continued to be comprehended as a basically noncommercial endeavor.

The Resurgence of National Heritage and Artistic Tradition

It is not just the use of Communist imagery that characterizes politicized art in the late socialist countries, but the use of nationalist symbols and images, as well. In the 1950s and early 1960s, a series of American artists, Jasper Johns the best known among them, painted the American flag. As Lucy R. Lippard noted in 1966, Jasper Johns is not "a Pop Artist in style or subject matter, though [he is] still considered to be such in Europe and by the mass media."[97] It is not impossible that Jasper Johns, with his well-known *Flag* (1954), may have at least in some instances served as the historical influence for the similar use of national and ideological symbols in late socialism that we find in various countries of the Soviet bloc.

In 1981, Sándor Pinczehelyi painted three paprikas in the Hungarian national colors, red, white, and green (see Plate 10). Two years later, he did the same with three sickles, exhibiting them on a floor covered with straw, after which he painted three chicken eggs in a straw nest and then even the grass and the trees, naming these works consecutively *Sickles from the Great RWG Farm*, *A Nest with RWG Eggs*, and *The Trees of the Great RWG Farm*. The "RWG" stood for "red, white, and green," the artist imposing a symbolic national ownership on these objects by painting the Hungarian tricolor on them. The gesture, of course, was ironical, but it nonetheless expressed the perceptive observation that the national components of the lived world were becoming increasingly important and were replacing the previous universal and transnational symbols of the hammer and sickle, which, in the photograph from 1973 (Figure 1), were devoid of any national appropriation.

Similar gestures include Russian and Chinese artists using their national alphabets or appropriating nationalist motifs in a narrative manner while at the same time exhibiting their "Russian" or "Chinese" nationality. It was in this vein that members of the Laibach group, in a video clip for their music album in 1989, displayed themselves in front of the Aljaž Tower, a metal shelter on top of Mount Triglav, the highest mountain in Slovenia and its national symbol. The Aljaž Tower was shown wrapped in a black flag with a cogwheel and Malevich's cross in the middle—the trademark of the Laibach group. In this manner, the group symbolically appropriated the Slovenian national icon.

The resurgence of national and local motifs bears witness to the end of modernism. Modernism strove to be international, urban, and elitist, with these aspirations even more pronounced in peripheral cultures in which the use of motifs that originated in the urban and cultural centers of Europe was for the most part also an attempt at cosmopolitanism, at breaking out of the narrow and provincial environments of these cultures. In the Soviet bloc countries, the appropriation of modernism (when and where it was allowed) also made possible an unpoliticized form of art that offered an escape from the ever-present political ideology.

The arrival and emergence of postmodernism in socialist countries thus resulted in a renewed interest in traditional motifs and the use of quotations from and references to classical works from these cultures. The works of the classical avant-gardes held a special attraction. In Hungary, Gábor Bachman employed the "picture architecture" of Lajos Kassák, who published a manifesto by the same name in 1922,[98] while in Slovenia, the theater section of the Neue Slowenische Kunst organization named itself after *Red Pilot,* an avant-garde revue from the early 1920s.

"Binary" Approaches

In the spring of 1968, Jean-François Lyotard held a seminar at Nanterre devoted to political posters.[99] Lyotard was especially interested in a poster by El Lissitzky, the *Street Poster* (1919–20) (Figure 7), which reads: "Beat the Whites with the Red Wedge." The work itself, which was intended for political propaganda (the "Red Wedge" is the Red Army, and the "Whites" are the counterrevolutionaries), was also one of El Lissitzky's first abstract works.[100] The poster represents a paramount example of what I call the "binary" approach—here, the juxtaposition of the textual and the figurative—in which each element retains its individual significance, as in a binary opposition. While giving a semiotic analysis of the poster and mainly referring to Roland Barthes, Lyotard acutely notices this visual paradox in Lissitzky's poster, for as "the written becomes form, the figure appears to become the text of forms. There is a deconstruction of letters and words, on one side, which bears not only upon the signified ('beat with the wedge'), but upon the graphism as well, dealt with in a plastic relation with the space: it is therefore a figural work."[101] The poster as a whole, besides being a work of political propaganda, thus also exhibits an overt aesthetic function. Its simple graphisms convey an excess of signification. Pure ideological statement and pure aesthetic object never meet in a single space, for this would destroy the perception and reception of each of them. The effect produced by the poster resembles visual paradoxes where, by changing our inner perceptual vantage point, we see the same object in a different way, or as a different object. In the case of the poster (and in many other works by the same artist or by Malevich), the aesthetic effect engendered by pure geometric forms augments the ideological effect of the written statement, and vice versa. The image and the narrative exist in two distinct spaces. They merely intersect, producing in our perception not a unified effect, but a doubled or parallel impression—a binary effect.

This binary approach strongly characterizes the work of numerous late socialist and postsocialist artists. It can be seen in Erik Bulatov's juxta-

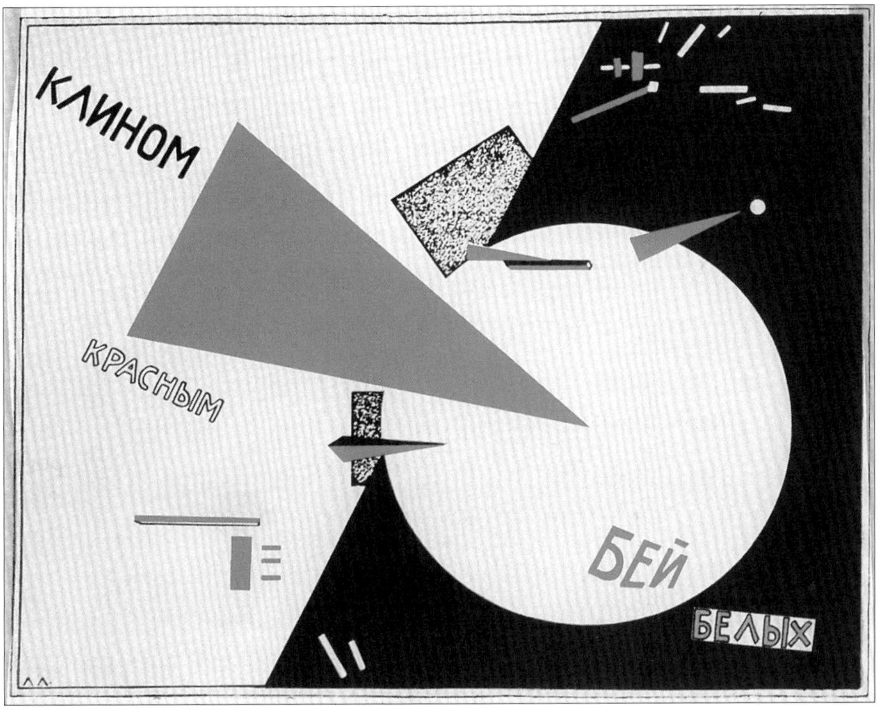

Figure 7 El Lissitzky, *Street Poster*, 1919–20, 54 × 72 cm.

position of a three-dimensional perspectival space of the picture and a two-dimensional political slogan superimposed on it, and, in a somewhat different manner, in Conceptualism as described by Epstein and enacted not only in fiction, but in the visual artworks of Pinczehelyi, Garciandía, and the subREAL group in Romania. In March 1990, for example, in Bucharest, subREAL exhibited portraits of President Iliescu (the immediate successor to Ceauşescu) that "raised a controversial scandal and a dispute between those who suspected a new adulatory attitude" toward the regime "and those who condemned the irreverent gesture. As usual, subREAL was misunderstood by everybody, and that was paradoxically satisfactory for this group."[102] With this exhibition subREAL achieved the paradoxical reception that group members wanted: one side accused the group of mocking Iliescu, implying a modernist critical or a typically dissident stance, while the other, the "dissident" side, comprehended the gesture as an accolade to the regime.

Both interpretations, as long they strive to attain exclusiveness, are erroneous, of course. They cannot simultaneously be grasped as a conceptual whole, for they are indeed incompatible. Just as in Fichtean dialectics, where thesis and antithesis never reach a synthesis, here, too, both interpretations exist side by side, never coexisting in a conceptual sublation, never attaining a unity, creating by this gesture an abyss between the visual and the conceptual, an unrepresentable whole:

> the impotence of the imagination attests *a contrario* to an imagination striving to figure even that which cannot be figured, and that imagination thus aims to harmonize its object with that of reason—and that furthermore the inadequacy of the images is a negative sign of the immense power of the ideas. This dislocation of the faculties among themselves gives rise to the extreme tension (Kant calls it agitation) that characterizes the pathos of the sublime, as opposed to the calm feeling of beauty.[103]

Perhaps the ceaseless fascination with Suprematism and Constructivism and their simultaneous use of purely aesthetic and purely symbolic or politically symbolic forms stems from the employment of a similar procedure, of what Lyotard called the "visual paradox." This approach, which Margarita Tupitsyn has called "the visualization of verbal concepts,"[104] found its first applications in the works of the Russian classical avant-garde and then in postsocialist Conceptual Art.

Related phenomena are the performances and statements of music groups. In the 1980s, the St. Petersburg group Pop Mekhanika, for example, staged its concerts dressed as a military band, often persuading the audience that they in fact were an official Soviet orchestra. The Laibach group, purportedly "one of the cleverest cultural manipulations since the Trojan horse,"[105] surpassed the ideological effects of the political populism of the late period of self-management socialism in Yugoslavia by incessantly repeating ideological statements and reenacting totalitarian rituals at their extreme. By presenting itself since its inception in 1980 as an excessive simulacrum of political ideology, it created a paradox similar to that for which subREAL strived. At the same time, it collapsed socialist, fascist, and national-socialist ideologies, the result being music that in Great Britain, for example, was equally well received—because of its ostensible political message—by the political Left and the nationalist, racist National Front. In Poland during the 1980s, the Orange Alternative movement likewise "staged street happenings to ridicule the reality of the communist system, including 'celebrations' of official holidays (the anniversary of the October Revolution) and mock festivals to commemorate Communist institutions (such as the police and militia)."[106] Such actions were designated "idiot art," "embarrassing art," or "decadent socialism."[107]

Such acts and actions bring to mind those started by the Zurich Dada in 1915. Nonetheless, while the Dadaists also carried out acts with overt political connotations, they existed within the very different social and political framework of Western Europe and New York. While their actions provoked public consternation and indignation, they did not carry a real political significance.

The actions of Laibach and subREAL, and the ironic works by Pinczehelyi, Kunc, Komar and Melamid, and Wang Guangyi, to mention but a few, emerged and then existed in very different social and political contexts: Within their socialist universe, every act was immediately transformed into a political act. Although under late socialism the political circumstances already have changed, artistic acts and works that were not codified, that is, that did not allow for a simple recognition and insertion within the extant frames of reference, were just as problematic as the traditional dissident art. In both cases, it was this problematic and politicized status of art that significantly added to its artistic relevance. As in the times of the so-called classical or historical avant-gardes and of the politicized segment of modernism, the political relevance and impact of art, although of a different kind, was also dependent on the political critique it engendered, and even on its prohibition.

While much of the earlier art in the socialist countries was either official, avant-garde in the nonpoliticized modernist sense, or dissident, the politicized art of the late socialist period profoundly differed from it, as well as from its nonpoliticized postmodern contemporary art, which was being simultaneously created in these very same countries. Since much of this art not only came into existence in countries that lacked a proper art market and related institutions and mechanisms known and abundant in the West, but also emerged at the time of the collapse of these regimes, it is not so surprising that as a homogeneous phenomenon, it has so far generated little recognition.

This book shows the common or similar traits of this distinct and specific artistic phenomenon, which in a limited time span existed on three different continents and in countries with very different kinds of socialism. Although such a project may appear dubious in a time when the deconstructive theoretical discourses are complemented by a disregard for totalizing narratives, I believe that the politicized art of late socialism warrants a critical analysis that reveals similarities while at the same time pays due attention to the differences. For a single person to accomplish this, that person would have to be not only fluent in Chinese, Russian, Hungarian, Slovenian, and Spanish but also well informed about the art and culture of the respective countries. For that reason, this volume was conceived not as a collection of loose essays by some of the foremost authorities in this field but as if it had been written by a single or even a "collective" author from the cultures and countries involved.

• • •

The obvious question that the reader may ask is what has happened in recent years to the artists discussed in this volume, especially since one of the basic arguments presented in this introduction is that the politicized art of late socialism is not only a transient phenomenon, itself being born out of transient historical and political conditions, but predominantly also already a past one. The conditions under which it appeared were special, for it was the highly politicized, ideologically distinct, and culturally specific context that allowed this politicized postmodern art to emerge in what often were unexpected places: in impoverished Romania, for example, where food was so scarce that the subREAL group in 1991 exhibited it as rare artistic artifacts, or in China, where, in the 1989 *China / Avant-Garde* exhibition, everything, whether the sale of shrimp or any other kind of performance, could become a political event with unforeseen consequences. Under such conditions, artistic events often developed into unique artistic phenomena that hardly find equivalents outside the confines of the postsocialist framework.

In the First World by the 1980s, art had, for better or worse, mostly lost that greater political impact that it possessed in the first half of the previous century and even in the 1960s. If it has retained political engagement, it has done so in relation to topics relevant not to "society" as such, but to special groups and to particular communities. In the passage from the previous ideological and cultural uniformity of socialism into the future capitalist cultural openness, the art of the postsocialist period, as well, has mostly lost political relevance and abstained from championing or opposing a political "cause."

A true artist always finds a way to express himself or herself and the lived world in ways previously unforeseen and unimagined. This is also true of many of the artists discussed in this volume: It suffices to glance at the list of the artists exhibiting in the forty-eighth Venice Biennial[108] to find there the group subREAL, representing Romania, and Komar and Melamid, representing Russia, with the Cuban artist Kcho, also discussed in this book, included in the prestigious APERTO section—where we also find numerous contemporary Chinese creators of works of the sort analyzed in this book.

Other artists discussed in this volume have followed very different paths. Milan Knížák from Prague, who had been dean of the Academy of Fine Arts, became the general director of the National Gallery in Prague after the political changes of 1989. Attila Kovács today spends most of his time in California, where he continues doing cinema stage design. In February 2002, his *House of Terror*, dedicated to the victims of totalitarian regimes of the previous century, was opened by the Hungarian prime minister, with one hundred and fifty thousand people attending the event. In Sándor Pinczehelyi's recent works, stars still appear, but they are now completely depoliticized, accompanied by a rose or a chain. His works show that the artists who were the most politicized in their works have the most difficult time adjusting to the changed and nonpoliticized circumstances.

As befits the avant-garde, today, the initial homogeneity of the groups and trends that existed in the 1980s and the early 1990s has disappeared. This is also a consequence of the current internationalization of art, which differs enormously from the situation in the 1970s and also the 1980s, when artists in socialist countries generally had very little knowledge of developments in the arts elsewhere in the world and, furthermore, political and cultural circumstances were also profoundly different. Where art of the late socialist period can still be found today, in China and Cuba, it usually builds on the tradition established in the 1980s, although the subject matter is often profoundly different, for it is concerned no longer with Communist symbols and political issues, but rather with consumerist ideology and artistic experimentation.

Today, most of the art discussed here is a past phenomenon. As shown, this does not signify that the artists are no longer there, or that they have ceased to make art. The art that they produce today, however, is more international, or, if it remains "national," it often exploits its own past. The original variety could emerge and exist only within its specific culturally and historically transient ambiance. Although artistically and historically unique, the politicized postmodern art of late socialism, like socialism itself, is no longer with us, except as a part of recent history.

Notes

1. Aleš Erjavec and Marina Gržinić, *Ljubljana, Ljubljana: The Eighties in Slovene Art and Culture* (Ljubljana: Mladinska knjiga, 1991), p. 9.

2. Leslie Holmes, *Post-Communism: An Introduction* (Cambridge: Polity Press, 1997), p. 63.

3. "By the late 1980s, the Chinese economic reforms had gone so far that many observers argued that China was rapidly becoming a capitalist country," redirecting itself under Deng Xiaoping toward "bureaucratic capitalism." Ibid., p. 120.

4. Zygmunt Bauman, *Legislators and Interpreters* (Cambridge: Polity Press, 1987), pp. 125, 117.

5. Mikhail N. Epstein, *After the Future: The Paradoxes of Postmodernism and Contemporary Russian Culture,* trans. with an introduction by Anesa Miller Pogacar (Amherst: University of Massachusetts Press, 1995), p. 95.

6. Kunc's art is yet another example of similarities springing up in unexpected places. Although his art strongly resembles that of the Russian Sots Art of Komar and Melamid, Leonid Sokov, and Boris Orlov, which all appeared at about the same time, "Kunc created his Ost-Pop without any contacts with these artists and was not even able to see reproductions of their works, for at that time they didn't exist." Milena Slavická, "Malíř kontrolovaného bláznovství: O díle Milana Kunce," *Výtvarné umění* (Prague), no. 3 (1992): 21.

7. Jean-François Lyotard, *The Differend: Phrases in Dispute,* trans. Georges Van Den Abbeele, Theory and History of Literature 46 (Minneapolis: University of Minnesota Press, 1988), p. 13.

8. Claude Lefort, *Les formes de l'histoire: Essais d'anthropologie politique* (Paris: Gallimard, 1978), p. 313.

9. Ibid., p. 315.

10. "Artistic production has boomed under communism. Never in the history of Eastern Europe have more pieces of art been exhibited. . . . The prosecuted artist is, on closer inspection, just not that unhappy one." Miklós Haraszti, *The Velvet Prison: Artists under State Socialism,* foreword by George Konrad, trans. Katalin and Stephen Landesmann (New York: Basic Books, 1987), p. 9.

11. Ibid., pp. 5, 8.

12. Piotr Piotrowski, "Post-modernism and Post-totalitarianism; The Poland Case of the 1970s," *Ars* (Bratislava: Slovak Academic Press, 1994), nos. 2–3 (1993): 235. Being an artist or a writer, of course, brought more than just a privileged social position, and it didn't bring that automatically. It also carried with it dangers and hardships, and I have no intention of minimizing these. What I want to point out is that in the socialist countries, as in the less-developed ones, intellectuals in general and therefore also artists were held in high esteem. In most cases, their political position was facilitated in the period of late socialism, which coincided with the beginning of the decomposition of socialist regimes, because repression was then generally less severe than before.

13. What this means is clear to anybody who ever went to a theater play, in Soviet Moscow, for example, and observed the audience laughing or giggling when spotting a veiled reference to a political figure or a political event—leaving the foreigner often completely baffled due to ignorance of the current local political context. Vladimir Voinovich, Russia's best-known satirical novelist, described this phenomenon in the following way: "There was a joke in those days about a director who was asked to define an allusion. He replied: 'An allusion is when you go to the movies and you see clouds, forest, or the sky on the screen, and you think: "In any case, Brezhnev is a bastard."'" "What Is Left to Mock? Interview," *Newsweek,* September 11, 1995, p. 60.

14. Sabrina Petra Ramet, *Social Currents in Eastern Europe* (Durham, N.C.: Duke University Press, 1995), pp. 3–4.

15. Neue Slowenische Kunst, *Problemi* (Ljubljana), no. 6 (1985): 24.

16. "Self-management socialism" in Yugoslavia, especially after the implementation of the 1974 constitution, was an attempt to build a socialism that resurrected the principles at the historical roots of the contemporary workers' movement, those of the Paris Commune. The aim of the Yugoslav legislators was therefore to establish mechanisms that would prevent the bureaucratization of socialism that was thought to be inherent to the Soviet system. In other words, the purpose of self-management was in part to dissociate the "Yugoslav way" from capitalism; but, more than that, it would avoid the pitfalls of the Realsozialismus of the Soviet Union and its satellites, with the Soviet Union being perceived since 1948 as the prime external political and military threat.

17. Slavoj Žižek, *For They Know Not What They Do: Enjoyment as a Political Factor* (London: Verso, 1991), p. 186.

18. Slavoj Žižek, *Tarrying with the Negative: Kant, Hegel, and the Critique of Ideology* (Durham, N.C.: Duke University Press, 1993), p. 222.

19. Holmes, *Post-Communism*, p. 124.

20. Ibid., p. 120.

21. Jean Baudrillard, *The Illusion of the End*, trans. Chris Turner (Cambridge: Polity Press, 1994), p. 37.

22. Emil Niederhauser, *The Rise of Nationality in Eastern Europe* (Budapest: Corvina, 1981), p. 334.

23. Luis Camnitzer, *New Art of Cuba* (Austin: University of Texas Press, 1994), p. xxii.

24. Tamás Hofer, "Construction of the 'Folk Cultural Heritage in Hungary' and Rival Versions of National Identity," in *Hungarians between "East" and "West": Three Essays on National Myths and Symbols*, edited by Tamás Hofer (Budapest: Museum of Ethnography, 1994), p. 48. The passages quoted by Hofer are by Georg L. Mosse.

25. Laura J. Hoptman, "Seeing Is Believing," in *Beyond Belief: Contemporary Art from East Central Europe* (Chicago: Museum of Contemporary Art, 1995), p. 2.

26. Katherine Verdery, *National Ideology under Socialism: Identity and Cultural Politics in Ceaușescu's Romania* (Berkeley: University of California Press, 1991), p. 12.

27. Epstein, *After the Future*, p. 6.

28. Verdery, *National Ideology under Socialism*, p. 120.

29. Slavoj Žižek, "Eastern Europe's Republics of Gilead," *New Left Review*, no. 183 (1990): 58.

30. See Giuseppe Carlo Marino, "Due borghesie, due modelli fascisti," *L'autarchia della cultura* (Rome: Editori Riuniti, 1983), pp. 99–111.

31. Gerardo Mosquera, "The 14 Sons of William Tell," in *No Man Is an Island* (Pori, Finland: Pori Art Museum Publications, 1990), p. 42.

32. Călin Dan, "Art + Politics = No Art / No Politics," *New Observations*, no. 91 (September–October 1992): 6.

33. Ibid.

34. Geremie Barmé, "Exploit, Export, Expropriate: Artful Marketing from China, 1989–93," *Third Text*, no. 25 (winter 1993–94): 67.

35. Li Xianting, "An Introduction to the History of Modern Chinese Art," in *China Avant-Garde: Counter-Currents in Art and Culture* (Hong Kong: Oxford University Press, 1994), p. 40.

36. Quoted in Andrew Solomon, "Not Just a Yawn but the Howl That Could Free China," *The New York Times Magazine*, December 19, 1993, p. 48.

37. Tuo Li, "Introduction," *China Avant-Garde*, p. 1.

38. Wolfger Pöhlmann, "Yu Youhan," *China Avant-Garde*, p. 177.

39. Charles Jencks, "The Post-Avant-Garde," *Art and Design (The Post-Avant-Garde: Painting in the Eighties)* 3, nos. 7–8 (1987): 20.

40. Fredric Jameson, *The Seeds of Time* (New York: Columbia University Press, 1994), pp. xvi–xvii.

41. Camnitzer, *New Art of Cuba*, pp. 301–2.

42. Ibid., p. 301.

43. Luis Camnitzer, "The Eclecticism of Survival: Today's Cuban Art," in *The Nearest Edge of the World*, p. 19.

44. Like Camnitzer, Péter György, referring to late socialist art in Hungary, speaks of "quotations and paraphrases that could be understood as very postmodern fragments."

45. Epstein, *After the Future*, p. xi.

46. Iurii M. Lotman and Boris A. Uspenskii, "Binary Models in the Dynamics of Russian Culture (to the End of the Eighteenth Century)," in *The Semiotics of Russian Cultural History: Essays by Iurii M. Lotman, Lidiia Ia. Ginsburg, Boris A. Uspenskii*, edited by Alexander D. Nakhimovsky and Alice Stone Nakhimovsky (Ithaca: Cornell University Press, 1985), p. 48. To find a more recent example it suffices to remember that the same ideas were proliferating at the time of Russian avant-garde. Thus, Goncharova and Larionov claimed, "Our future is behind us." Mikhail Larionov and Natalia Goncharova, "Rayonnists and Futurists: A Manifesto, 1913," in *Russian Art of the Avant-Garde: Theory and Criticism, 1902–1934*, edited by John Bowlt (New York: Viking Press, 1976), p. 88.

47. Epstein, *After the Future*, p. 330.

48. Boris Groys, *The Total Art of Stalinism: Avant-Garde, Aesthetic Dictatorship, and Beyond*, trans. Charles Rougle (Princeton: Princeton University Press, 1992), p. 108. Groys argues that since its inception in the early 1930s, Socialist Realism has represented the Soviet version of postmodernism, thus preceding its Western variant.

49. "At the moment of this uneasy reconciliation between officialdom and modernism, the presence of Sots Art, a form of postmodernism, was problematic. First of all, though somewhat unintentionally, the Sots artists created a new form of resistance to the cultural establishment, demonstrating once again that any art functioning beyond the framework of the system becomes potentially radical." Margarita Tupitsyn, "Sots Art: The Russian Deconstructive Force," in *Sots Art* (New York: The New Museum of Modern Art, 1986), p. 5.

50. Igor Golomshtok, "Unofficial Art in the Soviet Union," in Igor Golomshtok and Alexander Glezer, *Unofficial Art from the Soviet Union*, introduction by Sir Roland Penrose, edited by Michael Scammell (London: Secker and Warburg, 1977), p. 81.

51. Hans van Dijk with Andreas Schmid, "The Fine Arts after the Cultural Revolution: Stylistic Development and Cultural Debate," in *China Avant-Garde*, p. 15.

52. Lóránd Hegyi, "Hungarian Art in the Early 1990s: Individual Positions—Defining New Contexts," in *Free Worlds: Metaphors and Realities in Contemporary Hungarian Art* (Toronto: Art Gallery of Toronto, 1991), p. 33.

53. A statement to the author in Budapest on September 15, 1995.

54. Gábor Bachman, in *Free Worlds*, p. 71.

55. Gerardo Mosquera, "The New Art of the Revolution," in *The Nearest Edge of the World: Art and Cuba Now* (Brookline, Mass.: Polarities, 1990), p. 9.

56. Camnitzer, *New Art of Cuba*, p. 123.

57. Bauman, *Legislators and Interpreters*, p. 116.

58. Recounted to the author by László Rajk on November 7, 1994, in Budapest. Rajk was referring to the exhibition *Art and Revolution* (Budapest, November 1987–January 1988). See *Művészet és Forradolom Orosz (Szovjet Művészet 1910–1932 Art and Revolution), Soviet Art* (Budapest: Műcsarnok, 1987).

59. Milan Knížák, in "Milan Knížák: Kill Yourself and Fly: An Interview by Johan Pijnappel," *Art and Design: New Art from Eastern Europe*, no. 35 (1994): 37.

60. Katalin Néray, "Attila Kovács," in *Kovács Attila: Necropolis* (Pécs: Gallery Pécs, 1987), p. 3.

61. A statement to the author in Budapest on November 5, 1994.

62. Terry Eagleton, *The Ideology of the Aesthetic* (Oxford: Basil Blackwell, 1990), p. 373.

63. Žižek, *Tarrying with the Negative*, pp. 1–2.

64. Jochen Noth, "Beijing 1979–1992: Frequent Changes of Scene," in *China Avant-Garde*, p. 7.

65. Žižek, *For They Know Not What They Do*, p. 185.

66. Ibid., pp. 187–88.

67. Osvaldo Sánchez, "Dreaming of Tatlin's Spiral," *Poliester* (Mexico City), no. 4 (winter 1993): 16.

68. Eric Bulatov, "Malevich's Relationship of Space," *A-Ya*, no. 5 (1983). Quoted in *Russian Samizdat Art*, assembled by Rimma Gerlovin and Valery Gerlovin (New York: Willis Locker and Owens, 1986), p. 123.

69. Viktor Misiano, "Erik Bulatov and the Moscow School," in *Erik Bulatov: Moscow* (London: Parkett Publishers and ICA, 1989), p. 18.

70. Neue Slowenische Kunst, *Problemi* (Ljubljana), no. 6 (1985): 27.

71. Such are the works of Wang Qiang or the more recent works of Wang Guangyi. For other contemporary art in China, see *Inside Out: New Chinese Art*, edited by Gao Minglu (Berkeley: University of California Press, 1998), and *China! Zeitgenössische Malerei*, edited by Dieter Ronte, Walter Smerling, and Evelyn Weiss (Cologne: DuMont, 1996).

72. Epstein, *After the Future*, p. 202.

73. Elisabeth Sussman, "The Third Zone: Soviet 'Postmodern,'" in *Between Spring and Summer: Soviet Conceptual Art in the Era of Late Communism*, edited by David A. Ross (Boston: MIT Press, 1990), p. 63. Numerous authors use "Conceptualism" and "postmodernism" interchangeably. The above title (also the name of one of the more important exhibitions of Soviet art) exemplifies this.

74. Osvaldo Sánchez, "The Last of the Moderns," in *Cuba: La Isla Posible . . .* (Barcelona: Ediciones Destino, 1995), p. 250.

75. I owe this apt description to Martin Jay.

76. Lóránd Hegyi, "Sándor Pinczehelyi's Emblematic Art," in *Imre Bukta, Sándor Pinczehelyi, Géza Samu: Ungheria* (Venice: XLIII La Biennale di Venezia, 1988), unpaginated.

77. Slavoj Žižek, *Looking Awry: An Introduction to Jacques Lacan through Popular Culture* (Cambridge, Mass.: MIT Press, 1991), p. 143.

78. Groys, *The Total Art of Stalinism*, p. 82.

79. Ibid., p. 83.

80. Epstein, *After the Future*, p. 6.

81. Erik Bulatov, in "Interview with Erik Bulatov and Ilya Kabakov, Moscow, July 1987, conducted by Claudia Jolles," in *Erik Bulatov: Moscow*, p. 42.

82. Fredric Jameson, *Postmodernism, or, The Cultural Logic of Late Capitalism* (London: Verso, 1991), p. 9.

83. Gerardo Mosquera, "Carlos Rodríguez Cárdenas," in *The Nearest Edge of the World*, p. 44.

84. Antonio Eligio (Tonel), "Cuban Art: A Key to the Gulf and How to Use It," in *No Man Is an Island*, p. 74.

85. Margarita Tupitsyn, "On Some Sources of Soviet Conceptualism," in *Nonconformist Art: The Soviet Experience, 1956–1986*, edited by Alla Rosenfeld and Norton T. Dodge (London: Thames and Hudson, 1995), p. 303.

86. Groys, *The Total Art of Stalinism,* p. 94.

87. See Louis Althusser, "Cremonini, peintre de l'abstraction," *Democratie nouvelle,* no. 8 (1966): 10.

88. The notion of postmodernism is especially ambivalent in the writings of Russian authors. In the first comprehensive book on the more recent art from the Soviet Union, Margarita Tupitsyn identifies Sots Art with deconstruction and limits the notion of postmodernism mainly to the Apt-Art exhibitions and installations in private apartments in the early 1980s. See Margarita Tupitsyn, *Margins of Soviet Art* (Milan: Giancarlo Politi Editore, 1989), esp. pp. 60–114. See also Sussman, "The Third Zone."

89. V. I. Lenin, *What Is to Be Done? Burning Questions of Our Movement* (Peking: Foreign Languages Press, 1973), p. 51.

90. Erik Bulatov, "Ich bin überzeugt daß der Raum der Kunst und Raum unseres Lebens zwei verschiedene Räume sind: Ein Gespräch mit Heinz Schütz," *Kunstforum,* no. 106 (March–April 1990): 258.

91. Laibach, *Let It Be* (London: Mute Records, 1988).

92. Hans van Dijk with Andreas Schmid, "The Fine Arts after the Cultural Revolution," p. 19.

93. Boris Groys, "Milan Kunc: Cheerful Post-Modernism," in *Milan Kunc,* edited by Pavel Liška (Cologne: Edition Cantz, 1992), p. 25.

94. A statement to the author in Budapest on November 5, 1994.

95. For these distinctions, see, for example, *New Art from China: Post-1989* (London: Marlborough Fine Art, 1993).

96. Mosquera, "The 14 Sons of William Tell," p. 47.

97. Lucy R. Lippard, *Pop Art* (London: Thames and Hudson, 1966), p. 22.

98. For a history of constructivist tendencies in Hungary, see László Beke, "From Picture Architecture of Kassák to Post-Geometry and Beyond," *Fodor* (Amsterdam) 6, no. 4 (July–August 1987): 17–26.

99. This seminar paper was later included in Lyotard's *Dérive à partir de Marx et Freud* (Paris: U.G.E., 1973).

100. Lissitzky in effect plagiarized the unrealized project for a monument by Nikolai Kolli (1918). See Sergiusz Michalski, *Public Monuments: Art in Political Bondage, 1870–1997* (London: Reaktion Books, 1998), p. 112.

101. Lyotard, *Dérive à partir de Marx et Freud,* p. 302.

102. Călin Dan, "Art + Politics = No Art / No Politics," p. 7.

103. Jean-François Lyotard, "The Sublime and the Avant-Garde," in *The Lyotard Reader,* edited by Andrew Benjamin (Oxford: Basil Blackwell, 1989), pp. 203–4.

104. Tupitsyn, "On Some Sources of Soviet Conceptualism," p. 304.

105. *Performance Magazine,* quoted on the cover of the Laibach LP *Opus Dei* (London: Mute Records, 1987).

106. Piotr Piotrowski, "The Old Attitude and the New Faith," in *Beyond Belief,* p. 36.

107. Krystyna Czerni, "Spoiling Cannibals' Fun," in *Art from Poland: 1945–1996,* edited by Jolanta Chrzanowska-Pieńkos et al. (Warsaw: Galeria Sztuki Współczesnej Zachęta, 1997), p. 271.

108. See *La Biennale di Venezia: 48ª Esposizione Internazionale d'Arte,* 2 vols., edited by Harald Szeemann and Cecilia Liveriero Lavelli (Venice: Marsilio Editori, 1999).

The Other Gaze

Russian Unofficial Art's View of the Soviet World

Boris Groys

The unofficial art scene in the Soviet Union formed as early as the mid-1950s, almost immediately following the death of Stalin in 1953, and from then on developed parallel to the official culture industry. The artists belonging to that scene turned away from the official art of Socialist Realism, attempting to link up with the traditions of Western and Russian modernism. No longer as ruthlessly repressed as they had been under Stalin, these artists were assured of both physical survival and the possibility of continuing to pursue artistic work, yet they were almost completely cut off from the official museum, exhibition, and publication systems, as well as from the possibility of traveling abroad and establishing connections with the Western art institutions. As a result, the unofficial artists built their own scene in major cities such as Moscow and Leningrad, existing in semilegality at the margins of Soviet normality. They could earn a living by turning to applied art, by taking up another profession, or by selling their works to a handful of private collectors. Because of the precariousness of their social status, they felt insecure and threatened, but their social isolation also generated a kind of euphoria. They could practice a relatively independent and often extremely bohemian lifestyle in a country where such a thing was unimaginable for most of the population. Despite the lack of official recognition, their lifestyle was secretly envied, and during the three decades of the unofficial art scene's existence, from the mid-1950s until the opening of the Soviet system in the mid-1980s, many people in Moscow and Leningrad thought it a great and exciting adventure to have an unofficial artist as a friend.

Unofficial artistic circles also included independent authors, poets, and musicians, although these had even less opportunity than visual artists to survive on the margins of the Soviet system. Small exhibitions, poetry readings, and concerts were held regularly in artists' studios in an informal, closely knit social environment. The constant fear of possible repression forged solidarity among artists following very different and even opposite artistic programs. Indeed, the unofficial art scene of the 1950s and 1960s was very pluralistic and heterogeneous, reflecting the plurality of styles being oppressed by the officially dominant Socialist Realism. The unofficial artists adapted and brought into the Russian cultural context all kinds of art practices that were excluded by Soviet censorship, from icon painting through Cubism, Expressionism, Surrealism, and abstract art to Abstract Expressionism and Pop Art, which had already surfaced in Moscow at the end of the 1950s.

Behind this plurality of styles and techniques, however, there was a shared understanding of the role of the artist in the society: to manifest his or her individual truth in the midst of the official public lie. Most unofficial artists at this time saw their art in terms of a higher mission, as a way of bringing important truths and deep insights into the profane Soviet world that surrounded them. They tried to exhume the radical claims of modernist art in a culture that had forgotten them. The single utopia of Communism was suddenly replaced by myriad private, individual utopias, each of which, however, became thoroughly intolerant of all the others, even if the artists themselves remained on friendly terms. Such artists as Anatolii Zverev, Vladimir Yakovlev, Vladimir Weisberg, Mikhail Schwarzmann, Vladimir Nemukhin, Dmitrii Krasnopevtsev, Vladimir Yankilevsky, and Eduard Steinberg, among many others working in the 1950s and 1960s, embodied the paradigmatic figure of the modernist artist-hero suffering for individual artistic truth and struggling against a cold and hypocritical social environment.[1]

This claim to individual truth advanced by most of the Russian unofficial artists at that time appears to be somewhat problematic. Their almost complete isolation from the international art scene meant that they could not produce an innovative art that would give an objective, art-historical credibility to their claims to genuine individuality. After the Soviet system had opened itself to the outside world in the 1980s, they learned that if an artwork does not appear innovative or original in the international art context, it cannot be regarded as having developed out of an authentic inner impulse. This discovery was a painful realization for many of the unofficial artists, who had tended to appropriate and rather naively invest in the radically individualist rhetoric of modernism, above all in its radically oppositional posture, its contempt for all manifestations of contemporary mass culture. Soviet mass culture elicited from the unofficial artists an especially intense allergic reaction. The Soviet state was seen as an enemy, and Soviet mass culture was seen as an alien culture. Such an unreflective, oppositional stance was, incidentally, easily integrated into the Manichean worldview of the official Soviet ideology, which reserved a special place for its enemies, but not for an outside spectator. One could be for this ideology or against it, but a neutral, analytical position was simply unthinkable, unimaginable, impossible.

However, by the end of the 1960s and the beginning of the 1970s, several unofficial Russian artists had already begun to engage critically and ironically with characteristically Soviet mass culture. They tried to subvert the clear-cut opposition between official and unofficial, Soviet and anti-Soviet, high culture and mass culture. These artists tried to describe the specific Soviet ideological and visual context as neutrally and objectively as possible. They began to thematize Soviet cultural codes and visual clichés, which were completely ignored by most other unofficial Russian artists, who instead were searching for a reality hidden behind them. This attempt to stop looking behind the facade of official Soviet culture and to open the people's eyes to the structure of this facade was undertaken by a small group of artists who became known as Moscow Conceptualists.[2] This circle included the artists Ilya Kabakov, Erik Bulatov, Ivan Chuikov, and Andrei Monastyrsky, the poets Dmitrii Prigov and Lev Rubinstein, and the writer Vladimir Sorokin, to mention only a few. At the same time, Vitaly Komar and Alexander Melamid began to develop their own version of the critical, politicized art, "Sots Art." These artists and writers became models for the younger generations of unofficial artists of the 1970s and 1980s. As a result, they redefined the role of the artist in Soviet society from prophet to critical commentator.

To be sure, the artistic practice of Moscow Conceptualism was strongly influenced by the various trends in Western art at the time, from Pop Art to Conceptual Art, which dealt in diverse ways with the cultural codes and visual clichés of Western commercialized mass culture. But the highly ideologized Soviet mass culture was extremely idiosyncratic. Selling ideology is different from selling Coca-Cola—even if there are some obvious similarities. The Western artistic experience of dealing with mass culture could not simply be transposed to the Soviet Union of the 1970s. The artists had to develop new means to deal with Soviet culture, which was based much more on narrative than on images. That is why the art practices of the Moscow

Conceptualists can be seen retrospectively as the most original manifestation of Russian art in the international art context of the 1970s and 1980s. Among the Moscow Conceptualists, Ilya Kabakov and the artistic duo of Vitaly Komar and Alexander Melamid developed the most unmistakably original body of work, and they also exerted the greatest influence on younger generations of Russian artists, including the generation after perestroika that became active in the mid-1980s, when the Russian unofficial art scene slowly began to dissolve under the new conditions of political openness. In what follows I will focus on the work of these three main protagonists of the Russian unofficial art scene in order to characterize the specific strategies of this art in the Soviet era.

Vitaly Komar and Alexander Melamid: Searching for Lost Aesthetic Power

Following Lenin's definition, official Soviet art conceived of itself as "a part of the general Party work." Actually, this art was defined not so much according to political criteria as according to the aesthetic criterion of stylistic unity, which corresponded to the unity of the great Central Plan. The lives of Soviet citizens were shaped by this plan down to the most minute details. Viewed from the outside, the Party's relentless desire to establish absolute aesthetic control over the Soviet state and society appears, at times, to be completely inexplicable. It was, however, an indispensable component in creating the inner unity without which political authority would have lost its legitimacy.[3]

The relation between art and power may, in fact, be the main theme of art in the twentieth century. But with the exception of Germany in the 1930s, this relation was nowhere else as confused, ambiguous, and telling as in Russia during the Soviet period. The Soviet state understood itself as an avant-garde of mankind on its way into the communist future. Accordingly, the power of Soviet censorship was exerted not in the name of the past, but rather in the name of the future. The Soviet population had to be constantly on the move, constantly mobilized, inspired, and oriented toward utopian ideals. It had no right to stop, to relax, to look toward the past. In this sense, official Soviet art was also utopian, avant-garde art, because its main task was to visualize the communist future in order to inspire the Soviet people on the road to utopia.

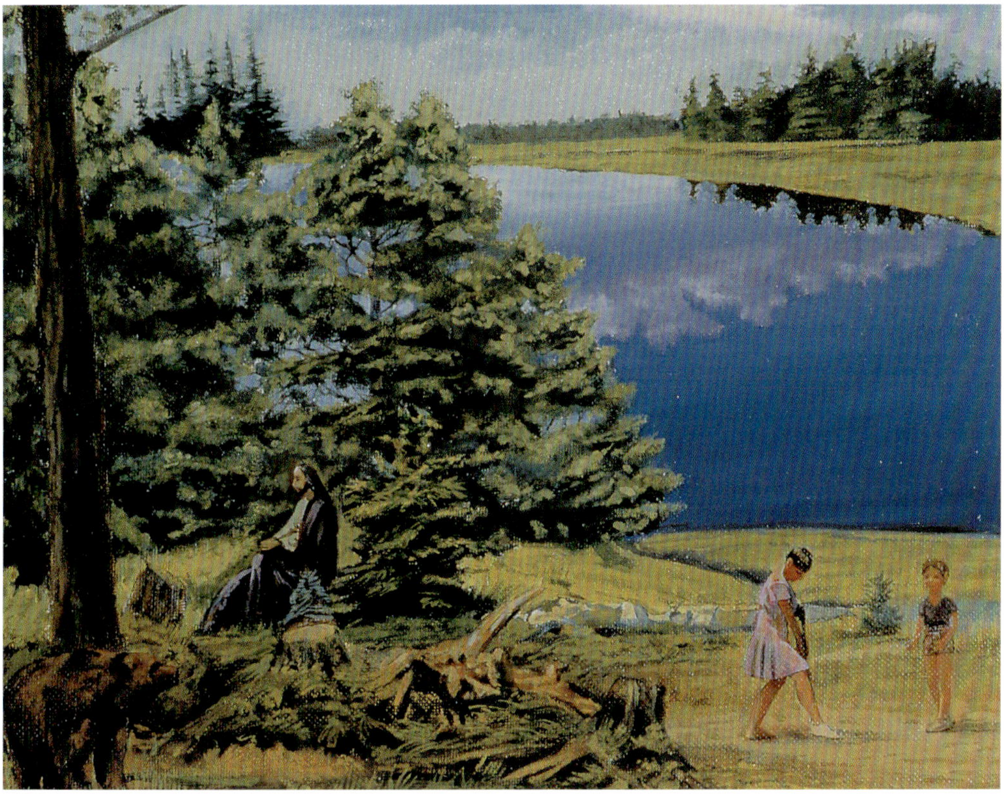

Plate 1 Komar and Melamid, *Russia's Most Wanted,* 1994, oil on canvas, 40 × 50 cm, TV size. Komar and Melamid's Archive.

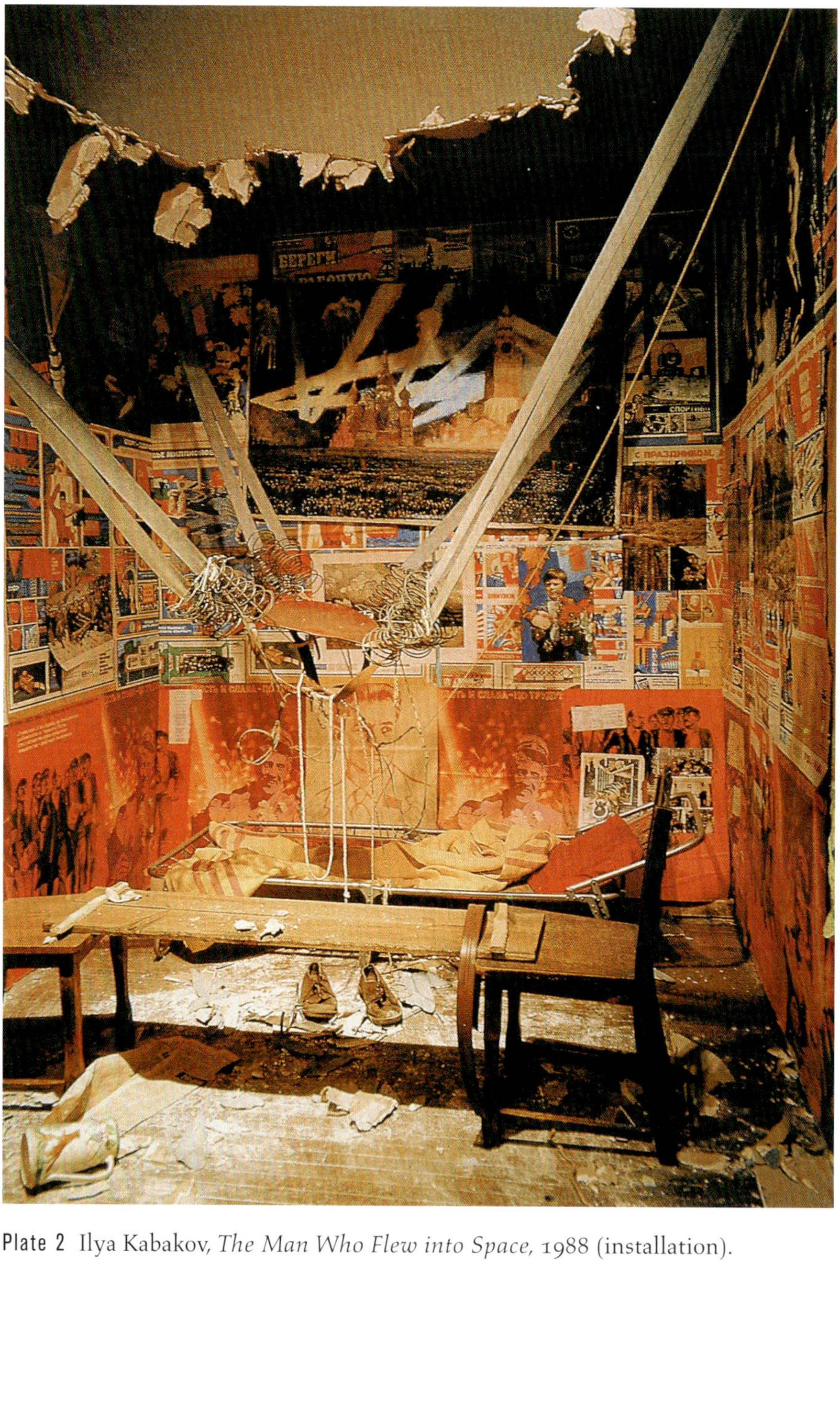

Plate 2 Ilya Kabakov, *The Man Who Flew into Space,* 1988 (installation).

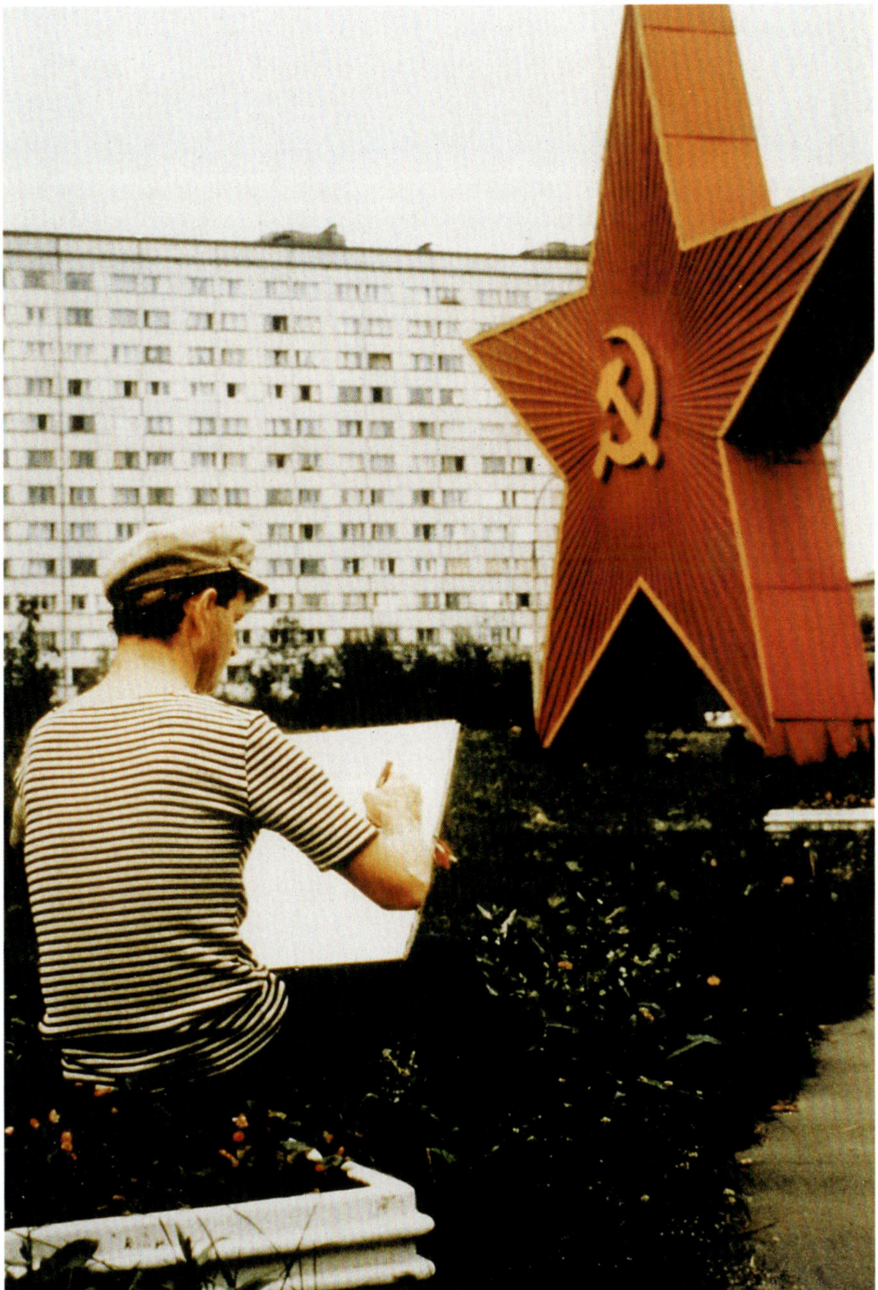

Plate 3 Milan Kunc, *Artist Working in Moscow,* 1979, performance, Cibachrome, 70 × 50 cm.

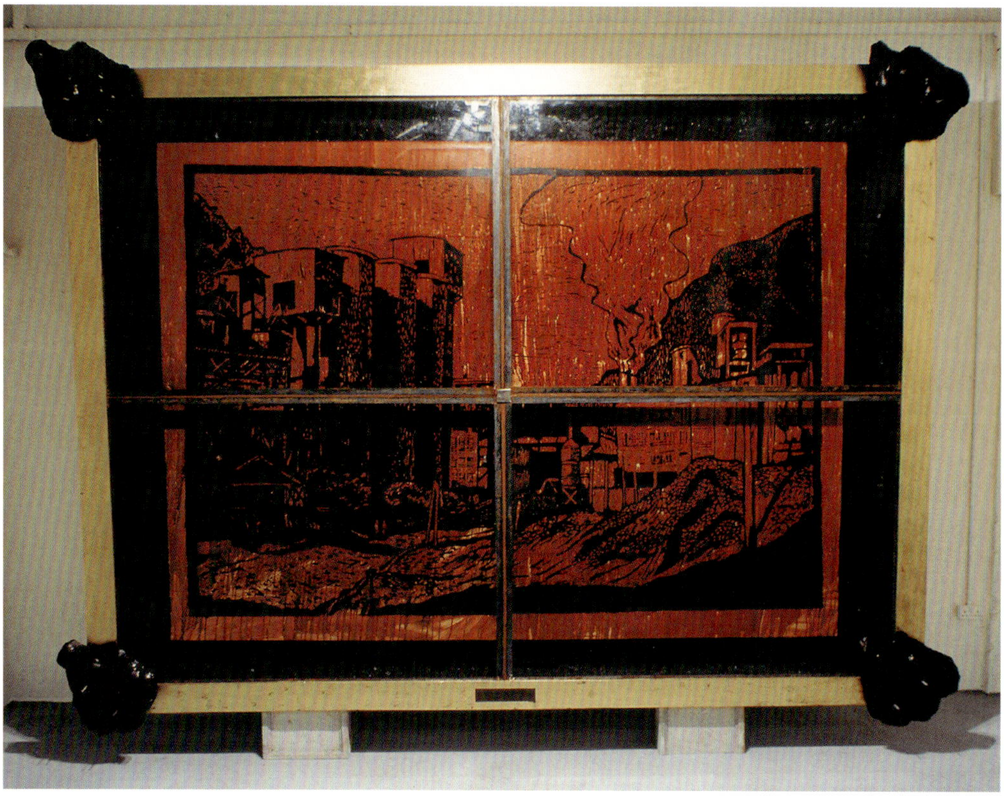

Plate 4 Irwin, *The Red Districts,* 1987, mixed media; picture object, 350 × 420 × 40 cm; collaborators Janez Knez and Tugo Šušnik. Ljubljana, Factor Bank.

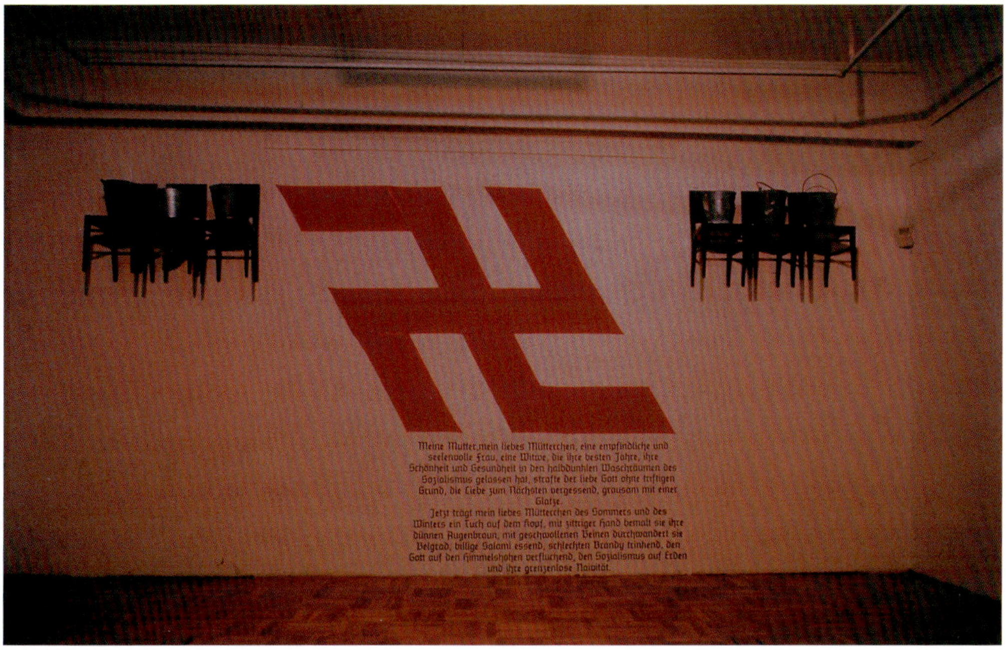

Plate 5 Raša Todosijević, *Gott liebt die Serben,* 1993, installation.

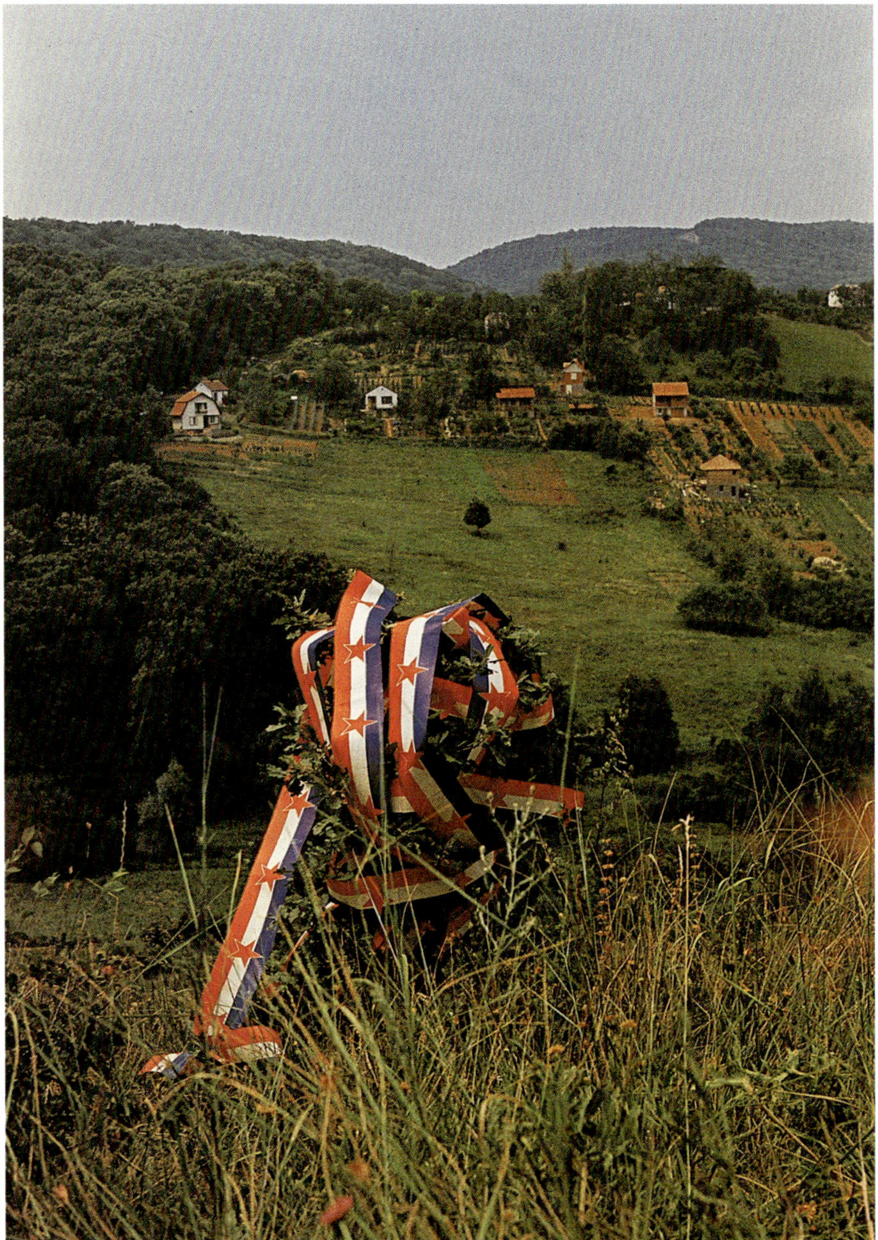

Plate 6 Balint Szombathy, *Flags,* 1972, installation.

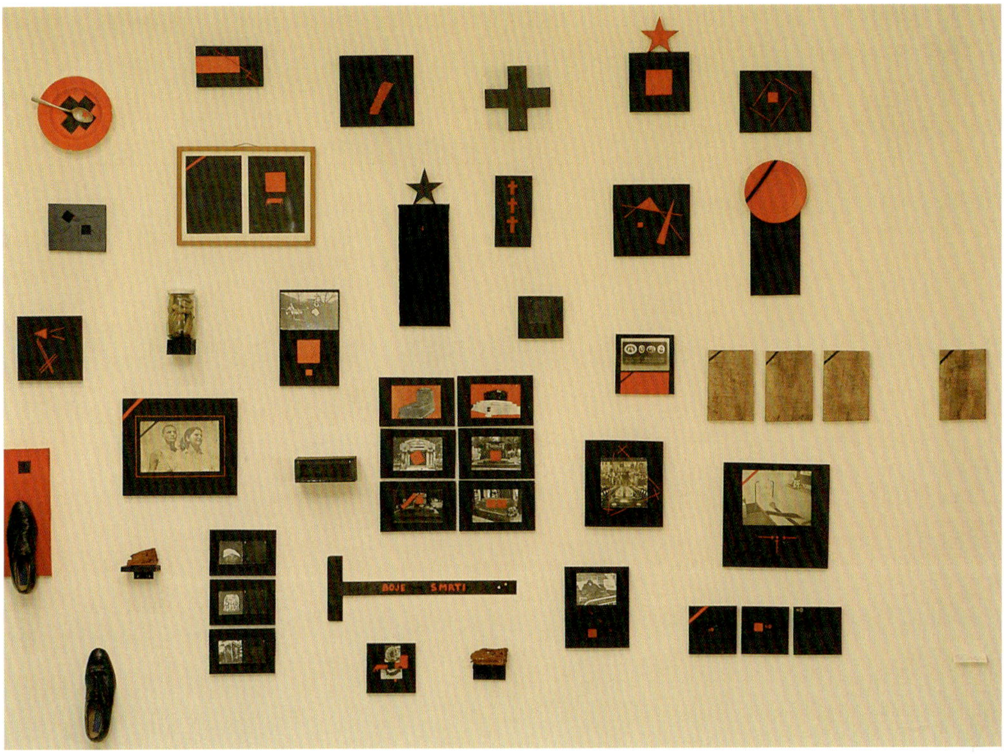

Plate 7 Mladen Stilinović, *Exploitation of the Dead* (detail), 1984–88, installation, 200 × 250 cm.

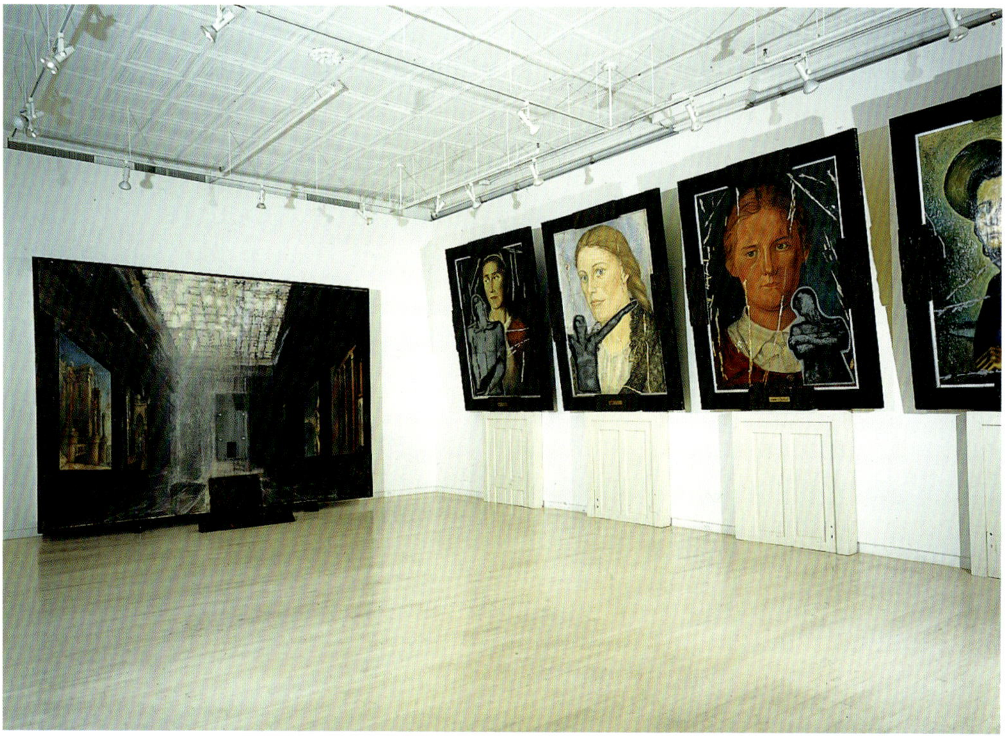

Plate 8 Irwin, *The Four Seasons* (from the *Was ist Kunst?* series), 1988, oil on canvas, each painting 260 × 200 cm. Collection of the artists. On the left side, Irwin, *The Resurrection of the Theater of the Sisters of Scipio Nasica,* 1984–85, mixed media, 320 × 400 × 50 cm. Ljubljana, Museum of Modern Art. From an exhibition in the Düsseldorf Kunsthalle.

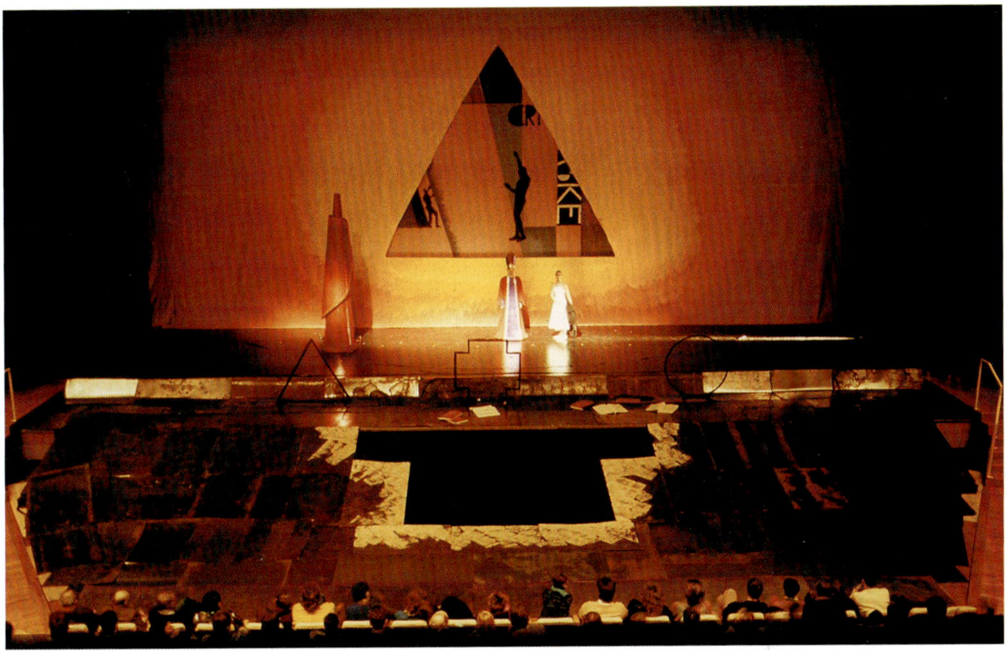

Plate 9 The Theater of the Sisters of Scipio Nasica, *Baptism under Triglav,* Cankarjev dom Cultural and Congress Center, Ljubljana, 1986 (photo: Marko Modic).

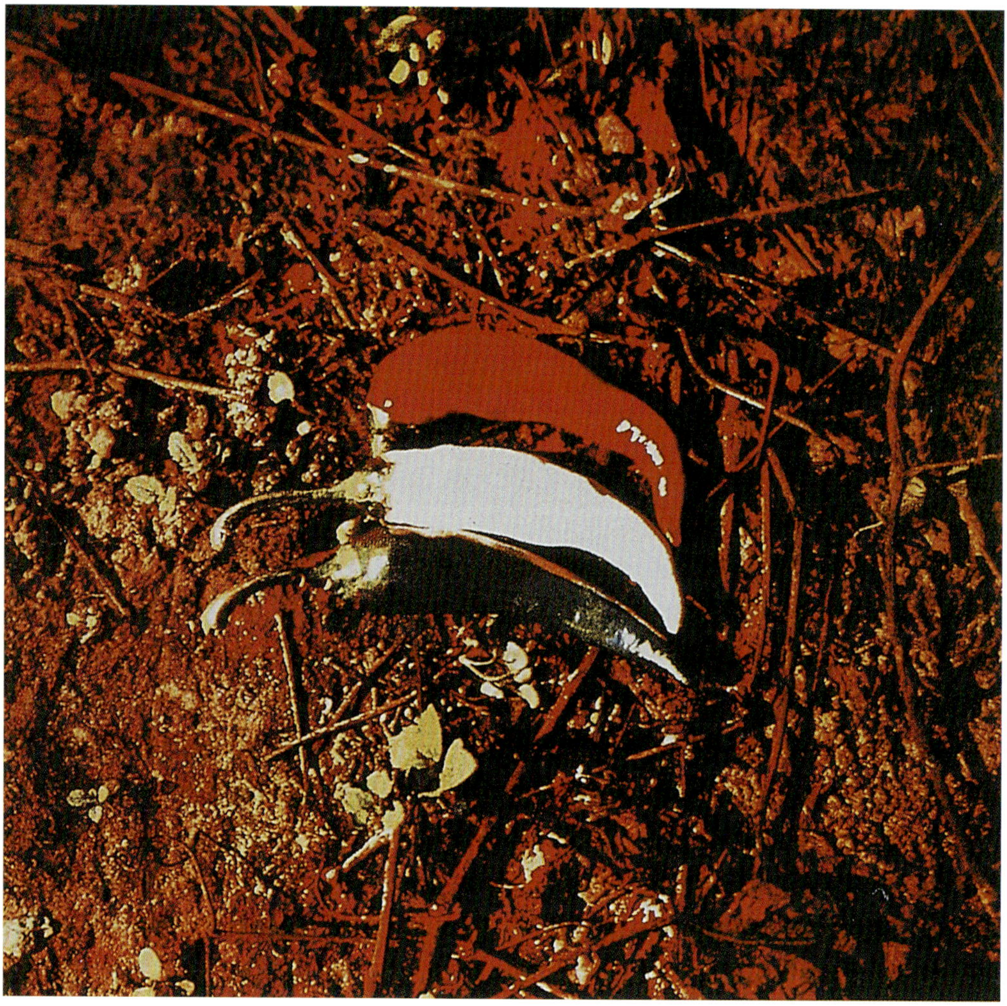

Plate 10 Sándor Pinczehelyi, *RWG Paprika,* 1981–83, screenprint on paper, 50 × 50 cm.

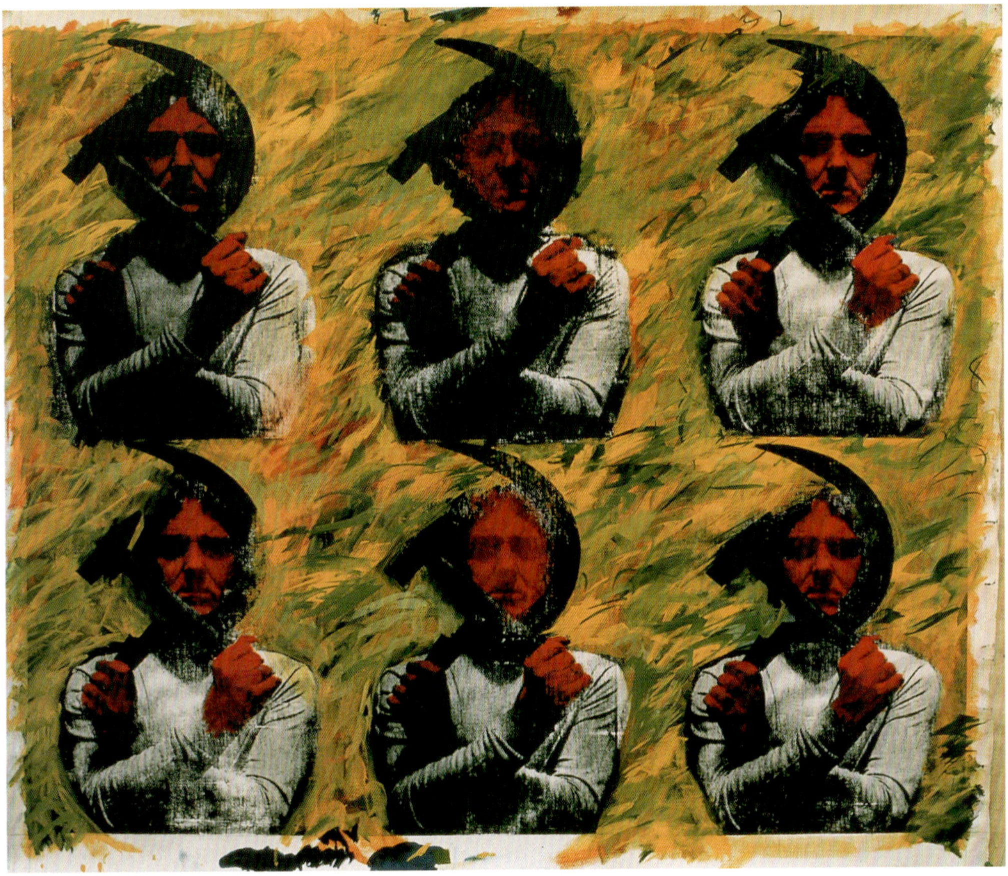

Plate 11 Sándor Pinczehelyi, *Hammer and Sickle I,* 1986, oil on canvas, 120 × 140 cm.

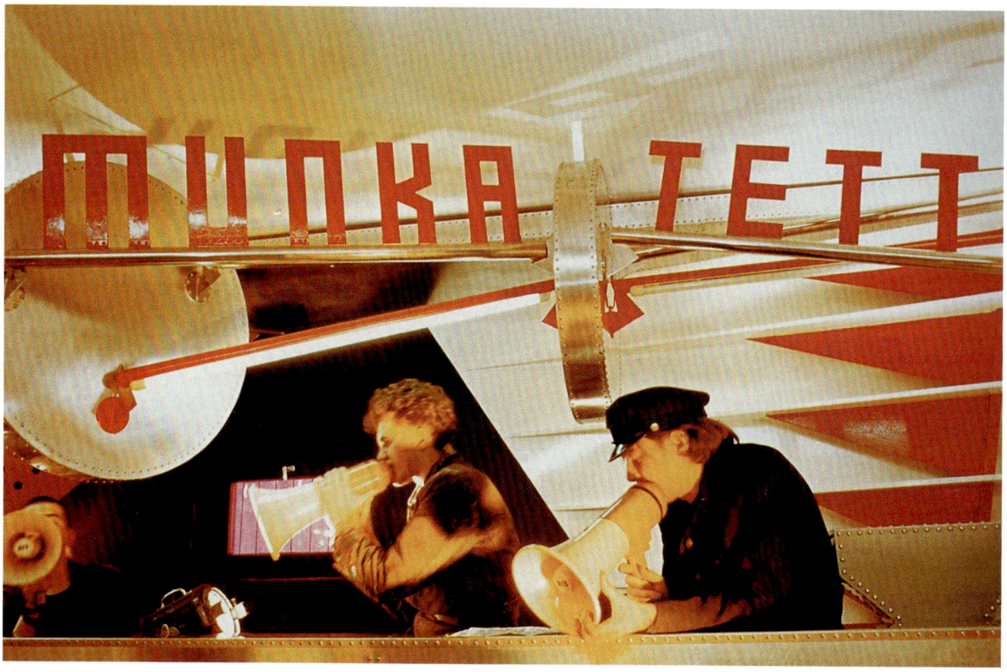

Plate 12 Gábor Bachman, *Work-Act,* 1985.

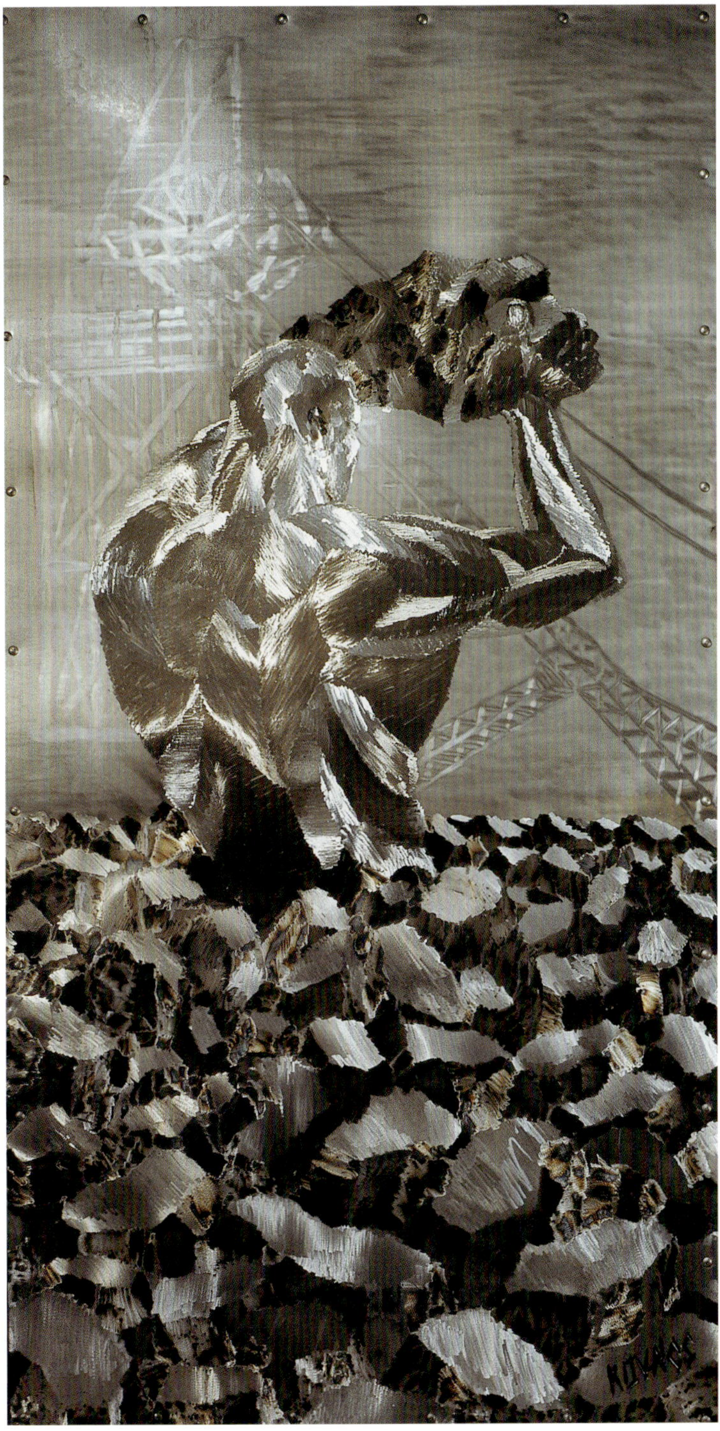

Plate 13 Attila Kovács, *Collapse,* 1987, polished iron sheet, 200 × 100 cm.

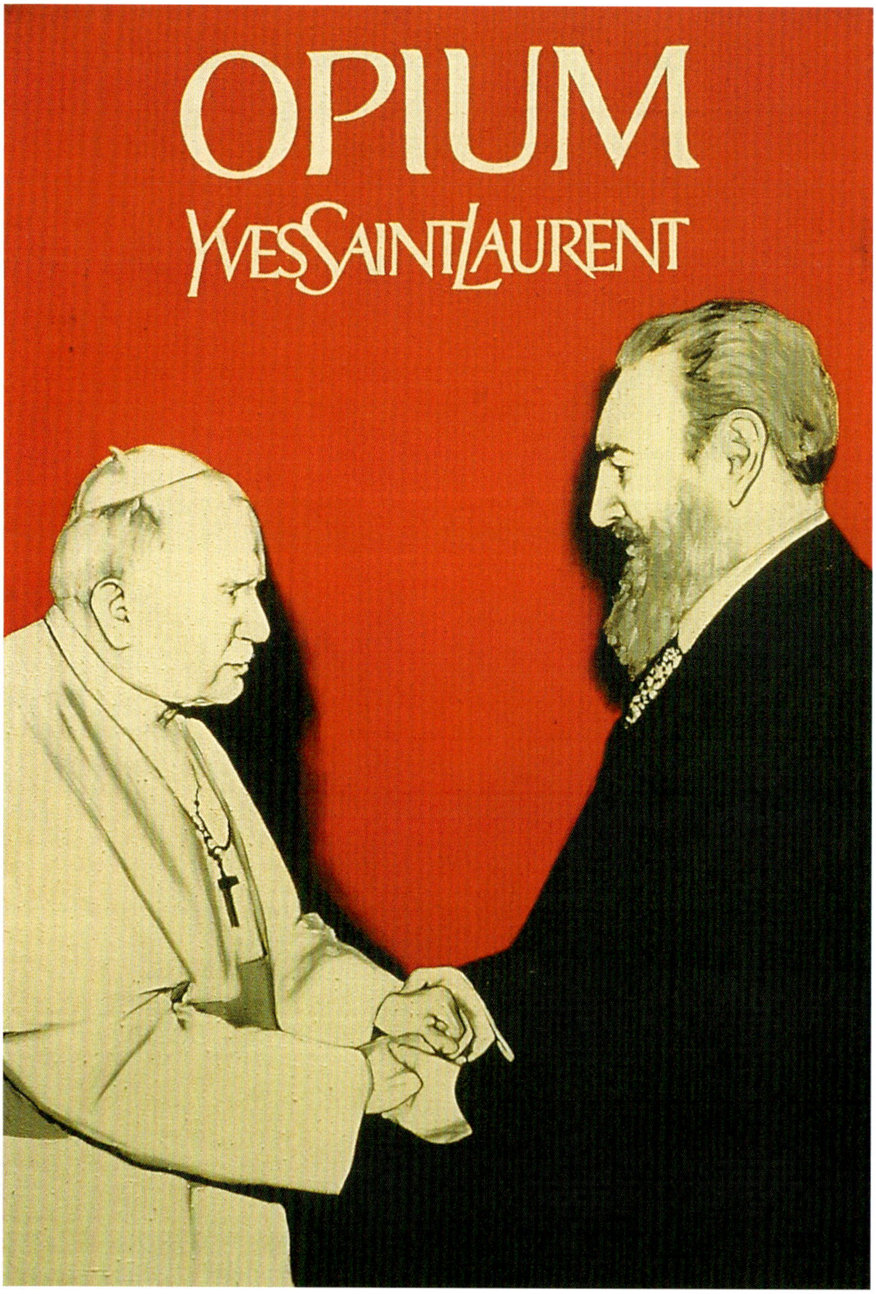

Plate 14 José Toirac, *Opium*, 1994, oil on canvas, 90 × 60 cm.

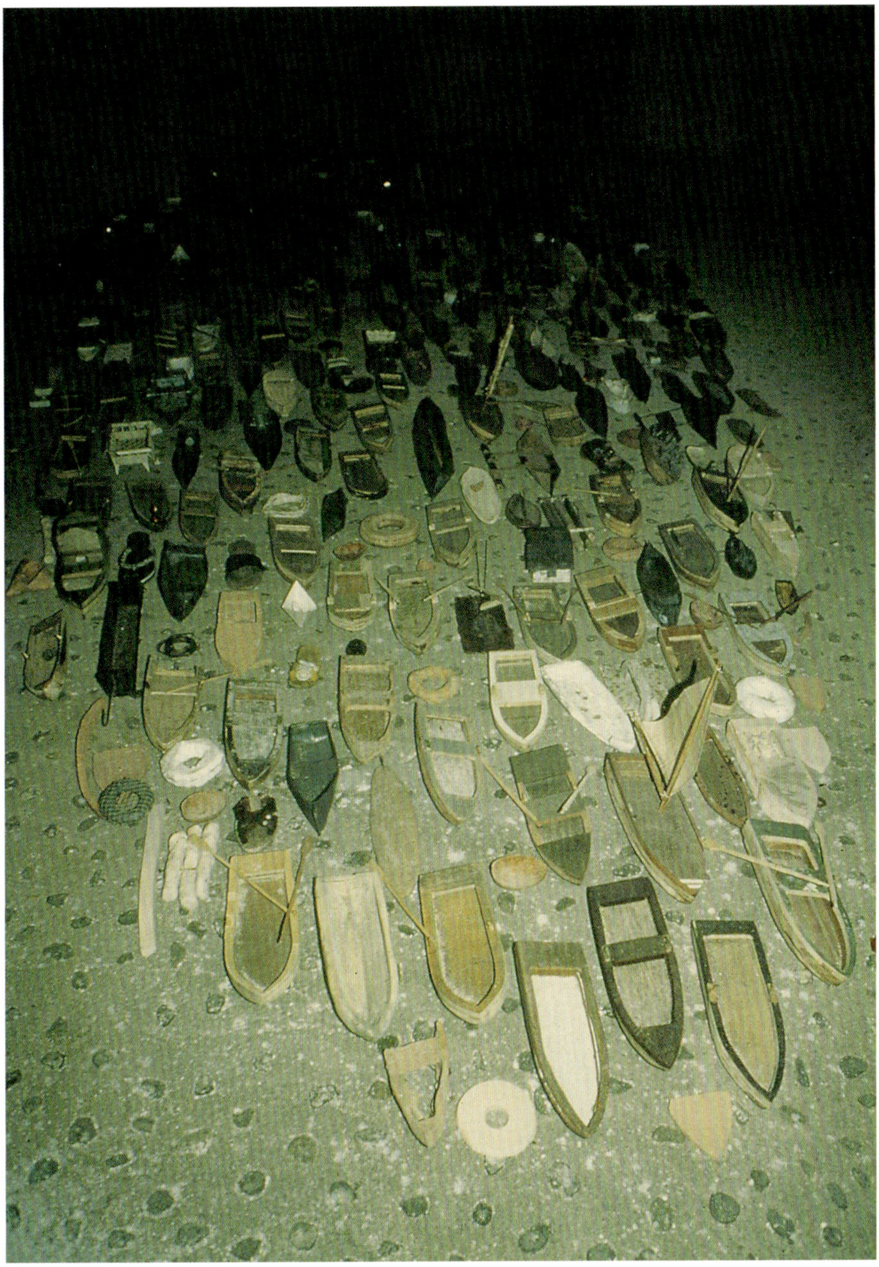

Plate 15 Kcho (Alexis Leiva), *Regata (Sailing Competition)*, 1995, installation.

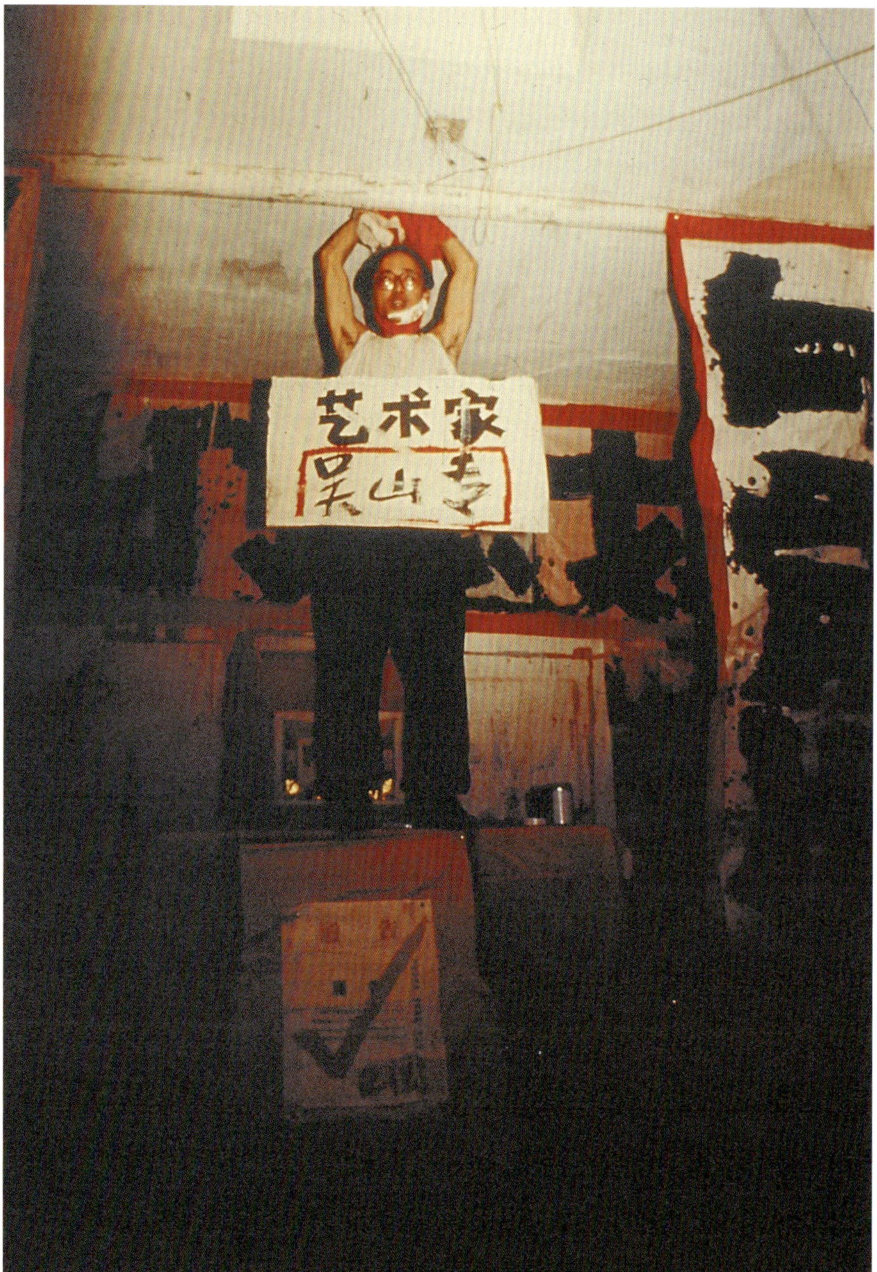

Plate 16 Wu Shanzhuan, *Red Humor: Red Windy Flags, Punishment,* 1987. Photographic documentation of an installation/performance; collection of the artist.

The history of avant-garde art is commonly viewed as the history of the symbolic liberation of the individual from the power of social traditions, ideologies, and state institutions. These all have at their disposal a repertoire of visual forms, and the artist's refusal to use these forms and to reproduce them symbolizes the highest stage of human freedom. The avant-garde artist thus becomes the sacrifice/priest of a new religion of individual freedom that opposes all forms of power and that has been canonized as such by contemporary political consciousness. With this canonization, however, the avant-garde itself becomes a new social convention and a new institution and, concomitantly, intricately imbricated with all other power institutions of modernity. While the Russian avant-garde rejected the clichés of the past, it did so only to adopt the clichés of the future. And the majority of the Russian avant-garde artists were ready to integrate their individual utopias into the collectivistic communist utopia and to serve Soviet state propaganda.

This relation to power is one source of late Soviet skepticism toward avant-garde art, toward its ability to be an enduringly effective opposition to the Soviet dictatorship and an "alternative" to its aesthetic censorship in the name of the communist future. In the West, one avant-garde movement was succeeded by the next, and no single movement had a chance to attain real power. The cultural and political dominance of the Russian avant-garde after the Revolution of 1917 represents the single exception. This brief period, which had come to an end by the mid-1920s, brought the entire potential of the avant-garde to power, a traumatic experience that even today informs the self-consciousness of Russian art. The Russian avant-garde artists saw in the revolutionary Soviet state a unique historical opportunity to realize their own dreams, and so, to that end, they were ready to accept its politics of terror and oppression. The Soviet state took on the same task as the avant-garde, to reshape humanity, to manipulate and shape the most elementary conditions of human existence, everyday life, the nervous system, and the unconscious. But from the mid-1930s on, the official Soviet art, Socialist Realism, tried to represent the communist future with the means of traditional academic painting, combined with photographically or cinematographically inspired imagery. The avant-gardist, futuristic artistic program thus was realized by official Soviet art with non-avant-gardist means.

At the beginning of the 1970s, Komar and Melamid began to thematize in their works this strange Soviet mixture of avant-garde utopianism and academic tradition.[4] They called their artistic practices, a combination of "Sotsrealism" (as Socialist Realism was usually called in Soviet times) and

American Pop Art, "Sots Art." First of all, the artists focused on the visual world of the Stalin myth and of Soviet ideological propaganda, which was also easy to recognize visually outside the borders of the Soviet Union. The Lenin and Stalin portraits with white slogans written on a red background, such as "Folk and Party Are One" and "Forward to the Victory of Communism," are just as closely associated with Soviet Russia and assimilated through the mass media and mass consciousness as the pyramids are associated with Egypt or Mickey Mouse and McDonald's are associated with the United States.

Russian unofficial artists had wrestled for decades with the question of how they could break out of their perennial provinciality and reach the international art world, and they initially attempted to do so by turning to "eternal," universal themes and archetypal images. However, around the beginning of the 1970s, they began to understand that the era of tourism and television rewards particular, regional flavors. Only the Soviet artist who could come to see his or her own land and its history with the eyes of an international tourist would be able to make something that could, potentially, be exported. Only such an artist would be able to achieve liberation both intellectually and practically from the state monopoly on culture.

Whereas Soviet culture conceived of itself as a closed totality, as "socialism in one country," a country that embodied the future of humanity and was separated by a kind of temporal abyss from the rest of the world, which supposedly lived in the capitalist past, Sots Art wanted to export itself into precisely this outside world through aesthetic self-stylization. It was therefore able to understand and describe the Soviet myth against the background of what this myth excluded. The moralistic critique of the Soviet system in the name of human rights attempted to demythologize the Soviet ideology by depicting Soviet reality "as it is." But the Sots Art artists saw in such strivings yet another ideological agenda, and they sought to overcome Stalinism by moving in the opposite direction. They wanted to remythologize Stalinism, so to speak, to integrate it into the broad, polymorphic mythology of the present and the past and, in doing so, to subvert the Soviet claim to the historical exclusiveness of the communist project. The Sots Art artist searched for a totality and symbolic power greater than those that the Soviet state possessed.

The work of Komar and Melamid went through several stages, the best known of which is from the early 1980s, when they had already emigrated from the Soviet Union and were living in New York. It featured large

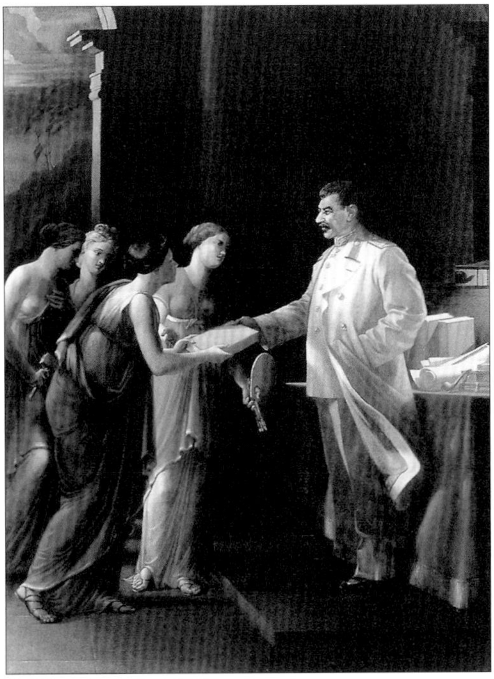

Figure 8 Komar and Melamid, *Stalin and the Muses*, 1981–82, oil on canvas, 183 × 137 cm. Komar and Melamid's Archive.

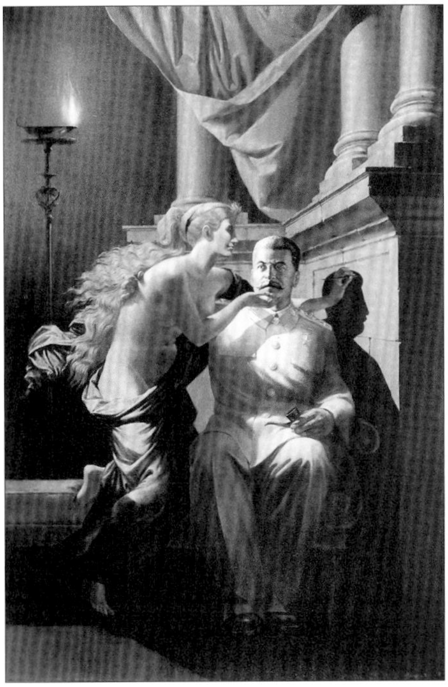

Figure 9 Komar and Melamid, *The Origin of Socialist Realism*, 1982–83, oil on canvas, 183 × 135 cm. Komar and Melamid's Archive.

compositions in the conventional, classicist manner of nineteenth-century historical salon paintings in which Stalin and his comrades take the place of antique heroes. The iconography of these paintings alludes to extremely diverse mythological traditions and situates the myth of Stalin within the context of a tradition that views art as the representation of power. Stalin appears as the great statesman of his era, as the creator of a great empire, the successor to Rome, and as the protector of the arts and sciences.

Of course, the pseudo-apologetic paintings of Komar and Melamid (Figures 8 and 9) stand in stark contrast to the actual aesthetics of the Stalinist era's Socialist Realism. Although "authentic" Stalinist art exhibits a proclivity for classicist and academic styles, it could not overcome the mandate to depict reality in realistic forms. The spirit of classicist stylization remained foreign to it. The mottoes of Socialist Realism read: "Paint the Truth" and "The Content Determines the Form." Soviet painters of the period were supposed to work in the knowledge that everything that appeared in their pictures was actually happening for the first time. No past era could be compared to Stalin's era with regard to sheer greatness, and the reality of Stalinism therefore needed neither beatification nor stylization. The art of past epochs could serve the art of the Stalinist era only as an anemic model, and only insofar as this art was progressive and life affirming, like the art of the classical Greeks and the art of the Italian Renaissance. Stalinist aesthetics resolutely opposed any kind of formalism and epigonal art. Otherwise put, it opposed any definite style that could be identified unambiguously and could be used as a formal model for Soviet art. This is the reason that classical Socialist Realism seems so murky, inexpressive, and eclectic. Soviet art had to be historically unique in order to be able to reflect the historical uniqueness of the Soviet state, even if, at the same time, it was also supposed to use techniques of pictorial representation developed in the past. The painting of an official Soviet painter had to be an expression of deep enthusiasm for Soviet reality, of gratitude toward the Party and its leaders. Therefore, a purely formal analysis of such a painting in terms of iconography, tradition, or school would seem blasphemous.

In fact, Komar and Melamid's works, which viewers not conversant with Socialist Realism could mistake for the real thing, struck the Soviet consciousness as blasphemous. They made visible the academic tradition of representation of glory and triumph that was concealed under the mask of official Soviet Socialist Realism. Komar and Melamid's paintings abound with complicated cultural historical associations, associations that their heroes, Stalin, Khrushchev, and their men, would not have been able to recognize, even though they half-unconsciously reproduced these archetypal representations of power. And the art of Komar and Melamid not only refers to the historicizing academic style, but also alludes to Magical Realism, Surrealism, Pop Art, and Conceptual Art, creating a net of associations and allusions transcending the borders between East and West as they were established by the Cold War.

In a certain sense, one can say that in the period of the Cold War, the border between the conscious and the unconscious, between thought and desire, between the self and the other was almost congruent with the political boundary between the two blocs. Each represented the dark side of the other; each threatened the other with destruction and with the fulfillment of its dreams. We know what kind of temptation the socialist East could be for Western intellectuals, while Soviet citizens imagined the West as, above all, the empire of sexual freedom, of luxury, of seduction, and of sweet degeneracy. In this realm of unconscious political and erotic symbolism, shifts in signification occurred constantly. For example, an object whose significance in Western culture was completely neutral could take on, in the East, the significance of a political and sexual fetish. Individual destiny was almost completely lost in this sea of the political-erotic unconscious. The individual dream had to lose its meaning in a world in which the subconscious was politically monitored and the psychological boundaries inside the individual psyche were identical to the military boundaries between the political blocs.

Komar and Melamid expressed through Sots Art a fundamental Marxist precept: the impossibility of "separating the personal from the social" and of separating individual biographies from historical processes. Komar and Melamid's works can be interpreted, to some extent, as the sessions of a psychoanalytic treatment that is supposed to shed light on the political unconscious and its images.[5] Both went through a double repression in the post-Stalin period in the Soviet Union: repression of the anti-Stalinist opposition and, after that, repression of the image, of the memory, of Stalin himself. While average Soviet citizens in the post-Stalinist period wanted to live out their lives peacefully and "as if it all had never happened," and while this wish has shaped the face of official and unofficial Soviet art since the last half of the 1950s, Komar and Melamid have evoked the realm of the repressed, foregrounding its dangerous and seductive potential. In their works, they constantly thematize the schism, the bifurcation, the rupture that can be interpreted as the political division of the world. They thematize it as an inner bifurcation, as the rupture caused by emigration, and as the splitting of their own images as individual artists, which they embody together. Together, they construct their own myth, as if they were "one" genius. They style themselves after the pairs Marx and Engels, Lenin and Stalin, and Stalin and Trotsky (Figure 10), demonstrating at the same time the inexorability of the original division: the inner rupture that inheres in the artistic will to power and in the pursuit of "tying down the bands of time," as well as in the general crisis of authorship that was acutely felt in the 1980s.

In the 1990s, this loss of individual authorship was combined with the loss of a socially and politically motivated interest in art. After the Cold War, there was no longer any need for the public or for the state to support or to contest a certain kind of art for ideological, political reasons. Art was now left alone. But Komar and Melamid never trusted the modernist promise to place the power of art solely in autonomous artworks that are supposed to have an unmediated effect on the soul of the recipient. Rather, these

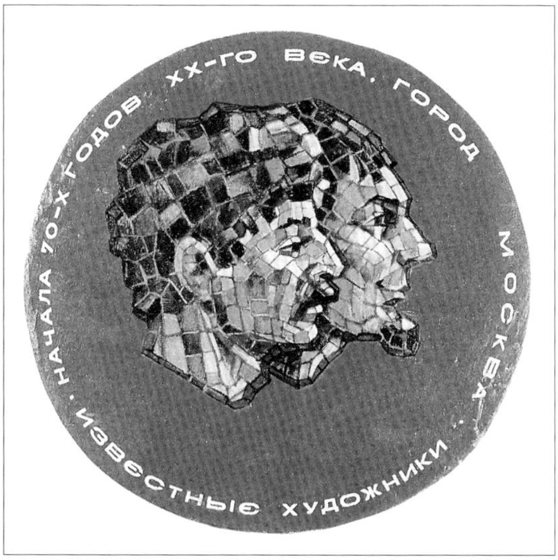

Figure 10 Komar and Melamid, *Double Self-Portrait*, 1973, oil on canvas, 91 cm diameter. Komar and Melamid's Archive.

Figure 11 Komar and Melamid, *America's Most Wanted*, 1994, oil and acrylic on canvas, 61 × 81 cm. Komar and Melamid's Archive.

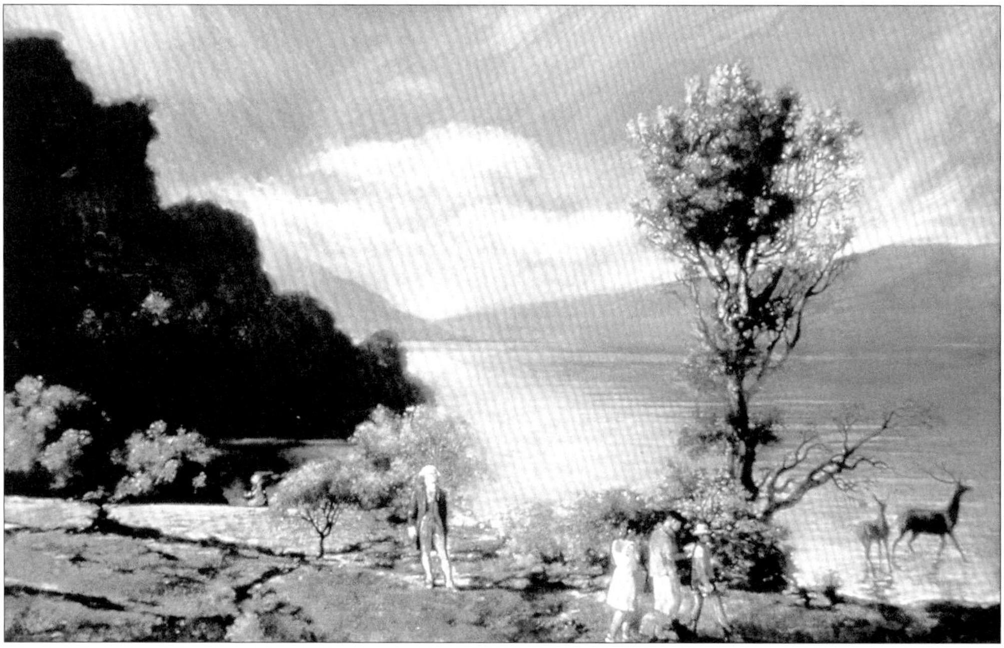

artists always believed that aesthetic power has its genuine source in political power. Thus, Komar and Melamid, after the end of the Cold War, again raised the question of the unity of political and aesthetic power. In their recent project *People's Choice* (which includes the works illustrated here as Plate 1 and Figure 11), Komar and Melamid once more confer all aesthetic power on the people by conveying popular aesthetic preferences statistically. The artists become enablers, servants of the people, since they simply lend visible form to the aesthetic sensibilities of the people.[6] With this move, Komar and Melamid renounce the greatest political-aesthetic accomplishment of modernity: They renounce individual authorship, as well as the related idea of aesthetic autonomy. The sacrifice is striking, even shocking, almost to the point of unseemliness. Yet we might ask here: Is this sacrifice really as great as it appears to be?

For thousands of years, the artist was above all a menial laborer who served the prevailing taste. In this way, great art was produced again and again. Russian artists who, like Komar and Melamid, lived and worked in the former Soviet Union must have had similar experiences. They were part of a society in which the artist was understood to be someone who worked for the people, the state, the Party. Those few Russian artists who, like Komar and Melamid, emigrated to the West encountered conditions with which they were in many respects familiar. Artist-émigrés who took the ideal of the autonomy of art too seriously would be immediately confronted in the Western art system with a fixed catalogue of demands and expectations that forced them to present themselves as innovative, original, and critical in accordance with relatively narrow criteria for what it means to be innovative, original, and critical. In essence, the idea here was simply to discover and fill empty spaces in the art market.

Not only is the mission of contemporary Western art narrowly defined; it is put forth in the name of a very small segment of the public. One might well claim that if art is to carry out a mission, then at the very least it should be carried out for the state and the whole people, and not for a fragment of the population, not for the institutionalized art establishment. If it must conform to a prescribed aesthetics, then it should conform to a great aesthetics with a broad effect and a long tradition, and not to a small subdivision of modern aesthetics. Above all, an artist-émigré asks, why is an artist no longer permitted to paint classically, realistically, traditionally? After all, the classicist artistic inheritance can be newly interpreted and implemented, as was the case in the Soviet Union. Thus, the artist-émigré experiences all Western institutionalized art prohibitions as irritating censorship, a censorship even worse than in the totalitarian home country. But in the 1990s, one could no longer respond effectively to this difficulty with the kind of appropriation strategy that was so successful in the 1980s and that was also used at that time by Komar and Melamid. It was no longer so important for the artist to assimilate an entire art-historical vocabulary in order to have it available as a way to escape the construction of a definite "personal" style. Such a gesture is relevant only within a modernist tradition and is valued because it takes up a certain possible art strategy that was overlooked earlier. Here the artist as appropriator remains a prisoner of the logic of artistic innovation and institutional demands and expectations.

The question, then, reads as follows: How can the artist become free from all these demands? The answer Komar and Melamid give is extremely simple and, for that reason, very convincing: through the artist's explicit renunciation of individuality, sovereignty, and autonomy. Appropriation is not the goal. Rather, the goal is self-expropriation: the renunciation of the claim to sovereign artistic individuality. Here one discovers that the power of censorship everywhere is based on a social consensus according to which artists are supposed to pour out their hearts, express their individuality, and be passionate and sincere in their art. It is well known, however, that every society has its own criteria for sincerity in art. In fact, we might ask: How can the question of whether a work of art is inspired by the inner life of the artist be objectively determined from outside? It is a great secret. The power of the art system, its arbitrariness, and its mechanisms of oppression all rest on this secret. Thus, in the West of today, a work of art is immediately rejected as insincere and unoriginal if it is not formally innovative. The artist was actually supposed to be sincere in the Soviet Union, as well, and art was supposed to come directly from the soul. The evaluative criteria, however, were different. Only what was made in harmony with the soul of the people was regarded as genuinely sincere. Here we see something that conjoins Soviet realism and Western modernism: the search for sincerity in art and the censorship of everything that does not seem to be sincere, even if the Soviet criteria for such a censorship seem to be opposed to Western criteria.

The *People's Choice* project signals Komar and Melamid's abdication of the demand for sincerity that makes the artist accountable for explaining everything. Komar and Melamid distance themselves from all personal responsibility for what they do as artists. The will of the people is defined and substantiated by written, verifiable, statistical data. The painters simply do their job and wash their hands afterward. What is at issue here is the last and most subtle freedom that remains available to us as moderns: the freedom of the radically alienated work for which the individual no longer bears any individual responsibility. This freedom is secretly exercised by all the democratically elected servants of the people. In contrast, Komar and Melamid have sincerely declared that they no longer want to be sincere. They have used their autonomy and personal responsibility to renounce both autonomy and personal responsibility. By deciding to mediate the will of the people scientifically and statistically, the artists have torn apart all inner, affective attachments to the people and have forsworn all inner solidarity with them. Instead, they have confessed that nothing binds them inwardly to their public any longer and that their public can no longer expect something sincere from them. Politicians have long known about this inner break with their constituencies. Artists must learn to negotiate it.

It is certainly easy to say here that statistics are misleading and that the servants of the people simply want to manipulate the will of the people. The Hegelian dialectic of master and slave is well known. It would be even easier to say that Komar and Melamid want to ironize public taste and make fun of the people. In my opinion, neither of these statements is true. To be sure, the *Most Wanted* pictures appear to be somewhat shabby, kitschy, and clumsy. But they are at the same time pleasantly poetic. They demonstrate a few of the purely personal preferences of the artists, which one will immediately recognize if one is familiar with their earlier works. The whole *Most Wanted* series is an allegory of fulfilled dreams. Instead of consciously disappointing the expectations of the public, as modern art putatively does, Komar and Melamid attempt to fulfill these wishes. And yet, we seem to be disappointed by the results. Many fairy tales and sagas tells us how difficult it is for us to accept that what we see before us is in fact the realization of our dreams. We have had many such an experience with modern utopias.

In the middle of the American *Most Wanted* picture (Figure 11), which is prototypical for the whole series, stands George Washington, lost and uncertain in the American dream he did so much to create. No one needs him any longer, either as a hero or as a criminal (one American meaning of "Most Wanted"). This figure of Washington evokes the figure of Stalin in several of Komar and Melamid's earlier paintings: also lost, lonely, and uncertain in the middle of a reality that he created. Certainly the artists identify themselves with these creators of reality who apparently no longer know whether they realized their own wishes or the wishes of others, just as one can no longer be certain about this in modern art.

Ilya Kabakov: The Artist as Fictitious Figure

Whereas Komar and Melamid, within the framework of their Sots Art, were primarily concerned with the aesthetics of power, other Moscow Conceptualists of the 1970s were more interested in the aesthetics of Soviet everyday life. In fact, the prevailing official Soviet aesthetics at this time had relatively little to do with the original Socialist Realism of the Stalin era, although an avowal of ideological allegiance to Socialist Realism was still a precondition for participation in the officially sanctioned art industry. The art of the Stalin era was optimistic, forward looking. The Socialist Realism of the Brezhnev era, in contrast, was retrospective, nostalgic. It wanted to take up cultural models of the past and to be worthy of them. The change in mood corresponded to changes in the legitimation needs of the dominant ideology. Stalinist culture always conceived of itself as a new historical beginning. The ideology of Brezhnev's era proclaimed the Soviet Union to be a place where traditional ideals and desires would be fulfilled, ideals and desires that were disregarded and betrayed by Western capitalism and its ruthless policy of modernization. This strategy corresponded to the general mood of the country, which wanted to pick up the thread of the past that had been severed by the October Revolution. At that time, Ilya Kabakov was the central figure in the artistic movement that reacted critically and ironically to this aesthetics of social stagnation.

The actual breakthrough and the discovery of his own artistic problematic came at the beginning of the 1970s for Kabakov, with the series of albums entitled *10 Persons* that he created between 1971 and 1976 (Figure 12). Each of these albums looks like a book with loose pages and tells in words and images the history of an artist who lives on the margins of society and whose work is not understood, or recognized, or even fully preserved. The images in the albums are meant as the inner visions or artworks of the artists-heroes. All these images have captions in which friends and relatives of the artists comment on their work. The final image in each album is a white page that announces the death of the hero. Each album also concludes with general commentary on all the works of the artist, spoken from the perspective of fictitious commentators, who, one should assume, represent the opinions of the educated class that has posthumous control of the artist's work and definitively evaluates it.

The private visions with which the heroes of the albums are obsessed refer in many cases to the glorious history of modern art in the twentieth

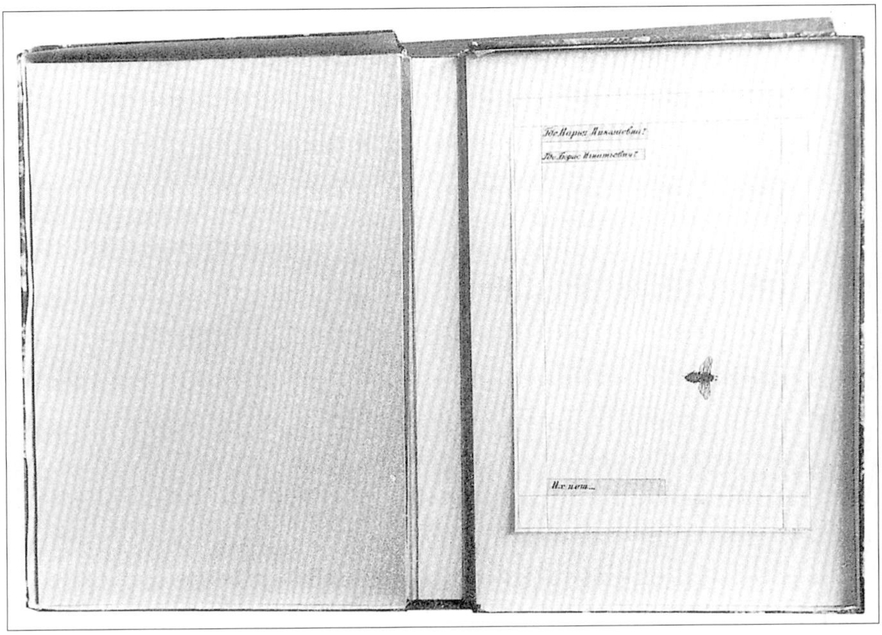

Figure 12 Ilya Kabakov, a view of an album, 1980.

century. The artistic execution of the albums themselves is performed, in contrast, first and foremost with reference to average Soviet children's book illustrations, which perpetuate the nineteenth-century tradition of drawing, a tradition over which Kabakov, who was active as a book illustrator in the official art industry, had a good command. The internal "avant-garde" visions of the heroes are largely discredited by the trivial visual language in which they are made manifest. In addition, the outsiders' commentaries on the visions of the heroes bear witness to the diverse misunderstandings to which all art is exposed. At the same time, these albums, admittedly, are wonderfully poetic, suffused with earnest artistic pathos, and the minute and precise execution of the illustrations is impressive. In this way, the albums aestheticize the limitations and anonymous failures of their heroes, so that their stories acquire a seductive aura. For the most part, it is an apt and fascinating as well as ironic depiction of the myth of modern art, whose resurrection did much to inspire the unofficial Moscow art scene.[7]

Furthermore, Kabakov created an imaginary audience for his artists-heroes through the accompanying commentary. This imaginary audience compensated him for the absence of a real audience for unofficial Russian art. Yet the imaginary recipients, as Kabakov sketches them in his albums, do not display a very deep understanding of art. The opinions of the recipients diverge radically. Their interpretations could accrue endlessly, and their sensitivity to artistic creation gets lost in this process of infinite interpretation. However, this circumstance results not in a pessimistic disposition on the part of the artist, but rather in profound optimism. The artist wants attention from the recipient, but not interpretive control, and the endless commentary promises endless attention.

In *10 Persons*, Kabakov tried for the first time the technique that would become the defining feature of his art: "personness" (*personazhnost*). Kabakov began to invent fictitious artists, and authors and to provide them with just as fictitious biographies, ascribing to them authorship of definite artworks. This technique enables Kabakov to take up the most diverse artistic attitudes, positions, and histories of development and to investigate their effects without fully identifying with any of these positions. In this way, the focus shifts from the production of individual works of art to the context in which they are produced. Individual artworks are shown by Kabakov to be projections of the hopes, self-deceptions, and disappointments of his heroes. He shows them to be the results of certain psychologically motivated artistic strategies that the heroes pursue. In doing so, Kabakov holds these strategies up against the background of a larger social and art-historical context, throwing the strategies into question without completely negating their force.

Instead of waiting for an interpreter steeped in art history who believes he or she can uncover the intentions and strategies that lie hidden behind an artist's works by contextualizing them, Kabakov himself thematizes the context of his works by telling the stories of the fictitious artists who are supposed to have created these works. To some extent, these stories can be trusted insofar as the heroes can certainly be understood as pseudonyms for or alter egos of Kabakov. Nonetheless, the distance and irony with which Kabakov describes these fictitious authors is not simulated. Kabakov identifies with the heroes of his stories only partially and, from the very start, takes certain of their artistic positions with ironic intent. Kabakov constantly stages a game of identification and nonidentification with his heroes. He often lays bare his own strategies by describing them as the strategies of his heroes, and he conceals them at the same time through this kind of description.

This strategy puts Ilya Kabakov in a special position, even within the Moscow Conceptualist circle with which he was intimately involved in the 1970s and 1980s. He does not believe that a certain art context can be described completely and objectively. On the contrary, Kabakov sees the context of art as an endless play of signifiers that can be neither described nor surveyed, so that his art evinces many similarities with poststructuralist theory. But Kabakov's primary interest is not in proving the impossibility of both completely mapping context and stabilizing authorial intention, because he regards authorship as fictitious. Rather, by introducing the fictive authors and the fictive art context in his albums, he wants to thematize explicitly the fictional character of all art. The real author is dead, as has often been asserted, and for just this reason, a fictive author can come alive.

The common mistake of a positivistic-sociological description of an art context and of authorship is that it overlooks the fact that art is created in the expectation of a different recipient, a different reception, and a different social context from the ones that, here and now, lend themselves to such a description. Art lives on the promise of its durability, which enables it to transcend the boundaries of the context in which it is produced. Works of art are produced with the expectation that they will outlast the context of their production, that they will be viewed in times and places that we, in the here and now, cannot predict, let alone describe, but can only imagine. Even commercial art is produced in the hope that it will be internationally enjoyable and profitable for a relatively long period of time. Thus, the context within which art orients itself is always utopian, fantastic, and impossible to describe positivistically. One cannot respond concretely to this other, phatasmatic context, which does not present itself in the here and now, but which announces itself only with insight. One can respond to it only with hope or fear. The context of art is never real, but always fictional, just like art itself.

Kabakov constantly thematizes the mixture of hope and fear that is characteristically exhibited by those who want to cross the borders of their world. This crossing creates hope, because artists want to believe that, in the new world, future recipients will perhaps understand their work better than their obtuse contemporaries, and that these future recipients will perhaps show these artists the respect, love, and admiration that all authors have lacked at all times in their immediate environment. At the same time, artists become anxious when they think about how foreign or future recipients might neglect their work or deem it utter garbage that might simply have possessed some sentimental meaning for the author and his immediate environment but is otherwise meaningless.

The first album in the *10 Persons* series, *Primakov Sitting in the Closet*, has remained, in many respects, paradigmatic for Kabakov's work. It is above all about the artist disappearing in a foreign place. The first pages of the album show the black square that evokes Malevich's *Black Square*. From the commentary, however, we learn that this black square is seen by a small boy who sits in a closet and, for the time being, refuses to come out. The child begins gradually to open the closet. First, he sees his family in their apartment, then his city, then the region, then the whole area, then the entire earth and the different levels of the sky, where objects and words begin to fall apart, as in modernist paintings. Then comes a white page that tells us that the boy disappeared out of the closet and was never seen again. The birth of the world is here equated with death.

The boy flies farther and farther in search of greater perspective, a greater horizon. The farther he flies, the more everything falls apart, until there is nothing more to see. At the end of the album, the consciousness of the hero is a void, a white piece of paper, a neutral surface. One could say that here, the definitive defeat of the hero is recorded. But the thoroughly banal commentary that follows the death of the hero is written on the white page that symbolizes the empty consciousness of the hero. One can therefore say that the death of the artist creates the space in which commentary becomes possible. However stupidly insensitive and foreign to the work the commentary may be, it does belong to the work, for it is written on the white piece of paper that belongs to the work.

The expanded art context reveals itself here to be purely phantasmatic. The reality of death alone corresponds to it. Death ironizes everything present and positive, everything that can be described, bringing it to dissolution. However, at the same time, death gives our hopes the chance to reach out over the narrow horizon of the living. The insight that everything present must disappear is sometimes disquieting. Yet it is also comforting, above all for someone who suffers under the conditions of the present and whose only hope lies beyond the immediate context of his life. This mood is very palpable in the Russian literary classics of the nineteenth century, in which, incidentally, Kabakov's work is much more deeply rooted than in the history of the plastic arts.

Kabakov's installations have their origin neither in performance nor in post-Minimalist, site-specific art, as is the case with most Western installations, but rather in narrative literature or, more precisely, in the novel. Characteristically, the first large installation that Kabakov made, in the Ronald Feldman Gallery, New York, after his immigration to the West was called *10 Characters* (1988).[8] In this installation, works that Kabakov had for the most

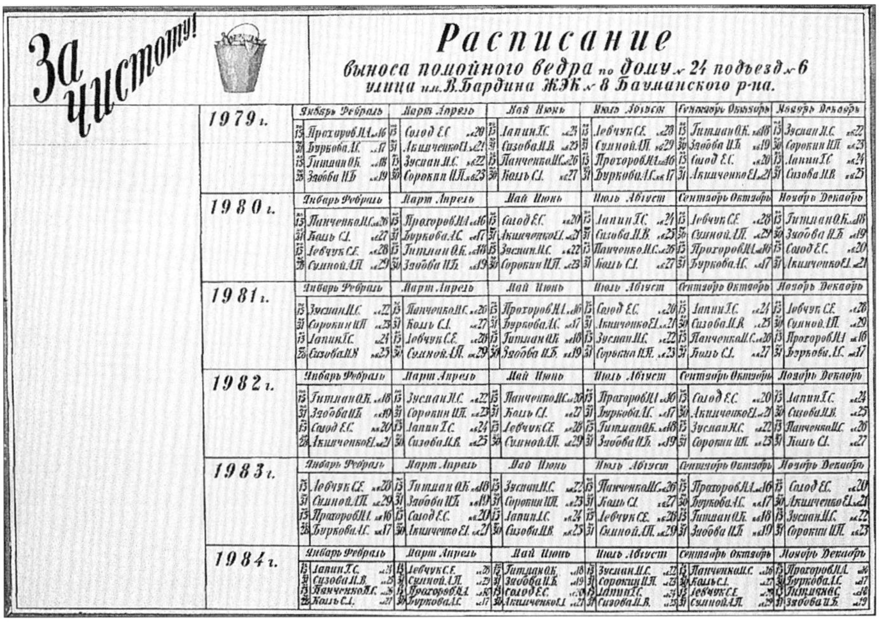

Figure 13 Ilya Kabakov, *"Schedule of Slop Pail Dumping,"* 1980, enamel on masonite, 150 × 210 cm.

part created in Russia during the previous decades were attributed to ten different fictitious authors, whom he depicted as lonely, isolated people who practiced their art in the seclusion of their small rooms. Each such installation by Kabakov tells a story, and it is almost always the story of a lonely artist in unpleasant, threatening surroundings (see Plate 2). They are Baroque installations that distance themselves programmatically from the "white cube" of Minimalist-Conceptualist installations and stage a play of shadow and light obscuring the perspective of the viewer, thus thematizing the difficulty of looking into the private sphere, of gaining insight into the intimate refuse of a strange life, while at the same time thematizing the attraction of such a voyeuristic look into the dark, hidden, and intimate. Not by accident was the whole space of the installation *10 Persons* staged as an average Soviet communal apartment in which previous tenants left refuse that should have been cleaned up. The Soviet communal apartment is also the theme of many other of Kabakov's works (Figure 13). All the tenants of a Kabakovian communal apartment are immersed in their personal dreams, and yet they all live in one apartment. At issue here is communication without communication, a crowded everyday coexistence coupled with complete inner isolation.

The communal apartment represents, no doubt, the general structure of life under the conditions of Soviet Communism. This life was forged by the fear that to express oneself would be to betray oneself. At the same time, people lived in extreme physical and spatial proximity to one another. The combination of inner isolation and external intimacy was certainly very disturbing. Yet, as always in such cases, Kabakov is out to discover in this unbearable combination a universal human condition, and even a utopia.

In *The Inoperative Community,* Jean-Luc Nancy attempts to define the communal by distinguishing its constituent properties from those of society and community.[9] His attempt is astoundingly close to the Kabakovian interpretation of the communal apartment. Nancy's theoretical construct can be described, needless to say, only cursorily here. Society, for Nancy, as it is for most theoreticians, is communication among autonomous individuals who enjoy certain rights, above all the right to anonymity, to a kind of protection against the public. Often counterposed to this society of individuals is a community—a community of love, of strong ties, of unity, whether seen as a family, an ecstatic religious community, perhaps a folk community, or a class-based community. The subject in a community, like the subject in a society, rules over its self-images. It is the subject's domination of its self-images, of its own aesthetic representation, that community and society have in common.

On the level on the communal, however, we produce images of ourselves that we cannot control. Others have an excess of vision, a visual advantage, over us. The communal is above all, for Nancy, this other, uncontrollable side of communication. Accordingly, Nancy defines the communal as "être exposé," as being exposed. He means: Even before I consciously produce images, I am always already on display on the level of the communal. One can therefore interpret the entire human pursuit of creating images as an attempt belatedly to correct the pictures others have of us or, at the very least, as an attempt to play with these pictures.

The Soviet communal apartment is, at bottom, such a place for Ilya Kabakov. It is a place where one is always already on display, exposed to the gaze of someone else. Here we no longer experience the private sphere, which stands in opposition to or is at least separated from the social sphere, as an area of private emotions in contrast to the coldness of society. The communal apartment is the place where the social is at its most terrifying, appearing most intrusive, where the individual is completely exposed to the mostly hostile gazes of others, who consistently exploit their visual advantage in order to gain temporary victories in the endless communal apartment war. In the extreme intimacy of the communal apartment, the whole visual field becomes a battlefield on which the war of gazes rages. To be able to observe others is just as important as to be able to conceal oneself from and protect oneself from the strange gaze. And even if Soviet Communism is no more, communal life remains the same. The others always have an excess of vision and power beyond ours, an excess that we want to protect ourselves against, but that we can also enjoy. Now that God, the intimate and all-seeing observer, is dead, only the communal remains as an observer interested in our intimate sphere. We know how many people have missed the excitement of being observed since the decline of Communism, the excitement of being the object of a stranger's constant interest, even if that interest was hostile.

The communal situation thus makes everyone an artist, and also an artwork. Not by coincidence, then, are all the tenants of Kabakov's communal apartment artists. The communal apartment serves as a metaphor for the "art community." And, indeed, what is a museum or a large exhibition, if not a communal apartment in which different artists, who, perhaps, have never even heard of one another and who pursue very different goals and interests, are pressed together by the will of a curator whom society has appointed? Thus, artists find themselves again and again in the forced intimacy of a common context, with strange, if not hostile, neighbors. At issue here is not the question of whether this context can be described, controlled, and articulated socially, politically, and institutionally. At issue, rather, are the remains of an uncontrollable communal being on display, something that cannot be consciously captured, articulated, and sublated by any such description.

In particular, Kabakov thematizes the tension between a private and a public place in his installation *Toilet*, which he built for the *Documenta 9* exhibition in Kassel in 1992.[10] He built this toilet as a separate building in the courtyard of the Fridericianum palace, where the majority of the *Documenta* works were shown. Through its structure, it evokes the common, primitive, hardly comfortable public toilets that can still be found in the south of Russia. Inside this toilet, Kabakov created private rooms that looked like a normal family apartment. What we had here was a family that lived quietly and undisturbed in a public toilet, without any dramatizing of this fact. The installation is at the same time a clever commentary on the *Documenta* exhibition. The interplay between private apartment and public toilet that Kabakov staged in this installation corresponds to the familiar structure of a contemporary large public art exhibit. Every viewer had the right to visit the private space of an artist in order to relieve his or her aesthetic need there. Of course, there is a certain tension in this metaphor, and it suggests that it is not without nostalgia that Kabakov thinks back on the time when he would receive the visitors who wanted to see his art in his atelier or apartment as a host who had the chance to dictate the conditions under which they could see his art. In the installations he made in the West, Kabakov attempted to win back this missing artistic control through purely aesthetic means, through direct or indirect instructions that steer the viewer's attention in this or that direction, establishing the sequence in which his installations should be seen.

Kabakov often labels his installations "total installations."[11] By this he obviously means that when he builds these installations, he does not simply place his artistic productions in an already existing space, but completely alters this space visually and makes it into his private exhibition place, if only temporarily. At the same time, however, these installations invoke a greater, totalitarian, project of omnipresent control and a system of direct and indirect orders that is reminiscent of the deceased Soviet Union. This impression is reinforced by the frequent application of Soviet-looking materials and spatial design. Here, Kabakov's relation to this totalitarian project seems to be divided and ambivalent. On the one hand, he sees this project as a kind of sinister oppression that was justly condemned to failure by history. But, on the other hand, he cannot overlook the fact that his own artistic drive to control and steer the gaze of the observer is intrinsically related to the totalitarian political project.

Many of Kabakov's "Soviet" installations make visible this ambivalence. Consider, for example, the structure of his powerful installation *The Great Archive* (Stedelijk Museum, Amsterdam, 1993). The first visitors were asked to fill out hundreds of different forms. Then they entered a room that looked like a Kafkaesque courtroom, where they apparently received some kind of sentence that sent them either to the garbage can of oblivion or to the archive of collective memory. The room evoked Soviet bureaucratic spaces: shabby, boring, depressing. The questions on the forms were so contradictory, inconsistent, and confused that the whole mass of forms seemed to be ready for the paper shredder and the wastepaper basket. The archive has collapsed because in claiming to be able to understand humans in all aspects of their lives, it accepted no criteria that would have allowed the essential and relevant to be distinguished from the inessential and irrelevant.

Without any sort of differentiation, the closing judgment can only be arbitrary and absurd.

This absurdity is reinforced by the fact that the installations are temporary and, after they are taken down, they remain only as vague memories in the minds of the visitors. In the best case, they are preserved in catalogues. Kabakov thematizes again and again the transience of his installations, whereby the demise of the Soviet socialist order functions repeatedly as a metaphor for transience of every civilized order. Thus, visitors entered the installation *The Red Wagon* (Düsseldorf, 1991) through a pseudofuturistic entrance that was evocative of the famous Tatlin's Tower, Vladimir Tatlin's 1919 *Monument to the Third International*, a projected 1,300-foot-high tower commemorating the Russian Revolution. They proceeded on through a room in which the dreams of Stalin's era were represented by a huge fresco and then at the exit found themselves at a landfill. Through the installation *The Red Pavilion* (Venice, 1993), Kabakov transformed the Soviet exhibition pavilion in the Giardini into something between a construction site and a storage shed. He also built a small provisional pavilion next door that remained off-limits to visitors, out of which the optimistic music of the Stalin era blared incessantly. One could not really enter either pavilion. The old pavilion was falling apart, and the new pavilion was merely a voice. And in the gigantic installation *We Live Here* (Centre Georges Pompidou, Paris, 1995), the deserted construction site of a mighty palace of the future was suggested. Only the ruins of the construction project and of the workers' provisional and shabby housing remained.

All of the installations in which Kabakov explicitly engages with the vanquished dreams of socialism constantly thematize the brisk transition between construction and decline, the moment between genesis out of garbage and dissolution into garbage (Figure 14). Civilization as such reveals itself to be a ruin in progress, a temporary installation that does not guarantee its own longevity and can vanish without a trace at any moment. Soviet civilization is the first thoroughly modern civilization that died before our eyes. All the other famous dead civilizations were premodern. The Soviet Union dissolved so completely and landed on the garbage heap of history so irretrievably because it left behind no unmistakable monuments comparable to Egyptian pyramids or Greek temples. This civilization simply fell apart and became the same modern garbage out of which it, like all modern, ready-made civilizations, was made.

Again and again, Kabakov stages the dissolution of Soviet civilization

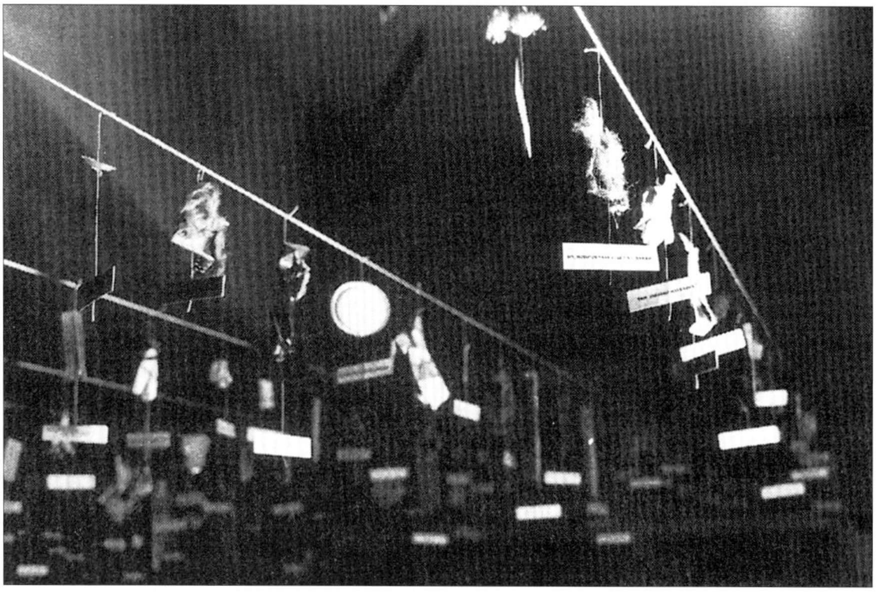

Figure 14 Ilya Kabakov, installation of garbage in his Moscow studio, 1982.

into extrahistorical garbage. Again and again, he shapes this sight as painful, cheap, repulsive, and, at the same time, sublime. The more radical and inexorable this decline is, the more exalted the image of this decline appears to be. The Communist utopia announced at its beginning the highest possible historical claims, undertook the greatest possible exertion in order to save humanity from its historical needs, only to collapse in poverty, squalor, and chaos. Its history offers the most extreme case of a historical defeat and, therefore, it may also offer an exalted historical image. Notwithstanding their heavy emphasis on Orwellian shabbiness and quasi-bureaucratic ugliness, Kabakov's installations, which thematize the fate of Soviet power, exhibit a kind of fascination with all the monuments of past glory.

It is not only utopian-messianic strivings that are transient for Kabakov, but all civilizing strivings. The museum is transient for him, as well. Kabakov may erect his short-lived installations inside the apparently stable institution of the museum, but he does not let his viewers forget that the museum itself is merely an installation, and that, in the end, it, too, will dissolve into garbage. Thus, in his installation *Incident at the Museum, or Water Music* (Museum of Contemporary Art, Chicago, 1993), Kabakov staged the dilapidated room of a provincial Russian museum in which the paintings of an unknown and extremely conventional Soviet painter were preserved. The ceiling in this museum was crumbling. Water dripped from above, and pots were arranged on the floor to catch it. As usual, Kabakov presented here the demise of civilization and its decomposition into refuse. And, as usual, this demise gave occasion for hope. The fall of the water was modulated by a special apparatus so that its dripping into the containers suggested a certain melody. Art survives every catastrophe, every falling apart, every decline, for what matters, in the end, is the ability to see everything with which we are confronted as art. This ability, we should note, does not have to do with total "aestheticization," which would anesthetize, dulling our sense of "reality." Rather, it has to do with the opportunity to create art under all possible circumstances. Art functions as a privatization of a social dream that transforms itself from a political utopia into an inner utopia after historical reality has failed. The utopian dream is no longer realized in the territory of a country but, rather, is constructed as an artistic installation on the grounds of a museum.

Privatizations: Strategies of Unofficial Soviet-Russian Art

The individualist privatization of a collectivist Communist utopian dream has been characteristic of all late Soviet Russian art since the beginning of 1970s. These artistic strategies of privatization announce in a very peculiar and telling way the strategies of economic privatization that were put into effect after the long-awaited but nonetheless sudden abdication of the Soviet powers in 1991, which transformed the gigantic territory of the Soviet Union politically and legally into a propertyless, empty space. One could argue that the old Leninist-Stalinist "dialectical" doctrine about the disappearance of the state as a result of an unlimited expansion of its power, which so many commentators treated ironically for so long, had, in the end, proven to be correct. The incessant domestic and international growth of the Soviet Union's power led, in fact, to its historical sublation. Here, in a certain sense, the October Revolution reached its completion: the death of the state as the last and only property owner left behind a society of the propertyless.

Of course, immediately after the demise of the Soviet state, individual citizens began to privatize everything that they could find. But this process of privatization should not be understood as the road that leads from a propertyless country (back) to a country of private property. Post-Soviet privatization is not a transition, but a lasting condition. At issue here is the condition of fundamental uncertainty about what belongs to whom and what belongs to no one. Otherwise put, what is at issue is the question of where the private begins and where it ends. The private thus reveals its fatal dependence on the public: Private spaces are necessarily formed out of the remains of state property. What is being played out is a violent picking apart and private appropriation of the dead body of the Soviet state, which evokes archaic, sacred festivals at which the members of a tribe have eaten the dead totemic animal. Everyone receives a piece. However, on the other hand, this festival is grounded in the supra-individual community of the tribe, which by far exceeds the bounds of the private.

Just as, after it expired, the Soviet state left behind a gigantic territory for private acquisition, so too, after the death of Soviet ideology, which had occurred much earlier, in the 1960s, the gigantic empire of desire, its legacy, was made available for private, psychological acquisition. The Soviet state invaded the souls of its subjects directly and manipulated their impressions, feelings, and experiences very effectively using the most modern propaganda tools. The traumatic experiences to which people in the Soviet Union were constantly subjected were incomparably stronger than all the individual traumas with which traditional psychoanalysis is concerned. This manipulative power of the Communist state was always stronger than all the powers of the personal unconscious. Thus, a huge reservoir of conscious and unconscious experiences formed that could not be attributed to individual souls in the traditional psychological sense and whose single subject was the state. In the Soviet era, every private psyche was subordinated to the official ideology and thus nationalized.

Soviet ideology was grounded in a particular desire: for a communism that signified the arrival of cosmic redemption and universal happiness. What was at stake was not simply a particular interpretation of world history. World history itself looked different within the Soviet Union. It had other names, dates, events, and patterns of narration. If Soviet history had been merely a national and regional history, it could easily be reintegrated into unified universal history with a few small changes. Soviet history, however, was a different narration of universal history, which, because of its claims to universality, could not be subsumed under neutral and scientifically conceived Western historiography.

This different, Soviet, universal history represents the territory on which the empire of state desire, or the nationalized psyche of Soviet citizens, was territorialized. With the death of the Soviet ideology, which actually occurred soon after the death of Stalin, the constitutional subject of state desire was dissolved. The empire of national feelings had lost the sovereign who had governed it earlier. Thus, this empire became rulerless, subjectless. Otherwise put: What had been the nationalized realm of feelings and experiences was transformed into the subjectless, nameless unconscious, into a psychological desert that could be appropriated and privatized by every single individual. The phantasmatic historical vision produced by the Soviet state was dissolved through the strategy of privatization and psychologization into the personal mythologies of individual artists who looked very modern, very up-to-date indeed. So-called totalitarian forms of culture are just as modern as liberal, democratic modernity itself. At issue here is another modernity, and not simply the survival of premodern identities. In fact, this totalitarian modernity is in many respects even more modern, because more radical, than liberal, democratic modernity. With it there emerges a rivalry that does not allow for the sentimentalizing of the other that represents the main artistic device of today's art for dealing with cultural identity politics.

Beyond Kabakov and Komar and Melamid, some other Moscow artists began the (re)privatization of the Soviet soul as early as the 1970s. By doing so, they tried to subvert the clear-cut border between the individualistic, Existentialist pathos of unofficial art of the 1950s and 1960s and the whole territory of the collective Soviet experience that was ignored or excluded by this pathos. One of the leading Moscow artists of the 1970s, Erik Bulatov (Figure 15), combined in his painterly practices the official symbols of Soviet power with the portraits of his personal friends and his wife. His paintings look in many respects like ordinary three-dimensional realistic representations. But in his works, Bulatov develops the device of combining the illusory "private" three-dimensional space of the realistic picture and the "social" two-dimensional space of the ideological propaganda poster. Bulatov achieves this goal by introducing into the space of the painting texts like "Glory to the CPSU," which he inserts into the painting with the same title (Figure 16) (1975), or ideological signs like the ribbon of the Order of Lenin that he inserts into *The Horizon* (1972). Thus, even as he uses the techniques of traditional, realistic painting, Bulatov demonstrates that he no longer trusts its immediacy or "naturalness" (Figure 17). In a world saturated with ideology, immediacy becomes impossible: *Lebenswelt* proves to be an ideological sign. But, at the same time, all ideological signs can become part of a painting. The tradition of painting opens for the artist the possibility of pri-

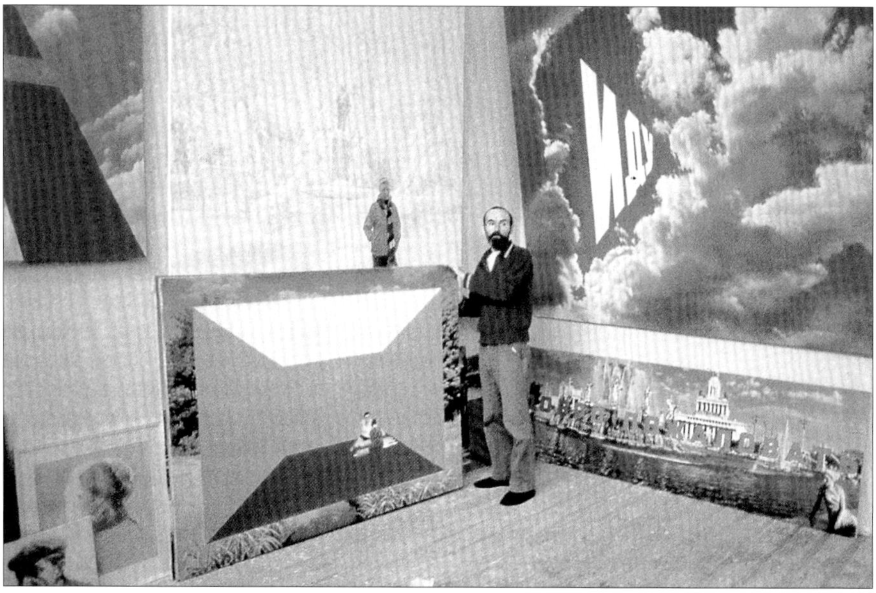

Figure 15 Erik Bulatov in his Moscow studio, 1970s.

vatizing all visual signs, of using them artistically, even the most ideologically dangerous ones.[12] The power of the painterly tradition also was demonstrated especially clearly in the works of Ivan Chuikov, which were made in the 1970s and 1980s.[13] In these works, quotations from the Soviet visual world were fragmented and integrated into the complex interplay of all kinds of other quotations taken from different periods of art history. As a result, the signs of Soviet ideology lost their symbolic power, because that power was based on their claim to absolute historical uniqueness.

It was not only by means of traditional painting, of course, that the artistic privatization of the Soviet cultural space was practiced. Artistic performances that were organized in the 1970s and 1980s by Andrei Monastyrsky, the leader of the group Collective Actions, were especially characteristic in this respect (Figure 18). These performances took place, as a rule, during the winter in a wide, snow-covered field on the edge of Moscow. The white surface of the snow evoked the white background of Malevich's Suprematist art or of Kabakov's early, quasi-Minimalist paintings. At the same time, it was a typical Russian landscape that could also often be seen on the paintings of the official Soviet artists: just the snow, the sky, and the woods on the horizon. The performances were extremely Minimalist and enigmatic: short fragments of strange, unfamiliar rituals. Here, the main interest of the

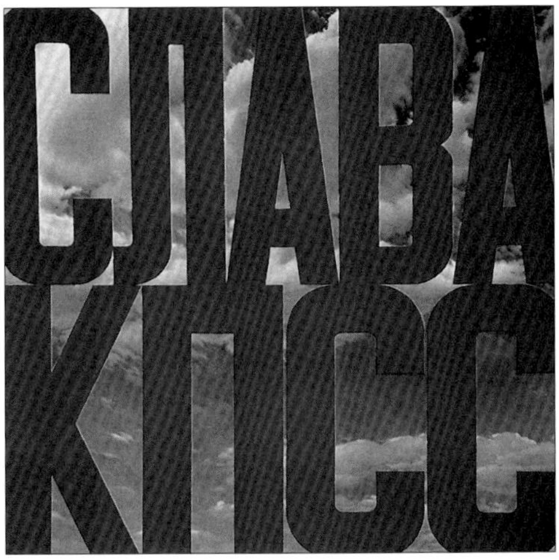

Figure 16 Erik Bulatov, *Glory to the CPSU*, 1975, oil on canvas, 220 × 220 cm.

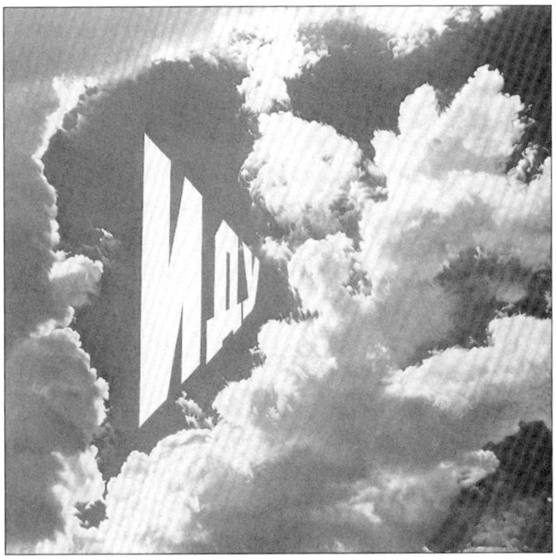

Figure 17 Erik Bulatov, *I Am Going*, 1975, oil on canvas, 220 × 220 cm.

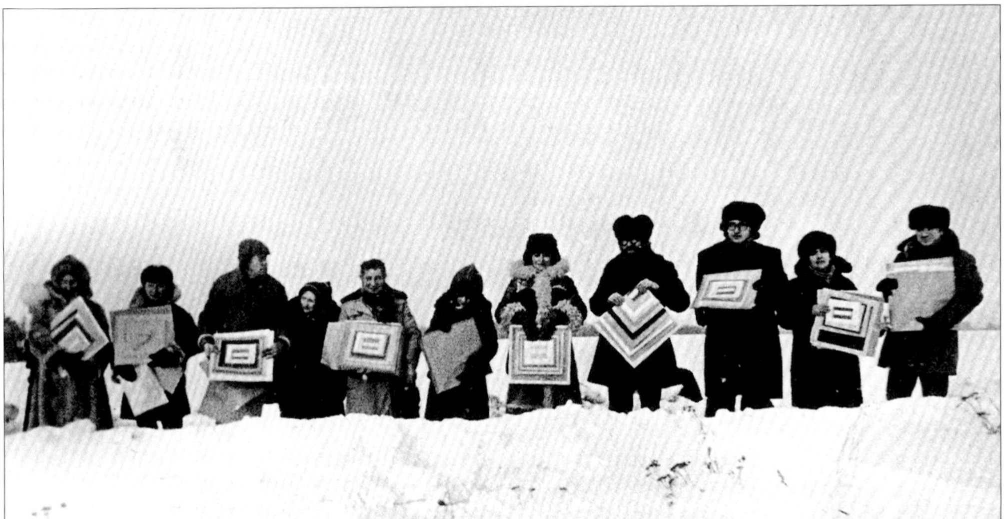

Figure 18 Collective Actions, *Pictures*, 1980, performance. Boris Groys's Archive.

organizers, as in the earlier work of Kabakov, was not so much the event itself as the process of interpretation that followed it. Instead of asserting the worth of their own work, they wanted, first and foremost, to provoke social commentary on this work. The individual performance only created the social space in which the discussion that followed among the participants and the viewers could take place. The commentary, conversations, and reactions were collected afterward and integrated into a multivolume work in progress entitled *Travels Outside the City.*[14]

The main characteristic of the commentary process inspired by Monastyrsky and his group was that it applied either exotic or purely private models of interpretation. The *I Ching* and Russian Orthodox mysticism were coupled with private memories, premonitions, obsessions, and associations. This did not have to do with any "actual belief" in the laws of the *I Ching* or any actual mystical epiphany. These were used, instead, to relativize the postulates of social normality and "realism." The mystical commentary was offered as one possibility among many of distancing oneself from the pressure of the quotidian. Andrei Monastyrsky's long-standing engagement with Chinese and, above all, North Korean Communism, as well as with the narrative structures of the classical Chinese novel, also served to thematize difference and otherness within international Communist discourse. Thus, Monastyrsky evaded the oppressive Soviet narrative, which conjoined the Russian realist novel of the nineteenth century with the nineteenth-century Marxist narrative, putting the familiar signs of Communism in a fully alien, Orientalized context.

This posture is also characteristic of the younger group Medical Hermeneutics (Pavel Pepperstein, Sergei Anufriev, and, earlier, Yurii Leidermann), which occupied an important place in the Moscow art scene of the 1980s and has programmatically inserted itself into the tradition of Moscow Conceptualism (Figure 19). Commentary on art and literature occupy more space in the activities of this group than so-called actual artistic production.[15] The interpretive practice of Medical Hermeneutics exhibits Kabakov's influence, as well as a fascination with psychoanalysis and a familiarity with the poststructuralist interpretive practices of Lacan, Deleuze, and Derrida. The readings that the Medical Hermeneuticians develop have to do with the basic relation of a work of art to its context. Every artwork, for Medical Hermeneutics, is always already contaminated by its context and is therefore sick, even half-dead. According to the discourse of Medical Hermeneutics, the artwork contains its context immanently, like so many bacte-

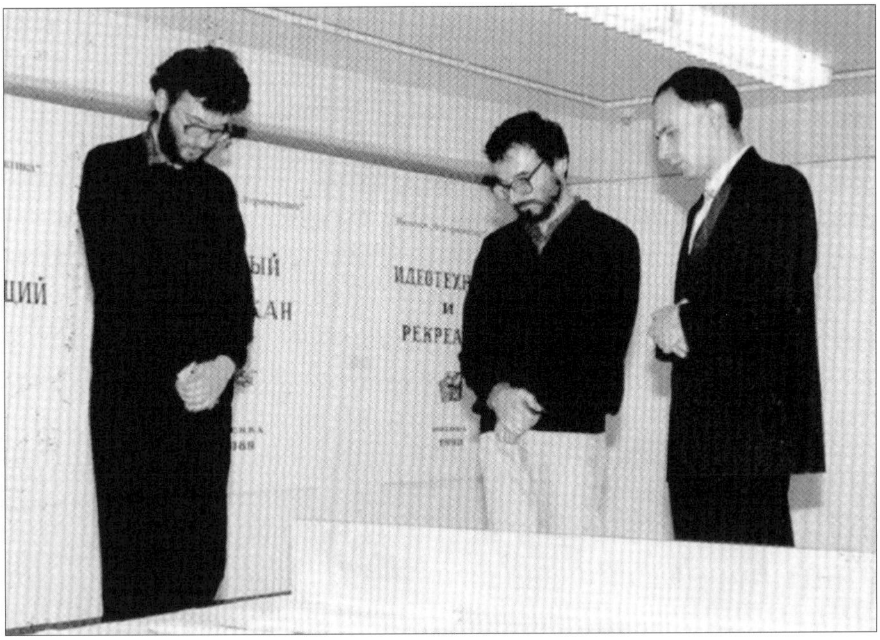

Figure 19 Medical Hermeneutics, *Orthodox Suckings*, 1990, installation (photo: Natalia Nikitin).

ria or viruses of which it can never completely rid itself, so that a liberation from contextual sickness is not possible. At the same time, one does not know whether the artwork's sickness is real or imagined, for its "inner context" emerges out of readings that do not possess logical necessity and that are of a purely private nature. The distinction between health and sickness, and thus between text and context, becomes impossible. The practice of Medical Hermeneutics consists in diagnosing the inner sickness of the artwork, with such a diagnosis regarded as being already a cure. An artwork is only actually sick when it regards itself as healthy.

Characteristic of the method of Medical Hermeneutics is a text by Pavel Pepperstein in which he describes, among other things, the following fictional situation: A grandfather watches his beloved granddaughter participate in a demonstration in Red Square in Moscow. As was customary, the young pioneers form the letters "CPSU" (Communist Party of the Soviet Union) with their bodies, and he discovers the beautiful body of his granddaughter somewhere near the bottom of the last letter. Afterward, writes Pepperstein, whenever the grandfather sees the letters "CPSU," he thinks lovingly and longingly about the small point at the bottom right where his granddaughter's body was. The story's references to Lacanian psychoanalysis and Derrida's theory of writing are easily recognizable. At the same time, the text alludes to a picture that is well known in Russia, Erik Bulatov's *Glory to the CPSU*[16] (Figure 16).

But above all, the story suggests that the old grandfather will still love "CPSU" after the repressive character of Soviet power has been exposed and the crimes of the CPSU have been revealed, because the reason for this love lies elsewhere and cannot be criticized. Since this love is not rationally, socially, or politically motivated, but rather is motivated by private reasons, it cannot be destroyed through political argumentation. This love, we should note, has not been determined by an "aestheticization of the political" or a "fascination with power." The grandfather is in no way fascinated by the demonstration as a demonstration. He sees only his granddaughter. The pleasure he takes in her body is of a purely private nature, and it has nothing to do with the official festivities. This private character of love for the CPSU renders every critical analysis at once impossible and superfluous. The letters "CPSU" are not changed in appearance or meaning by the fact that one of the points out of which they are formed was once a warm, beautiful young female body. The private sphere is not made political and public here. Rather, the public is privatized and thus made safe from foreign, critical, judgmental interventions. After losing its historical power, "CPSU" survives as this private, hallucinatory vision.

There are, then, no scientific, analytic means by which to describe completely the context of the letters "CPSU." Every such description will overlook the meaning they have for the old grandfather. The story can thus only be recounted narratively. It therefore undermines all claims to an objective description of context, for one can imagine that those who claim to be able to reconstruct the meaning of "CPSU" scientifically and politically are in some cases such grandfathers themselves, grandfathers who are pursuing private obsessions. Context exists only in art and literature, not in reality itself. Every "realistic" description of a context is merely a description of an image or a text. There will be in this description private truths that cannot even be guessed at. These private truths cannot legitimate the artwork, as Romantic or early avant-garde aesthetics would have it. However, these truths are legitimate perspectives within a context that cannot be arbitrarily reduced to a small number of positivistic, sociopolitical perspectives. For this reason, every context that is conceived "realistically" is internally infected, sick, in need of medical hermeneutics.

The strategies of privatization through personal memories are also characteristic of other artists of the 1980s who belong to the tradition of Moscow Conceptualism. Vadim Sakharov makes the tradition of Moscow Conceptualism itself into the object of his art, reinventing it in his one-man journal *Pastor,* as well as in the installations that serve as illustration for the journal. Thus, Sakharov functions as the chronicler of a group that is extraordinarily ephemeral. It is not defined as an organized art movement. Its practice is bound together by hardly any exhibits, publications, or collections. Moscow Conceptualism, at bottom, is nothing more than a rumor, a supposition, a suspicion. To create an archive for such a movement and to document it is to invent it. Sakharov's works move in the spaces between documentation and production, archivization and creation, remembering and inventing.[17]

The works of Yurii Albert, which also belong to the tradition of Moscow Conceptualism, offer ironic commentary on the rituals of discursive emptiness that his friends perform. He confronts their Mannerist, esoteric, ideological languages with, for example, the languages of deaf-mutes and blind people, or with professional languages, like the language of seamen. In doing so, he ironizes the incomprehensibility of much of contemporary artistic discourse that separates initiates from the uninitiated—the uninitiated are, obviously, those who are waiting for a higher meaning. At the same time, however, Albert shows in one of his installations how van Gogh's unpainted pictures, which van Gogh described in letters to his brother, suddenly become visible to blind people when these descriptions are reproduced in Braille. Imagination allows the blind person to see pictures by van Gogh that remain concealed for the seeing.[18] This disbelief in the capability of the ordinary public to see reflects Albert's experiences as an unofficial artist in the Soviet Union. And these experiences belong by no means only to the past.

• • •

Meanwhile, though Ilya Kabakov and Komar and Melamid have achieved considerable international success, and the younger generation of Moscow Conceptualists, as well as other groups of the new Russian art, are becoming part of the international art scene, they remain marginal in the context of the post-Soviet Russia. At least as of today, the end of the Soviet Union has not resulted in any great domestic changes for advanced Russian art.

The Russian public, upon being suddenly confronted with the success of their own, formerly unofficial, artists, artists of whom they had not known earlier, tend to interpret this success as dictated by the West, which wants to impose foreign criteria on Russian art. Various conspiracy theories circulate. Far from embracing the international successes of a few Russian artists, many Russian observers receive these successes as a personal insult. The sudden opening to the outside that today's Russia has experienced and that has bolstered its financial dependence on the outside world frequently elicits a nationalistic reaction. The Russian domestic art market orients itself toward the new ruling class of entrepreneurs, bankers, and political functionaries who have only a vague conception of "Western" culture of the twentieth century and who prefer an art that revives the atmosphere of Russian life before the revolution. Russia was not especially happy in the twentieth century. That is also one reason why the Russian public does not like any art of this century, whether Western or Russian, realist or avant-garde. In this post-Soviet time, as the majority of Russians try either to forget that unhappy century altogether or to glorify the Soviet past without actually remembering it, the unofficial art of the Soviet era functions, paradoxically, as the only cultural space where the private memories from the Soviet era are still kept.

Translated from the German by Paul Reitter

Notes

1. For the history of Russian unofficial art, see *Nonconformist Art: The Soviet Experience, 1956–1986,* edited by Alla Rosenfeld and Norton T. Dodge (New York: Thames and Hudson, 1995), *Non-Konformisten: Die Zweite Russische Avantgarde 1955–1988. Sammlung Bar-Gera,* edited by Hans-Peter Riese (Cologne: Wienand, 1996), and *Ich lebe—ich sehe: Künstler der achtziger Jahre in Moskau,* exhibition catalogue (Bern: Kunstmuseum Bern, 1988).

2. For the history of Moscow Conceptualism, see Boris Groys, "Moskovski ro mantichesky konceptualizm," *A-Ya* (Paris), no. 1 (1979): 3–11, and Ilya Kabakov, *Noma, oder der Kreis der Moskauer Konzeptualisten,* exhibition catalogue (Hamburg: Kunsthalle Hamburg, 1993).

3. See Boris Groys, *The Total Art of Stalinism: Avant-Garde, Aesthetic Dictatorship, and Beyond,* trans. Charles Rougle (Princeton: Princeton University Press, 1992).

4. See Carter Ratcliff, *Komar & Melamid* (New York: Abbeville Press, 1988).

5. See Fredric Jameson, *The Political Unconscious* (Ithaca, N.Y.: Cornell University Press, 1981).

6. *Painting by Numbers: Komar and Melamid's Scientific Guide to Art,* edited by JoAnn Wypijewski (Berkeley: University of California Press, 1998).

7. See Ilya Kabakov, *Am Rande,* exhibition catalogue (Bern: Kunsthalle Bern, 1985).

8. Ilya Kabakov, *Ten Characters* (New York: Ronald Feldman Fine Arts Gallery, 1988).

9. Jean-Luc Nancy, *The Inoperative Community*, edited by Peter Connor, trans. Peter Connor et al., Theory and History of Literature 76 (Minneapolis: University of Minnesota Press, 1991), pp. 9ff.

10. See *Documenta IX*, vol. 2, catalogue of the Kassel *Documenta IX* exhibition (Stuttgart: Cantz Verlag, 1992), pp. 248–49.

11. Ilya Kabakov, *Über die Totale Installation / On Total Installation* (Stuttgart: Cantz Verlag, 1995).

12. Boris Groys, *Zeitgenössische Kunst aus Moskau: Von der Neo-Avantgarde zum Post-Stalinismus* (Munich: Klinkhardt and Biermann, 1991).

13. Ivan Chujkov, *Werke von 1966–1997*, exhibition catalogue (Moscow-Leverkusen, 1998).

14. Collective Action, *Poezdki za gorod* (Moscow: Ad marginem, 1998).

15. See Medical Hermeneutics, *Binokel und Monokel: Leben und Werke* (Zug: Kunsthaus Zug, 1998).

16. See Boris Groys, "Der ein-gebildete Kontext," in *Kontext-Kunst*, edited by Peter Weibel (Cologne: DuMont, 1993), pp. 257–82.

17. Vadim Zakharov, *Der letzte Spaziergang durch die Elysischen Felder: Retrospektive 1978–95*, catalogue from the exhibition in Kunstverein Köln (Stuttgart: Cantz Verlag, 1995).

18. See *Kräftmessen*, catalogue of an exhibition in Munich (Stuttgart: Cantz Verlag, 1995), pp. 91–93.

Art as a Political Machine

Fragments on the Late Socialist and Postsocialist Art of Mitteleuropa and the Balkans

Miško Šuvaković

The term "Mitteleuropa" usually designates a cultural, not a geographical, space. "It does not quite correspond to the English phrase 'Central Europe.' Mitteleuropa suggests something that resonates in historical mystique; it is a cultural idea and cannot be reduced to geo-political definitions."[1] It points to the complex relation of cultures, national cultures, communities, and states that occupy the center of the European continent: not only Austria, Hungary, the Czech Republic, and Slovakia, but also Poland, Slovenia, northern Italy, Croatia, and Vojvodina (northern Serbia). The idea of Mitteleuropa embraces countries and cultures that have built their cultural identity under the influence of the Austro-Hungarian Empire. After the Second World War, with the exception of Austria and Italy, they became socialist and a part of the East or Soviet bloc. During the Cold War, they were most often identified by the less geographical and more political term "Eastern Europe."

Today, the idea of Mitteleuropa is determined by the myth of the unity of European culture, the myth of the enduring integrative nature of Austro-Hungarian culture, and the ambivalent idea of the shared socialist past.

The Balkans represent the geographical space of the Balkan peninsula, occupied by Turkey, Greece, Albania, Bulgaria, most of the former Yugoslavia (Macedonia, Serbia, Montenegro, Bosnia and Herzegovina, and part of Croatia), and Romania. The Balkans as a cultural space do not carry much weight. The term instead denotes a loose historical entity and a provisional geographic area.

Postmodernism and Postsocialism

Let us start with two banal observations concerning postmodern art: Postmodern art is a plural art. It is an art consisting of the different and mutually irreducible worlds of art and culture, this being valid whether we observe it from a historical or a geographic and geopolitical perspective. Postmodern art, moreover, is an art in which styles and genres of art, culture, and politics become codes for the representation, expression, and production of social reality. As a consequence, the geoaesthetics of postmodern culture of the late twentieth century, between the late 1970s and early 1990s, doesn't possess a globally consistent status. In this it differs from the European cultural hegemony that prevailed in the first half of the twentieth century and from the cultural hegemony of American culture that prevailed during the century's middle period and during its third quarter. On the contrary, postmodern art and culture exhibit different functions and effects that depend on different specific historical, geographical, and social backgrounds.

Postmodern art and culture emerged in Mitteleuropa and the Balkans after the hegemonic project of European modernism, which had first fractured into bourgeois and socialist political and cultural projects, gave way to a pluralism founded on the irreducibility of difference itself and to a variety of projects, from the politically ironic to the politically nostalgic. From the late eighteenth century to the end of the Second World War, modern culture was established as European bourgeois economic, social, cultural, and artistic domination over the world. As a bourgeois culture, modern culture provided the means for establishing autonomous institutions and for attempting to realize the project of international technological, cultural, and artistic progress. The concept of modernism was constituted in the larger European countries (France, England, Germany, Austro-Hungary, Russia), as well as in small, nonparadigmatic Central European, Eastern European, and Balkan cultures.

Modernism is "a set of beliefs about the practice of art, of criticism and of history, and about images, values and techniques of representation."[2] It is not some external, neutral culture that resembles nature (in spite of modernists' often believing the opposite) but a body of political beliefs that determine the artistic practice and its theory. This body of beliefs enters into the conception of every individual modernist painting because the painting is a representation of these beliefs and of the modernist horizon of creating art. In the cultures under discussion, modernism from the beginning of the twentieth century possessed certain distinctive traits. It coincided with the final transformation of late feudal societies into bourgeois societies and with their industrialization and the introduction of the first notions of mass culture. It thus resulted in the establishment of modernist forms of representation and expression, as well as in the transformation of national cultures from folk identities into cultures that defined themselves in terms of national bourgeois modernism.

After the Second World War, however, two conflicting political and cultural projects appeared. The liberal bourgeois modernist project was built primarily on the notions of technical and social progress—progress from an industrial to a postindustrial society and from imperialism to late capitalism. The socialist modernist project was built primarily on the notion of political revolutionary progress—progress via the dictatorship of the proletariat and a bureaucratic system of management to the utopia of a classless society and self-management. Postwar modernism thus was characterized by a crucial difference in understanding and realizing social, technical, and artistic progress.

The previous hegemonic relation of European culture to non-European civilizations was replaced by a dialectical opposition or tension between the two military and political blocs. Simplifying somewhat, we can say that the ideal of autonomous, abstract, individualistic, and highly aestheticized bourgeois art represented by "existential" art such as Abstract Expressionism, Lyrical Abstraction, and Informel stood opposed to the ideal of revolutionary, utilitarian, collective, and realist proletarian art represented by a mixture of socially critical art, post-avant-garde movements, and apologetic Socialist Realism or, as it is sometimes called, Romantic Realism. While Western bloc culture was characterized by a clear institutional difference between high elite art and popular media art and mass culture, the culture of the Eastern bloc promoted the idea of unitary new socialist and realist art conflating the needs of elite art and mass (folkloric, working-class) culture.

In this binary division of the world, the majority of small, nonparadigmatic Central European, Eastern European, and Balkan cultures ceased to be participants in and contemporaries of the modern bourgeois project. Since they were forced to accept the model of revolutionary realist art, the evolution of bourgeois modernism was interrupted. The introduction of officially sanctioned Socialist Realism meant that after the Second World War, these countries followed a modernist trajectory different from that of Western European and American modernism.

In most socialist countries during the 1960s, explicit revolutionary Socialist Realism was replaced by an implicitly utilitarian art derived from the model of European "Sober Modernism,"[3] an art that was decorative, neither abstract nor figurative, and politically neutral. It expressed values and beliefs compatible with those of the new postrevolutionary bureaucratic governments. Postrevolutionary governments, in turn, found ways of maintaining the power and influence of communist ideology by this Sober Modernist art, which promulgated autonomous aesthetic values and was oriented toward mass culture. This process evolved completely in Yugoslavia, while in Poland, Czechoslovakia, Romania, and Hungary, an idealized socialist art (the art of Socialist Realism) and Sober Modernism coexisted simultaneously. Sober Modernism served the state but was devoid of revolutionary realist iconography and was also called by some authors "Socialist Aestheticism."[4] Although such art was a major step in the direction of Western modernism, at the same time, it constituted a major obstacle to radical, subversive, critical, or experimental art such as neo-avant-garde, Conceptual, or early postmodern art. Sober Modernism, a belated and diluted form of Western capitalist art, was employed as a means to revitalize and perpetuate socialist culture.

In the European socialist countries of the 1960s, the 1970s, and part of the 1980s, art existed in three different worlds. The first was the art world based on the historical ideals of the socialist revolution as expressed by the aesthetics of Socialist Realism and supported by the state, the Party elite, and by the revolutionary old guard, who idealized the rhetorical world of the revolution. The second was the art world of Sober Modernism. Later, in the period of late socialism, such art was supported by state institutions and disseminated internationally via official exchanges. The third art world was that of the experimental and intermedial activism of neo-avant-gardes and Conceptual Art. At the beginning, this existed outside any institutional framework, but later it was exhibited and internationally represented through marginal cultural institutions such as student and other youth organizations.

Finally, when the division into blocs disappeared in the Mitteleuropean and Balkan countries, a postmodern megaculture, a culture of irreducible differences, or differends, set in. Postmodern pluralism marked a global plural existence of differences (multiculturalism and transculturalism) and, in conformation with this global pluralism, local and regional (political) totalitarianisms and (religious) fundamentalisms.

The era of late socialism and postsocialism is one of postmodern art and culture: the signifier exists without the signified. The sign from the epoch of Realsozialismus, "actually existing socialism," has declined into a signified that has disappeared and a signifier that continues to exist as an institutional order, a historical trace, and a mimesis of a mimesis of a lost social phantasm. The postmodern nature of late socialism and postsocialism is well illustrated by Mikhail Epstein's depiction of the situation in the Soviet Union:

> Brezhnev was a simulacrum, a copy without an original. He was not an image of communism, which simply did not exist at the time. Stalin was an image of communism, in the real sense of the word. It was an awful, a horrible communism, but it was something that did exist then. Brezhnev, however, was signifying nothing. He was a splendid figure as a simulacrum, although we did not have that word to designate him. We had not yet come to the epoch of open postcommunism, so his words were perceived as outright lies, and a lie is not postmodern. A lie is told when truth is concealed—but when truth in fact exists. We now understand that no truth existed then at all. We came not to the *zero level of writing* in the Barthesian sense, but to a zero level of being. Postcommunism is the zero level of being: empty being, empty writing, so that now we live in a vacuum, in empty space where all words and all actions seem to have no meaning at all. They can only be traced on the level of surface, with no depth, no truth standing beyond them.[5]

Art as a Political Machine

Different and contradictory kinds of high art emerged in Mitteleuropa and the Balkans during the late 1970s and early 1980s, that is, during the period of late socialism, and during the late 1980s and 1990s, the era of postsocialism. These included what I will call "National Realism," a second wave of modernism, deconstructive postsocialist political art, and a postmodernism resembling that of the First World. Since the last essentially imitates its Western counterpart, however, it is not relevant to our discussion here. In this essay, I will primarily discuss deconstructive postsocialist political art, but we need to begin with a preliminary understanding of National Realism and the second wave of modernism if we are to place this art in context.

By "National Realism" I mean art that employs traditional means of expression and representation such as figurative painting, landscape painting, monumental sculpture, and the architecture of national styles in order to restore styles from the past (the national style, folklore, early bourgeois art, nineteenth-century Romanticism, and, less frequently, realism) and to reactivate them as strategies of anti-Communist, antimodernist, and anti-Western art. In the philosophical sense, these orientations are fundamentally ontological. They search for or project ideas of national, religious, political, and, less often, racial self-containment, exclusiveness, foundationalism, and historical authenticity. They thus are oriented toward restoring religious and especially national identities in these states. In a political sense, these forms of expression are connected with the heterogeneous corpus of patriotic and nationalist forces, and therefore with postsocialist political forces in Russia, Romania, and Serbia that came into being by the fusion of nationalistic and Rightist political parties with the power machinery of socialist institutions that had lost their Leftist ideology.

The second wave of modernism[6] was a pluralistic attempt at establishing elitist high art—esoteric modernism and abstract painting and sculpture. It questioned and further developed modernist ideas (originality, the strong subject, flatness, abstraction, pure forms, sharp edges, literal meaning), thereby revealing the traumatic place of the socialist culture, in which abstract high modernism was censured, oppressed, and obstructed. The second wave of modernism, furthermore, employed posthistorical citations, collage, and montage and reinterpreted modernism in a manner similar to that of the early postmodernism of the 1980s, the Trans-Avantgarde and Neoexpressionism that reinterpreted the iconography of Baroque, Mannerism, Symbolism, Secession, and Metaphysical Painting. The second wave of modernism, moreover, exhibited an ambition to reverse the socialist and late socialist entropy and restore to its grotesque, cynical, and projectless culture the ideas of utopia and its projects, be they contemporary or future oriented. In this manner, it represented a modernist response to premodernist regressive National Realism.

In contrast with these movements, the artists who create deconstructive postsocialist political art, conceptualize it, and thematize it seek to present the limits and paradoxical sites of subjectivity, rationality, individuality, contemporaneity, historicity, and politics in late socialist and postsocialist environments. Their works are sometimes referred to as "retro-avant-garde," as in the case of the Slovenian Neue Slowenische Kunst organization, because they use the avant-garde strategies of penetration, attack, subversion, and excess while simultaneously revealing that there exists no hope, no utopia, and no progress.

The artistic practices of deconstructive postsocialist political art could well be termed "nomadic," for they are characterized by displacement, travesty, mimicry, and transgression. An artist changes, consumes, reactivates, recycles, and rejects different stylistic possibilities and those offered by different genres or media. The work becomes a map of political, cultural, and artistic traces produced by a combination of collage and montage. These practices are deconstructive because they come into being as conceptual, visual, behavioral, or environmental investigations (representations, simulations) of meanings, values, metaphysical borders, and fetishizations of socialist culture. Postmodern artists in late socialism and postsocialism show their dirty hands, their manipulations, mimicries, and tricks. The artist appropriates the procedure by which he or she was manipulated by institutions, ideologies, and culture. By manipulating the manipulatory procedures of the manipulators, these artists carry out a deconstruction of the artistic metaphysics of overdetermination.

The position of such artists is a complex one, for they deconstruct not only postsocialist culture and history, but also the wish of the Western art system to see and identify the artist in such a culture as an asymmetrical and exotic Other. In this way, these artists take over the cynical wish of Western culture and its art institutions to see the postsocialist artist as a caricature or degeneration of Socialist Realism and socialist culture. The postsocialist artist multiplies, varies, deforms, empties, and makes nonsensical the representation of this wish of the West. It seems as if the artist is saying: "Yes, I am the fulfillment of your wish, but I also make complete nonsense of this wish. I am but an empty signifier that consumes and destroys ideology. I am the phantasm of the reality. I am a political machine producing art, a machine that produces and consumes for you your horrors, the power and weaknesses of politics." The deconstructive postsocialist artist behaves as a machine that quickly, obscenely, and ecstatically consumes the meanings, sense, and values of capitalism, as well as the remnants of the actually existing socialist politics. For such an artist, politics is his or her material and tool, and politics in its obscenity and exhaustion is his or her effect or trace. In the philosophical sense, the use that postsocialist art makes of deconstructive devices results in relativism (there is no ontological, axiological, and ideological obligation imposed by class, nation, religion, ethics, aesthetics, or market) and antiessentialism. There is not just one essence that a society projects as reality—the ideology of a given society is a mimesis of a mimesis.[7] An artwork is an illusion of culture, which itself is a form of representation, expression, and overture of signification. In Baudrillard's terminology, it is a simulacrum.

The Sublime and the Kitsch: Czech Socialist and Late Socialist Art

Czech culture in the twentieth century is a characteristic example of a national culture experiencing a traumatic break with authentic European modernism and then its renewal through alternative movements during the epoch of the socialist regime.

During the first part of the twentieth century, Czech high culture was developed with all its stylistic and genre nuances. Avant-garde art began in painting, sculpture, and architecture with its own authentic Cubism—a movement different from French Cubism. The pioneering abstraction appeared in the art of František Kupka (1871–1957) around 1912. Distinctive avant-garde movements also appeared: Dada, Constructivism, Surrealism, and Leftist radical art. Modernist art developed in all its varieties, from Symbolism and Expressionism to Art Deco and the modern style. Here the extraordinary figure of artist and art theoretician Karel Teige (1900–1957) is paramount. During the 1920s, he anticipated the changed relations between high and popular culture, as well as critical revolutionary art and the consequences that the October Revolution would have for art in the decades to come.

In 1948, a Communist government was installed, with Socialist Realism consequently becoming the dominant art. In this way, further development of international modernism was interrupted. Hereafter, Socialist Realism in its rigid or sometimes more tolerant forms remained the invariant official state policy in culture until the fall of the Berlin Wall and the Czech Velvet Revolution in 1989. The exception to this rule is, of course, the period of the Prague Spring. The ideas for it started to develop in 1963; it ended with the military intervention of the Warsaw Pact military forces in August 1968.

Parallel to the official art of Socialist Realism, a Czech alternative art developed. It consists of two distinct trends. The first could be designated as Sober Modernist and highly aestheticized art (Lyrical Abstraction, Informel, Lyrical and New Figuration, fantastic painting, associative geometric abstraction). The second is very different and, from the 1950s up to the 1980s, is represented by subversive, critical, and experimental avant-garde, neo-avant-garde, and post-avant-garde art (Bretonean late Surrealism, kinetic art, concrete and visual poetry, Fluxus events, happenings, body art, Conceptual Art, Neoexpressionism, the Trans-Avantgarde, and political deconstructive art). The principal exponents of this art in Czechoslovakia were Milan Knížák, Milan Kunc, and the practitioners of Czech body art.

Milan Knížák

In the 1960s, the extraordinary figure of Milan Knížák (born in 1940) appeared. He is one of the inventors of the European happening. His early works were made in the spirit of ludism and individual anarchism, for example, his happenings *A Short Carting Exhibition* (1963), *An Individual Demonstration* (1964), *A Demonstration for All the Senses* (1964), and *A Game of War* (Prague, 1965).[8] In *A Short Carting Exhibition*, Knížák's friends collected trash from urban spaces and built assemblages out of it. In *A Game of War*, a children's game was simulated: Prague intellectuals imitated an infantile mock combat in a city park, with wooden swords, nonsensical flags, and army caps made of newspapers. Fragments of everyday life, courage, intellectual self-irony, and channeled normality became forms of destructive action. The artist argued that every act of everyday life has to be evaluated by placing it into the "container" of art.[9]

In Western societies (the United States, France, and West Germany), happenings were an expression of resistance to consumer society and its expansionist values. In Czechoslovakia, however, happenings were staged as political excesses. In the Czech environment of the 1960s and 1970s, tying a red scarf around one's mouth or having a group of people dressed all in green walk around in a Prague square expressed pronounced political messages in the eyes of many, despite being simple happenings and performances. In such an environment, ludism, individual anarchism, and experimental art were viewed exclusively as a political provocation and an attack on social normality. It is therefore perhaps no wonder that Milan Knížák was arrested as a counterrevolutionary in 1973. In January 1980, Allan Kaprow gave the following description of his work:

> Does art teach man how to live? This is the question Knížák asks at the beginning of his "Why Just So" lecture-demonstration of 1964. It is asked as a continuous refrain throughout the lecture. Knížák knows it as an old question, an essential question for him, and he knows it has not been answered. In the sixteen years since then that question has remained central to his life and to how and why he does art.[10]

In the eyes of the West, his activities in the 1960s made Knížák a leader among the artists of the Eastern European Fluxus movement and happenings.[11] He also founded the Aktuel group (the Aktuel band, Aktuel University, A-City): "We wanted to talk directly to the people. We didn't want to

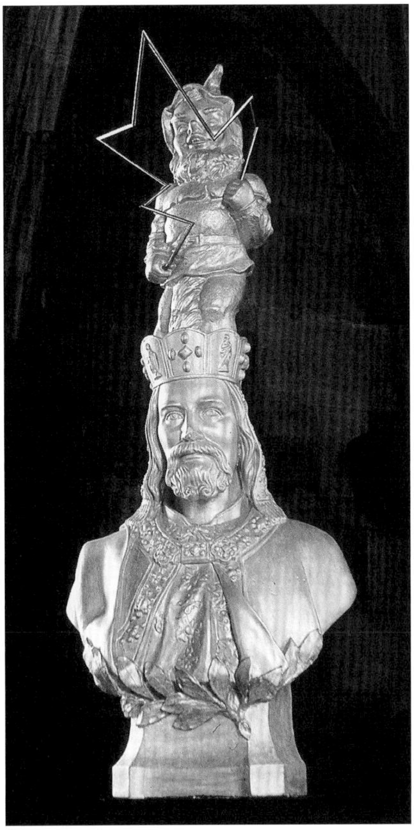

Figure 20 Milan Knížák, *Fathers of the Homeland I,* 1989, acrylic, plaster, iron, plastic, 155 × 60 × 33 cm.

create complicated media, complicated galleries. We wanted to influence people directly with anything which is strong and direct. You know, at that time we had the idea that art is something which can change a lot."[12]

Over time, his work spread in different directions: poetry, fashion, design, music, and the visual arts. In the late 1980s, he worked on statues and dolls that were at the same time expressions of Czech folklore and fairy tales, symbols of national state identity, and expressions of the socialist appropriation of values and of historical characters. As in the 1960 and 1970s, when he wrote songs such as "I Love You and Lenin," and "Sons of Bolshevism," Milan Knížák continued to question the presence or remnants of historical and national kitsch in socialist and postsocialist culture, fusing the figures of Czech kings, fairy-tale dwarfs, and socialist politicians in ironic and transgressive works such as *Fathers of the Homeland* (1989–91) (Figure 20) and *An Idea for the Monument to the Velvet Revolution Serving Also as an Antenna* (1990). Knížák's artistic positions are quite clear:

> I am interested in kitsch as a material, but I don't want to start with kitsch and end with kitsch. The Koons piece I saw at the Venice *Biennale* I didn't like it. . . . My work is more sharp and ironical. Maybe violent. It is always changing. The period of the dwarfs, presidents, and kings is already over. I am currently involved in castles and animals, and then the work might go somewhere else. . . . I do not take influences from art, which is the typical postmodern thing to do, I am deeply involved in irreality, that is the way I have always worked. First of all I am a voyeur, I just love to look.[13]

Knížák's words and works conceptualize and fuse the eclectic, the arbitrary, and the ecstatic in a postsocialist universe and the world beyond it. They are an amalgamation of the national, real, irreal, mythic, voyeuristic, socialist, kitschy, marginal, ironic, rational, regional, historical, and international. His humor is at the same time typically Czech. It is a humor that tends toward subversion of every institutional power and is at the same time also a Fluxus analogy to the Zen koan. It tends toward transformation of the human being.

Milan Kunc

The artistic career of Milan Kunc (born in 1944) started in the Realsozialismus of Czechoslovakia of the late 1960s and continued in Germany at the Düsseldorf Academy of Arts. Kunc was born into a family of musicians. He grew up with Western rock music (Chuck Berry and Jerry Lee Lewis), which under socialism functioned as a utopian promise of a prosperous and free world beyond the Iron Curtain. He was thrown out of the Prague Academy of Art before graduating. In Düsseldorf, he studied under Joseph Beuys, and after Beuys was dismissed because of his political activities, Kunc joined Gerhard Richter's class. He studied with the leading artists of German postmodernism: Jorg Immendorf, Imi Knobel, Anselm Kiefer, and Felix Droese. In his own words, he didn't feel quite at home in Beuys's class, because Beuys taught about art after the death of painting:

> After Beuys had to leave the academy, I went to Gerhard Richter's class, where I made sort of "Action-Abstract-Expressionist" large-scale paintings. In the end I was making monochromes. Richter was impressed, but I already started to find it boring. I changed to comics and illustrative-looking paintings with happy banalities, which at this time were being developed independently by Sigmar Polke. Richter was not thrilled by this new work, and he recommended that I should go into advertising instead. I told myself, my painting

has to be better, and decided to make them unbeatable—into masterpieces. Around 1974, I developed quirky, provocative paintings, based on kitsch and Socialist Realism with a touch of naiveté, which I called "Embarrassing Realism" or "Painful Realism." It was a kind of Socialist Realism with a Surrealist undertone. I painted heroic, sentimental, large-sized war pictures. And to make them even more heartbreaking, I draped them in chains and safety pins. With that I anticipated the punk style, which came out of the music trend in England first in 1978.[14]

For Kunc, painting became a tool for representing the traces of Socialist Realism, French painting from the Salon era, and Viennese Biedermeier. At the beginning of the 1980s, his work began to resemble German Neo-expressionism. Beginning in the mid-1980s, he started working on "sweet paintings" that merged neoclassicism and thematizations of ecology. He was fascinated not only with the classical and modern masters, but also by Western mass culture, and in this respect he was different from his contemporaries among the Russian painters: "I was in love with Renoir and Walt Disney."[15]

His nomadic life, characteristic for many Eastern European artists, including Gerhard Richter, A. R. Penck, and Braco Dimitrijević, allowed his work to be conceptually open, morphologically indeterminate, and polysemic. Kunc used both the "post-object" strategies of nonpainterly expressions and representational devices immanent to classical historical, fictional, and narrative representational painting. His naive and purportedly expressive art is an ironic, provincial, and hedonistic degradation of serious and sublime Western historical painting from Delacroix and David to Rothko and Newman. Kunc looks back with irony and cynicism at his own country and its political follies, but at the same time has a patriotic streak.

In his paintings and installations Kunc points to the universal invariant of the contemporary world, the multiplicity and infinite presence of consumer and ideological kitsch. His works from the late 1970s, wherein he employed everyday objects and materials (a toolbox, a framed portrait of Lenin, a knife and fork, and a hamburger and Coca-Cola can resting on a map [Figure 21]), reveal that for contemporary international culture there is no difference between a representation of Lenin and that of a hamburger, between the purportedly sublime symbol of a political and social revolution and a trivial symbol of mass consumption. The trivial and the sublime construct a homogeneous grid of rhisomatic expressions and representations that obliterate the notion of a consistent autonomous and elite work of art. Instead of cultural or political values, there are only consumed and faded rep-

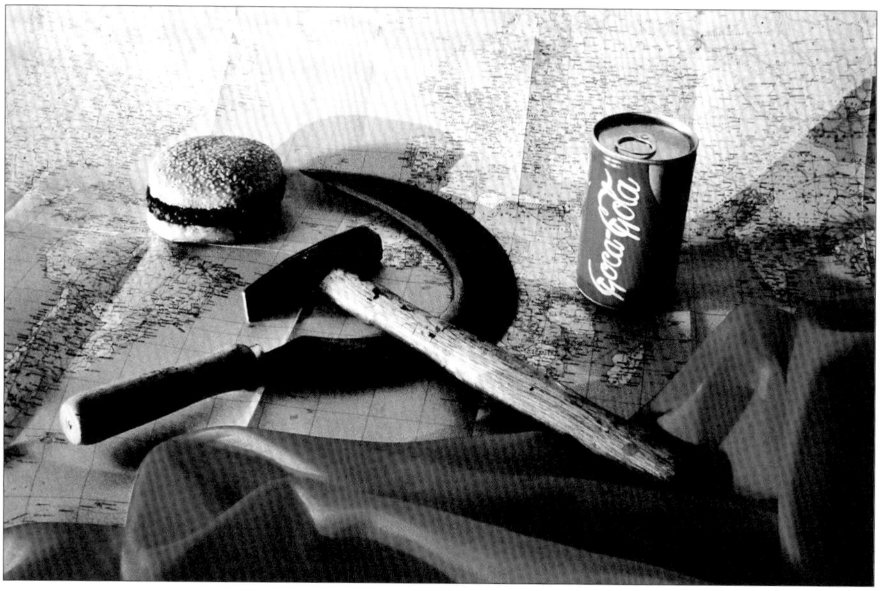

Figure 21 Milan Kunc, *And Tomorrow the Whole World!* 1978.

resentations produced by the fleeting seduction between the painter and the spectator.

Kunc named the particular style of his early period (1974–79) Ost Pop. This "East Pop" not only relates ironically to Pop Art, as was the case in the early 1960s with French Narrative Figuration and German Capitalist Realism, but brutally opposes the metaphysical and ideological confines of Western consumer signification to the metaphysical and ideological confines of Eastern ideological signification. In his works, different economies and metaphysics of the sign as an identity are displayed in their nonsensical nakedness. When Kunc uses photos from his childhood and youth, there is no sentimentality, only an ironic gesture pointing to the trivia of everyday life under socialism. His use of this trivia may be related to the Czech "New Cinema" of the 1960s, such as Milos Forman's films *Black Peter* and *The Loves of a Blonde*. When Kunc takes photos of himself while painting in front of a Communist monument consisting of a monumental red star with a hammer and sickle (see Plate 3), he ironically replaces the sublime symbols, archetypal landscapes, and eroticized figures of Western painting with trivial, consumed, and vacuous signs of postrevolutionary socialism. In Kunc's photographs, objects, and paintings, these signs are not the signs of a conquering, revolutionary, and victorious socialism, but the signs of a postrevolutionary sluggish, banal, manipulatory, worthless, deceiving, and provincial bureaucratic society. They are signs in which no one believes anymore, and with which no one identifies.

The artist's next step consisted of relating, in a collage or a montage, everyday symbols of capitalism (Coca-Cola or a hamburger) and of socialism (a hammer and sickle, a Lenin portrait, and Soviet slogans written in Cyrillic capital letters). Symbols of Realsozialismus are mirrored in the symbols of capitalism. Kunc deconstructs the painting by presenting it is as a trace of a symbolic order of political paradoxes. The painting (a landscape, still life, or figurative composition) is filled with and emptied of political meanings and values. This procedure is most pronounced in works such as *Jeans Coca-Cola* (1978), *Post-Tsarist Still Life* (1978), *Do Not Drink Alcoholic Beverages, Comrades!* (1978–90), and *Campaign in Moscow* (1979).

It was not possible to deconstruct Western representational painting by turning toward abstract painting, as many modernists believed. On the contrary, this could be done by confronting the painting with the political mechanisms of the production of sense. Pictorial representations of traces of capitalist and socialist kitsch are those forms and signs of mass culture by which the artist raises suspicion about the idealism of modernist autonomous painting and, on the other hand, destroys the apparent visionary power projecting the new and better world in Socialist Realist painting. Nonetheless, the traces of ideology and consumerism that are represented in an ironic and distorted way are not yet destroyed and abandoned by this gesture. In the work of Milan Kunc there is no revolution, for ideology and consumer products are, nevertheless, enjoyed in their perverted and rhetorical exaggerations. Kunc shows how to consume politics with enjoyment and consume the enjoyment with politics. The artist discloses how to enjoy a sign emptied of sense.

Kunc's art is that of an artist who cannot discard his or her origin (the corpse of socialism), but who cannot be integrated into the world of late capitalism, either. With his art, Kunc reveals to our gaze his intelligent and cynical impotence. He tries to seduce the gaze of the viewer and to play with his or her wishes, pleasures, and consumption. He doesn't try to offer a new utopia, for he knows that behind every utopia there is the lie of the market or of political totalitarianism, and that every truth is structured as fiction. He reveals the political power machines: Western consumerism, which is desired by the people from the East, and the false Eastern utopia (the philosophy of hope) of which the Western leftist intellectuals dreamed and which was purportedly offered by socialism—but only under the guise of the "actually existing" bureaucratic negation of this same existential hope.

Boris Groys persuasively argues that Kunc enters the logic and economy of the functioning of any ideology: "Milan Kunc's 'Ost Pop' series is an exploration of the actual structures of the ideology that prevailed in Eastern Europe, including their secret codes and the social subconsciousness of their subordinates. The same game of signs looks different from the Western perspective. Here, Coca-Cola and McDonald's are not any kind of ideological symbols indicating Western values."[16] Political signs and ideologies are revealed as arbitrary structures in Milan Kunc's painterly semiology. The pain and horror of their arbitrariness are offered as a necessity of consumption in Western culture and as a necessity of the realization of ideology in Eastern culture. Signs exist, but legitimate frameworks and conditions of use are no longer there. The demise of totalitarian regimes and the binary division of the world resulted in the loss of the legitimacy of the necessary identity of the sign. The death of the identity of the sign in the West was hidden by the uncontrolled production of goods, while in the East, this death appeared on the surface of pure everyday reality, which in its totality was marked by political intentions, expectations, and consequences. While in late capitalism the death of the identity of the sign was hidden, in "actually existing socialism," and especially in postsocialism, it was seen everywhere. This was so because actually existing socialist society and the political forces that connected it and held it together lost their capability to advocate and represent reality. The cause of this was the disappearance of the legislative metalanguage that gave legitimacy to socialist reality.

The distinctive qualities of Knížák's and Kunc's art, of art as a political machine, can be illuminated by comparing their use of kitsch with the use of kitsch in the works of two Western artists, Andy Warhol and Jeff Koons, who also profusely employed kitsch for artistic purposes. Warhol elevated the kitsch of everyday consumerism to high art, making it sublime, valuable, and exclusive. Warhol showed how high modernist art is capable of transforming trivial kitschy everyday objects, situations, and events into exclusive ones by employing avant-garde devices derived from Duchamp's "ready-mades." When Warhol exhibited his *Hammer and Sickle* in 1977, he showed how capitalist power machines (the mechanisms of the capitalist artistic system) could transform anything into commodity value, and how in Western society, Communism, too, could become a commodity.

In Knížák's works, in contrast, kitsch is unreal, almost transcendent.

He seems to promise a certain hope in the possibility of an imaginary leap from superficial everyday triviality into the singularity and depth of art. Knížák is a combatant who in a dialectical employment of ludism, humor, irony, cynicism, and grotesqueness finds the means of continuing the project of transformation and progress.

Unlike Knížák's works, those of Jeff Koons are inexpressive, cold, calculated, and multiple. His is an art without any subject or emotion. The object is in the center of the world, and the obscenity of the detail attracts attention. His approach to reality is pornographic and nihilist. There is no program, and the critical and cynical provocation allows for no hope or positive expectations. East and West reflect each other in a desperate illusion. The pornographic detail of the industrially produced object is the final instance of the evolution of Western humanism.

Milan Kunc, however, uses kitsch differently. He presents it as a border case of the expression of any (Western or Eastern) politics. The kitsch of politics can no longer exist in everyday reality, but only as a theme that the cynical artist employs to attain pleasure in painting—in painting that has reached its historical end.

Milan Kunc's paintings from the 1990s obsessively thematize the functions and effects of kitsch. The confrontation between the signs of the East and the West is replaced by representations of the absurdity of everyday life. "Again and again, Milan Kunc pictures paradise in everyday visual language. But there is always something amiss in it, some jarring note, suggesting that it has a morbid underside."[17] The representations of kitsch in Kunc's recent work are not kitschy representations of late capitalist mass culture. They are the small, sweet, blushing worlds of the Central and Eastern European provinces, visual representations of the wish and search for the romantic, sublime, and disinterested world of tenderness, weakness, private concerns, and self-pity. In the visions of German, Czech, or Russian provincial middle-class kitsch (sunsets, pigs, idyllic villages, a young couple, a kiss), horrific aggression is hinted at, the aggression that sprang up in totalitarian times and reached its apogee either at Auschwitz under National Socialism or in the Gulag under actually existing socialism. In the images of such a paradise, for example, in the paintings *The Mysterious Taiga* (1990), *From a German School Book* (1990), *Tuscan Landscape* (1991), and *Penetration of the Dialectic* (1992) (Figure 22), there is always something that conceals hell. The paradise represented is the index of the hidden hell. By painting the paradise, the sweet landscape, Kunc anticipated their Other. Kitsch is a

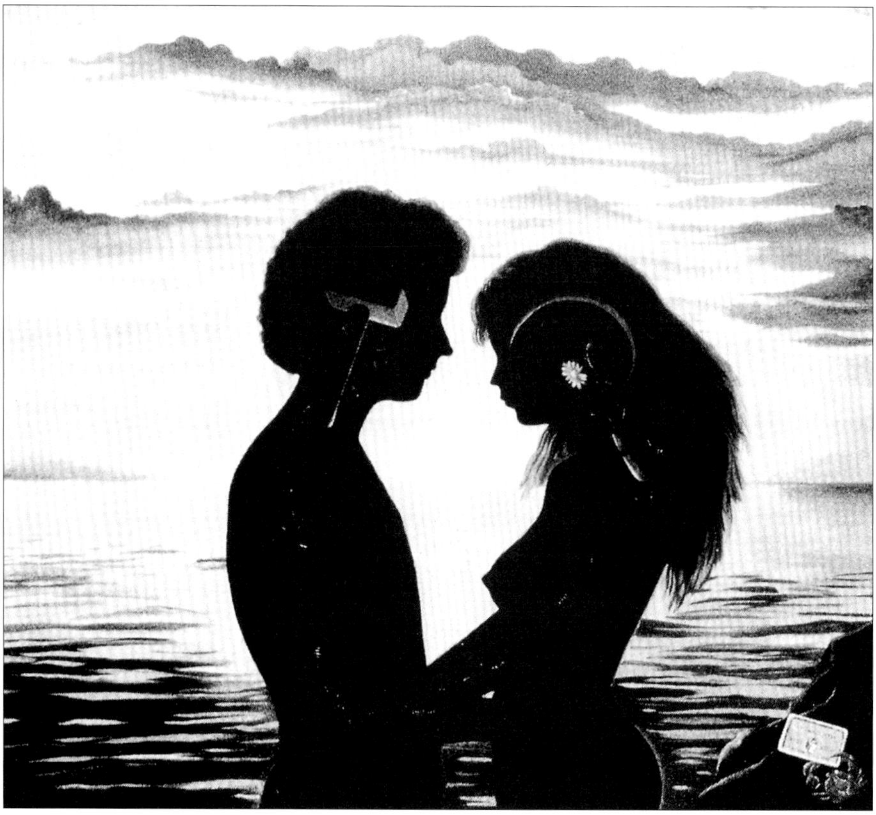

Figure 22 Milan Kunc, *Penetration of the Dialectic (Young East European Lovers in the Caribbean for the First Time)*, 1992, oil on canvas, 140 × 150 cm. Collection of Václav Havel.

symbolic and retarded expression of the sublime, and sublime is the last shelter of kitsch. Thanks to the recent paintings of Milan Kunc, we have arrived at the question posed by Michel Foucault: "But what if, on the contrary, the Devil, the Other, were the Same? What if Temptation were not one of the episodes of the great antagonism, but the subtle insinuation of the Double? What if the duel took place in a mirror world? . . . God who so closely resembles Satan who so cleverly imitates God."[18]

Czech Body Art

During the 1970s, Czech body art appeared.[19] It consisted of private, secret, and public actions, performances, and rituals by Karel Miler (born in 1940), Peter Štembera (born in 1945), Jiři Valoch (born in 1946), and Jan

Mlčoch (born in 1953). These works were appreciably different not only from Knížák's optimistic ludism and anarchism, but also from the complex apocalyptic deconstruction of the culture of Realsozialismus carried out by Milan Kunc. Czech body art emerged as an expression of resignation and horror arising from the defeat of the Prague Spring. With his body, Miler measures nature, smells the grass, or collects trash on the street with his bare hands. He has confidence only in his own minimal and unexpressive physical gestures, which are situated within his marginal, vacuous, and impossible everyday world. Štembera exposes his body to pain: he sticks thorns into his hand, the blood flows out of the vein, and, millimeter by millimeter, the knife penetrates the stomach. In a nonsensical ritual Mlčoch, blindfolded and barefoot, jumps across a fire. There is no game, no challenge and excess. On the contrary, these are rituals of exposing oneself to real pain, suffering, and resignation. These works are the final stage of the modernist dream of confronting art with life and death, of confronting sense with the existential act and with non-sense.

Politics and Art in Serbia and Vojvodina

Since 1991, Serbia has been a constitutive unit of the Federal Republic of Yugoslavia, the other being Montenegro. Kosovo is the southern province of Serbia, the majority of its population being Albanian, and Vojvodina is the northern province. Vojvodina, which was a part of the Austro-Hungarian monarchy before the First World War, is a multinational region with the majority of the population consisting of Serbs, Hungarians, Croatians, Slovaks, Ukrainians, Gypsies, and Romanians.

After the Second World War, some developments in culture and art in Serbia and Vojvodina reflected those in the rest of the former Yugoslavia, while others were specific to and dependent on the cultural traditions arising from the prewar period.

The late 1940s and 1950s were dominated by Socialist Realism and related state, utilitarian, and revolutionary figurative art. These forms were followed by Socialist Aestheticism and Sober Modernism, which were related to the postrevolutionary ideology of socialist bureaucracy. Within this period, which lasted until the 1980s, a dissident movement existed from the late 1960s on that was nationalistic in character and that developed a figurative art (New Figuration, fantastic painting) with a politically thematized national and religious content. During the 1970s, along with the New Left, "post-object" movements (Conceptual Art, performance and environmental art) emerged. The ideas of the New Left in this art were discernible in its activism, which subversively and critically provoked the stable socialist bureaucratic system.

In the 1980s, politically oriented art used irony and the grotesque to thematize the end of socialism, while in the 1990s, an alternative urban culture and art appeared in response to the restoration of National Realist modes of expression, including the renewal of the premodern and of patriarchal and rural values. Major exponents of this politically oriented and alternative art included Raša Todosijević, Goran Djordjević, and Balint Szombathy, among other artists.

Raša Todosijević

Raša Todosijević (born in 1945) was the first to criticize the dominant aesthetics and cultural ideology of Sober Modernism in Serbia after 1971. Leaving behind painting as a form of expression, he started to lead the open and unstable life of an artist-nomad. His works existed in the spaces between traditional realms of art. He made neo-Dadaist use of objects (ready-mades), did performance art, environmental works, sculpture, photography, and abstract analytical as well as figurative painting, and wrote theoretical treatises, reviews, and other kinds of prose. For him, every product, mode of expression, and representation or behavior allowed for very different interpretations. The multiplicity of meanings could be seen as extending the freedom of artistic expression and expanding the notion of art, in contrast to the closed and autonomous notion of art (especially painting and sculpture) in the aesthetics and ideology of Sober Modernism. It could be seen as a strategy for developing an art without an ontological and morphological obligation, an art that is art, not because of its artistic material essence, but because of its ability to imitate culture in producing, exchanging, and consuming various sets of values. It also could be seen as establishing an ironic distance from a sincere, "natural," and politically verified discourse on and evaluation of art and culture.

The performances that Todosijević realized in his first period, from 1971 to 1973, were under the influence of American neo-Dadaism and its subversive use of objects and the human body. After 1973, he created a series of performances, *Decision as Art* (1973), *Drinking Water* (1974), and *Art and Memory* (1975), in which he established relations between the primary powers of his own body (he drank water until he began to vomit, and explored the boundaries of memory) and the powers of discourse (of slogans and statements that frame the social, cultural, and artistic identity of an artist).[20] Afterward, he made a series of works in the manner of analytical painting, where the empty, pure, monochrome surface of the painting was not represented as an aesthetic ideal (as was the case in American Formalism, the tradition extending from Newman to Ryman), but as a trace of the consumption of modernist values (the powers of representing and expressing truth, essence, being, and existence). With the series of wall drawings *One Line in an Empty House, 20,000 Lines in a Gallery,* and *200,000 Lines for the Paris Biennial* (1977), he questioned the relation between a work of art and the institution in which it is exhibited. What was at stake here was the relation between the seemingly formal complexity and dimensions of the work and the significance supplied by the place in which it is exhibited. The latter is the context that gives economic, artistic, and historical value to what is otherwise a trivial order—a bundle of horizontal lines, for example.

Among Todosijević's most important writings was "The Edinburgh Statement 1975: Who Makes a Profit on Art, and Who Gains from It Honestly?"[21] The text was provocative in two ways. First, it appeared as a cynical question by an Eastern European artist about the economic determination of the Western art system, and second, it appeared as a cynical question about the art system under the conditions of late socialism, where the effect that politics had on art was weakening and where there was no real art market yet, only the effects of arbitrary bureaucratic cultural institutions. With this text, Todosijević showed the political decentering and paradoxes of Yugoslav self-management socialism, which strove simultaneously to be openly pro-Western and to remain a socialist society. The idea of art that in modernism was regarded as the ideal, innocent, and sublime area of creation and expression was presented here as the realm of social relations such as interests, profit, and exploitation.

In 1977, Todosijević started a series of performances entitled *Was ist Kunst?*[22] (Figure 23). They were performed in Paris and Belgrade (1977), Warsaw (1978), Vienna (1978), and elsewhere. His political, expressive, and aggressive performances based on the question "What is art?" grotesquely showed the repressive relation between the investigator (the artist) and the investigated person (the participant in the performance). In the performance, the artist hysterically and threateningly shouted the question "Was ist

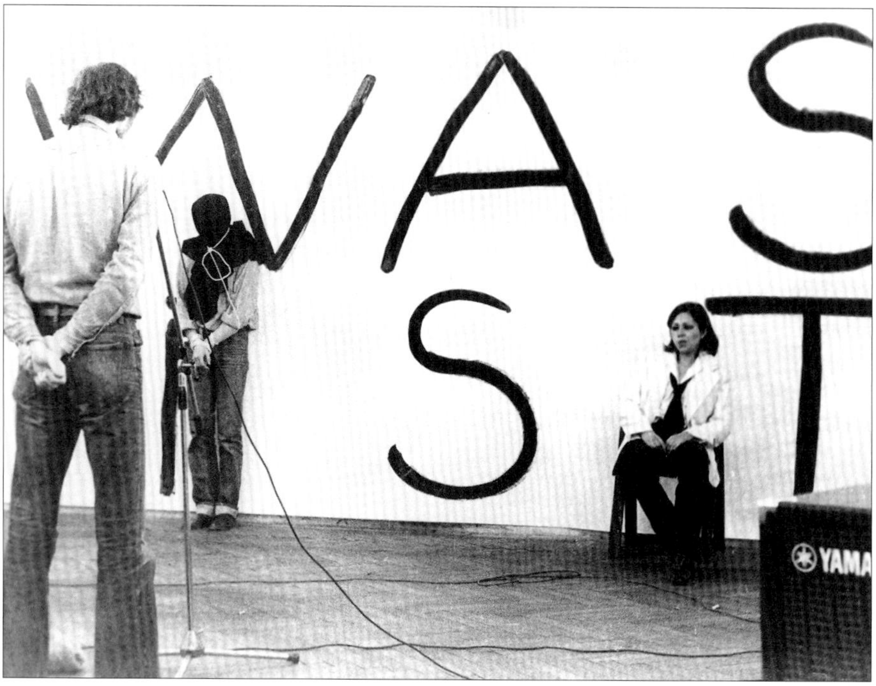

Figure 23 Raša Todosijević, *Was ist Kunst?* 1977, performance.

Kunst?" at his passive audience. According to Todosijević, the way in which an artist asks the question about art is an artwork. He thereby points out that an artwork has a performative form, its sense being realized by the act of speaking. Enunciating the question in German ironically underscores the traumatic relations of the various national cultures of Yugoslavia with German culture and the memories of the German occupation during the Second World War, Nazism, political terror, and totalitarianism. In socialist Yugoslavia, National Socialism, German cultural identity, and political repression were viewed in an exceedingly negative way. Todosijević introduced the signifying structure of the taboo of Nazism as an artistic symptom of the end of socialism.

The question "Was ist Kunst?" was taken over from Raša Todosijević and reinterpreted by the Slovenian retro-avant-garde group of painters called Irwin. In contrast to Todosijević's neo-Leftist, critical, ironic, and parodic provocation of political taboos, the group Irwin simulated the ideological and artistic atmosphere of totalitarian art in the series of paintings entitled *Was ist Kunst?* (1986) (see Plate 8) using the postmodern techniques of citation, collage, and montage.

In the 1980s and early 1990s, Todosijević proceeded in three directions, in all of them deconstructing the refurbished pillars of contemporary Serbian culture. He deconstructed and subverted Sober Modernism by painting inflated copies of works from Picasso's late period, he wrote short stories that ironically depict the everyday life of local artists,[23] and he made paintings, sculptures, objects, and installations in which the German phrase "Gott liebt die Serben" appears. The sentence "God takes care of Serbs" (or "loves the Serbs") is directed at Serbian nationalism, with its reemergent paranoiac phobia of everything German and, speaking more broadly, everything Western.

The series *Gott liebt die Serben*, exhibited from 1990 on, is realized in different ways: as an assemblage (plates on metal supports give a parodic semblance of small decorative sculptures), as a monumental metal monument (400 × 300 × 50 cm) placed in a public space and then destroyed, as a symbolic sculpture in gallery-scale dimensions (a menorah, the Jewish candlestick, again inscribed with "Gott liebt die Serben") (Figure 24), as a Neo-expressionist painting (a painting with a Suprematist cross, an Expressionist skull with crossbones, and the usual German inscription), and as an installation in a gallery (large red swastikas, chairs that hang on a wall, a can, six tape recorders, and again the German inscription, this time in Gothic script) (see Plate 5). These works are arbitrary combinations of different elements made strange, confusing, mysterious, and allegorical by the always-present inscription "Gott liebt die Serben." By this gesture, Todosijević produces absurd, unexpected, unresolved, and horrible representations that place their viewer in the uncanny and unpleasant position of a voyeuristic political accomplice.

These works were intentionally targeted at a specific political situation in Serbia in the late 1980s and early 1990s. Serbia was then at the mercy of opposing nationalist political movements. Their members championed the premodernist values of nineteenth-century Romanticism and the Rightist and Leftist nationalist ideas of a postsocialist society and promoted rural patriarchal and anti-Western euphoria and civil disobedience. All this resulted in simultaneous totalitarianism and anarchy, in a violent agony caused by the effective continuation of a one-party system, and in an ecstatic postmodern entropy of the senses. In such an eclectic situation, the seemingly arbitrary works of Raša Todosijević simulated the extant spiritual, intellectual, social, and political confusion, the chaos and entropy. It is Todosijević's intention that his works cause surprise and confusion. And, really, although

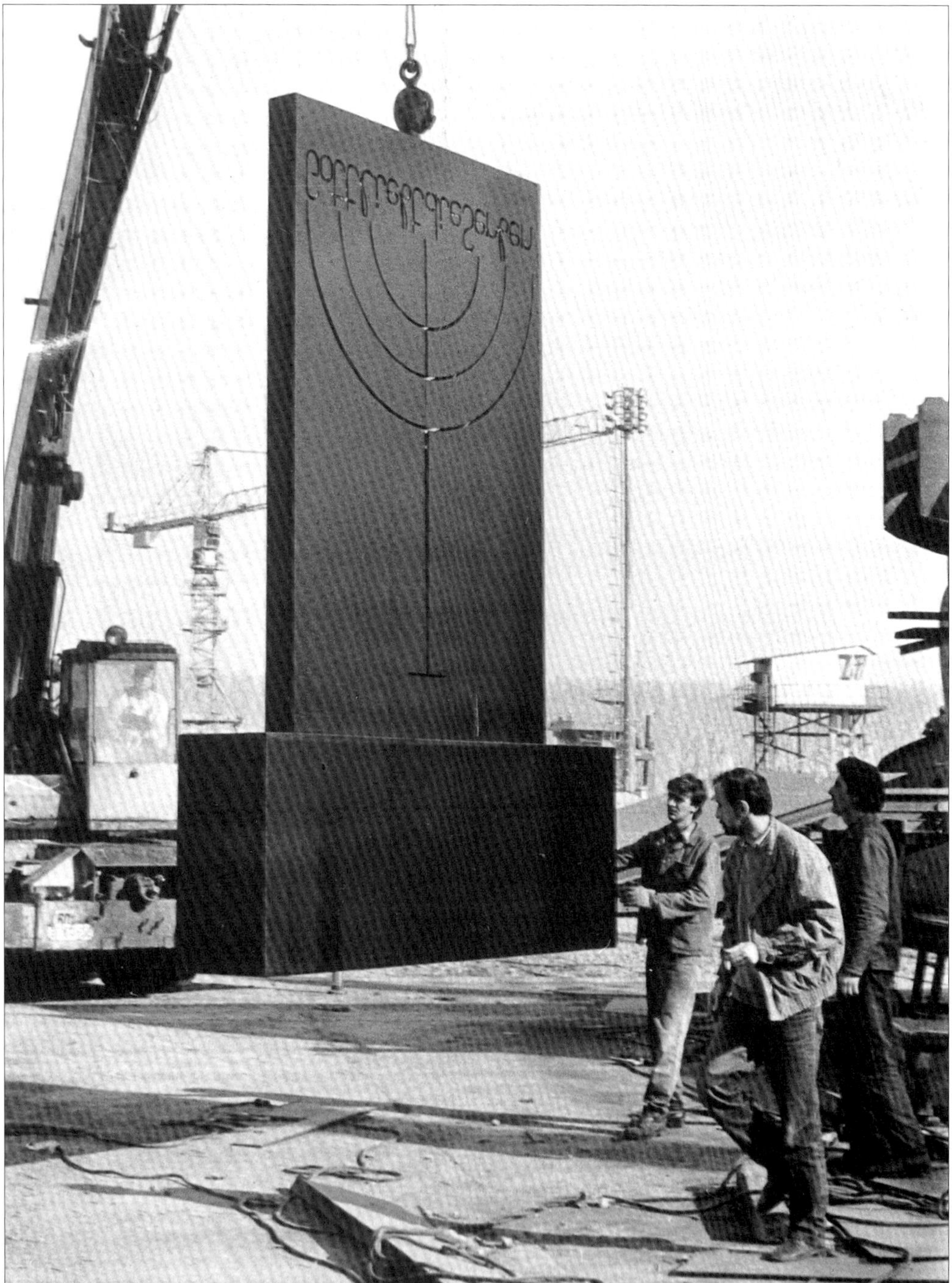

Figure 24 Raša Todosijević, *Gott liebt die Serben,* 1989, sculpture, 400 × 300 × 50 cm.

the viewer at first simply looks and reads, the continuous gaze then reveals paradoxical and disconnected levels of signification: a Serbian nationalist slogan and the German (Gothic) inscription, a Jewish religious symbol and a German Gothic inscription with a message that is actually a Serbian nationalist slogan (only, of course, if it is not in German), and an arbitrary connection between the political slogan, specific national or religious symbols, and objects from everyday life (plates, a can, chairs, etc).

In this manner, Todosijević relates conflicting objects and narratives, suggesting the arbitrary dramas of what could perhaps be called a "neo-postsocialist," eclectic, and posthistorical populist society. Everything is confronted with everything. Everything is contemporary and retro; everything is present and absent: as a trace, a symbol, existence.

Goran Djordjević and Some Other Artists

Goran Djordjević (born in 1950) began in Belgrade in the early 1970s as a Conceptual artist by investigating formal and analytical mathematical and sign systems. He approached formal and analytical systems as theoretical ready-mades, models taken over from the formal sciences and transmitted into the art world, and also as models that represent the thinking process: "This work of mine tends to investigate and set up a visual method which would serve to present and carry out the thought process. Since thought is a function of time (a process), the problem of the inclusion of this dimension is resolved through a series of successive visual states of the system under analysis."[24] In the mid-1970s, his work became theoretically complex and increasingly connected with mathematical theory—with theories of how to represent formal systems, the theory of graphs, for example.

Parallel to formal and linguistic investigations of the visual representation of thinking, Djordjević began to investigate and to discuss theoretically the political system of art and culture. He based his discourse on a critical analysis within the frame of late neo-Marxism practiced in the circle of artists in the New York faction of the Art & Language group. His critical discourse in the mid-1970s was characterized by a confidence in the conceptual and ideological analysis of social conditions and in understanding and interpreting the social mechanisms of power: "The known history of human society is principally a history of class reflections."[25]

By the end of the 1970s, however, Goran Djordjević had left behind the devices of analytical and critical Conceptual Art. The positive utopia of late modernism (criticism, analysis, and understanding the mechanisms of culture and art) was replaced with emergent apocalyptic postmodernism. Poststructuralism, and postconceptual art as well, could be understood as the theory and the art of negative dialectics: a theory and an art of transgression and the violation of prohibitions, laws, and contracts. Djordjević started using the device of copying, of representing another artwork or cultural artifact, thus erasing the borders between high and popular culture. He made use of kitschy motifs, reproducing the misinformation, mystification, and fictionalization of existence and of the object and functions of the artwork and the artist in contemporary culture. He focused his attention on the grotesque relations between avant-garde art, Western modernist art, the art of Realsozialismus, and kitsch. The idea of kitsch is realized by the use of kitschy objects, which is characteristic of Western capitalist art, and kitschy ideas, which is characteristic of socialist culture. For example, Djordjević makes copies of reproductions of kitschy paintings bought in the market (*Self-Portrait with the Model,* 1979), copies of paintings that he painted as a child (*Harbingers of the Apocalypse,* 1980), and copies of Mondrian's painting *Composition II* from the late 1920s (copied in the Belgrade National Museum in 1983).

In the middle of the 1980s, Goran Djordjević disappeared from the art scene. In the same period, "mysterious artists" appeared: an anonymous artist, "Adrian Kovacs," "Walter Benjamin," "Piet Mondrian," "Kazimir Malevich," and so on (Figure 25). Exhibitions devoid of artists re-presented (reconstructed and simulated) historical modernist and avant-garde exhibitions. The *International Exhibition of Modern Art—Armory Show* of 1913 was held in Belgrade and Ljubljana in 1986, Kazimir Malevich's *Last Futurist Show 0.10* of 1915–16 was presented in Ljubljana in the same year, and so on. In 1993, a remake of the Salon de Fleurus from 1904 to 1920 appeared in a flat in Soho in New York.[26]

Goran Djordjević adamantly disclaims any relation to these artists, thereby offering us two options to resolve this enigma of identity. The first is to accept his claim that his artistic oeuvre came to an end in the mid-1980s, while the second is to hypothesize that Goran Djordjević and these artists are all the same person. Given the fact that this dilemma is unresolvable, I choose quite arbitrarily (but resolutely) the second option, although it is built on a hypothesis and unproven speculation.

The ideas of Goran Djordjević were of crucial importance for the work of numerous artists from the former Yugoslavia, some of whom borrowed

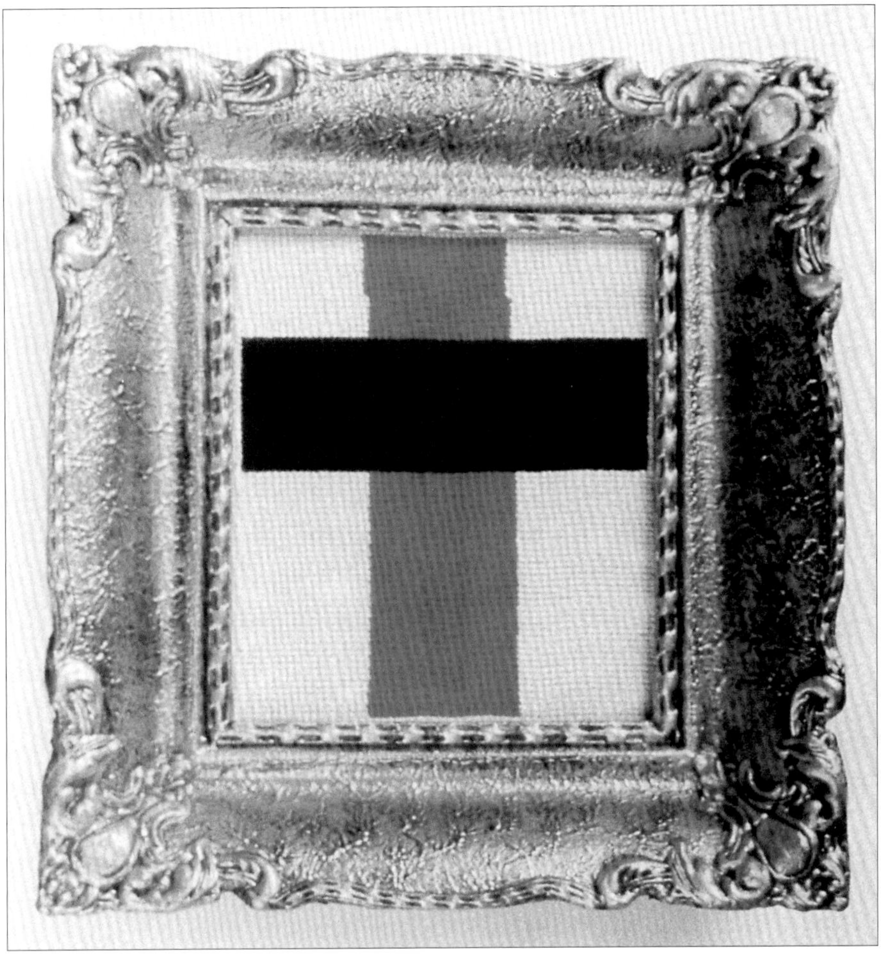

Figure 25 "Kazimir Malevich," *Suprematist Icon*, 1985, embroidery, 29 × 27.5 cm.

just as unscrupulously from him as he did from others. His ideas and works also bear witness to a different political and cultural situation in the former Yugoslavia when compared with the countries that were formally parts of the Soviet bloc.

Djordjević's strategies relate directly or indirectly to postmodern culture and its artistic devices. Djordjević's copying annuls the essential modernist assumption of the artist as a "genius" who creates original and unrepeatable exclusive statements or who intuits them in nature (the universe, biology, Spirit, or Being). At the same time, simulation and the use of the simulacrum imitate history (the history of representation, of the represented in history). The experience of and knowledge about art becomes relative, consumable, and free-floating. Since we are confronted with a consumption of facts, an entropy of experience, and a destabilization of the stable metalanguage of history, it becomes possible that "experience may also be reconstructed, re-membered, rearticulated. One powerful means of doing so is the reading and rereading of fiction in such a way as to create the effect of having access to another's life and consciousness, whether that other is an individual or a collective person within the lifetime called history."[27] Finally, Djordjević's relativization of the artist's identity questions the historical, private, and interpretative identity of the modernist subject of art. In retrospect, Djordjević's obsessive destruction of the artist's autonomous and integral identity allegorically points to the tragic destruction of the identity of citizens coming from nationally mixed families at the moment of disintegration of the former Yugoslavia.

Balint Szombathy

The work of Balint Szombathy (born in 1950) could be described as a nomadic traversing of the avant-garde, the neo-avant-garde, and the post-avant-garde traces of the history of modernism. Szombathy lives in Subotica, near the Hungarian border. Subotica is a town in Vojvodina that is on the margins of Mitteleuropa and the Balkans and, therefore, in a political sense, on the dead-end street of Eastern Europe. While a distant province and a cosmopolitan place, it culturally still remains divided between the Mitteleuropa of the Austro-Hungarian monarchy and the more recent multinational and multicultural state of the former socialist Yugoslavia. Subotica is a town where the visitor meets Hungarian, Serbian, and Croatian cultures in a shocking and unexpected way, encountering them in their heterogeneous, dispersed, and decentered modes.

Szombathy's work exists at what Slavoj Žižek would call the "quilting point" of different avant-garde traditions, the point of their libidinal attachment—primarily the Serbian and the Hungarian traditions. That is why when I consider Szombathy's art, I see it as a cognitive map of traces, and not as a collection of art products. Displayed before our eyes is a language, and not a piece of work. Whether within the order of visual, written, or behavioral discourse, no element could function as a sign without pointing to some other, absent, element. This linkage causes every element in Szombathy's work to be constituted from the traces of other elements of the chain or the system therein. This linkage produces the artistic (visual, linguistic, behavioral) text that is being created through transformations of other texts (images, manners of behavior, visual expressions, semiotic codes). Szombathy mirrored and multiplied the traces of effects of the classical avant-gardes through neo-avant-garde experiments and post-avant-garde transfigurations of meaning, sense, and value.

From the very beginning, Szombathy's work had an extremely political intent: to show political power and its expressions in the society of socialism and self-management. Often he described his work as a "semiotic investigation," showing how it is possible to reconstruct mechanisms of the production, exchange, and consumption of meaning, sense, and value in concrete culture: "For me . . . creativity is not connected with production, the creation of material objects, but like Enzo Mari, I strive to set up models of new linguistic systems, or to be more precise, to detect the already existing but still insufficiently known linguistic forms."[28] He uses different strategies and art forms, ranging from visual poetry through processual art, land art, and performance to Conceptual Art. His performances have been focused from the beginning on questioning the political identity of the artist in Eastern Europe and on the representation of the relation between the artist and the artwork in the hiatus between hegemonic Western culture and Eastern European underground culture. In the 1960s and 1970s, high modernist art was the dominant art in the West, while in the East, there was an underground art, an active member of which was not only Milan Knížák, but also Balint Szombathy.

Szombathy's early performance *Lenin in Budapest* (Budapest, 1972) (Figure 26) is an example of how to introduce disorder into the culture of Realsozialismus. In the Soviet bloc countries, posters of Lenin, the leader of the Soviet Bolshevik Revolution of 1917, were, of course, symbols of power and objects of idolatry. Posters of Lenin were displayed on stands during celebrations and in military or workers' parades along with posters of Marx, Engels, and local political leaders. Szombathy carried a poster of Lenin through Budapest as an advertising poster, taking away its function of fetish and idol and placing it in the trivial everyday life of "actually existing socialism." By this act, he not only symbolically expressed disobedience to the leader of the first socialist revolution, but also appealed to the socialist society to return to itself, to the originary existential act of the not-yet-bureaucratized revolution—to return to rebellion and excess. Szombathy knew such an appeal was futile. His intent was to reveal socialist society as at the same

Figure 26 Balint Szombathy, *Lenin in Budapest,* 1972, performance.

Figure 27 Balint Szombathy, *Flags II,* 1993, performance.

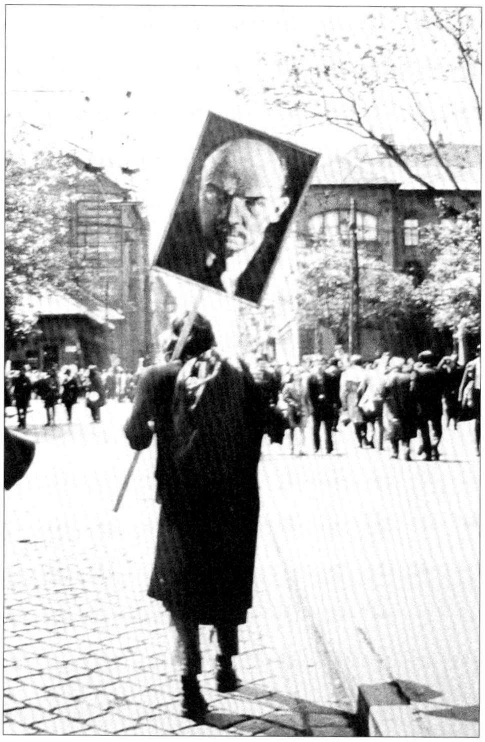

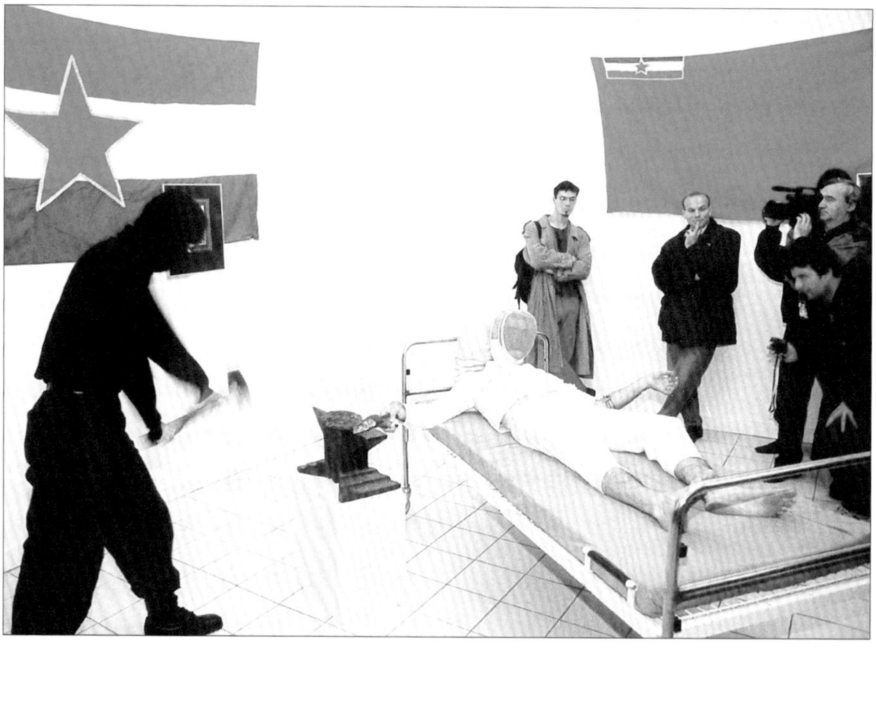

time a lost dream and a society on which the bureaucratic order of the Party was imposed.

The installation *BAUHAUS* (1972), realized in several versions, was similar to the *Lenin in Budapest* project. A poster with the word "BAUHAUS," written in capital letters, that is, the name of the modernist school that created purist and modernist aesthetics, was exhibited in front of flats in different poor urban environments. The Bauhaus ideology that became the ideology of international postwar modernism was thus contrasted with the concrete reality of socialist everyday life. Szombathy confronted the ideals of modernism as the culture of progress with the quotidian environment of the great majority of members of the socialist society. In other words, he confronted the phantasm of modernism expressed by the word "BAUHAUS" with the penetration of everyday socialist reality into the phantasm itself.

In his works, Szombathy used everyday language to show and express the grand themes of ideology. Leninism, Stalinism, totalitarianism, Socialist Realism, and, on the other hand, the utopias of modernism are revealed not as grand metaphysical themes, but as individual and singular representations, absurd expressions, disorders, and symbolizations of the everyday socialist lived world.

From the late 1980s on, Szombathy focused on late socialist and post-socialist themes within the specific situation of the former Yugoslavia—its political disintegration and the concurrent civil war. He made use of his exclusive position as simultaneously a member of Yugoslav culture and someone who is its interior, asymmetrical Other, a Hungarian among Slavs. As a Yugoslavian, he belonged to the culture that had disintegrated into national cultures and national states, but as a Hungarian, he was someone to whom the intrinsically "Yugoslav" national identities (of Serbs, Croatians, Slovenians, Muslims, etc.) related as toward some outer voice that was exempt from their internal "Yugoslav" identity.

The 1993 project *Flags II* (at Ludoško Lake near Subotica, and in the Fruška Gora hills) consists of the state flag of the former Yugoslavia exhibited in a pristine natural environment (Plate 6) and then in an urban space (Figure 27).[29] By exhibiting the flag of the former Yugoslavia, Szombathy pointed to the dramatic erasure of a symbolic trace that related to a reality for innumerable people, the citizens of the former Yugoslavia. A similar exhibition of the same flag in 1972 had been very different, part of a political game with the state, for the sanctity of the flag was protected by law. The flag was the symbol of Yugoslav unity and (because of the star on it) of the victorious socialist revolution. In this first project, preceding the second by twenty-one years, the artist exhibited flags in a bush at the foot of a hill. In another sequence of the same project, the artist stood in front of a decrepit wall with a small flag in his hand. The state flag was decontextualized and used as a ready-made. In that context, it ceased to be a sign of power or identity and became a toy and an instrument for the artist's transgressions. The flag exhibited in 1993, in contrast, was used in a performance dedicated to the civil war and was the flag of an already nonexistent country. It was an erased trace of a political symbol that already belonged to history. What in 1972 was an artist's transgression became in 1993 the locus of the code of the posthistorical memory.

Performances carried out in the 1990s were events in which Szombathy tried to break with mimesis and mimicry. A performance is a simulacrum and is actually present in the world: "In performance everything is as in life, one to one; when it comes to using materials and requisites, a knife is a knife, and if I cut myself, I really cut myself, and if blood is in question, it is real blood, not paint. There are no tricks. I cannot lie."[30] The artist exposes his body as an object in a space that is full of traces of socialism and of the state of Yugoslavia. This former state exists now only as an erased trace, as a reconstructed and simulated visual and scenic order of codes.

In the installations *The Balkan Dialogue* (Dessau, 1995), *Binoculars* (Belgrade, 1995), and *Installation* (Novi Sad, 1996), Szombathy worked with concrete and literal traces of socialist culture: a portrait of the Yugoslav president Josip Broz Tito, a gun, bullets, corn, shoemaker's tools, plaques with the names of final train destinations in the former Yugoslavia, plastic soldiers, video monitors that emit the political program of Serbian and Croatian national television stations, and so on. These are not innocent readymades, but brutal traces of civil war, of a state that is now decomposed, where clean ethnic territories are now being created and culturally closed national cultures are emerging. Szombathy artistically petrifies the moment when one history in its political, artistic, cultural, national, ethnic, and geographical dimensions comes to an end. He selects this moment out of the time continuum and repeats it through his performances and installations. It is as if he is imitating with political, state, and national symbols the toy that the child in Freud's famous example was throwing under his bed, shouting: "Fort, Da!, Fort, Da!, Fort, Da!"

The Exploitation of Dead Signs: Art and Politics in Croatia

Beginning in the early 1950s, after Socialist Realism and related art ceased being the officially sponsored doctrine, art in Croatia[31] developed in several directions. Through lyrical abstraction and fictional figuration, it established Sober Modernism. It also started to embrace the (neo-avant-garde) radically modernist "new tendencies" that in the 1960s were the dominant artistic trend (Neoconstructivism, geometric abstraction, computer and kinetic art), and it appropriated neo-Dadaist and Fluxus strategies, as witnessed by the works of members of the Gorgona group. In fact, in the 1960s, Croatian culture became the only culture in the socialist world in which neo-avant-garde art became the dominant institutional art. As in some other socialist countries, however, certain Croatian artists became exponents of fantastic and primitive painting and sculpture using strong national symbols.

However, the activity of a group of six artists, Mladen Stilinović, Vlado Martek, Željko Jerman, Boris Demur, Sven Stilinović, and Fedor Vučemilović), along with their later individual work, could be designated "post-avant-garde." Post-avant-garde art followed the last avant-garde movement, the New Tendencies and the corresponding cultural ideology of the progressive and technical development of modern society. It criticized the fundamental values and horizons of artistic and aesthetic expression of institutional high and late modernism, primarily the aesthetic formalism of late abstraction and the fetishization of the culture of industrial design in the New Tendencies. While the art of the New Tendencies prepared modernist culture for the new cybernetic and techno-aesthetic age, and the early Conceptual artists in Yugoslavia such as Goran Trbuljak and Braco Dimitrijević believed that critical and subversive works of art could offer a political, or at least an ethical, corrective to anomalies of the predominant modernism, the activity of the Croatian group nihilistically showed that the art of today takes place at the scene that lies behind the principle of hope promised by the Marxist utopia.[32]

Mladen Stilinović

The discursive and visual art of Mladen Stilinović (born in 1947) falls between Conceptual Art and postmodernism. The elements of Conceptual

Art in his work are its linguistic functions, tautologies, and critical investigations of the value systems of cultural institutions. What is postmodern in his work is the use of eclectic and inconsistent paradoxes, appearances, and errors expressing the repressed sites of ideological discourses, a multiple reading of the metaphors and simulations of everyday language, a discursive use of the nondiscursive aspects of ideological imagery, accentuated artificiality, and the arbitrary use of political signs.

> The subject of my work is the language of politics, i.e. its reflection in everyday language. These works are not just made up. I would like to paint. I paint, but the painting betrays me. I write, but the written word betrays me. The pictures and words become not-my-pictures, not-my-words, and this is what I want to achieve with my work—not-my-painting. If the language (the colour, the image, etc.) are possessed by ideology, I too want to become the owner of such a language. I want to think it with consequences. This is neither criticism nor ambiguity. What is imposed upon me is imposed as a question, as an experience, as a consequence. If colours, words and materials have several meanings, which is the one that is imposed, what does it mean and does it mean anything—or is it just idle run [idling in neutral], a delusion? The question is how to manipulate that which manipulates you, so obviously, so shamelessly, but I am not innocent either—there is no art without consequences.[33]

Stilinović doesn't conceal the fact that he approaches art with the language of politics and behaves in a manner characteristic of the world of politics. He shows what happens to the artist, art, and artwork when relations in the art world are replaced by the relations of politics, of belonging to the Party, by repression and manipulation. His works are not a simulacrum of avant-garde, socialist, or modernist culture; they are a simulacrum of the totalitarian world of art in its most dramatic and tragic aspect.

What the works of Mladen Stilinović offer at first glance is a surface. Many of his works contain words and are in fact word works or sentence works, reminding us a little of the works from the 1980s of Ilya Kabakov or Andrei Roiter, but are situated in a completely different context and have no direct connection with them whatsoever. In works such as *Sing! (Thoughts about Money)* (Figure 28), *Rose Environment* and *Red Environment (Thinking about Color, Language, and Society)* (1980), and *The Conditions of My Work Are Not in My Hands, but, Fortunately, Neither Are They in Yours* (1989), he enables us to see from a distance what we cannot see up close. Here, discourse reveals the glossed-over mechanisms of utilitarian communication.

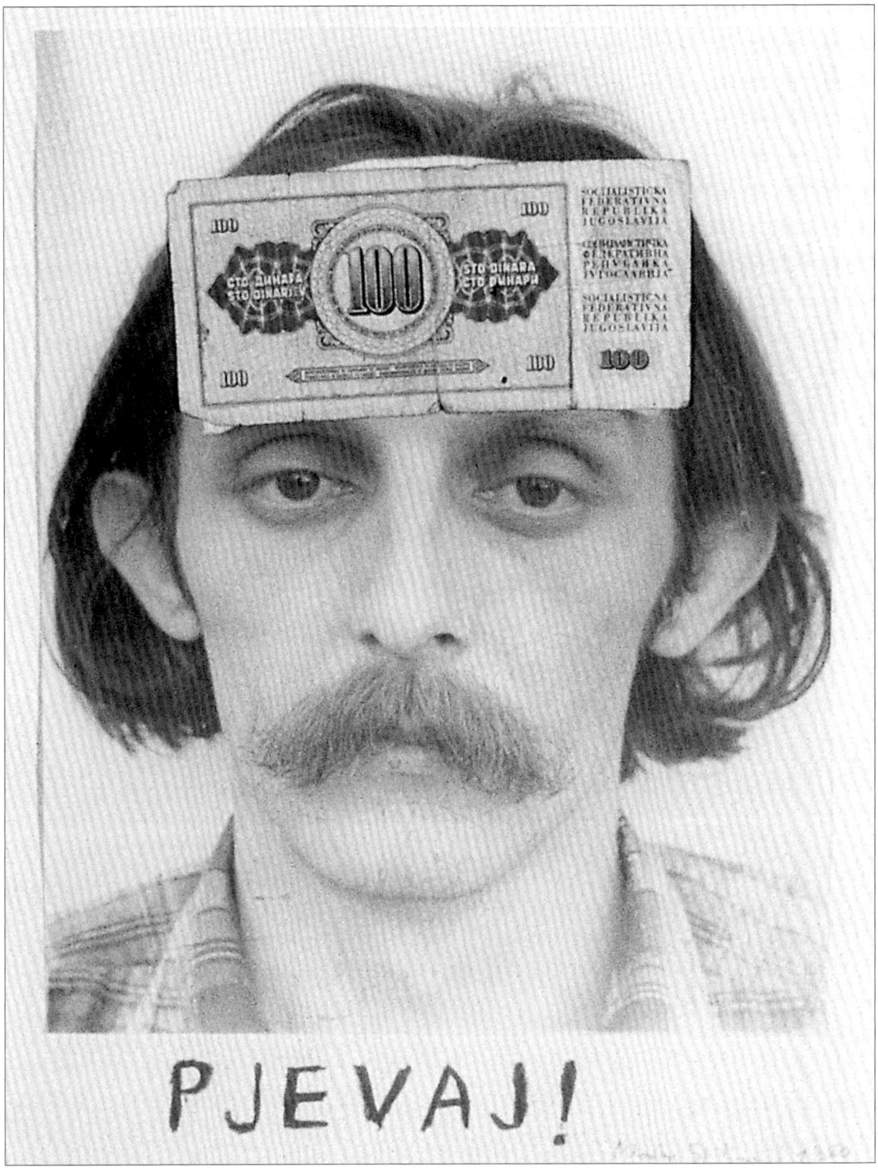

Figure 28 Mladen Stilinović, *Sing! (Thoughts about Money)*, 1980, b/w photograph, pastel, paper, imitation silk, 52 × 48 cm.

That is why an artist is not innocent, clean, transparent, and untouchable, but is a symptom of the political projection of everyday reality. A symptom is a place where the totality (of art, politics, religion, or everyday life) slips. Stilinović's acts are simple. He removes the political or social trauma and deposits it in one of the symbolic grids offered by art—and vice versa: If one of the definitions of practice is to act with the Symbolic on the Real, then Stilinović acts with the Symbolic of art on the Real of politics and acts with the Symbolic of politics on the Real of art. There is no hope, no promise, and no redemption.

The series of works entitled *Exploitation of the Dead* (see Plate 7), from the 1980s, consists of paintings and objects installed on a wall in the artist's flat or in a gallery. The signifier is what remains of the sign. Stilinović displays the way in which the sign is dying. He focuses our gaze at the empty signs, showing signifiers such as black crosses or Communist stars, the signs of the classical avant-garde or of Socialist Realism. In his view,

> the exploitation of the dead refers to several things: first, to the exploitation of the dead poetics of painting—Suprematism, Socialist Realism, and geometric abstraction. Second, to the exploitation of dead signs: for me, these signs are dead because they have lost their meaning or their meaning is so transparent that it is in fact dead. For other people, of course, these signs are not dead. Third, the signs of the cross and star initially represented man and were later used by religion and ideology for their purposes; today, and this is a personal interpretation, they have turned into signs in cemeteries, not dead signs, but signs of death.[34]

With the idea of exploitation of dead signs, Mladen Stilinović suggests that in late capitalist Pop Art, Conceptual Art, and Neoconceptual Art there is an uncontrolled consumption of various products (values, objects, and representations), while in the cultures of late socialism and postsocialism there is an uncontrolled exploitation of aesthetic and ideological meanings. The aesthetic as ideological and the ideological as aesthetic are the manipulative devices he employs in his series of installations *Geometry of Cakes and . . .* (Figure 29), for example, in his defictionalizations of power and political rule. He confronts us with a dramatic, horrible, and grotesque process of the use and consumption of the meaning of art, politics, religion, and everyday life. Everyday life and its apparent superficiality are the realm in which power, manipulation, consumption, the deadly game of politics, rationality, and subjectivity are displayed.

This cynicism is neither the pedagogical cynicism of the Enlightenment, which carries out the rational criticism of society and its conditions, nor the cynicism of the modernist artist who wishes to engender the avant-gardist dialectical turn from a given reality into a new world. Instead, this is the cynicism of modern subversion, as exemplified by self-destructing slo-

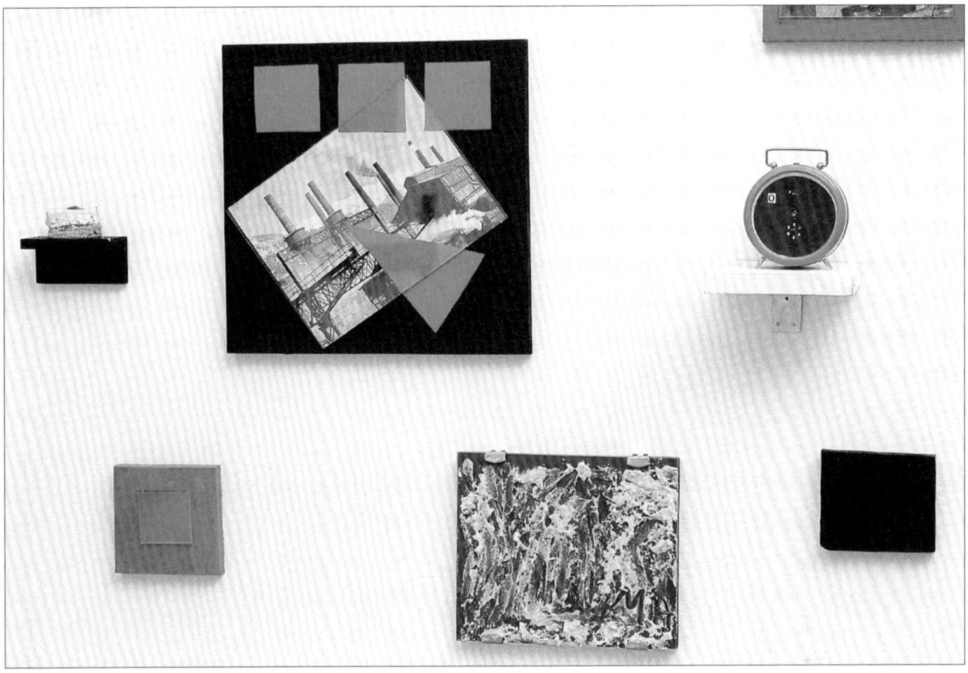

Figure 29 Mladen Stilinović, *Geometry of Cakes and . . .*, 1993 (detail), installation.

gans from his series *Geometry of Cakes and . . .* : "He Who Will Not Work Shall Not Eat. Death," "A Poor Man Has No Friends" (Figure 30), and "Who Works, Eats. Death." It is a situation in which, following Slavoj Žižek, the artist subverts cynical acts of ideology, politics, and the social reality itself.[35] His is the cynicism of postmodern entropy. Nothing remains at the end: The end itself should be consumed and thereby be lost, as well.

Impossible Histories: Postmodern Art and the Avant-Garde in Romania

Some histories are impossible. The roots of Balkan art, for example, remain within the framework of European history of modern art, but Balkan art remains excluded from it. It is art that is forgotten, repressed, and erased. Its history is impossible.

Such is the impression when approaching the small, nonparadigmatic avant-gardes of the Balkans, the avant-gardes of Romania, Bulgaria, Serbia,

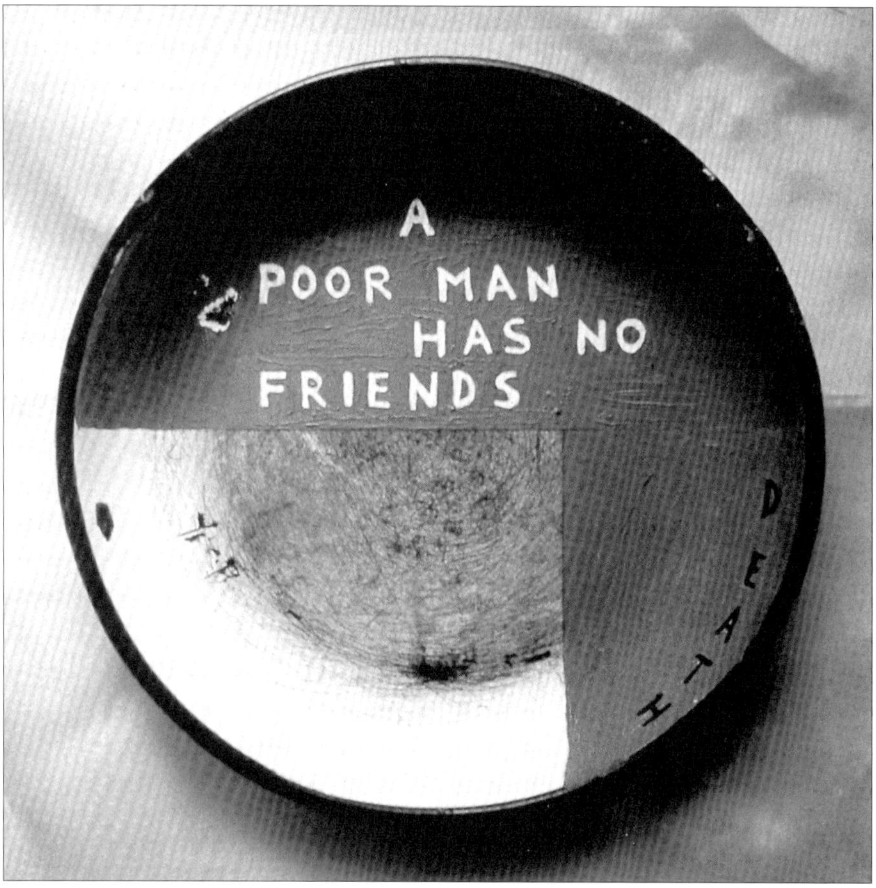

Figure 30 Mladen Stilinović, *A Poor Man Has No Friends,* 1993, installation.

and Croatia. Something existed, but it was not identified, classified, and represented as a part of the history of modern Europe. Among the reasons for such a situation, I wish to highlight two: the geographic and political marginality of these countries and the effect of Realsozialismus.

Modern and avant-garde Romanian art started at the beginning of this century and paralleled Western European artistic tendencies.[36] French culture had a huge influence on Romanian culture. Some of the Romanian artists who left the Balkans became leading European modernist and avant-garde artists and intellectuals: Constantin Brancusi, Tristan Tzara, Eugene Ionesco, Emile M. Cioran, and Mircea Eliade. Although after the Second World War Romania became a part of the Soviet bloc, in the 1960s, it started down a somewhat insular path toward Communism by combining socialist and nationalist ideas. It thus became isolated in relation to the Eastern bloc, as well, a kind of cultural void in the Europe of the second part of the twentieth century, a country "in the middle of nowhere." Its recent culture consisted of "exotic" Balkan folklore, in the West allegorically represented by the tales of Transylvania and Dracula, and at the same time of the work of numerous intellectuals and artists who, like their predecessors, left Communist Romania and found their place in the intellectual capitals of Western Europe.

subREAL

The group subREAL was founded in 1990 in Bucharest. Today its members are also active in Berlin and the Netherlands,[37] its permanent members being Călin Dan (born in 1955) and Iosif Király (born in 1954). The expressive media of the group are photography, video, installations, and performances. The group came into existence after the fall of the Ceauşescu regime in December 1989.

SubREAL works under a postsocialist zero degree of existence. In the historically and existentially emptied space of Balkan postsocialism, there is no difference between art and culture. Culture and art exist as various arbitrary remnants and traces. The basic activity of subREAL is therefore gathering notes, recycling and recombining the arbitrary traces of art and culture. The group doesn't create artworks or an art world. Under these peculiar circumstances, it makes use of the consumed traces of society, culture, and art, of public and private identities. The sense of their works is not determined by an ontological order of art, but by the powers of organizing language games as the vital activity of the artist.

A language game is not a ludic act of liberation and emancipation, but the use of consumed traces of ideological and everyday discourse in desperate confrontation with a world that has gone to waste:

> When subREAL took shape in the depressive Romanian summer of 1990, it was hard to predict that it would be more than another short-term survival-operation. A lot of them have been launched in the darkness of the eighties and killed immediately by the non-exhausted political censorship. But this time we were lucky: the oppressive system in Romania was too busy elsewhere after the big shake-up of December '89. That is why next July we can celebrate the amazing 5th anniversary of when the (old/new) Power allowed us to exist.[38]

Călin Dan here outlines the world of Balkan postsocialism, a world composed of gaps and lost in the European unconscious (in "the other scene" of Europe), a world that exists not as a presence, but as an endless process of deferring.

Thus, subREAL is an activity or practice of creating and producing art as a postponed expression, as a failure of understanding of the original sense. Its work appeared as a reaction to its unique existential environment. The project *East-West Avenue*, realized in Bucharest in August 1990, for example, points to the geopolitical position of Romania between the East and the West, manifests the artists' wish to cross from the East to the West, and ironically imitates the megalomaniac avenues built by the Romanian dictator Ceauşescu.

Another example: the installation *Alimentara* (The Food Store) (Figures 31 and 32), realized in Bucharest in February 1991, exhibits the lack of food in Romania. The stores are empty, and there is no food to buy, except on the black market. Installing the food store as an artwork is not only an act of irony; it also exhibits the public scene: unspoken dramas of hunger, deprivation, and the loss of human dignity. The installation representing the food store becomes an allegory of hunger.

Hunger can be existential and political. If we compare, for example, the Romanian food store *Alimentara* and the food store (*The Store*, 1961) realized by the Pop artist Claes Oldenburg, we immediately discern that in spite of the food store realized by subREAL being the store of real poverty, and the store realized by Oldenburg being the store of grotesque plenty, the former possesses primarily an existential significance and the latter a political one.

In this environment, subREAL perceives itself as a certain kind of signifier: It aims at becoming any sign in any place and in any relation. It is,

> first of all, a certain way to react towards an environment. Which just happened to be Romania. Then, it became a concept covering the ambiguous faces of that reality. Then again, the fact that Romania is just a piece in a huge subREAL context became obvious. But what is subREAL remains a question potentially addressed to everybody and everything. For the moment, let's say that subREAL is all the information coming from the territory where stupidity and cynicism become one.[39]

Stupidity and cynicism for Russian artists of Sots Art or perestroika art, not to mention the Slovenian retro-avant-garde, were a theme (the stupidity of

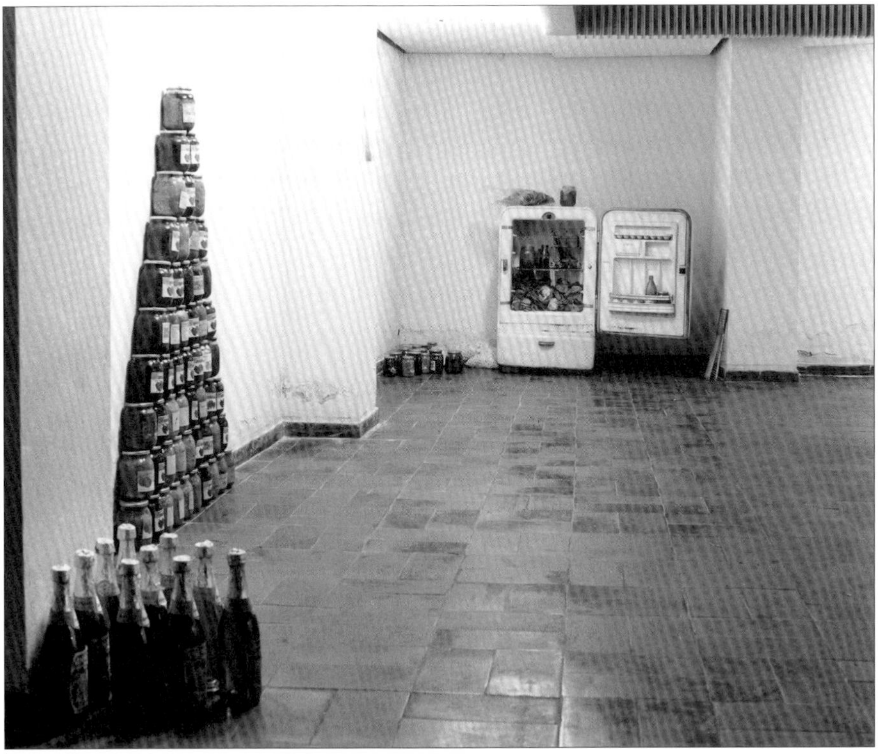

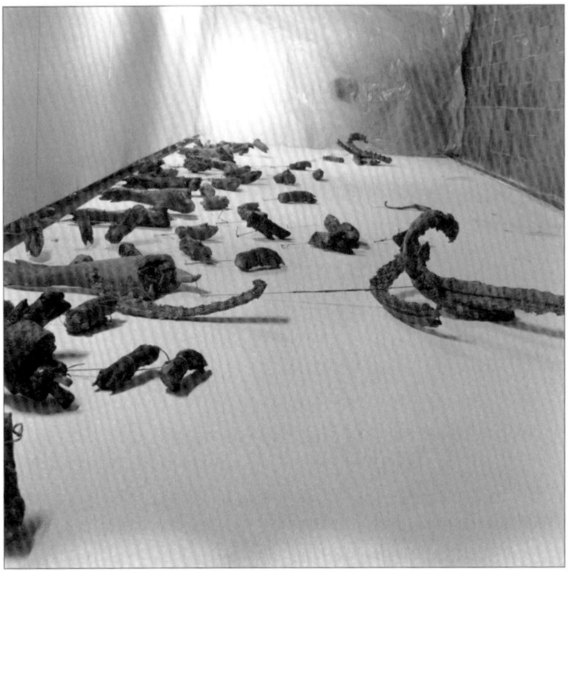

Figure 31 subREAL, *Alimentara,* 1991, installation; with D. Mihaltianu and friends.

Figure 32 subREAL, *Alimentara* (detail).

ideology and politics) and a device (cynicism, the grotesque), for there existed at least a certain recognizable difference between the world of politics and the lived world. Stupidity and cynicism for subREAL, however, were the reality of the lived world itself, the only extant one.

Out of the confrontation with such a reality, subREAL's concrete poetical devices came into being. The material poverty of Balkan cultures confronted the group with a dilemma: how to make a work when all that is at hand is the aura of an artwork. In such a situation, they used a magician's trick: Who will cheat whom? Will the artist cheat culture, history, and art, or will the institutions of art, culture, and history swindle the artist? Works, by being faked, can become art:

> In the case of subREAL, that experience was changed by the revelation that people can make history if they know how to fake it. What matters in the postindustrial era is not the fact but the information, not the object, but its carrier. An aura of photographs, videos and texts surrounds the subREAL art pieces. What is an installation? A very demanding sculpture, which needs more room, and more technical assistance than a *normal* art piece, is very difficult in terms of transportation and very fragile in the fight with natural enemies of art—dust and light. Installations, like humans, get old and ugly. Installations are time based; this is why they need photography.[40]

The installation *Draculaland* (1993) arose out of the revelation that it is the document that makes a monument, that is, an artwork, and that the mythology produced by mass culture should not be discarded, but used. In it, subREAL simultaneously evoked the Romanian culture of folklorism and the Hollywood use of Bram Stoker's character.

A related project was subREAL's *Art History Archive Deconstruction*[41] from 1995, an absurd collection of works constituting an impossible history of Romanian and international art:

> "Datacorridor" is a part of the "Art History Archive" (AHA), a serial project based on the experience of Călin Dan & Iosif Király, both as artists and (for a period) editors of the—at the time—one and only art magazine of Romania, *Arta*. The magazine collapsed after the political shifts of 1989, and the archive (accumulated since 1935) stayed as a floating deposit of photographs documenting Romanian & international art history from antiquity to postmodernism. Presented until now in several locations, "Datacorridor" is a dynamic sculpture meant for multi-layered readings, and a place with the ideological and cultural filters which interfere in the process of reading cultural

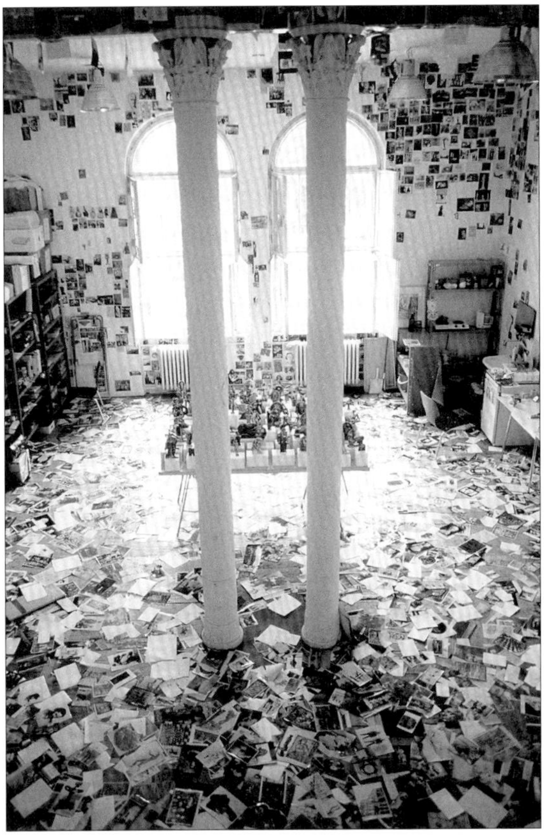

Figure 33 subREAL, *Art History Archive Deconstruction,* Berlin, 1995, installation.

> information. Description: A corridor is the inside completely covered with about 10,000 b/w photographs of various dimensions. The corridor is lit by 8 lamps mounted in the ceiling. A 60 min. audio tape with a female voice announcing names of artists provides a sound archive replicating the photo archive. The names alternate with the ringing of an electronic bell.[42]

The history of Western (French, German, Italian) avant-garde art is thus deconstructed and transformed into a history of modern art and the Balkan avant-gardes, with the established history of art used as material for constructing the art of subREAL (Figure 33).

The performance *Communication 1:1,*[43] from 1994 (Figure 34), is realized as a blood exchange between the two permanent members of the group. They sit, one beside the other, and exchange their blood with an apparatus for blood transfusion. The blood exchange is simultaneously an event that points to the subtext of the Dracula tale, a simulacrum of nature, and an al-

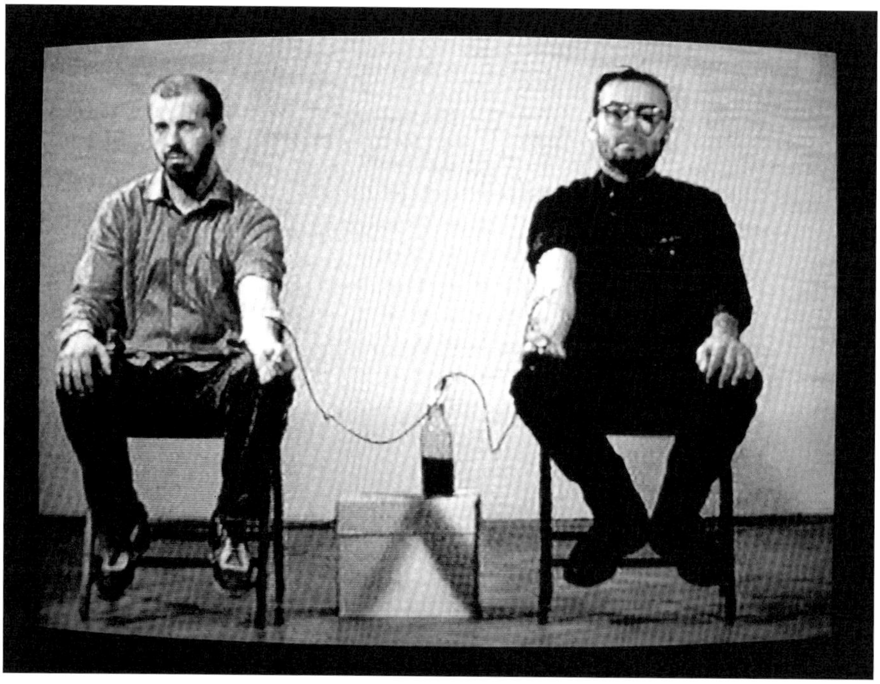

Figure 34 subREAL, *Communication 1:1*, 1994, performance.

legory of total communication (the politics of the body). It furthermore represents the ultimate use of the life substance. "Art takes place between life and death," wrote Walter de Maria thirty years ago.[44] It seems as if subREAL answers: Art is made *from* life and death—literally.

Notes

1. Gerard Delanty, "The Resonance of Mitteleuropa: A Habsburg Myth of Antipolitics?" *Theory, Culture and Society* 13, no. 4 (November 1996): 94.

2. Charles Harrison and Fred Orton, *A Provisional History of Art & Language* (Paris: Éditions E. Fabre, 1982), p. 5.

3. See Ješa Denegri, "Šest decenija—period posleratnog modernizma," in *Petdesete: Teme srpske umetnosti (1950–1960)* (Novi Sad: Svetovi, 1993), pp. 5–19, and Ješa Denegri, "Socialistički estetizam," ibid., pp. 104–10.

4. Denegri, "Socialistički estetizam."

5. Mikhail Epstein, in Ellen E. Berry, Kent Johnson, and Anesa Miller-Pogacar, "Postcommunist Postmodernism: An Interview with Mikhail Epstein," *Common Knowledge* 2, no. 3 (1993): 103–4.

6. The idea of the second wave of modernism in the context of Western art is discussed by Heinrich Klotz in *Kunst in 20. Jahrhundert: Moderne—Postmoderne—Zweite Moderne* (Munich: Verlag C. H. Beck, 1994).

7. See Miško Šuvaković, "Asymmetries of Language and Sight: Introduction to a Philosophy of Art," *Filozofski vestnik* (Ljubljana) 17, no. 2 (1996): 203–15.

8. For the early works of Milan Knížák, see Udo Kulterman, *Art-Events and Happenings* (London: Mathews Miller Dunbar, 1971), pp. 43, 70–71, and Adrian Henri, "Eastern Europe," in *Environments and Happenings* (London: Thames and Hudson, 1974), pp. 128–29.

9. See Milena Lamarova, "Knížák's Universe," in Milan Knížák, *Novi Raj: Vyber praci z let 1952–1995* (Prague: Galerie Manes, Umeleckoprumyslove Museum, 1996), unpaginated.

10. Allan Kaprow, "Milan Knížák (Who Never Fell in Love with Art)," in Knížák, *Novi Raj*.

11. Pierre Restany, "Carpe Diem!" in Knížák, *Novi Raj*.

12. Milan Knížák, in "Milan Knížák: Kill Yourself and Fly. An Interview by Johan Pijnappel," *Art and Design: New Art from Eastern Europe*, no. 35 (1994): 38.

13. Quoted in Valerie Smith, "King of Dwarfs: A Conversation with Milan Knížák," *Arts Magazine* (May 1991): 62–63.

14. Milan Kunc, "Notes on Being in the Wrong Place at the Right Time," in *Milan Kunc*, edited by Pavel Liška (Cologne: Edition Cantz, 1992), p. 14.

15. Ibid., p. 15.

16. Boris Groys, "Milan Kunc: Cheerful Post-Modernism," in *Milan Kunc*, pp. 25–26.

17. Donald Kuspit, "Milan Kunc's Fool's Paradise,' in *Milan Kunc*, p. 62.

18. Michel Foucault, "The Prose of Actaeon," *Art Press*, no. 195 (October 1994): 59.

19. See "Vzpominka na akčni umèni 70. let: Razhovor Ludvika Hlavačka s Petrem Štemberou a Janem Mlčochem," *Výtvarné umènί* (Prague), no. 3 (1991): 61–77, and Jiři Valoch, "Land Art and Conceptual Art," in *Krajina: Landscape* (Prague: Soros Center for Contemporary Art, 1993), pp. 29–40.

20. See Jasna Tijardović, "Marina Abramović, Slobodan Milivojević, Neša Paripović, Zoran Popović, Raša Todosijević, Gergelj Urkom," *The New Art Practice in Yugoslavia, 1966–1978*, edited by Marijan Susovski (Zagreb: Galerija suvremene umjetnosti, 1978), pp. 59–63, Raša Todosijević, *Great Southern Performances* (Belgrade: Studentski kulturni centar, 1980), and *Raša Todosijević* (Zagreb: Galerija suvremene umjetnosti, 1982).

21. Raša Todosijević, "The Edinburgh Statement 1975: Who Makes Profit on Art, and Who Gains From It Honestly?," in *Texts* (Tübingen: Edition Dacić, 1977), unpaginated.

22. *Raša Todosijević*.

23. Raša Todosijević, *Stories on Art* (Belgrade: Studentski kulturni centar, 1995).

24. Goran Djordjević, "Examples of Process in Square System," quoted in Ješa Denegri, "Goran Djordjević," in *The New Art Practice in Yugoslavia, 1966–1978*, p. 63.

25. Goran Djordjević, "On the Class Character of Art," *The Fox* (New York), no. 3 (1976): 163.

26. See Marina Gržinić Mauhler, "Fiction Re-Constructed," *Filozofski vestnik* (Ljubljana) 15, no. 2 (1994): 235–46.

27. Donna Haraway, *Simians, Cyborgs, and Women: The Reinvention of Nature* (London: Free Association Books, 1991), p. 113.

28. Balint Szombathy, "Landmarks in the Work of the Group Bosch+Bosch," in *The New Art Practice in Yugoslavia, 1966–1978*, p. 52.

29. See Balint Szombathy, *Zastave* (Novi Sad: Galerija Most, 1993).

30. Balint Szombathy, quoted in Majda Adlešić, "Krv a ne boja: Razgovor sa Balintom Szombathyjem," in *PerformaNS 95*, edited by Sava Stepanov (Novi Sad: Centar za vizuelnu kulturu "Zlatno oko," 1995), p. 7.

31. For a broader survey of radical Croatian art, see Branka Stipančić, *The Horse Who Sings: Radical Art from Croatia* (Sydney: Museum of Contemporary Art, 1991).

32. I have already mentioned the "principle of hope." *Das Prinzip Hoffnung* was also the title of the best-known work by the German philosopher Ernst Bloch, published between 1953 and 1959. With his unorthodox Marxist treatment of the notions of hope, utopia, and

freedom, Bloch had an enormous influence on the European Left of the 1960s, an important part of which included intellectuals from Eastern Europe, too.

33. Mladen Stilinović, "Footwriting" (1984), *M'ars* (Ljubljana) 6, nos. 1–4 (1994): 73.

34. Mladen Stilinović, in Darko Šimičić, "Interview. Mladen Stilinović," in *Mladen Stilinović: Exploitation of the Dead, 1984–1989* (Zagreb: Edicija Šimičić, 1989), p. 1.

35. See Slavoj Žižek, *Filozofija skozi psihoanalizo* (Ljubljana: Analecta, 1984), pp. 100–129.

36. For a review of the classical or historical Romanian avant-garde see *Avangarda, Arhitekst Magazine of Architecture, Construction and Visual Arts*, no. 3 (Bucharest, 1993), and Krisztina Passuth, *Les avant-gardes historiques de l'Europe centrale* (Paris: Flammarion, 1988), pp. 209–26.

37. See subREAL, *Akten/Files* (Berlin: Berliner Kunstverein, 1996).

38. Călin Dan, "Untitled Celebration," *Imago: Another Europska Photography* (Bratislava) (winter 1995–96): 31.

39. Ibid.

40. Ibid.

41. See subREAL, *Art History Archive: La Biennale di Venezia 1999* (Bucharest: Ministry of Culture, 1999).

42. subREAL, "Datacorridor: Art History Archive (AHA)," in *Manifesta 1* (Rotterdam: European Art Manifestation, 1995), p. 15.

43. See the catalog *Naturally—in Central Europe* (Budapest: Ernst Muzeum, 1994), pp. 219–27.

44. Walter de Maria, motto in *Minimal Art: A Critical Anthology*, edited by Gregory Battcock (New York: Dutton and Co., 1968).

Neue Slowenische Kunst—New Slovenian Art

Slovenia, Yugoslavia, Self-Management, and the 1980s

Aleš Erjavec

The Slovenians are a nation of two million people living in mountainous terrain bordered by Austria, Hungary, Croatia, Italy, and the Adriatic Sea. From the eighth century until 1991 they had no independent state of their own. National aspirations that emerged mostly in the nineteenth century caused Slovenians to join the newly formed Yugoslavia after the end of the First World War, which thus became the "Kingdom of Serbs, Croats, and Slovenians." In Tito's federal Yugoslavia, Slovenia retained and strengthened its cultural autonomy, this being equally true for language, education, art, and literature. Before independence in 1991, Slovenia's overall culture, political system, and economy were inextricably linked with those of the rest of Yugoslavia.

Throughout most of Slovenian history, national identity was built almost exclusively on the Slovenian language and culture. With no kings and conquerors to speak of, streets in towns or villages in Slovenia were named not after royal figures and generals, but mostly after writers, painters, scientists, and a few statesmen. In the early twentieth century, Josip Vidmar, one of the leading Slovenian intellectuals, promulgated the idea that small Slovenia could excel, not in economy or politics, but in culture and art.[1] From this wishful thinking arose his idea of the "Slovenian Athens"—the idea that the capital of Slovenia, Ljubljana, could become another Athens or Florence, renowned for its culture, making a mark in the world in this way.[2]

Not only before the emergence of Yugoslavia, but also after its creation in 1918, the Slovenian national identity and the role of Slovenia within the broader Yugoslavia raised numerous problems and were the cause of many unresolved ambiguities. Through the centuries, Slovenians and their predecessors found their principal national foe in German culture, and Slovenian intellectuals established an uneasy defensive posture toward it. After the integration of Slovenia into Yugoslavia, however, the source of the danger of assimilation slowly ceased to be German culture and was replaced by Serbian or a unitary "Yugoslav" culture. While German culture was still the centuries-old enemy, because of historical distance and a vastly changed political framework, its relation to Slovenian culture proper now began to be perceived in a more benign way. Serbian culture, on the other hand, started to exert its influence, a culture that much later, in the 1970s and 1980s, strove toward a similar all-Yugoslav identity. It has to be pointed out, however, that for a large segment of the younger generation in Yugoslavia, Slovenians included, a Yugoslav "identity" started to supplement the ethnic identity in the 1970s and 1980s.

In Tito's Yugoslavia after the Second World War, a federal system of republics was established in which Slovenian culture retained its autonomy. More recent conflicts with the other republics or the federal government in Belgrade erupted mainly in relation to the amount of GNP that Slovenia should contribute to the federal government and to the less-developed parts of the country, since the relationship between the national and the federal economy and between cultural and political uniformity and autonomy remained underlying issues. Because Slovenia was the most highly developed republic, having the largest income from exports and the strongest economic links with Western market economies, it opposed centralization and the extant economic system of increased federal redistribution of wealth.

After the break with Stalin and the Soviet bloc countries in 1948, Tito's Yugoslavia faced a series of dilemmas, some of which also infringed on art and even art theory. In politics, Yugoslavia helped create the nonalignment movement and played the Cold War blocs against each other while retaining a shaky equidistance from them. Beginning in the early 1960s, Yugoslav citizens could possess passports, travel abroad, buy foreign publications, and so on.

Because of the break with Stalin, Yugoslav Party theorists could no longer rely on Soviet theoretical sources and references. They started to use as their reference points Marx's own writings and, increasingly, those of the early Marxist dissidents and of what Perry Anderson has called "Western Marxism": the authors of the Frankfurt School, Ernst Bloch, and the early Georg Lukács among them.[3]

A similar situation occurred in the arts and literature: "Yugoslavia broke with Stalin and its life depended upon its opening to the West. Yugoslavia had to prove to the world that a freedom of thought exists here and for this purpose the most adequate were artists who made works resembling those in the West."[4] As the artist Milan Butina explained in the late 1950s, he considered it "patriotic" to employ the Cubist painterly style,[5] while in the 1960s, Existentialist literature was de rigueur in Slovenia and Croatia, with Heidegger becoming probably the most influential single philosopher of the time.

Under such conditions—and in this, Yugoslavia differed from the Soviet bloc countries—there was nothing politically incorrect in being an Abstractionist, an Expressionist, or a Surrealist in the fine arts, an Existentialist or a Conceptualist in literature, or an atonal avant-gardist in music. It is true that Social Realism was the artistic style often preferred by the politicians, but the degree of such preference was strongly dependent on the particular milieu and its provincialism or cosmopolitanism. In Slovenia since the late 1960s, Social Realists had become an increasingly rare (and unfashionable) breed, consisting mainly of a few artists and writers of the prewar generation. One exception, but someone belonging to the younger generation, was the painter Janez Knez, who earned his living in one of the few proletarian areas of Slovenia.[6]

The consequences of identifying Socialist Realism with Stalinism not only made Socialist Realism politically unacceptable but made it and its discursive argumentation one of the main targets of literary and art criticism. From the late 1960s the label "Socialist Realist" signified the worst aesthetic critique, for it denoted not only artistic worthlessness, but also an attempt to politicize art in an obsolete and dogmatic way unworthy of a real artist. As early as 1956, a controversy between Josip Vidmar and Boris Ziherl, the leading Party ideologue and defender of the social role of art, signaled the demise of the interpretation of art as a vehicle for social ideas and legitimized modernism in literature.

From Self-Management to a Multiparty System

The purpose of accepting unorthodox Marxist theory was not only to distance Yugoslavia from the Soviet bloc, but also to develop a Yugoslav socialist theory proper—self-management socialism. Although it was claimed that it began to develop in the 1950s, self-management really took off in the 1970s, when in 1974 the amended constitution and in 1976 the Law of United Labor became "the foundation for the real development of self-management socialism."[7] A huge reorganization of the country was begun, accompanied by an equally extensive change of vocabulary, turning Yugoslavia into a country where practically no political or economic organization or institution had a terminological equivalent in other countries, be they parliamentary or people's democracies.

The person most responsible for much of this specific Yugoslav path to a classless society was the Slovenian theorist Edvard Kardelj (1910–1979). Kardelj wanted to put to use the political ideas and practices of the Paris Commune in an attempt to avoid the Western market economy, on the one hand, and to circumvent the pitfalls of the bureaucratized "actually existing socialism," on the other: "In that [it] was contrasted not only with capitalism but also with 'bureaucratic' approaches to the building of socialism and communism in the Soviet bloc, the ideology of self-management was *in part* a form of official nationalist legitimization."[8] It was also something more: an attempt to bridge the gap between the "iron laws of history" of which Marx wrote in *Das Kapital* and the free world of unharnessed subjectivity found in Marx's early writings and championed by the Yugoslav Praxis group and other promulgators of anthropological Marxism. It may have been the consciousness of the uncircumventable necessity of existential issues within the communist universe that caused Kardelj to state that "no state, no system and no political party can bring man happiness. Man alone can create his own happiness."[9] Nonetheless, such a liberal and humanist statement also starkly reveals that its author was aware of the futility of attempting to change the human condition by outside means only. Unfortunately, his ideas, when put into practice, proved almost as inefficient as those of the Soviet-type socialism.

Theoretically, the aim of self-management was to allow for decision making at the lowest possible level and to make social relations and decisions direct and transparent. In reality, social organization in the least-developed parts of Yugoslavia, where modern industrialization has not yet really taken hold, started to revert to the premodern state, while in the country as a whole, a complex system that was almost impossible to fathom caused decision making to become even more opaque and chaotic. Then, in 1980, Tito died at eighty-eight. Politicians coming to power after him unsuccessfully attempted to counter the decentralization that had been augmented and institutionalized by self-management in the increasingly disparate parts of the country, with their economically disparate interests. Some of the measures taken by the federal government in the late 1970s and the 1980s may not have been too unpopular in some parts of Yugoslavia, but in Slovenia, the introduction of a deposit for exiting the country in 1982, for instance, and a drastic reduction of the sale of foreign press and literature due to the purportedly wasteful spending of foreign currency were seen as visible symptoms of dogmatization, ossification, and bureaucratization of what under Tito used to be a relatively open and liberal society. It was perhaps in the humanities and in art that this change first began to be detected and reflected.

One of the increasingly visible consequences of self-management socialism was populism and anti-intellectualism. Previously, although the Yugoslav League of Communists had employed a typical Party discourse, it had managed nonetheless to update it somewhat so that it often functioned as the consciousness of an epoch and not as false consciousness. In the late 1970s and early 1980s, however, the gap between the symbolic reality offered by the official political discourse of self-management newspeak and the social reality of the *Lebenswelt* became increasingly visible. In the humanities, this self-management populist discourse was analyzed and criticized by Slovenian adherents of Louis Althusser who gathered around the revue *Problemi*. Althusser's theories of state apparatuses and ideology offered one of the rare effective theoretical tools for a critique of the discursive opaqueness of the self-management discourse and the power relations hidden behind its apparent benevolence toward various disparate interests. Such a critique began with thorough analyses of Stalin's own discourse. It soon became clear, though, that the same discursive mechanisms functioned in the self-management discourse, too, thus revealing that despite the officially proclaimed fundamental differences between Soviet Stalinism and Yugoslav self-management socialism, the two, unfortunately, shared common traits of a fundamental character. A similar type of discourse was moreover discerned in National Socialist discourse, leading to the obvious conclusion that they all belonged to the same group of ideological discourses engendered by related social orders.

The 1980s

The inextricable mixture of politics and art of the 1980s is what warranted this historical survey. It also needs to be stressed that Yugoslavia and hence Slovenia in the 1960s and early 1970s were in a different position from the Soviet bloc countries and cultures, but that in the 1980s, the similarities between the situation in the Soviet bloc countries and that in Yugoslavia visibly increased. The Slovenian art under discussion arose from such conditions, and it is for this reason that it so strongly resembled the concurrent art of most of the other postsocialist countries in its forcefulness and exceeded that art in its political effects. Elsewhere in Central Europe, politicized postmodern art was mostly the work of scattered individuals or small groups, while in Slovenia, a whole organization sprang up, an organization that, in the eyes of innocent observers, functioned like a well-oiled military machine.

Traditionally, in Slovenia, the artistic creative form par excellence was literature. Theater and, later, cinema were mostly viewed and treated as its extensions, with the fine arts and music playing second fiddle. Until a few decades ago, in this respect, Slovenian culture was not only similar to the cultures of other small European nations, but also patently a traditional one, with a few modernist islands existing in the small urban centers.[10] In prewar Yugoslavia, Slovenia remained culturally traditional and dominated by the conservative Catholic Church, the power base of which was the rural countryside—the whole of Slovenia, except for a few larger towns.[11]

With the postwar advent of socialism, a more urban and more cosmopolitan culture took hold in Slovenia. Since the late 1960s, Yugoslav artists have been well informed about cultural and artistic events, whether these came from capitalist, socialist, or Third World countries. In the late 1970s and the early 1980s, the Yugoslav lifestyle started to change: a youth and underground culture developed in urban centers, and mass culture proliferated. In Slovenia, these started to replace the previous literary high culture with one that was predominantly visual.[12] A mixture of various genres, high and low, profane and elitist, characterized the 1980s. This was possible partly due to the autonomy that self-management offered to individual republics and their constituent parts. What was artistically or politically still acceptable in Slovenia could be unthinkable in Montenegro or Belgrade. In the 1980s, Slovenia thus became a safe haven for political dissidents from the rest of Yugoslavia. The first gay club was opened in Ljubljana in 1984, and punk as an intellectual cultural form became fashionable—all this occurring within the confines of the ever-increasing populist self-management discourse and amid ominous threats from Belgrade and the more traditional parts of Yugoslavia directed at the excessively liberal Slovenia.

Although "Slovenia was in the vanguard of pressures for the liberalization and democratization of Yugoslav public life in the 1960s, as well as later, in the 1980s,"[13] it carried insufficient political weight, and its interests were probably too different from the rest of Yugoslavia's to change the country as a whole in any substantial measure. In most of Yugoslavia, the transformation into a postindustrial society, which had only just begun, was stalled because of fear of its social and political consequences and because of sheer incompetence. Much of this incompetence was linked to the populism promoted by a peculiar social revolution in which workers, peasants, and the lower echelons of the bureaucracy were seizing political power. A suffocating political climate reigned, and, at least in Slovenia, it seemed as if clouds of populism were closing in from the impoverished and decrepit industrial basins of central Yugoslavia, an increasingly provincial, anti-intellectual, disparate, disorganized, and corrupt country.

In 1989, the Slovenian League of Communists consented to a multiparty system. In the fall of 1990, a referendum in support of a merely confederate Yugoslavia was passed, asserting the will of Slovenia to become independent in six months' time if such a proposal was not embraced at the federal level. Since the proposal was not accepted, Slovenia proclaimed independence in June 1991.

Of Art and Culture

One of the typical features of politicized postmodern art in the other socialist countries discussed in this book is the lack of references to contemporary or simultaneous art from Western Europe or the United States. In Prague, Milan Knížák acknowledged his happiness in 1964 when for the first time he saw Western art magazines on modern art,[14] and in Hungary, Attila Kovács did not see the numerous paintings by Magritte that are similar to his Stone Room of 1982 until much later (see Figure 54).[15] The works from the 1970s and 1980s in the USSR depict at most only the best-known characters and icons of Western popular culture. Conceptual Art in the European socialist countries had certain links with similar trends in the West, but it predominantly developed in its own indigenous way. Even if communication existed, it remained for the most part inconsequential, for the more recent politicization of such art under socialism could find no parallels in the Western democracies.

Yugoslavia and Slovenia represent a different case. Yugoslav citizens could travel freely abroad, and since the late 1960s, artists had been not only familiar with international developments in art, but formally taught and informed about both past and recent international art. Slovenia was traditionally a crossroads country, and its different parts gravitated in different directions culturally. The southern part looked more toward Italy, where in the late 1970s and early 1980s the Italian Trans-Avantgarde under the theoretical and critical guidance of Achille Bonito Oliva reached its apogee, while in Ljubljana, artists, curators, and writers followed a variety of cultural paths. Such circumstances prevented a single culture from exerting a pronounced influence on Slovenian culture and its artists. At the same time, other cultures within Yugoslavia made their influence felt via the artists themselves or via immigrants from those cultures who came to Ljubljana to work or study and then stayed in Slovenia.

The influence of other cultures in Slovenia was not balanced, however, for cultural influences from the other European socialist countries was rarely present. Yugoslavia supported the Prague Spring of 1968 and other similar political events occurring in the Soviet bloc countries. While the Czech cinema and Polish design were held in high esteem, most of the more recent culture in that part of Europe was either unknown or perceived as lacking in interest and as obscure, if not altogether obsolete. Eastern European artists were seen as being either supported by the Soviet-type state or hard to reach (in the case of "alternative" artists), since they usually had no institutional support whatsoever. Such a perception of the culture of the Soviet bloc countries was prevalent in Slovenia, although some other parts of Yugoslavia that had historical links to or borders with the Soviet bloc countries kept closer ties with them and their art and culture.

In an interview for London's *Audio Arts* in December 1988, the Slovenian group of painters called Irwin explained the multifarious nature of Slovenian culture in terms of its use of the Malevich cross, which it frequently employed:

> For us the cross, with all the connotations and significations it has acquired until today, is one of the symbols from the picture book of European culture. The cross in Irwin's picture is therefore a way of translating this culture into consciousness, its mimesis. Nonetheless, the cross carries for us, as members of a small nation, another, fatal significance, as well. With our culture, we are chained to the center of the cross, at the meeting point of the mad ambitions of the East and the West. This is an empty space, geometrically defined, but with its meaning never completely clarified.[16]

In the early 1980s, Slovenian culture represented a crucial part, but still only a segment, of the broader culture of Yugoslavia, with its bands, visual artists, and writers frequently visiting, exhibiting, and performing in the large urban centers such as Belgrade, Zagreb, Rijeka, and Sarajevo. At the center of this culture stood a multifaceted association of artists that combined music, performance art, graphic arts, theater, and design: the punk and rock group Laibach, the group of graphic artists that came to be known as Irwin, the Theater of the Sisters of Scipio Nasica and the Red Pilot Cosmokinetic Theater, and the New Collectivism design group, all of which came together under the banner of Neue Slowenische Kunst—New Slovenian Art.

Trbovlje and Ljubljana: Laibach

It was popular music and alternative art and culture that retained and even strengthened the cultural links among the Yugoslav republics in the early 1980s and that brought Slovenian artists onto the broader European stage. Not that other cultures didn't possess strong ties with foreign cultures, but at that time in Slovenia, the division into elite art and popular culture did not permit any substantial exchange between the two. It was only the emergent postmodern culture that disregarded this segregation into "high" and "low."

In 1977, the first Slovenian punk band, the Bastards, came into existence, soon to be followed by many others, one of them the Laibach group, founded in 1980 in the coal-mining town of Trbovlje, in the cellar of a house belonging to Janez Knez, the father of group member Dejan Knez. In September of that same year, the group wanted to hold an art exhibition accompanied by punk music played by various bands. The black-and-white linocut posters that the group hung throughout Trbovlje (Figure 35) provoked a strong protest from the local socialist youth organization and from ordinary citizens and became a cause for a lengthy debate about artistic freedom, violence, fascism, and law and order. What the Trbovlje populace found most revolting about the posters was their purported visual and graphic violence and political obscenity. In December, the Trbovlje Youth Organization sent a letter to the youth journal *Mladina* stating:

> Everything a young worker, farmer, miner and student are striving for is present in all working people, in self-managers, in all of us who are building on the basis of our achievements. All these people who even in this quick

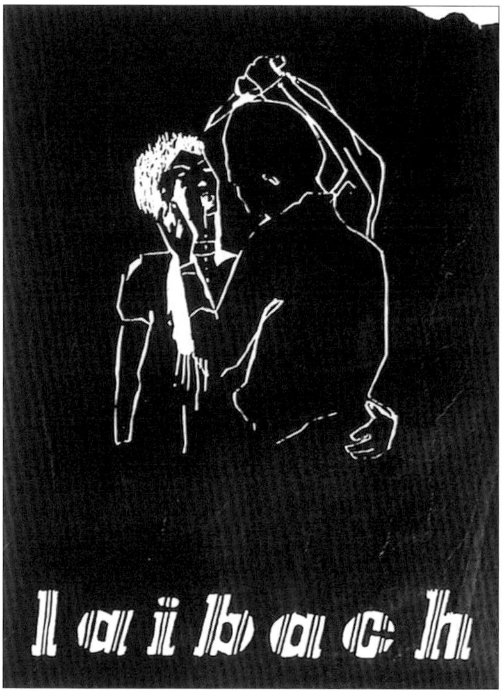

Figure 35 Laibach poster, 1980, linocut, 59 × 43 cm. Design Laibach Kunst.

> pace of life still manage to find a few moments for relaxation, who search through and draw in national tradition, were humiliated by these posters—their work, their creativity, their past were all humiliated. They were surprised by the propaganda material for the art exhibition and punk concert, and they publicly expressed their unwillingness to tolerate such things in their midst. We, the young, feel that not everything, especially not what our elders went through during the war, can be pasted on the wall under the cover of the word "punk."[17]

Provocation didn't end there: The very name of the group, Laibach, was the German name for Ljubljana, used officially for the last time during the German occupation of the city from 1943 to 1945. Because of its name, the Ljubljana City Council prohibited the group from performing in the city, causing its members to stage concerts there under a different name.

From the beginning until the present, the Laibach group has functioned as an impersonal collective. When asked how they understand freedom, the group replied: "The image of freedom changes over time; freedom that is possible in the time of plenitude is no longer viable when want reigns. Our freedom is the freedom of those who think alike."[18] This and similar statements, the detached stance of their public appearances, and their discourse and performances, which recalled martial music, only confirmed what they explicitly stated: "Every art is subjected to political manipulation except that which speaks the language of this very manipulation."[19]

Initially, Laibach was no different from other Slovenian punk bands except that its members were perhaps more articulate. Although its music was politicized from the very beginning, this politicization was carried out in a different way from that encountered in the traditional protest lyrics of singers such as Bob Dylan (and his local Slovenian counterparts) or in the music of more subversive bands such as the early Rolling Stones or, later, the Sex Pistols, Clash, and so on. The punk movement in Slovenia, and often elsewhere in socialist countries, was a predominantly intellectual phenomenon, and not primarily a creation of socially marginalized individuals, as was the case in the United Kingdom. British punk was assimilated to Slovenian conditions (not that those in Croatia were much different), under which it was often middle-class youths who formed punk bands with names such as the Bastards, Ljubljana Dogs, the Berlin Wall, and the Children of Socialism, with the audience divided about equally among suburban youth and high-school and university students. In their lyrics, most of them deplored the hypocrisy of socialist society, their marginal status, and emergent conflicts between Slovenians and the workers from southern Yugoslavia, creating on the way their own jargon, dress codes, and behavior. "[In Slovenia], too, the phenomenon of punk was tied to social and economic circumstances on the basis of which it emerged and attained certain specifics that are typical only for [Slovenia]. These are low living standards, unemployment, incessant inflation and devaluations, housing problems, special measures introduced by the government, scarcity of certain commodities, national intolerance, etc."[20]

Sometimes punk bands and their adherents used anarchist and Nazi symbols, and just as often socialist and official ones, although in most cases this was done in a straightforward ironic manner, as when the lead singer of the Bastards draped himself in a red flag at a concert in 1982. Such behavior was not politically very provocative, nor did it draw any repercussions, but it did reveal the antigovernment stance of the nascent "alternative culture." The institutions and positions attained by the students' movement in the late 1960s and early 1970s formed a strong base for that culture: Radio Student, founded in Ljubljana in 1969 and the first independent student radio station in Europe, was joined by journals such as *Mladina,* youth clubs, and the Students' Cultural Center.

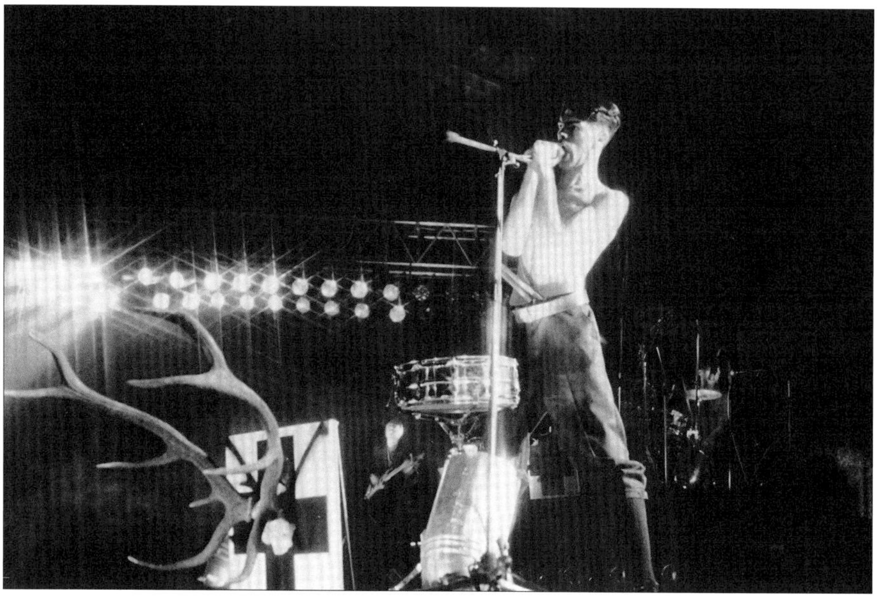

Figure 36 Laibach concert in Ljubljana, 1987.

What distinguished Laibach at first glance from the other bands was its "image." Its members soon began to wear a specific garb consisting of traditional Alpine breeches, vest, jacket, and cap, using "Germanic" and Alpine paraphernalia onstage, such as antlers, flags with the Malevich cross or the swastika, and dramatic lightning effects, staging these concerts in decrepit industrial buildings, conflating in this way the ambience of Wagner, *Blade Runner,* and the *Heimat* films (Figure 36). The industrial element was introduced under the influence of the industrial music of British groups such as Test Department. However, as Alexei Monroe observes, "in Slovenia, industry never played the type of role in popular consciousness that it did in Britain or in the USSR, despite the imposition of an artificially populist worker's culture in the postwar decades."[21] Instead, in its songs, Laibach used segments from political speeches—be they Mussolini's or Ronald Reagan's—often enunciating them in German, the somber voice of the lead singer being accompanied by trumpets, various drums, and sometimes a philharmonic orchestra and even the children's choir from Trbovlje.

By its impersonal behavior, explicit self-designation as ideological and political, its use of folk motifs, which before were considered unacceptable in avant-garde art, and its use of explicit national and political discourse in its music, Laibach completely contradicted the established perception of what artists and "serious" musicians were supposed to be like. In its "Ten Edicts of the Convention," written in Trbovlje in 1982, Laibach claims:

> (1) Laibach works in a team (collective spirit), modeled after industrial production and totalitarianism, which signifies: it is not the individual that speaks, but the organization. Our work is industrial and our language political. . . .
>
> (3) Every art is subjected to political manipulation (indirectly—consciousness; directly) except that which speaks with the language of this manipulation itself. To speak with a political expression means to reveal and admit the omnipresence of politics. The role of the most humane form of politics is the overcoming of the distance between reality and spirit by the mobilization of the masses. Ideology is the locus of authentic social consciousness.[22]

In these statements, Laibach already clearly shows that it has discovered a novel approach to grasping and opposing the extant political and ideological reality, one that avoids the traditional dissident method of criticizing or mocking ideology. Like some other artists from the socialist countries, Laibach has discovered the crack in the homogeneous membrane of socialist symbolic reality. When referring to Conceptual artists in the Soviet Union, Mikhail Epstein observed that "Conceptualists grasped and unmasked the artificial nature, not only of Soviet literature, but of Soviet reality itself."[23] The same holds true of the Hungarian artist Sándor Pinczehelyi, for example. By photographing himself in 1973 holding a hammer and sickle (see Figure 1), he "showed the object itself," the literal meaning of these two objects, which at that time, as representations, still existed essentially as ideological symbolic entities. By these and similar gestures Russian, Slovenian, Hungarian, Romanian, and other artists showed political reality "itself," devoid of its symbolic and ideological dimension. They exhibited a social reality that had lost its previous all-embracing and unquestioned meanings and symbolic interpretations ("ruling ideas"), for, imperceptibly, its symbolic power had been almost completely chipped away. Slowly, its desymbolized reality started to reveal itself underneath what not long ago had appeared to be indestructible layers of the symbolic reality of the socialist socioeconomic formation. "In order to function properly," as Žižek puts it, "power discourse must be inherently split, it must 'cheat' performatively, to disavow its own underlying performative gesture. Sometimes, therefore, the only truly subversive thing to do when confronted with a power discourse is simply to *take it at its word.*"[24] Žižek interpreted the strategy of the group as deliberately frustrating

> *the system (the ruling ideology) precisely insofar as it is not its ironic imitation, but over-identification with it*—by bringing to light the obscene superego underside of the system, over-identification suspends its efficiency. . . .
>
> The ultimate expedient of Laibach is their deft manipulation of transference: their public (especially intellectuals) is obsessed with the "desire of the Other"—what is Laibach's actual position, are they truly totalitarians or not?—i.e. they address Laibach with a question and expect from them an answer, failing to notice that Laibach itself *does not function as an answer, but as a question.* By means of the elusive character of their desire, of the undecidability as to "where they actually stand," Laibach compels us to take up our position and decide upon *our* desire.[25]

Laibach was among those who went furthest in this direction, for it functioned mostly in the small society of Slovenia, where every event carries much weight, and used expressive means not available to painters, designers, or theater directors. A Laibach concert was not only a musical event, but also a musical performance similar to a Wagner opera. Each production, each location, was planned to the minutest detail, and the knowledge of the group's banned status, its ambivalent (or rather indefinable) political position, and its growing success elsewhere in Europe and overseas all added to its aura of an almost sublime cultural phenomenon. Still, the small size of Slovenia offers only a partial explanation for the Laibach phenomenon, for the group had a similar (although certainly more limited) effect in other countries, including the larger Yugoslavia. The two features that probably attracted audiences to the Laibach concerts and made them listen to the music were the force (part of the overall image of the group) of its dramatic Wagnerian effects and the undefined and not obviously definable nature of their discourse.[26]

Their approach is a specific postmodern cultural phenomenon, different from previous procedures that bore a similar purpose. It no longer reevaluates a given meaning—showing the "real" reactionary nature of purportedly progressive events or actions, as Pasternak and Solzhenitsyn do, or satirically exposing provincialism, narrow-mindedness, petit bourgeois human nature, cruelty, and selfishness, in the manner of Gogol, Brecht, and Jonathan Swift—or redefines a given term. Instead, Laibach, as well as the other groups that founded the Neue Slowenische Kunst organization, used what I have called the "binary approach," simultaneously deploying two unreconciled and irreconcilable realities. They appeared traditional and traditionalist, even *völkisch,* on the one hand, while on the other they were cosmopolitan and global, attracting fans and intellectual adherents in places as different as Seattle, Budapest, and Göteborg. Almost from the beginning, Laibach intentionally projected this ambivalent self-image, showing at the same time that in reality there was "nothing behind" it. Their image was not some sophisticated prop hiding the "real" Laibach. Instead, heads and tails on this coin were the same.

To put it another way, the procedure employed by the Laibach group and also by some other groups of what became the Neue Slowenische Kunst organization, especially New Collectivism, was to articulate a secondary discourse on ideology in the form of the primary ideological discourse. Their explicit use of ideological statements and the ensuing complete identification with political ideology prevented the actual political ideologues of self-management socialism from establishing any distance between that ideology and postmodern critique, as carried out by Laibach, that would have allowed for a rebuttal and hence would effectively have neutralized that critique. The critique by Laibach was no ordinary critique of the kind encountered in dissident literature and art, or even in the detached stance of Conceptualism. It was not even a proper critique, for this always requires a certain distance from its object and symbolization in one form or another that allows the public to distance itself from the object of the critique. The approach of Laibach in Slovenia, of the subREAL group in Romania, in some of its works, and of the Russian, Hungarian, and Cuban artists under discussion was, on the contrary, to eradicate the distance between the representation and the represented, to create a simulacrum of the represented, thereby hindering or even destroying the power of the represented to react, to counter such an attack. The reactions at the disposal to the ruling ideology were hence either straightforward elimination, that is, the prohibition of this bothersome entity and its activities (which was much more difficult to do in the relatively liberal Slovenia than in Moscow, for example), or its reduction to straightforward dissidence or to youthful anarchism. Still, neither of the two approaches eliminated the feeling of discomfort, of an encounter with an entity that did not play by the rules of the familiar modernist approaches of partisan and dissident art.

In the years that followed, Laibach became one of the more visible music groups emerging from socialist countries. Punk groups became a trademark of not only Great Britain and West Germany, but also Slovenia and Poland. Not all of the music that emerged bearing a political message in Second World countries in the 1980s was or has remained punk. Its broader common denominator would more appropriately be called rock,[27] and also pop.[28]

Often, the crucial meeting point for the alternative culture and these music bands was Berlin, which until the fall of the Berlin Wall in 1989 carried the aura of a border city between the East and the West with a specific lifestyle and culture.

The late 1970s and early 1980s were the time of *Blade Runner, Mad Max, Terminator,* and similar films that were congenial with the music of industrial groups such as Throbbing Gristle, Cabaret Voltaire, Einstürzende Neubauten, Test Department, Sonic Youth, and Joy Division. Many of the features of these films and groups can also be found in Laibach's performances, style of dress, exhibitions, and other public appearances. The use of the German name was a useful provocation that exploited what was evidently the last unconquered terrain for the artistic avant-garde: patriotic sentiments. Just as the historical avant-gardes and the neo-avant-gardes discovered and consumed the provocational potential of nonacademic art, abstraction, and inner truth, of violence, war, and sexuality, and of the attack on bourgeois hypocrisy *en épatant le bourgeois,* Laibach and its adherents made use of the provocational potential of patriotism and the struggle against fascism. The blasphemy of such an attitude could find its equivalent not in John Heartfield's antipatriotic, anti-Nazi posture, but in the behavior of the French Surrealists—in Georges Bataille, for example. But Laibach, while supporting freedom, was also upholding Slovenian national culture and promoting its music and art as *Slovenian.* It really was true, as Laibach claimed, that the way for art to escape political manipulation was to speak the language of this manipulation itself.

A good, although perhaps somewhat benign, example of the use of Nazism and, at the same time, of the double-sided nature of Laibach is their Occupied Europe Tour of 1983. They gave the concerts in Vienna, Budapest, Warsaw, West Berlin, Copenhagen, Hamburg, The Hague, Amsterdam, and London, among other places. The question was, how would different audiences interpret the title of the tour? For the "Easterners," it could mean that they were occupied, but the two Nazi figures on the concert poster (Figure 37) also implied that "occupied Europe" was actually the Europe that was occupied by the Nazis during the war. "Westerners," on the other hand, could interpret the "occupation" of Europe either as the former Nazi occupation

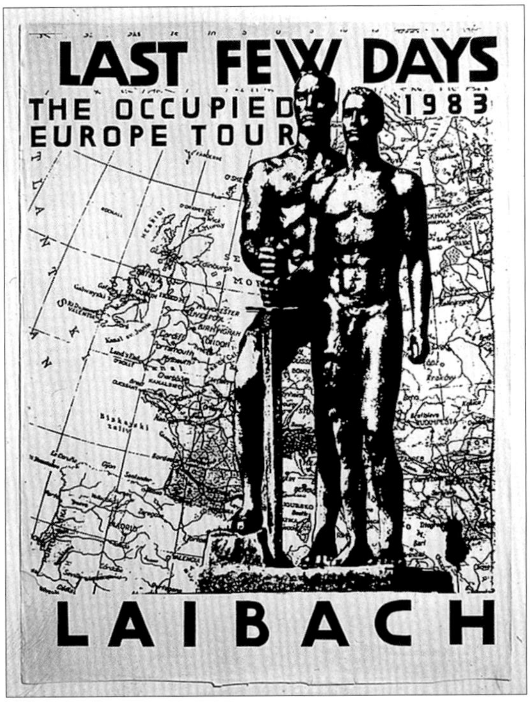

Figure 37 Laibach, *The Occupied Europe Tour* poster, 1983, silk screen, 96 × 71 cm. Design New Collectivism.

or as their own countries' impending occupation by Laibach and what it represented—and all such interpretations were correct.

Laibach and Neue Slowenische Kunst

Because it avoided the usual status of pop singers and artists, Laibach retained an aura of inaccessibility. It led a phantomlike existence as an oblique entity that was never really domesticated, that never allowed the public gaze to be directly fixed on it. Laibach never "gave in" to individual fame and the pleasure of individual public appraisal.

In 1984, Laibach, along with two other artistic groups, Irwin and the Theater of the Sisters of Scipio Nasica, formed the Neue Slowenische Kunst organization.[29] Laibach, however, retained a special position within the framework of the NSK. It was the root from which other groups sprang, and also the one most exposed to political and public adversity. At the same time, from the very beginning, Laibach's members remained individually anonymous, delegating the role of their voice to one of them and commonly answering interviews in writing. Even when the five members were individually identified, they dissociated Laibach from themselves as if it were an organization, a political party, or a state.

The theater component of the Neue Slowenische Kunst organization retained a similar anonymous character at the beginning, in part because its actors were appropriated from other, already existing, Slovenian theaters and it therefore was a different troupe with each new play. The group of painters called Irwin, which consisted of five persons, never strove to retain the same anonymous posture, however. Almost from the outset, they were identified by their names and pictures, working, exhibiting, and commenting on their works as individuals, and some of them also were active in the group of the NSK designers, New Collectivism. For this reason, they appeared more accessible, more benign, and more akin to other "standard" artists.

When founded in 1984, Neue Slowenische Kunst developed a complicated scheme of laws and a complex internal organizational structure. It started to function as an enlarged version of Laibach itself. In the years to come, Neue Slowenische Kunst was involved in music, painting, installation art, theater, design, television, and video, to name just a few media, transgressing traditional divisions of genres and the need for a clear and individualized identity of the artists.

In short, it behaved as a veritable political party. In 1990, it started to issue "NSK State" passports,[30] proclaiming NSK embassies and consulates in various European cities—Moscow, Ghent, Venice, Berlin, Florence, Sarajevo, Amsterdam among them. Clearly, Laibach and Neue Slowenische Kunst filled a crucial cultural role in Slovenia and beyond at the moment of transition from socialism to postsocialism. To understand that role more fully, we must look at the broader context of what was going on in Yugoslavia.

"Ce à quoi vous aspirez comme révolutionnaires, c'est à un maître. Vous l'aurez."

On December 3, 1969, when revolutionary students at Vincennes attacked Jacques Lacan for his skeptical stance toward the idea of a new society, he responded by claiming that "revolutionary aspiration always ends in the discourse of a master. Experience is the proof of this." He added: "What you aspire to as revolutionaries is a master. You will have him."[31]

The situation in Yugoslavia in the 1980s was revolutionary, too: self-management socialism was supposed to become the beacon of an emergent social order with no equal in the world. Soon, however, the only support it could find was in faraway Third World lands whose friendship was based more on weapons sales than on ideology and the fascination with novel political theory. The incessant claims about the freedom of self-managers that were associated with the concurrent inconspicuous militarization of Yugoslav society were combined in Slovenia with the repeated promotion and praise of culture as the vehicle for Slovenian national identity. However, this culture now was neither the high culture of the urban communities nor the alternative culture of the younger generation of intellectuals, but the amateur culture of "culture lovers," of ordinary people who were now told that their choirs, creative writing, or amateur theater productions were artistically just as relevant as those of professional artists and that their efforts therefore warranted equal institutional support. In art and culture, people began to be valued according to their desire to be "creative," and not according to the professional or public evaluation of such creativity. Tito was eulogized, and his speeches were to be included in the school curricula, with newspapers continually printing reports of various self-defense activities of the populace at large.

It was within such an atmosphere that Laibach appeared and in a few years became the leitmotif of numerous cultural and political debates, controversies, and criticisms. The public attitude toward the group was generally negative or ambiguous. Were they Nazis? Were they anti-Nazis? Were they a totalitarian group, or were they mocking the extant system—and if the latter was the case, why was everybody made to feel so uncomfortable?[32]

In Slovenia, culture was always a sacrosanct national realm in which excesses were allowed and expected, but only as long as they remained within the traditional bourgeois moral and political confines. Although it had become more intellectual, more cosmopolitan, and more progressive, in retrospect it is clear that Slovenian culture under socialism nonetheless continued to be traditionally bourgeois. The importance that the theorists of self-management populism ascribed to amateur culture often meant privileging a transmogrified folk culture and its aesthetic tastes, bringing Yugoslavia, which previously was so averse to the Soviet bloc type of culture, into its close proximity. The more backward the environment, the greater the popular support that such a tendency received, for it not only provided entertainment, but also built on national and populist sentiments.

The gap between urban and provincial culture, indirectly promoted by the provincialism and narrow-mindedness of the promoters of self-management, increased throughout the 1980s. Not only was a gap widening in Yugoslavia between the north, which was slowly entering the postindustrial age, and the south, which was remaining or drifting back into premodern times, but a similar gap was emerging between the urbanites and the peasants, workers, and petty bureaucrats.

The suffocating populism of the self-management era of the late 1970s revealed itself later as the period of late socialism and hence as the nascent stage of postsocialism, the period of disintegration of the previously stable social and political system, which saw in the future nothing but an infinite development. In this respect, self-management socialism was a typically modern social project. In Slovenia, at least, during the 1980s, no radical remedies were offered, no firm political action was taken against opponents, and no politician dared to criticize publicly the regime's intellectual critics. A cynicism similar to that found during the same decade in Hungary set in. For example, in Slovenia, it was not only the critics of self-management who argued that it was a mistake. Its official defenders tacitly agreed with them, increasingly identifying self-management with the Belgrade government. At the same time, nobody knew how to reverse its further expansion, for the only two options existing until then were either to offer a critique from within the system and pursue the infinite and often futile attempt at change from within the institutions themselves or to offer a dissident critique that simply equated self-management with Soviet-style "actually existing socialism." Neither of the two options was viable. The first never achieved much outside narrow intellectual circles, and the second simplified matters to the extreme, for even if populist, Yugoslavia and especially Slovenia during the 1980s hardly resembled Honecker's German Democratic Republic, Husak's Czechoslovakia, or Jaruzelski's Poland.

In this muddied cultural pond, the appearance of Laibach made waves. It represented an unprecedented transgression not only of quotidian social norms but also of those appertaining to the artistic social universe. What Laibach thus seemed to offer to its adherents and critics alike was a master, but a master who intentionally restricted his activity to the symbolic realms of music and culture and never transgressed their frontiers, in spite of frequent statements that gave a semblance of the opposite.

The group employed a totalitarian discourse, equated art with politics, quoted Hitler, praised law and order, denigrated artistic freedom—all in the name of art. Before in Slovenian history, artists may often have been moral misfits, but they hardly ever transgressed the narrow borders of provincial bohemia. This time, self-management politicians who, in accordance with this political theory, were for the most part amateurs in cultural politics, had to defend artistic freedom from a group of people who for all practical purposes were themselves artists. Furthermore, the members of Laibach were intellectuals, a segment of society that throughout Slovenian history defended artistic freedom, often either from politics or from the church. The Laibach group reversed such familiar perceptions of what an artist, art, freedom, and artistic freedom are.

Even as the official ideological discourse overflowed with words such as "freedom," "liberty," "decision making," "equality," "the nonconflictual solving of social problems," and so on, social reality increasingly became oppressive. Nonetheless, this course of events—with the exception of the circle around the revue *Problemi*—met with no discourse capable of theorizing these ongoing historical processes without being immediately assimilated into the ruling discourse. The discourse of self-management was like AIDS: there was no traditional way to combat it. With its incessant praise and promotion of freedom and the peaceful and nonconflictual adjustments of various interests, it never permitted any straightforward conflict.

Laibach, however, found a discursive tool with which it was able to overcome symbolically the deadlock between a social reality that had drifted into populist totalitarianism and the discursive reality of an official ideology in which the official discourse promoted unlimited freedom. It overcame the deadlock by bringing the official discourse to its final limits. If, for example, the official ideology of self-management praised art as the highest form of creativity (following in this respect the theories of the young Marx), it simultaneously had to conceal the fact that it *also* claimed (as a Marxist theory) that art *may have*—and indeed must have—political consequences. If society is a whole of interrelated structural relations that are based on class antagonisms, it makes no sense to speak of nonpoliticized art, nonideological art history, "pure science," and so on. Such claims only conceal the extant social relations of art, science, or the humanities, turning them into forms of consciousness that are more bourgeois than they are (or were) in bourgeois countries. Laibach shattered this illusion by overtly claiming that art *is* politics, and that artists *are* politicians.

A good case in point is a Xerox copy that Dejan Knez, a member of the Laibach group, made in 1981 and sent to his friends as a New Year's card. On the copy, he superimposed the picture *La condition humaine* (1933) by René Magritte on the background of a photograph depicting Hitler's rise

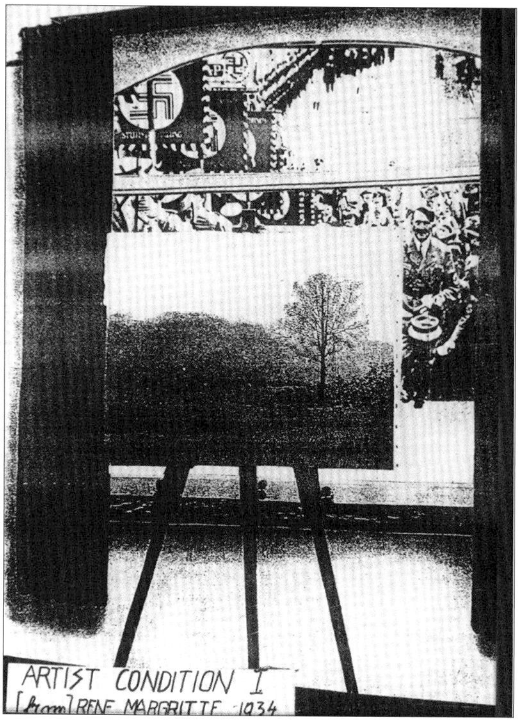

Figure 38 Dejan Knez, *Artist Condition I*, 1981, A4 Xerox copy.

to power. On the Xerox copy he wrote "Artist Condition" and "1934" (Figure 38).

Knez here showed the direct relationship between art and ideology, between the symbolic reality of Magritte's painting, the personal reality of the artist, and the historical reality of Hitler's ascent to the German and global political stage that framed the Surrealist painting and its nonpoliticized *paysage* and formed its literal background. He juxtaposed in a brutally direct way two social spheres that modernity has held separate since the advent of Dutch painting and the Reformation, but that Romanticism and anarchist aesthetics brought together again. In contradistinction to traditional modernist criticism of politics, which either used irony and Aesopian language or ignored politics altogether, and also in contradistinction to Walter Benjamin's "politicization of art" (as in Brecht, for example), Knez's postmodern approach repeated that of the early avant-garde artists such as Malevich and Lissitzky, who presented in their art two realities, the link between which was now severed, for they possessed no obvious common or shared space.

Knez's work, as a parallel to and a premonition of Laibach's, revealed at the same time a detached position from which the artist consciously avoided the typical gesture of modernist partisan art, presenting one's own subjective position. The formerly homogeneous social space had now disintegrated, shattered into a series of fragments, and in that space, the modernist partisan position was impotent, for it was immediately integrated into the system it aimed to criticize. In another part of Europe and in a much larger country, one where artists had almost none of the influence or effect on political events that they had in Slovenia, another artist explained the postmodern situation of the 1980s in a related way: "While there is no obvious mockery or irony in my work, there is also no evident enthusiasm. I always just showed things the way I saw them—as a bystander, not an advocate or ardent participant."[33] Laibach, too, was neither an advocate nor an ardent participant, but it certainly was a very loud and unpleasant bystander.

Dejan Knez's gesture revealed not only a new consciousness concerning the relation between and integration of politics and art, but also a novel approach to different media. Never before had artists in Slovenia drifted so easily between different artistic genres, and only at the time of the historical avant-gardes did they so easily slide between high and low culture. Although it appeared initially that their combinations of music, painting, installations, theory, philosophy, theater, film, video, design, and architecture (not to mention lifestyle) followed the tradition of the historical avant-gardes, it would be more proper to call this "mixed media" in the sense in which Fredric Jameson uses the term: In "'mixed media' (the contemporary equivalent of the *Gesamtkunstwerk* . . .), the 'mix' comes first and redefines the media involved by implication a posteriori."[34] It is true that in retrospect, the works of Laibach and the groups that merged in 1984 to form the Neue Slowenische Kunst organization appear to be less a Wagnerian and Romanticist *Gesamtkunstwerk* or the honest attempts of the historical avant-gardes to accomplish the same aim—with their endeavors resulting in the juxtaposition of paintings and theater, poetry and music, and so on—than a mixture of various media that in the meantime have attained an unprecedented measure of exchangeability via history. The recent "pictorial turn" not only has enhanced the role of the image, but also has collapsed various artistic and cultural genres.

Rrose IRWIN Sélavy

The component of the Neue Slowenische Kunst organization that deals predominantly with graphic media is the group called Irwin. In 1920,

Marcel Duchamp created one of his many puns, Rrose Sélavy, thereby referring to a fictitious person whom he impersonated. In 1983, the group Rrose IRWIN Sélavy, which eventually deconstructed its name, first to R IRWIN S and finally simply to Irwin, had its first exhibition in the student discotheque F.V., which also served as an exhibition place for graffiti art—and in fact the early work of the group members also partly belonged to that genre. It was also strongly related to the simultaneous work of the Belgrade artist Goran Djordjević, who experimented with the relation between the copy and the original. Djordjević's works were completely international, with a direct link to similar trends in New York, and devoid of any detectable connections with his native Serbia. Rrose IRWIN Sélavy also used procedures such as accentuating the tension between the original and the copy as a means of artistic expression and subversion of the role of the author and artist, but in the socialist circumstances of Slovenia in the early 1980s, such acts had only theoretical relevance, for no real market existed for the kind of works that the group executed. Even more than in the case of punk music, the artistic act here bore mostly an intellectual significance and had no repercussions on the extant art market in Slovenia.

Early paintings and installations by Rrose IRWIN Sélavy visibly echoed the ideas of Djordjević. They betrayed the strong presence of Malevich's motifs and his practice of exhibiting paintings as if they were icons (Figure 39). Past works by others also continually kept appearing, but remade, recontextualized, and appropriated within a different, usually pronouncedly Slovenian, framework, thereby also exhibiting similarities with the concurrent Trans-Avantgarde movement in Italy and its equivalents in West Germany. A good example of this technique of appropriation and recontextualization in terms of national and local traits is the use Irwin made of a well-known painting by the Slovenian artist Ivana Kobilca, *Woman Drinking Coffee* (1888). The Laibach group first used a black-and-white graphic image of the same painting for its exhibition in 1983, with the same work reappearing as *Woman Drinking Coffee* (1989) painted by Irwin, only this time crossed over with Suprematist geometric forms. Another such appropriation was *The Red Districts* series (1985–89), in which the group copied engravings and graphics by Janez Knez, impregnated them with pig blood, and asked Janez Knez to sign them (see Plate 4).

Such motifs very often reappeared in different contexts, executed for different occasions, including the sets for Laibach concerts, the jackets of Laibach LPs, concert posters, and stage designs for the theater group that be-

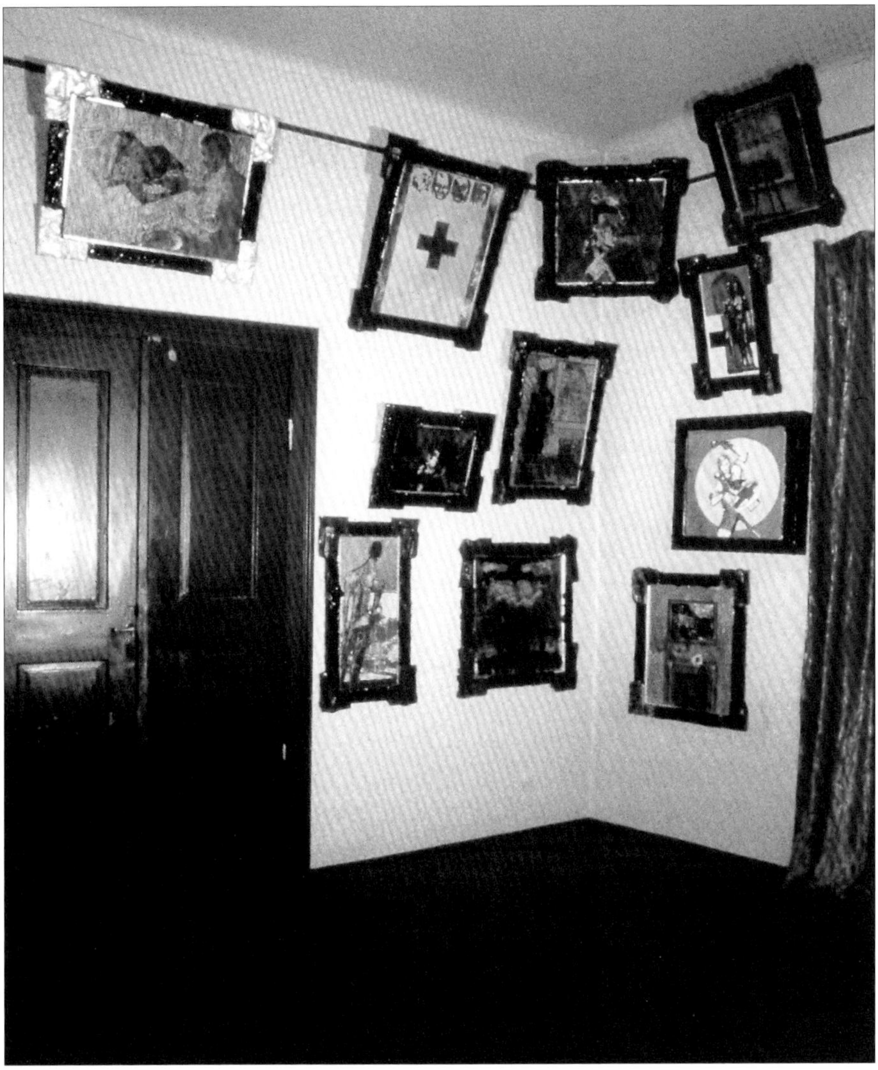

Figure 39 Irwin, exhibition in a private apartment in Ljubljana, 1985.

came a part of the NSK in 1984. Another favorite motif was the sower, the history of which goes back to Jean-François Millet's first *Sower* of 1850. In 1907, the Slovenian Impressionist painter Ivan Grohar created his own *Sower*, which became an archetypal painting for Slovenian art history, a status it shared with the original *Woman Drinking Coffee*. Laibach executed its *Sower* in 1982 (Figure 40). Since 1985, the motif has been used by the Irwin group, with the sower appearing sometimes alone (Figure 41), sometimes as part of a pair, and in the 1990 project *Laibach Kunst* as a series of paintings within

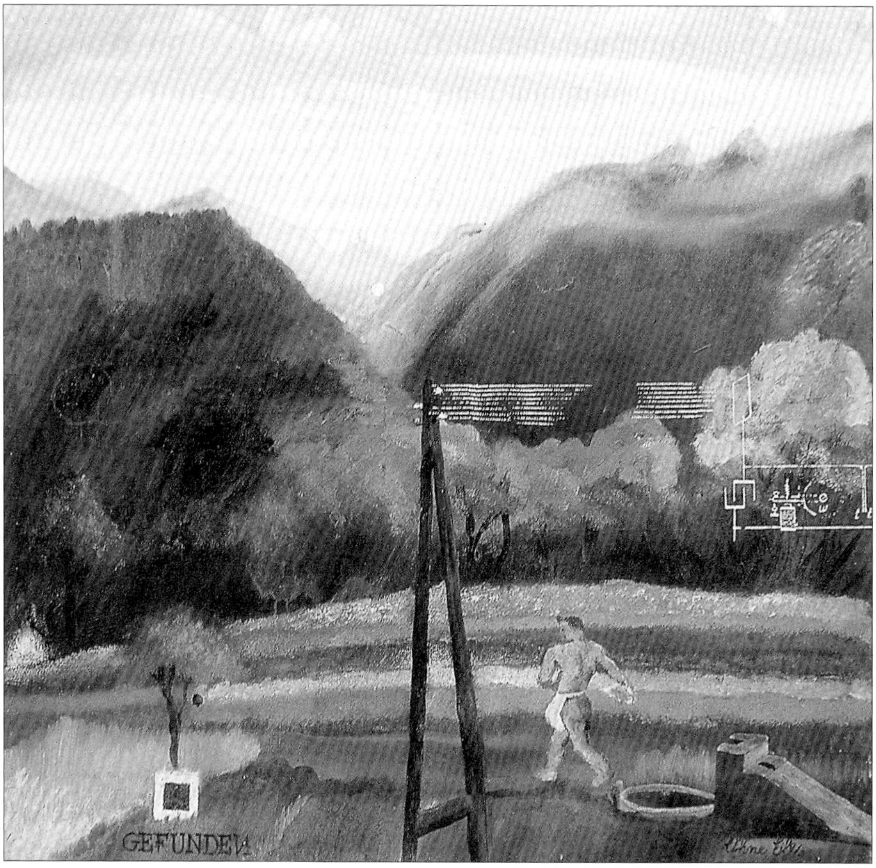

Figure 40 Laibach, *The Sower,* 1982, oil on canvas, 71 × 71 cm. Collection of Neil K. Rector.

paintings that resemble Magritte's *La condition humaine* and that echo at the same time the Xerox from 1981 by Dejan Knez.

Most of the time, Irwin's paintings or mixed-media works were literally framed by the cross and by the coal from the native town of the Laibach group, Trbovlje (Figure 42). The picture frames were actually made of pieces of coal, with the four corners constricting the frame into a cross. On other occasions, the four corners of the frame were made from coal. The motif of the sower is also seen on the relief (this time made exclusively from coal) for the jacket of the Laibach LP *Slovenian Acropolis* (Figure 43), made by the New Collectivism group of NSK.

Since the beginning, the members of the Irwin group have collaborated with Laibach, which is also the reason not only for the frequently

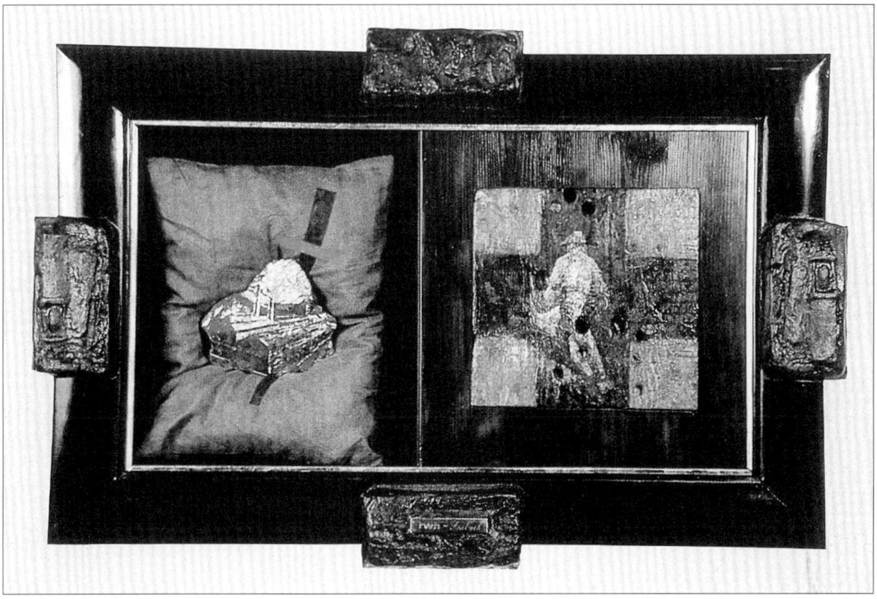

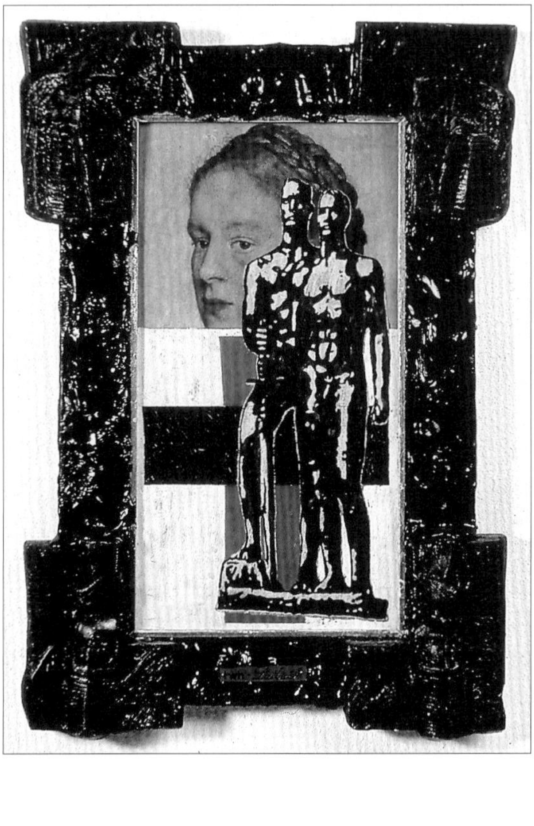

Figure 41 Irwin, *Sower II,* 1989, mixed media, 62 × 93 cm.

Figure 42 Irwin, *Malevich between the Two Wars,* 1984, mixed media, 55 × 28 cm. Collection of the artists (photo: Franci Virant).

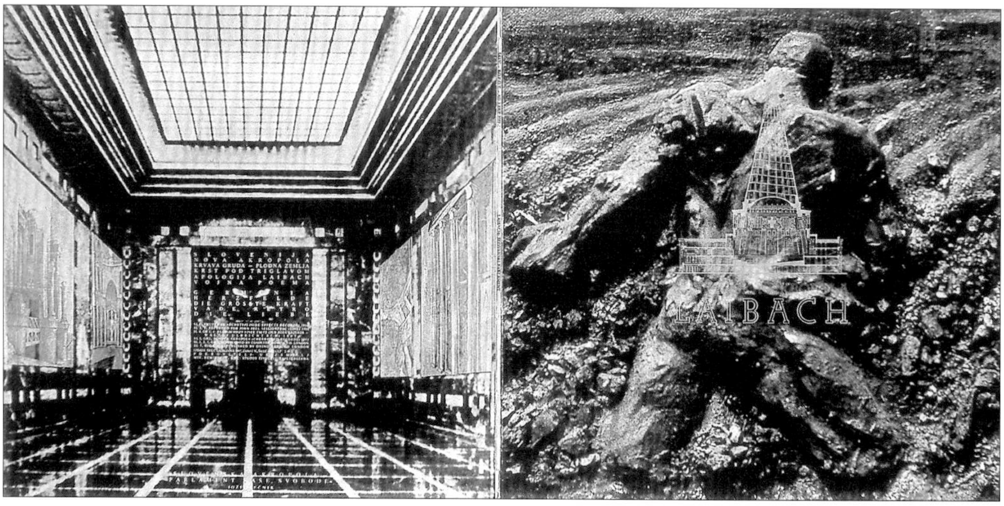

Figure 43 Laibach, the jacket for the Laibach LP *Slovenian Acropolis,* Ljubljana: ŠKUC N.o.i.s.e., 1987. In the center is an outline of Plečnik's Slovenian Parliament. Design New Collectivism.

obscure authorship of their works (appearing sometimes signed by Laibach, sometimes by Laibach Kunst, and, of course, sometimes by Irwin), but also for their great resemblance. The activity of Laibach and the members of Irwin was intertwined even before NSK formally came into existence.

A pronounced feature of Irwin's art is its use of national and folk motifs, ranging from those from Slovenian Baroque churches to the archetypal images from the history of Slovenian art and the motif of the Slovenian Parliament developed in 1947 by the Slovenian Neoclassicist architect Jože Plečnik (see Figure 43). Although Laibach, too, frequently related to Slovenia and Slovenian culture, it was international almost from its very beginning. However, Irwin, because of the nature of the visual medium it used, made every possible use of Slovenian national motifs, proclaiming as its credo: "There exists Greek, German, French art and not art in itself. Our art will be the better the more Slovenian it will be."[35] In this respect, Irwin followed the precept of Achille Bonito Oliva that "the current artist has no intention of losing himself behind the homologation of a uniform language, but aims at recovering an identity corresponding to the 'genius loci' that inhabits his particular culture."[36] What has been claimed of Anselm Kiefer would be equally valid for Irwin, for each offers us "both art and history as an incomplete mosaic, never adding up to a whole. It must be emphasized that Kiefer deconstructs German tradition and modern artistic tradition simultaneously, showing that for all its momentousness there is something hollow in both, since neither affords the perspective necessary to create a total world picture."[37] Irwin did the same with Slovenian artistic tradition and visibly helped to integrate folk, popular, and elite art into what started to function as an integrated whole, no longer excommunicating one another. In fact, Kiefer was another important influence in Irwin's work. Their painting *Resurrection of the Theater of the Sisters of Scipio Nasica* (1984–85) (see Plate 8) is an explicit remake and homage to the German artist.

However, the most obvious feature of Irwin's work is its infinite eclecticism. The works of Duchamp and Malevich,[38] Magritte and Landseer, Slovenian Baroque Madonnas and Nazi Kunst motifs, Lenins and Stalins—they all appear on various Irwin paintings, installations, and art objects. Yet Irwin saw the artistic eclecticism professed by the artistic trends of the 1980s as synonymous with Slovenian culture: "Traditionally Slovenian artists, as well as the Yugoslav ones, have been under the predominant influence of three or four cultures. . . . It is clear now that what constitutes the specificity of Slovenian culture is incessant eclecticism. We therefore defined ourselves as the carriers of organic eclecticism."[39]

Irwin explicitly referred to its art as "Trans-Avantgarde," and also "postmodern(ist)" (a self-designation also used by Laibach), introducing in its work the "retro" principle,[40] the method of using and referring to past works, trends, and ideas, using them indiscriminately, but nonetheless with the clear aim of promoting Slovenian culture. In many of its paintings and installations, Irwin used a picture of a stag, which was very familiar to the Slovenian audience, although in fact the picture the painters used (and copied) was by the Scottish painter Sir Edward Landseer. In addition to its use of ideas and works by Goran Djordjević, Irwin employed the performances of another Belgrade artist, Raša Todosijević, *Was ist Kunst?* (see Figure 23), using its title as the title of an artistic project that was started in 1985 and consisted of exhibitions and approximately a hundred paintings, posters, and photographs (see Plate 8). One of their frequent motifs was also the so-called Laibach worker, a black-and-white image of an industrial worker, with smokestacks in the background and the Laibach logotype in the foreground (Figure 44). While Laibach was more industrial, Irwin was more rural, frequently making use of images of the Slovenian countryside, the sower, and so on, all in an attempt to bring to life the Slovenian Athens of which Josip Vidmar wrote back in 1932.[41]

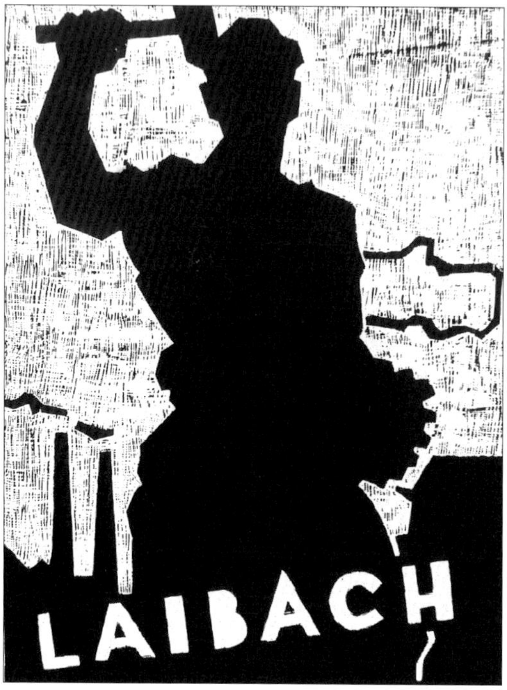

Figure 44 Laibach, *The Metal Worker,* 1980, woodcut, 59 × 43 cm. Design New Collectivism.

During the 1980s, Irwin was probably the least problematic segment of NSK politically. Its works were exhibited worldwide and often were seen as related to somewhat similar works of the Russian artists. In recent years, Irwin has created more installation art, drifting away from easel painting.

"Theater Is the State"

One of the many sources of the Neue Slowenische Kunst organization has been the historical or classical avant-gardes. Not only Malevich and Suprematism and Constructivism, but also Italian Futurism and the Slovenian avant-gardes of the early 1920s were an important ingredient of NSK ideas. The NSK group that was, in this respect, the most visibly dependent on the Slovenian avant-gardists was the theater group. The Theater of the Sisters of Scipio Nasica[42] came into existence performatively. On October 13, 1983, the Act of Foundation was proclaimed, in which the self-liquidation of the theater was announced in four years' time. The "First Sisterly Letter" of 1983–84 states: "Theater is not an empty space. Theater is the State."[43] In the Act of Foundation, the theater publicly announced that it would not

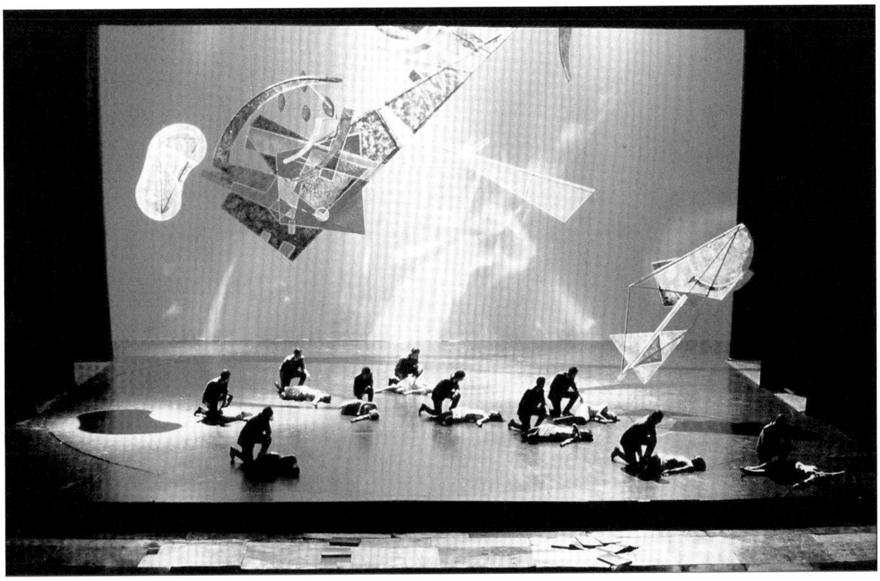

Figure 45 The Theater of the Sisters of Scipio Nasica, *Baptism under Triglav,* Cankarjev dom Cultural and Congress Center, Ljubljana, 1986 (photo: Marko Modic).

have a stage of its own, but would unite all theater institutions in Slovenia. In the years of its existence, some of its plays were staged in private apartments with a very limited audience, and one, the biggest and also the most controversial, the "retro-garde event *Baptism under Triglav* (Figure 45; see Plate 9) was presented on the big stage of Cankarjev Dom, the large conference and arts center in Ljubljana. Like Irwin and Laibach, the theater group employed extant motifs, in the case of *Baptism under Triglav,* the poem "Baptism at the Savica Waterfall" by the Slovenian Romantic poet France Prešeren (1800–1849). The play was a postmodern spectacle using all the technical possibilities offered by the newly built stage. Constructivist motifs, the Malevich-Laibach black cross, fireworks, and other effects were used, leaving the elite theatergoers astonished and confused. It was evident to everybody that something unprecedented was happening, but it was very difficult for the audience or the critics to define exactly what it was, except that it certainly exploited the letter and the spirit of the poem.

At the start, a replica of Vladimir Tatlin's *Monument to the Third International* (1919–20) appeared on the stage, proving in hindsight William Tucker's words that the character of this project, "like so much Russian Con-

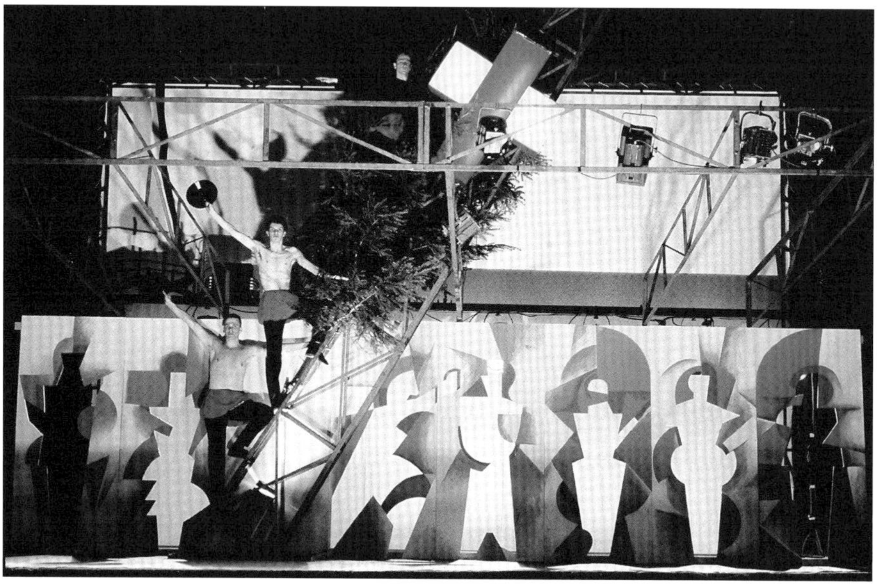

Figure 46 The Red Pilot Cosmokinetic Theater, *The Zenith Ballet Observatory*, Ljubljana, 1988.

structivist work, is closer to stage design than to sculpture, or architectural engineering."[44] What followed was a detached presentation of the conflict between the church and the main character and his beloved, exposing the incessant power play between the state (or church) and the individual, whether an artist or a free spirit—in whatever case, the Other. The theater production affirmed in this play what Laibach and its adherents had argued all along: that art is a form of politics and that in Slovenia, art always has a relation to ideology and hence to politics.

The Red Pilot Cosmokinetic Theater (named after the Slovenian avant-garde revue *Red Pilot* of 1922), which emerged after the dissolution of the Theater of the Sisters of Scipio Nasica, staged a Futurist ballet, *The Zenith Ballet Observatory*, in 1988[45] (Figure 46). The last project of the Red Pilot Theater was *The Zenith Drama Observatory* of the same year, which took place on an abandoned track of Ljubljana railroad station in a railroad car that was rebuilt like an SS-20 rocket (Figures 47 and 48). The audience was led into the car in complete darkness, amid a banging on the metal walls of the car that resembled the herding of Jews into similar trains on their way to concentration camps. The plot of the play was taken from T. S. Eliot's theater piece *Murder in the Cathedral* and was related to issues of the Catholic

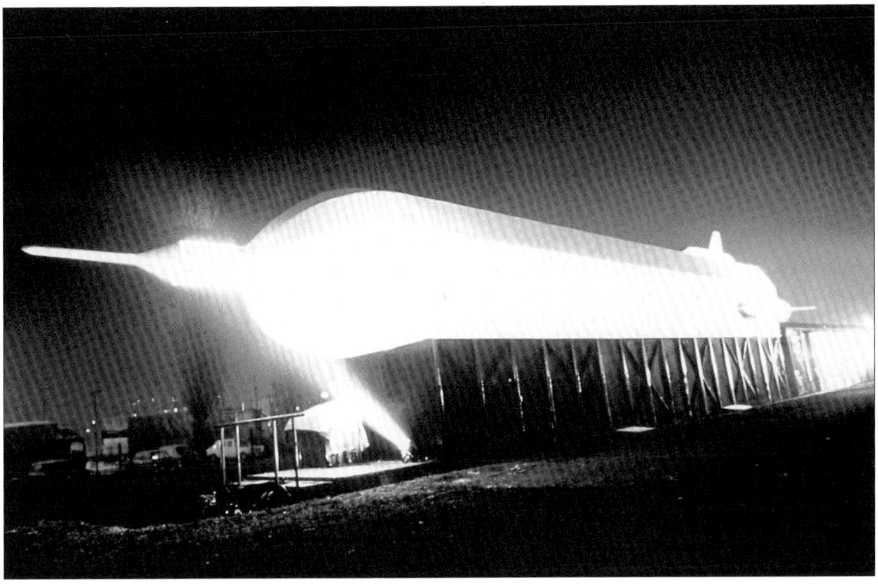

Figure 47 The Red Pilot Cosmokinetic Theater, *The Zenith Drama Observatory*, Ljubljana, 1988. In coproduction with Mladinsko Theater, Ljubljana (photo: Franci Virant).

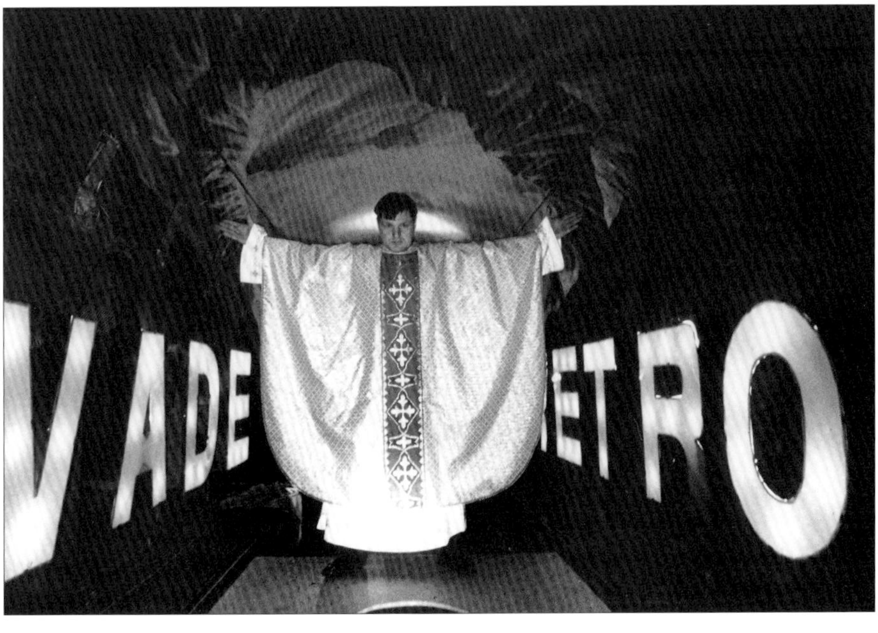

Figure 48 The Red Pilot Cosmokinetic Theater, *The Zenith Drama Observatory*, Ljubljana, 1988, interior (photo: Franci Virant).

Church, power, belief, and ideology. At the end of the performance, a part of the car started to move, literally squeezing the audience out of it. The play toured Europe on railroad tracks, and in Zagreb in March 1990, the car, intended for "Western Yugoslavia," was reunited with its Eastern counterpart, which was "launched" in Subotica, north of Belgrade.

New Collectivism

In the late 1980s, a crucial part of the Neue Slowenische Kunst organization became the New Collectivism group. It was founded in 1984 and consisted of a technical director and one representative each from Laibach, Irwin, and the Theater of the Sisters of Scipio Nasica. Its purpose was to "become a technical group that would create the public image of the NSK and images of the Slovenian and global cultural and political institutions."[46] In the years to come, the principal activity of the group was to design posters, LP jackets, and so on for the three main groups of NSK. Thus, its activity was publicly visible and useful to NSK, but still modest and auxiliary in comparison with the other constituent groups' works and public appearances.

All this changed drastically in 1987 when the New Collectivism group designed the official poster for the Day of Youth Festival, the annual youth festival celebrating Tito's birthday. Although Tito had been dead since 1980, the youth festival in Belgrade still carried much political weight, for it symbolized Tito's socialist and federal legacy in Yugoslavia and the equality of different nations and ethnic groups in that economically, ethnically, and culturally disparate country. In short, it was one of the main, if not the main, public manifestations of the common Yugoslav spirit, the importance of which was further enhanced by the fact that it was devoted to and carried out by youths coming from various parts of the country. "The youth," Tito used to say, was supposed to be "our future."

New Collectivism submitted their poster on the basis of a public competition and received first prize. But to a reader of a Belgrade daily in which the poster was reproduced, the picture seemed familiar. On investigation, he discovered that the poster (see Figure 6) was, in fact, a remake of the Nazi painting *The Third Reich* by Richard Klein, from 1936. As was to be expected, a huge scandal broke out, and the Slovenian political leadership was accused of complicity in this act of blasphemy, especially since Slovenian public opinion, in spite of not being fond of Nazism, perceived the designers as Slovenians first and as guilty provocateurs second. This was the second half of the

1980s, and the relations between the central government in Belgrade and Slovenia were already tense. Since by that time the decentralized political system that formed a part of the self-management project was firmly in place, the federal government and its courts could not touch Slovenian citizens on the territory of Slovenia. The main Slovenian daily, *Delo*, announced a year later, in 1988, that the prosecutor's office had concluded that what was at stake "was nothing more than a manner of artistic expression."[47]

Again the work of an NSK group was interpreted as a purely artistic work, in spite of possessing all the characteristics of an ideological and political artifact. Although the prosecutor's decision was certainly also politically motivated, since acquitting the defendants meant a rebuff of the federal government and the federal League of Communists, the reason given was the traditional "freedom of artistic expression" argument.

The affair with the Day of Youth Festival poster raised uncomfortable questions, the main one being how it was possible that a remake of a Nazi poster—in a country that had suffered so much from National Socialism—could be selected as the best. It was obvious that Yugoslav political reality in the 1980s must have had much in common with Nazism, in spite of fascist ideology being portrayed as the central political and ideological adversary, be it in Nazi Germany or in some postwar parliamentary democracies. New Collectivism defended its act in the following way:

> The "Day of Youth" poster has for ever erased the negative symbolics of the dark recent past. The swastika was covered by a five-pointed star and the blue-white-red Yugoslav flag, just as the [Yugoslav] Partisans, under the cover of night, used to strike out Fascist symbols with a red star. The Nazi coat of arms has been erased, to be replaced by the six torches of the six Yugoslav nations. The German eagle has been supplanted by the symbol of peace—the white dove.[48]

Epilogue

The Neue Slowenische Kunst organization also comprised the Department of Pure and Practical Philosophy, a group of video artists (Retrovision), and a group of architects (The Builders), but Laibach, Irwin, the Theater of the Sisters of Scipio Nasica, reappearing later under other names, and New Collectivism were and remain the focal groups. In the early 1990s, the NSK organization slowly weakened, as befits an avant-garde movement. This trend gained a further impetus from the disintegration of Yugoslavia and, especially, from the independence of Slovenia and the transformation of the political system into a parliamentary democracy. The old foes were gone, and the NSK groups found themselves in a void, as did many other artists in the postsocialist period. As the Slovenian state emerged as an independent political entity, the poetic potential of the NSK state declined. As socialism disappeared, the artistic potential of ideological and politicized discourse also diminished.

In the late 1980s and early 1990s, Laibach and NSK sided with the Russian views on the West, bringing its imagery closer to that of its Russian contemporaries who reproved the effects of capitalism. Nonetheless, this did not last, because in Russia proper such a trend diminished, as well. In the past decade, Laibach and the other NSK groups no longer have employed German as their principal language, but have switched to English instead, in this way symptomatically revealing their displacement from the context of the continental Europe of the 1980s into the more global, English-speaking context of the 1990s.

The New Collectivism has become a somewhat more traditional designers' studio, although in its present work it still possesses features that are immediately recognizable. In the late 1990s, the Laibach group found a new target for its music and texts: the Catholic Church, which in Slovenia has been attempting to regain and to consolidate its power and political influence.[49]

How are we to assess the effect that Laibach and the Neue Slowenische Kunst organization as a whole had on political changes in Slovenia in the 1980s? In the period of late self-management socialism and the period of postsocialism in Slovenia and Yugoslavia, Laibach and NSK emerged and existed in a unique situation. Slovenia is so small that every cultural or political event has a visible effect, and art and culture were partial surrogates for a national state that did not yet exist. Under the conditions of self-management socialism, every public act thus became a political act. That is why Laibach found it easy to claim that "politics is the highest and all-encompassing art and we, who create contemporary Slovenian art, consider ourselves to be politicians."[50]

The process of the Slovenian nation becoming a nation-state may also shed some light on the obsession with the state present in the ideas of Laibach and the whole of NSK at that time, ideas that were materialized in the NSK "state in time" with its passports, stamps, and embassies and that allowed

NSK members and supporters to create and carry on an imaginary state that at the same time possessed visible symbols of a real political entity. Previous Slovenian intellectuals thought that Slovenia, because of its tiny size, could make a mark in Europe only via culture, and NSK, in its own way, to a certain extent actually carried out this project. Laibach and NSK thus formed one of the "new civil movements" that appeared at approximately the same time in various parts of Europe.

Slovenia, in which the tectonic upheavals of the historic demise of socialism manifested themselves as the decentralizing movements and the centrifugal forces induced by self-management socialism, slowly distanced itself from the rest of Yugoslavia and the idea of Yugoslavia as such. In the 1980s, art and culture in Slovenia, perhaps for the last time, played a political role equal to or exceeding that of political groups and parties, for they formed a social realm that in Slovenia always found public support. In Yugoslavia, as in other socialist countries, social attitudes and political ideas that could not be enunciated in political discourse proper could be manifested in art and culture. As a crucial part of the so-called alternative culture or subculture, Laibach and NSK were eloquent, enigmatic, and at the same time persuasive critics of a political frame of mind that was visibly disintegrating, but at that time rarely encountered a discourse that would offer a new cognitive mapping and would "make sense" of what was going on in those years. In that specific Slovenian late socialist and then postsocialist situation, Laibach and NSK offered a mapping that came as close as any to what art and culture can offer in a time of such profound historical change.

Notes

1. Vidmar's ideas regarding the role of culture were influenced by Johann Gottfried von Herder.

2. Josip Vidmar, *Kulturni problemi slovenstva* (Ljubljana: Tiskovna zadruga, 1932), p. 92.

3. For example, a selection of Walter Benjamin's essays was published in Belgrade in 1960, while the first American edition (*Illuminations*) appeared in 1968, and the first volume in French in 1966.

4. Milan Butina, in "Milan Golob in Robert Lozar, Pogovor z Milanom Butino: Interview with Milan Butina," *Likovne besede: Artwords* (Ljubljana), nos. 35, 36, 37 (May 1996): 134.

5. Milan Butina on TV Slovenia 1, September 4, 1994.

6. Janez Knez lived in Trbovlje, in the heart of the coal-mining area of central Slovenia. He earned much of his living executing realist (and what would today be viewed as Socialist Realist) graphics and frescoes for the local mining companies and mining unions.

7. *Leksikon* (Ljubljana: Cankarjeva založba, 1988), p. 442.

8. Leslie Holmes, *Post-Communism: An Introduction* (Cambridge: Polity Press, 1997), pp. 50–51.

9. Edvard Kardelj, *Self-Management and the Political System*, trans. Margot Milosavljević and Boško Milosavljević (Belgrade: Socialist Thought and Practice, 1980), p. 67.

10. For a comprehensive survey of Slovenian modern art, see Steven A. Mansbach, *Modern Art in Eastern Europe: From the Baltic to the Balkans, ca. 1890–1939* (Cambridge: Cambridge University Press, 1999), esp. pp. 205–17.

11. Ljubljana, the Slovenian capital and largest city, which now has approximately 270,000 inhabitants, had 123,000 in 1948.

12. Cultural and political changes in Slovenia during this time are discussed in more detail in Aleš Erjavec and Marina Gržinić, *Ljubljana, Ljubljana: The Eighties in Slovene Art and Culture* (Ljubljana: Mladinska knjiga, 1991).

13. Sabrina Petra Ramet, "Democratization in Slovenia—the Second Stage," in *Politics, Power, and the Struggle for Democracy in South-East Europe*, edited by Karen Dawisha and Bruce Parrott (Cambridge: Cambridge University Press, 1997), p. 190.

14. Milan Knížák, in "Milan Knížák: Kill Yourself and Fly. An Interview by Johan Pijnappel," *Art and Design: New Art from Eastern Europe*, no. 35 (1994): 37.

15. A statement to the author in Budapest on October 4, 1995.

16. Quoted in *Neue Slowenische Kunst* (Zagreb: Grafički zavod Hrvatske, 1991), pp. 121–22.

17. Quoted in Erjavec and Gržinić, *Ljubljana, Ljubljana*, p. 92.

18. Quoted in *Neue Slowenische Kunst*, p. 46.

19. Quoted in *Neue Slowenische Kunst*, p. 21.

20. Andreja Potokar, "Pank u Lublan," in *Punk pod Slovenci*, edited by Nela Malečkar and Tomaž Mastnak (Ljubljana: RK ZSMS & UK ZSMS, 1984), p. 32.

21. "In Britain, heavy industry was so associated in the popular consciousness with certainties like the Empire that its decline and the end of the associated lifestyles (hard as they were) caused a (temporary) outpouring of sentiment and a sense of loss far beyond the 'devastated' labor movement and the 'devastated' communities. In Slovenia, the development of more media-friendly high-technology sectors is celebrated while heavy industry is seen as a source of pollution and embarrassment at odds with the self-image of the 'new' post-socialist Slovenia." Alexei Monroe, "Laibach & NSK: Industrial Diagnoses of Post-Socialism," *M'ars* (Ljubljana) 8, nos. 3–4 (1996): 18.

22. "Laibach: Deset točk konventa," *Neue Slowenische Kunst*, p. 18.

23. Mikhail N. Epstein, *After the Future: The Paradoxes of Postmodernism and Contemporary Russian Culture*, trans. with an introduction by Anesa Miller Pogacar (Amherst: University of Massachusetts Press, 1995), p. 202.

24. Slavoj Žižek, *Tarrying with the Negative: Kant, Hegel, and the Critique of Ideology* (Durham, N.C.: Duke University Press, 1993), p. 237.

25. Slavoj Žižek, "Why Are Laibach and NSK Not Fascists?" *M'ars* (Ljubljana) 5, nos. 3–4 (1993): 4, italics in the original. The following response to an interview question exemplifies the point made by Žižek:

> *Q:* In different parts of Europe (and Yugoslavia) you were "scolded" as fascists, Communists, spiritual terrorists, radicals, elitists, reactionaries, artists. . . . How do you comment upon such extreme designations?
>
> *A:* When the need arises, we allow ourselves the luxury to be aristocrats and plebeians, reactionaries and revolutionaries, legal and illegal, as we see fit in the place, time, and surroundings in which we have to work and act. (Quoted in *Neue Slowenische Kunst*, p. 51)

26. A related explanation would be that Laibach learned how to make use of totali-

tarian and classicist cultural effects without succumbing to their totalitarian political effects. What this means could be illustrated by Lionel Jospin's phrase "Yes, to the market economy; no, to the market society." Quoted in *Newsweek,* January 7, 2000, p. 64.

27. For a useful overview, see *Rocking the State: Rock Music and Politics in Eastern Europe and Russia,* edited by Sabrina Petra Ramet (Boulder: Westview Press, 1994).

28. Ramet calls Laibach "a pop totalitarian group." Sabrina Petra Ramet, "Making the Scene in Yugoslavia," in *Rocking the State,* p. 117.

29. See *Neue Slowenische Kunst,* p. 53.

30. Komar and Melamid made a similar project in 1977: *Language of TransState* and *Passport for TransState* for "a new nation created by the artists with passports, money, and a Declaration of Independence, etc. Anybody can be a citizen of TransState 'who in his own opinion falls outside the structure of all known functioning state systems.'" *Russian Samizdat Art,* assembled by Rimma Gerlovin and Valery Gerlovin (New York: Willis Locker and Owens, 1986), p. 119. See also "Appendix: TransState Documents," in Carter Ratcliff, *Komar & Melamid* (New York: Abbeville Press Publishers, 1988), pp. 198–204. The NSK project went a step further: since the NSK passports were being issued at the time of the disintegration of the former Soviet Union and Yugoslavia, in the ensuing confusion at border checkpoints, some people actually used these passports to travel around Europe. In 1994, NSK also issued a series of NSK stamps, which were then used as the official stamps of Slovenia.

31. Jacques Lacan, *Le séminaire (livre XVII): L'envers de la psychanalyse* (Paris: Seuil, 1991), p. 239.

32. It was not coincidental that the members of Laibach, and especially their later adherents, studied the works and deeds of Slovenian avant-garde artists from the early 1920s, who likewise met with a complete misunderstanding when introducing Constructivism into the Slovenian cultural atmosphere. The result of their nonstatus was that their works drifted into complete cultural oblivion. They were partially resurrected in the 1960s and especially in the early 1980s, when theoretical historical research on them coincided with a similar interest among the artists.

33. Erik Bulatov, in "Perestroika in New York: A Conversation with Erik Bulatov," *Arts Magazine* 64, no. 3 (November 1989): 85.

34. Fredric Jameson, *Postmodernism, or, The Cultural Logic of Late Capitalism* (London: Verso, 1991), p. 172.

35. Irwin, in *Neue Slowenische Kunst,* p. 87.

36. Achille Bonito Oliva, *The International Trans-avantgarde / La transavanguardia internazionale* (Milan: Giancarlo Politi Editore, 1982), p. 52.

37. Donald Kuspit, *The New Subjectivism: Art in the 1980s* (New York: De Capo Press, 1993), p. 109.

38. Irwin's exhibitions often resembled those of Malevich, especially his *Last Futurist Show 0.10* (1915–16).

39. Irwin, "Interview," *Neue Slowenische Kunst,* pp. 122–23. First published in *Opus International* (Paris) (September–October 1988).

40. The notion had already been introduced by Laibach, which defined its aim as the "triumph of 'monumental retro-avant-garde.'" Laibach, *Problemi* (Ljubljana), no. 6 (1985): 19.

41. *Slovenian Athens* was also the title of another Irwin project. Although conceived in 1985, it was actually carried out in 1991 as an exhibition in the Museum of Modern Art in Ljubljana. It consisted of works by forty-three artists who executed the motif of Grohar's *Sower* in various techniques and media.

42. The name of the theater was taken from a note in Artaud: "Scipio Nasica, the great pontiff, ordered that the theaters of Rome be leveled and their cellars filled up." Antonin Artaud, *Le Théâtre et son double, Œuvres Complètes,* vol. 4 (Paris: Gallimard, 1964), p. 32.

43. *Neue Slowenische Kunst,* p. 163.

44. William Tucker, *The Language of Sculpture* (London: Thames and Hudson, 1977), p. 123.

45. Named after the avant-garde revue *Zenit* (Zenith), which was published by Lubomir Micić from 1921 to 1926, first in Zagreb and then in Belgrade.

46. *Neue Slowenische Kunst,* p. 267.

47. *Delo,* February 11, 1988, reproduced in *Neue Slowenische Kunst,* p. 275.

48. New Collectivism, quoted in Erjavec and Gržinić, *Ljubljana, Ljubljana,* p. 90.

49. For this reason, Laibach's compact disc *Jesus Christ Superstar* (London: Mute Records, 1996) was condemned in 1997 by the Catholic archbishop of Ljubljana.

50. Laibach Kunst, *Problemi* (Ljubljana), no. 6 (1985): 23.

Hungarian Marginal Art in the Late Period of State Socialism

Péter György

When discussing the relation between postmodernism and late socialism or postsocialism and the issues arising in the Soviet art world in general, one faces complex questions of narrative, politics, and art. There are various theoretical discourses on postmodern art and on late state-socialist societies, for example, the narrative of Sovietology and, a few decades later, of transitology. There are classical and traditional theoretical fields such as history and art history. Other approaches, like cultural studies and the cultural anthropology of state-socialist societies, were developed only later. Every theoretical discourse has its own classification, expectations, and demands. Every tradition has its own system of language games, allusions, and linguistic horizons.

In this investigation of marginal and politicized art in Hungary during its transition from Soviet-style socialism to postsocialism, the methods and approaches I have mentioned above are intermingled.[1] The confluence of categories such as postmodernism and deconstruction, as well as those of the cultural logic of late capitalism and of late socialism, both promotes and frustrates our discussion. On the one hand, it appears promising to combine different theoretical traditions, but on the other, this may also give rise to a mutual misunderstanding, for there is no single ruling discourse in this field.

To avoid possible misunderstandings, double meanings, and confusions, I wish to offer a few introductory explanations and clarifications. To begin with, we need to remember that Socialist Realism is the common inheritance of Soviet art and of the former Soviet world. The essence of this common tradition is its totality:[2] Stalinism became the greatest and, from the Western point of view, an almost unimaginable "avant-gardist" artistic, social, and political practice. The historical practice of totalitarianism and the Wagnerian idea of *Gesamtkunstwerk* have been a common state practice in these countries and have even characterized the legacy of Socialist Realism. In fact, behind the Berlin Wall, there were stylistic similarities among different official artistic genres, making this common legacy a valid historical framework. In the former Soviet bloc countries, the tradition of total(itarian) art later became subjected to artistic interpretation: from the Russian artists Komar and Melamid to the Hungarian architects/artists, there were numerous successful attempts to create art that would be connected to individualistic, sarcastic, or highly parodic versions of this tradition.

The social meaning, function, and subsequent interpretation of this common legacy diverged drastically in different countries, however. Socialist Realism, like every social phenomenon, has a global and a local aspect. Consequently, the historical meaning of this term is closely associated with each country's own spiritual and political legacy. The national traditions of individual countries, as well as the characteristics of their presocialist artistic heritage, largely determined the reception and the original interpretation of the demands imposed by Socialist Realism. Hungarian society—and this is very significant concerning the interpretation of its marginal art—was drastically different, for example, from the society of the former Yugoslavia or that of the Soviet Union, where Socialist Realism and oppression of the different national traditions were deeply correlated. In all these cases, the art-historical meaning of the tradition of Socialist Realism and the notion of Soviet art depended on the local social context. The concrete local context influenced the abstract meanings of the Socialist Realist tradition and created the semantic field of its metaphorical usage. The local social, historical, and political context created the interpretative horizon for artistic invention. The Socialist Realist legacy thus was a common language, but every country made its own translations. Such a common language was also the heritage of the historical events and social circumstances of the Cold War. The differences that developed began to become especially apparent during the 1970s.

The historical meaning of Socialist Realism is inseparable from the political background of the history of art. We must recall that the history of Western high culture is connected with freedom of expression in the arts. In the political debates of the 1950s, such freedom became the characteristic difference between the Soviet art world and the art worlds dominated by Western values.[3] Today, we know that abstraction, namely, Abstract Expressionism and the New York School, has become a symbol of such a division. Abstract Expressionist artists—from Pollock to Rothko—became living myths on the eastern side of the Oder-Neisse border. For the Easterners, such artists signified the undamaged freedom of art and the right of personal expression, but in the Soviet art world, nobody had any idea about the origin of the broad success of the New York School, about the local context of their struggles against the market, or about the local meaning of the Leftist theoretical convictions of Clement Greenberg and Harold Rosenberg. Behind the Berlin Wall, nobody had any idea about the local context of market-based society. They were informed only about the independent, decontexualized artworks and about the symbols of what they perceived as "freedom." Very few knew anything about the American avant-garde artists' problem with the politics of the Cold War. The silent appropriation of this art by politics was almost impossible to imagine. Until recently, that is, before monographs by Serge Guilbaut, Diana Crane, and Erica Doss, almost nobody investigated the political conditions and the background of the New York School, the way these artists left the isolated avant-garde ghetto and became popular cultural heroes.[4] Thus, from the 1950s until the late 1970s, permanent mutual misunderstandings occurred. Before we can begin to analyze the artistic interpretation of Soviet art, the "post-utopian"[5] practice of the 1970s and 1980s, we therefore must take a brief look at the origins of these historical misunderstandings, because contemporary Western ideas and art—ideas such as postmodernism—were received through the structures of interpretation that these misunderstandings produced.

The nature of the Soviet art world had resulted from the political and economic divisions between the two worlds. These divisions produced the dearth of information that was characteristic of these decades. In the Soviet art world, nobody knew enough about the West, and in the West, nobody wanted to know much about the contemporary Soviet art world. This lack of information caused Easterners to entertain mistaken ideas about the decontextualized pieces of Western art and to underestimate themselves while admiring everything that came from the "other side" of the world. The members of the Soviet art world wanted to learn everything about Western art history. They wanted to follow all the Western fashions and movements. Only in rare cases did they believe in themselves as members of a universal art world. The artists of the Soviet art world naturally wanted to belong to universal art history, to this imagined community, but they remained imprisoned within their social reality and the divided world system. They wanted to emancipate themselves and dreamed about Western artistic freedom. Their self-emancipatory struggle became the common interpretive framework of these artists, the common ground of their self-evaluation, even as their concrete art-historical solutions were connected with local culture and with the levels of domination and political oppression that prevailed there.

Against the background of the aspirations, misunderstandings, and self-evaluations that had developed in the Soviet art world, the world of Socialist Realism, and, last but not least, Soviet Constructivism, the generation of post-utopian artists in the late 1970s, both in Hungary and Central Europe in general, began to further their aspirations to enter universal art history and realize the artistic freedom they imagined must prevail in the West. The Socialist Realist and Constructivist traditions were a kind of lingua franca that developed differently in each social context, receiving new meanings in each. The tradition of Socialist Realism—the level of domination and oppression—in particular, influenced the interpretation of contemporary Western art fashions. The degree of cultural shock they caused depended on the extent of the lack of information or on the measure of misinformation. The social reality of these countries thus radically influenced and determined not just the interpretation of the legacy of Socialist Realism but also the perception and the appropriation of contemporary Western ideas. It is not accidental that a few years ago, according to a Russian participant in the first Internet symposium on Russian postmodernism, the Soviet Union served as the best example of a Bermuda Triangle,[6] where the traditional meanings of terms like "postmodernism" disappear.

In this essay, I will attempt to map a portion of the Hungarian variety of postmodernism and show how and in what way the recognition and reception of postmodernism were determined by the social reality of the last decade of the regime, and in what way Neoconstructivism—and sometimes Deconstructivism—became the leading force and spiritual essence of marginal art. This occurred at a very rare moment in history when, for a brief while—during the months of transition—the Hungarian "post" artists became almost official artists. During that moment, in Hungary, the received legacy of international avant-garde traditions became more strongly represented officially than official or popular art and culture.

Prohibition, Tolerance, Support

Focusing on some of the key events of recent art history and of politics in Hungary will help clarify the specific characteristics of the Hungarian postsocialist art scene, both its more universal motifs and its local social contexts.

When attempting to characterize the position of Hungarian society in the former Soviet bloc, there are two basic facts that we should not overlook. Hungarian national identity had never been threatened by the Communist Party to the same degree as in many other countries of the Communist bloc. On the contrary, after the shock of the First World War, when millions of Hungarians found themselves outside the borders of Hungary, Communism offered some degree of hope for Hungarians who had become minorities in Romania, Yugoslavia, and Slovakia. The other fact is the historical and geographical position of Hungary. According to Hungarian mythology and national traditions, Hungary historically always has belonged to the imagined community of the "West." The deep—sometimes almost comical—conviction that we, too, are Westerners is one of the most important factors in Hungarian national and cultural identity. The "imagined community" for Hungarians always had been the little-known West, and from this perspective, becoming suddenly a part of the Soviet world was naturally a shock.

As a result of Hungary's place in the Soviet sphere, Socialist Realism in Hungary was a compulsory style that reigned during the 1950s, but after the suppression of the Hungarian revolution of 1956, the Kádár regime changed its cultural policy. The new slogan became the cultural policy of the "Three Ts" (*Tiltás, Tűrés, Támogatás,* "Prohibition," "Tolerance," "Support").[7] The Party tried to make a new contract with both the masses and the intelligentsia. In Hungary, the Communist Party gave up the ideal of *Gesamtkunstwerk,* the idea of total art. They no longer wanted to regulate and influence the forms of everyday life and therefore suspended the previous strong control over every detail of the public sphere and space.

Thus, although the 1950s were dominated by the aggressive colonialization of everyday life in the name of socialism, after the 1960s, liberalization commenced. By the 1970s, Hungary had become an economically developed Soviet bloc country where the traditions of compulsory Socialist Realism had almost disappeared. In the meantime, a culture of what might be called "sincere cynicism" had developed, and the Party practically lost its self-identity. Sincere cynicism involved a permanent and public power game played using the terms of the "Three Ts." The Party expected no one to believe in the ideas of Socialist Realism; it only expected the artists to abide by the rules of the game. It no longer wanted to convince anybody about the superiority of Socialist Realism and of the Party itself; it was instead satisfied with orderly public behavior. Under such conditions, local traditions such as Hungarian Impressionism reemerged.

Only one politically provocative artistic realm remained, that of the social issues. The Party tried to avoid social topics in art, the easily understandable social meanings by which different social groups and minorities could have represented themselves. They did not want to let the simulacrum of happiness, the peaceful surface, be destroyed. The Communist Party, having no aggressive ideology for the 1970s, tried to build up and support an art scene in which late Impressionism and a certain kind of kitschy realism would represent the mainstream. Ironically, in the age of state-sponsored cynicism, the middle-of-the-road style became a peculiar sort of global kitsch in which Monet was mixed with Norman Rockwell.

Sándor Pinczehelyi, the Hungarian Provincial Pop Artist

In this social context, the artist Sándor Pinczehelyi started his career. In the mid-1970s, analytical Conceptualism and geometrical abstraction became common currency among Hungarian neo-avant-garde artists. Pinczehelyi (born in 1939) was perhaps the first to break with this tradition. He radically changed his former artistic position, discarded the very sophisticated and metapolitical style, and began to create paintings and carry out actions that were connected with well-known socialist symbols such as the hammer and the sickle. At first glance, his inventions were simply an imitation and a variation—or a reception—of Andy Warhol's globally known decorative and empty surfaces, but in reality, his method and adaptation radically differed from the activity of the American Pop Art celebrity. However, there are similarities in their work, such as the reinterpretation of the meanings of truisms and of almost meaningless commonplace symbols.

When making five-pointed stars of cobblestones (the five-pointed star was the symbol of the proletariat's struggle in the preceding century and more recently had become the icon of the Paris revolution in 1968) (Figure 49), for example, Pinczehelyi reinvented Pop Art traditions and adapted them to the Hungarian social context (Plate 10). He became a veritable troublemaker when he started to analyze and paint other political symbols, such as the hammer and the sickle, in different contexts (Plate 11). These were the symbols of the current social system, but, of course, nobody could believe that the artist's intention was meant as a simple affirmation of its authority.

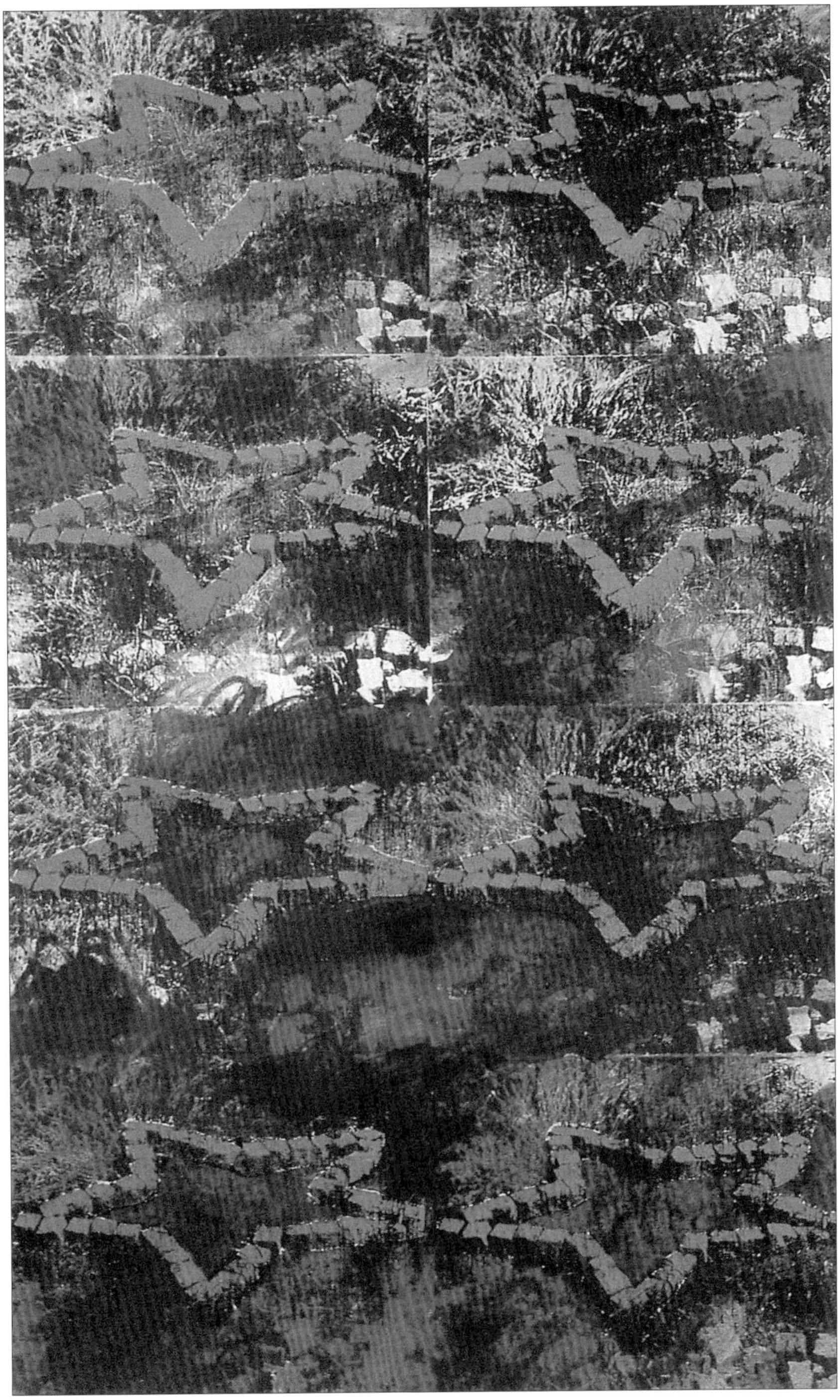

Figure 49 Sándor Pinczehelyi, *Star, Cobblestone I,* 1986, oil on canvas, 200 × 120 cm. Ludwig Forum für Internationale Kunst, Aachen. Ludwig Collection.

When Pinczehelyi took a photo of himself with a hammer and a sickle in his hands during the period of sincere cynicism (see Figure 1), he expressed something very frustrated and ironic. He revised the rules of the "Three Ts" game, mixing and combining different kinds of cynicism. He kept his independence, but at the same time started to attack the extant system with irony and a typically Central European absurdist sense of humor.

The artist started to develop a strategy of double meanings in the early 1970s. He combined American Pop Art symbols, the icons of consumerism, with traditional Hungarian nationalist and Communist icons. In a very sensitive way, he combined two different life worlds, thus ironically following the policy of the Hungarian Communist Party, which tried to navigate between the East and the West. Pinczehelyi created a montage of political and metapolitical icons and carried out a reinterpretation and a conflation of Pop Art, national symbols, folk art, and Communist and Socialist Realist icons. At the same time, he imitated Warhol's prints. He also adapted the technique of classical Pop Art, in which high and low culture confronted each other. He analyzed the consumer society, but at the same time politicized it.[8] He appropriated the method of consumerism, using the style of photorealism and perfect technology, inventing in this manner one of the most interesting artistic hybrids of these decades. Pinczehelyi was a provincial artist—he never lived in Budapest—yet at the same time a cosmopolitan and a universal one. In spite of having a critical and ironic attitude toward the system and caring about politics, he never belonged to any of the dissident political artist groups. He was simply not interested in direct political struggles. Pinczehelyi never attempted to leave Pécs—a town in the southern part of Hungary with a very strong cultural legacy and a population of 170,000—which meant that he tried to avoid Budapest and the inner circles of the art scene. He remained an outsider and a "double agent" when he appropriated Pop Art and privatized the common socialist myths.

What did the reinvention of a Western style and the application and reception of universal symbols mean in this local context? Pinczehelyi became the first postmodern artist and the first practitioner of *bricolage* in Hungary. The lack of a coherent ideological and cultural canon, which consequently had no semantic structure, created the essence of his art—if the lack of the essence can be considered an essence at all. Pinczehelyi was the first to realize—many years before the New Painting, Neue Wilde movement, and New Figuration arrived in Budapest—that the lack of a coherent cultural canon and ideological order in the political world had become an es-

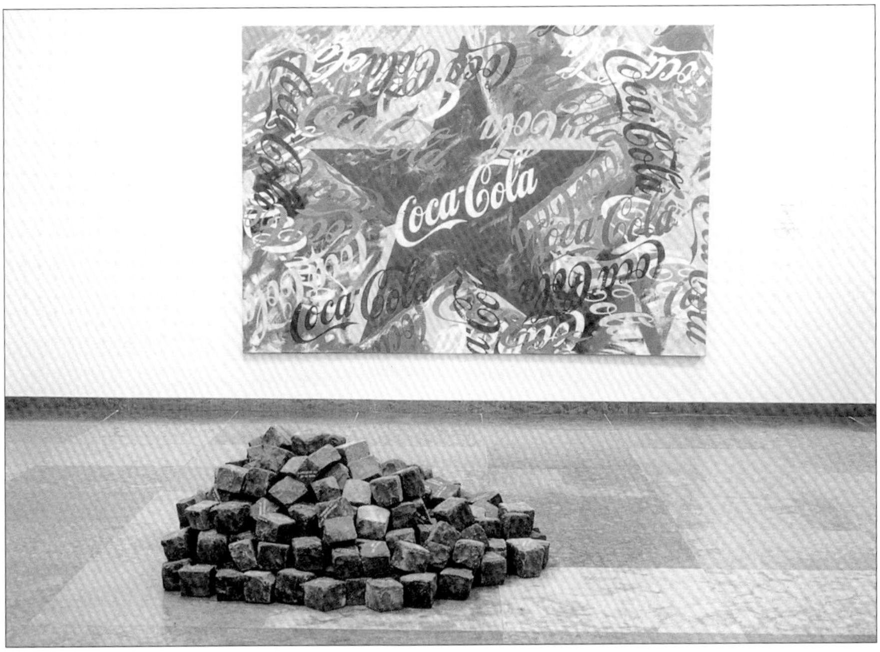

Figure 50 Sándor Pinczehelyi, *Weapon of the Proletariat,* 1974–88, 350 cobblestones, each 7 × 7 × 7 cm, and *Star, Coca-Cola I,* 1988, acrylic, oil on canvas, 200 × 280 cm (Collection of Hungarian National Gallery, Budapest), Venice Biennial.

sential part of the art world. The lack of coherent semantic connections and the rapid disappearance of the established models of representation revealed the presence of the cultural logic of late capitalism. Here, depthlessness is everything. Depthlessness is the "essence" of the Warholian turn of the avant-garde and is the main category of Jamesonian aesthetics.[9] Postmodernism as the cultural logic of Western late capitalism and of late socialism is represented by the depthlessness, the lack of a deep structure, of a coherent semantic canon, and thus the lack of strict metaphors. Pinczehelyi didn't want to search for an underlying correlation between the signifier and the signified because he realized that there wasn't anything beyond the surface. Allusions had lost their metaphorical meaning. Anything could represent anything. Only the ruins of the coherent canonical structures remained. This could be the sickle with a Coca-Cola bottle or the red star with the logo of Coca-Cola (Figure 50), or the colors of the Hungarian national flag on a Campbell's soup label.[10]

It was this spirit of the time—which had very little to do with mere fashion—that Pinczehelyi expressed in his works. He was the first to invent an artistic procedure for expressing a consciousness of this new and different situation.

Architects in Art—Politics and Aesthetics

It is no mere coincidence that we can find many architects among the artists who were involved in the invention of Hungarian Neoconstructivist and Deconstructivist art. Gábor Bachman, László Rajk, Attila Kovács, and Tibor Szalai started their careers as practicing architects. In the late 1970s, they worked in architectural studios, but they very soon realized that as pure architects they wouldn't be in a position to carry out their own ideas. The political demands and aesthetic coercions were too strong, and they found the dull and uninventive day-to-day grind of Hungarian architectural practice intolerably narrow and meaningless.

Bachman and Kovács were originally influenced by Imre Makovecz, who in the 1970s was perhaps the most important Hungarian architect, as well as the spiritual leader of the counterculture. Makovecz belonged to the tradition of organic and fantastic architecture. He was influenced by Rudolf Steiner, Antoni Gaudí, and later Paul Virilio, as well as by Hungarian folk art. Makovecz, an anti-Communist, represented for many an uncorrupted and traditional way of thinking and way of life. He was much appreciated by the younger generation because he remained outside the existing system—and, as an architect, never got a commission in Budapest until 1989. He remained in the shadows, building family houses and a few community centers, libraries, and restaurants around the country, mostly in small villages. In the name of organic local traditions, he refused the heritage of Bauhaus, the spirit of superrationalism, and the nomadic global village. This architect became perhaps the first well-known Hungarian radical regionalist, criticizing modernist architecture in general and constantly mixing criticism of international modernism with criticism of current socialism while combining environmental issues and nationalist politics. Makovecz hated socialism, which, according to him, had destroyed the traditional Hungarian lifestyle. His antimodernism very much resembled some of the ideas proposed by postmodernism. From him, Bachman and Kovács learned the importance of organic structures. Makovecz, who admired Heidegger's essays on technology, also introduced Budapest to Virilio and his theories on the aesthetics of German bunker architecture—the world of the bunkers of the Third Reich, which referred both to militant German mythology and ancient, biological forms.

Traces of his influence, that is, elements of organic architecture, are revealed in the early works of Bachman and Kovács. Their antimodernism or postmodernism was mixed with Romanticism. Both were interested in mythology and, among other things, in the analysis of cemetery traditions.

At this time, in the early 1980s, since they and Rajk were dissatisfied with their jobs as architects, all three quit. Architecture was under very strong state control, and consequently, they tried to find new possibilities. Fine art, stage art, and film design provided them with new territories. Rajk, Bachman, and Kovács started to work in the Hungarian State Film Company, for example, and, later, in various theaters.

Unlike ordinary painters, they very soon learned where the sometimes invisible boundaries of the political permissiveness of the system lay, lessons that enabled them to destroy their velvet prison and understand their own social reality. Painters were more independent of the system because painting didn't belong to the public space the way architecture did. Unlike painting, architecture had never been a lonely genre. Cooperation and group efforts focused on different kinds of temporary artistic forms thus played a very important role for these artists. It is not a coincidence that they very frequently exhibited their artworks together. Bachman and Rajk worked as a pair, while Szalai worked together with his other friends in the Brettschneider group. Their projects were extremely successful and popular.

László Rajk's name, however, was usually taboo with the officials. Rajk belonged to the heart of the Hungarian dissident circle. His father, the first Communist foreign minister, was executed in 1949, when János Kádár was the minister of the interior. Because the regime did not want another martyr, Rajk's family name protected him from police investigation, and Kádár was afraid to harass him. Consequently, the state police never dared arrest him, but sometimes they frustrated his jobs, stage plans, and film designs. This was one of the reasons why he and Bachman together founded Studio Plus in 1984 (Figure 51), which existed under this name until 1991–92. There they designed film and stage sets.

The marginalized and sometimes dissident Hungarian architects could not get real, serious jobs during the time of socialism, and the film and theater sets offered only temporary employment. Nevertheless, this work had some social effects. The architects weren't completely isolated and in this way were able to break out of the velvet prison of the high-cultural environ-

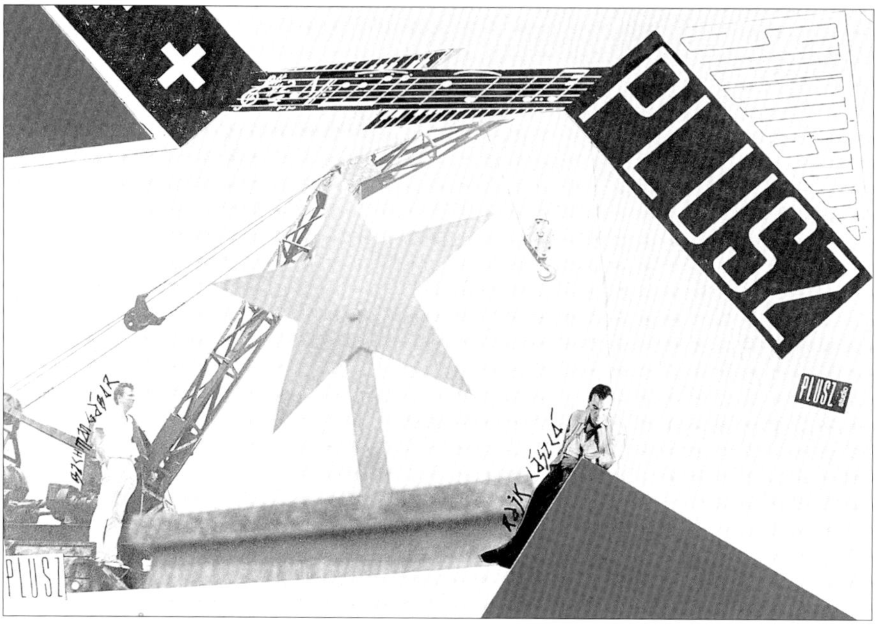

Figure 51 László Rajk, poster for Studio Plus, 1984, presumably destroyed.

ment and out of the hopeless and ineffective silence of the exhibition halls. Temporary and experimental architecture, with its contradiction between permanence and transience, expressed their position, and thus their social position and their artistic message were firmly correlated. The social disadvantage of the architects became their artistic advantage.

In Hungary, this kind of architecture turned out to be the most influential and coherent icon of late socialism. Film and stage sets have a symbolic meaning. Architecture as employed by the film industry is the architecture of dreams. These late socialist architects didn't live isolated lives within the ineffective high culture, but they were unable to reach social reality, either. They lived and worked within the boundaries of reality and unreality. Their art represented different stages and circles of the world beyond that of everyday socialism. In the beginning, they turned to the legacy of Surrealism and to the organic tradition of Rudolf Steiner (1861–1925), who reintroduced biologism and the spirit of organic forms into architecture and who conflated anti-Communism with radical antimodernism and an attack on Bauhaus. Rajk was the only member of this generation who had never been interested in the reinvention of Steiner's legacy. He always remained in the present, within the inner borders and problems of rationality. His political and artistic careers were always intertwined, however. His "Samizdat Boutique" provided a place where artists and members of dissident political circles could meet.[11]

Szalai, who belonged to a younger generation, had never been touched by the problems of politics. His fantastic architecture originated more from Kurt Schwitters's *Merzbau* than from the Wagnerian, the Steinerian, or the Russian Constructivist traditions of *Gesamtkunstwerk.* Szalai, like Schwitters, favored private spaces and metaphysical architectural visions that were devoid of actual functions. Just as the early Schwitters rearranged the space of the gallery so that it became a scene for the display of his structure, the museum piece, Szalai used the exhibition space as a constantly altered private space in which he located his occasional architectural constructions or "structures." Szalai was much more closely related to the Dadaist tradition, which preferred metaphysical problems, than to Constructivism, which used revolutionary solutions and was thinking almost always in communal terms.

In the late 1970s and mid-1980s, unlike the emerging and, in Hungary, soon very successful practitioners of international postmodern painting and of the fashionable new and radical eclecticism,[12] this group of architects turned to the reinterpretation and reinvention of the legacy of Constructivism, the Russian avant-garde, and the inheritance of political and agitprop art. Until the mid-1980s, there was a very perceptible tension and contradiction between the fine art of the pseudo-avant-garde mainstream and the visual art produced by Rajk, Bachman, Kovács, Szalai, and the Conceptualist and later Constructivist art of György Jovanovics. The younger generation of Hungarian painters started to enter the Western-style art gallery system, and as they followed the demands and norms of galleries, these artists became more and more successful in economic terms.

Unlike such mainstream artists, the group of architects turned to the politico-aesthetical criticism of the system, each as half architect, half *Gesamtkunstwerkman.*[13] These fashionable postmodern painters were completely uninterested in social issues and lacked any sense of social responsibility. The depthlessness and sensuality of postmodernism, its enjoyment of the artistic activity for its own sake, its sincere lack of any social, political, or existential message, and its evident and contradictionless impressionism were very comfortable for the political establishment. In the late 1970s and early 1980s, Hungarian society had become rotten through and through. The Socialist Party lost any convictions it may have had, and its politics was characterized by simple and meaningless compromises. In this period of Hungarian history, therefore, a postmodern emptiness and a lack of a serious artistic message were often the most convenient positions in art.

The activity of the alternative architects, however, was becoming more and more annoying to the official cultural politicians and more and more fascinating to the inquiring audience interested in contemporary art. At a time when the cultural identity of the mainstream art world was becoming an integral part of the international gallery business, the alternative architects instead explored local traditions, working-class culture, and Leftist art history. Bachman and Rajk, in particular, began to analyze the legacy of Constructivism. The symbolic turning point may have been the International Shinkenchiku Residential Design Competition in 1985. The theme of the competition was "Bulwark of Resistance." Bachman and Rajk worked on their projects together with György Konrád and Miklós Haraszti, eminent members of the Hungarian liberal Leftist intelligentsia. Konrád's role was crucial, for not only was he a famous writer and a good friend of Rajk and Bachman, but he was himself interested in architecture.[14] His second novel, the *City Founder* (1977), dealt with the social role of architects in a socialist society. The *City Founder* had a key position in the reinvention of Constructivism as a metaphor for the Hungarian architects. Through architecture, Konrád criticized the philosophy of state planning, with architects becoming symbols of the suprarational socialist bureaucrats who controlled every possible segment and element of quotidian life.

After 1985, these artists—together or alone, in a group and in individual exhibitions—continued to investigate the legacy of Constructivism. Again, however, their reinterpretation of this avant-garde movement was situated within local frameworks. They used the emblems of Constructivism and its abstract structures, the styles of Rodchenko, Popova, Tatlin, and Malevich. For these Hungarian artists and their audience, the use of such quotations signified a very obvious attack on the system. For example, the Munka-Tett Kocsma (Work-Act Pub) by Bachman, which was built near Budapest in a proletarian environment, expressed his social and political sentiments (Figure 52).

These architects continued the tradition of experimental architecture when they built their paper models. Paper models played an important role in their activities. Such models were the only way to participate in different collective and, later, individual exhibitions in Budapest and abroad. Programmatic texts such as the "Architecture of Nothing" reminded the politicians

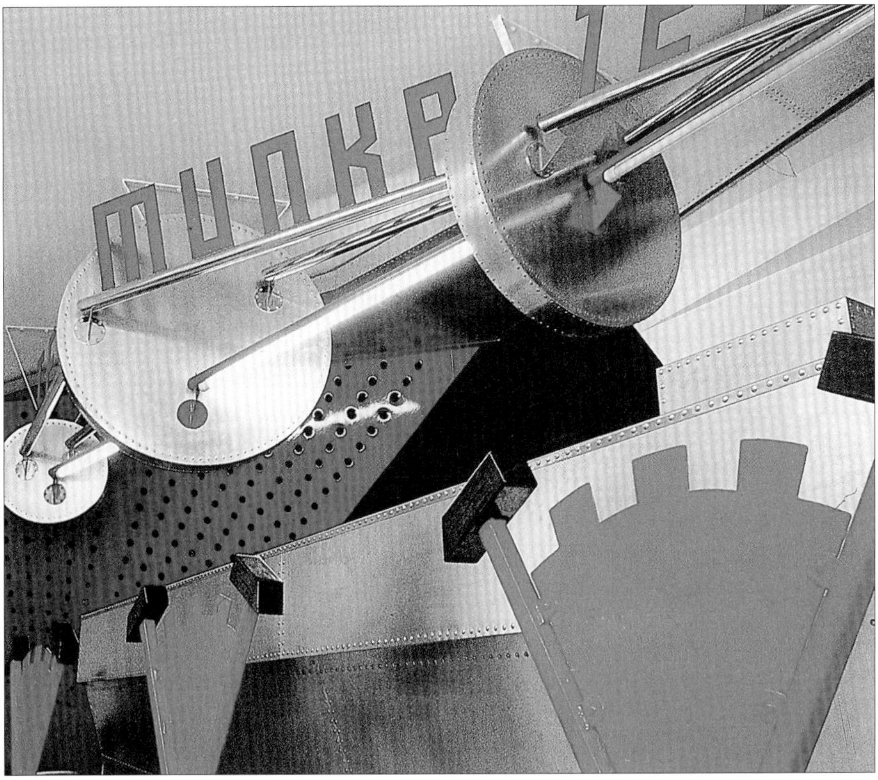

Figure 52 Gábor Bachman, Work-Act Pub, 1986 (photo: Zoltán Bakos).

and the mass audience of the lack of any structure in contemporary Hungarian society. The architects built temporary structures in a world that was visibly and definitely disintegrating. The collapse of late socialism formed the social context within which they reinvented symbols that once had expressed the ideas and ideology of socialism. Tatlin made models of huge structures, while Rodchenko and Malevich investigated basic structures of the world and of spirituality—and decades later, a few Hungarian artists started once more to use these symbols. In their local context, their meaning was very explicit: very political, very direct, and very sharp. At the same time, from the point of view of an international art historian, these artworks had a different meaning. These models and structures were primarily quotations and paraphrases that could be understood and interpreted as postmodern fragments.[15] This whole practice confirms the theoretical efforts of Rosalind Krauss: The myth of originality was the myth of high modernism, and the loss of this originality is the evident symbol of postmodernism.

László Rajk, Political Dissident and Post-Utopian Artist

László Rajk was born in 1949 in Budapest, the same year in which his father was executed. Rajk studied at the Technical University in Budapest and later at McGill University in Montreal, where he received his M.A. in 1978.[16] With his key position as an intermediary between the avant-garde art scene and the political dissidents, he was one of the few well-informed artists and very soon learned about contemporary Western architectural and art-historical debates. From the very beginning of his career, he was a typical *Gesamtkunstwerkman.* He worked as a practicing architect and made experimental projects. He became an exhibiting artist, gave lectures, and made film designs, stage sets, book and CD cover designs, sculptures, environmental art, and, last but not least, comic books and cartoons. He was perhaps the first artist in Hungary to realize the social importance of this genre.[17]

In the 1970s and early 1980s, Rajk was influenced by experimental architecture and by the sociological analysis of architecture. His political criticism went hand in hand with his architectural ideas. He was a good example of an "alternative architect," one who also wholeheartedly embraced Kenneth Frampton's "critical regionalism."[18] Rajk strongly criticized the failures of modernism, but never turned to the romanticism of nationalism and the traditionalism of organic architecture and never was influenced by Imre Makovecz. Rajk investigated local conditions and interpreted the possibilities and role of architecture within contemporary society. He always combined critical and experimental elements with linguistic and visual ones. In 1978, for example, he a gave a lecture called "Rubbish Heap—Rubbish Flat."[19]

As a practicing architect, he planned the workers' home at the Budapest recycling factory,[20] but his first avant-garde house was built outside Hungary. In 1983, he designed a studio house in Saint Paul de Vence,[21] in the south of France, together with Gábor Bachman and another friend, Bálint Nagy. The studio in Vence—the Károlyi Foundation—was probably the first postmodern Hungarian building, and it is not a coincidence that it was built outside the country. It is a good example of the "do-it-yourself" architecture of the culture of *bricolage*[22] and the spirit and style of classical postmodernism. Rajk entered many international competitions, and his plans are closely linked to his stage designs, which he created during the 1970s and 1980s—increasingly frequently together with Bachman. His ability to interrelate different activities was perhaps his greatest merit. After the mid-1980s, both men turned to Neoconstructivism and Deconstructivism, the architectural movement instigated by Jacques Derrida and Bernard Tschumi. Rajk's film sets were made in the same eclectic spirit. One of the most important projects—made together with Bachman—was the design for the congress of the Radical Party in Budapest in 1988. The congress was held in a building built in the style of Stalinist architecture with a statue of Lenin in front of it. It was redone using provisional architectural elements of the Neoconstructivist/Deconstructivist style so often employed by both architects.

For Rajk, the design for the Radical Party was a turning point. Prior to that, Rajk had never been in the position to get communal, public commissions and lived in the experimental theater and film "ghetto." This was the first time that he and Bachman could cross that border and work in the public arena.

The Radical Party was one of the manifestly cosmopolitan international political organizations in Europe. It was originally founded in Italy—Cicciolina[23] was a member of this party—and its politics always balanced theatrical events, artistic performance, and serious traditional political struggle. Its congress in Budapest in 1988 was one of the first signs of the emergent multiparty system in Hungary and of the reinvention of the European parliamentary tradition. The building in which the party held its congress also had a political role, for it was the headquarters of the Trade Union of Architects. The environment designed by Bachman and Rajk was probably the first clearly Neoconstructivist and at the same time Deconstructivist project in Budapest. They used the well-known spatial, building, and color elements of the Russian classical avant-gardes: black and red-and-white surfaces, sharp cuts, and the imitation of metal structures. The stage design recalled Tatlin's designs and Bachman's Work-Act Pub and hence referred to classical Constructivism and to the historical reinvention of this tradition. Rajk and Bachman weren't postmodern artists who would simply imitate the original Constructivism. They admired the heroes of the avant-garde revolution and through the reinvention of their work and ideas expressed their critical historical position.

Rajk's most personal artwork is perhaps his *Letatrajk*—the title is a paraphrase of Tatlin's *Letatlin.*[24] The black paraphrase and copy of the *Monument to the Third International* is combined with red industrial structures and white wings. The spirit of Constructivism, of public and social revolution, is the essence of the original work. Rajk's work, on the contrary, belongs to Deconstructivism, to individuality, and to revolution in art. There are several symbolic elements in this narrative. The fate of the *Letatrajk* speaks for itself: Today, it decorates a private flower shop.

Nevertheless, Rajk's own fate also is symbolic. Not only has he become a member of parliament for the Alliance of Free Democrats, but he also has started to work as a practicing architect, for now he has received real commissions—he designed the reconstruction of the largest movie theater in Budapest and the interior of the largest bookshop there. He also did work abroad. The design of the Collegium Hungaricum in Vienna is his accomplishment, and in the Austrian town of Hollein, there will be a Neoconstructivist Hungarian official building built according to his plans. If the history of architecture is any proof of social changes, this building proves that the transition to democracy in Hungary has not been just a dream.

Gábor Bachman: From Biological Romanticism to a Memorial to the Heroism of the Working Class

Gábor Bachman, born in Pécs in 1952, was not just Rajk's friend and coauthor, but also a successful architect and a painter in the new generation of Hungarian artists. He first studied architecture at the Technical University in Budapest, but finished his university years at the Academy of Applied Art and Design.

At the beginning of his career, he was inspired by the mystical decadence and the biological Romanticism of Imre Makovecz. Bachman was a very close friend and colleague of the avant-garde film-maker Gábor Bódy,[25] and in Bódy's film *Narcissus and Psyche,* Bachman had an opportunity to try out almost every creative idea that entered his mind. In the images and landscapes made as parts of the set for *Narcisuss and Psyche,* one recognizes a visual imitation of German Romanticism, the dreams of a preindustrial age and of the collapse of industrial society. This film is perhaps the most aggressive attack on modernism in the name of individuality, independent personality, and "bio-radicalism," as Bódy sometimes called their shared sensual radicalism. *Narcissus and Psyche* was a very forceful reaction to both the legacy of abstract, insensible Conceptualism and the sad moral vacuum of everyday Hungarian life. This film was a *Gesamtkunstwerk* and represented a monument to and catalogue of the dreams of a generation. These artists loathed contemporary socialist society with a revulsion that was positively physical, but had no idea about the reality of contemporary capitalism, didn't understand the cultural environment of a market-based art world, and escaped into the Romantic past and the admiration of sensual love.

After the *Narcissus and Psyche,* their attempt at a *Gesamtkunstwerk,* Bódy and Bachman continued their cooperation. They made a theater and a film version of *Hamlet* (subtitled *The Armed Philosopher*). The stage design was a concave cerebrum with passages, blood vessels, and outer protective walls. It was the culmination of their "bio-radicalism" and Romanticism. Their version of *Hamlet* is one of the best keys to the spiritual and intellectual environment of late socialism. This interpretation is an expression of their general contempt, for these artists held the whole society in contempt. Hamlet was their agent, their "mask," because he disdained the world itself.[26]

After this depressed period, they made a film in the mid-1980s about the legacy of Bauhaus. Bachman and Bódy started to overcome their early Romanticism and understood the advantage of the "Neue Sachlichkeit," the early-twentieth-century art grounded in the representation of reality. In 1985, however, Bódy killed himself.[27] His death was a personal tragedy for Bachman, for he remained alone, without his master. That same year Bachman, together with Rajk, Miklós Haraszti, and György Konrád, entered the "Bulwark of Resistance" international competition. In the project they submitted, the *Striker's House,* they combined traditional Constructivist elements with elements of Deconstructivism, the Constructivist structures and the symbolic colors of Communism with the ruins of the industrial age. In December of the same year, Bachman, together with his wife, Judit Vida, held an exhibition in their native town of Pécs. This was to be the turning point of Bachman's career. The title of the exhibition was *Munka-Tett (Work-Act),* and the design combined and reinvented the elements, colors, and typography of classical Constructivist and Socialist Realist iconography (see Plate 12).

The exhibition carried a very powerful message. The hammers, the red-and-black cogwheels, and the geometrical elements resembled not only the Russian Socialist Realist heritage, but also the design of the Slovenian Neue Slowenische Kunst organization. The text of the exhibition catalog was written by Péter Esterházy, the famous and fashionable writer of that generation.[28] He wrote the essay "Construction of Nothing," which became a cult text not only for Bachman and his friends, but almost for their whole age group. Nine years later, Bachman himself wrote a programmatic essay called "Architecture of Nothing" that was based on "Construction of Nothing." The postmodern textual pastiche written by Esterházy, which contains texts by Goethe, Alpár Bújdosó, János Megyik, and Lautréamont, is the best expression of the double meaning of this project. The *Work-Act* exhibition made use of the political gestures of Constructivism and Bauhaus, but it was also very ironic. Bachman cited the collective Total Art, but its participants never belonged to the Communist movement. The *Work-Act* exhibition forcefully revealed a typical Central European irony and sense of humor. Nothing is simple in this context. Everything has an additional meaning.

There is something ironic and incomprehensible in the reinvention or reintroduction of socialist demagogy and Constructivist tradition during late socialism. Is the "Construction of Nothing" an example of a double meaning, or of a conspiracy with the audience? Is this a stylistic game with the common past, as it was in the case of Irwin? (The Neue Slowenische Kunst organization was more complicated and difficult to understand than the Hungarian late socialist artists. The Slovenian artists played with the Nazi Kunst tradition and socialist heritage at the same time. Their intention was to show the common features of the two totalitarian artistic endeavors.)

A year later, in 1986, Bachman further developed his stylistic remakes and montages by building the Work-Act Pub (see Figure 52) in Szigetszentmiklós, the suburbs of Budapest. In my view, together with the Striker's House, this pub was the most important and fascinating work of its decade in Hungary. The Work-Act Pub is a typical *Gesamtkunstwerk*. In other words, it is a materialization of the idea of total art, but set against totalitarianism. The refurbished pub resembled a classical Constructivist structure. The metal surfaces, red letters, and iron chairs recalled the inventions of Russian classical avant-garde—Rodchenko's design and Mayakovsky's *Windows of RosTA*. It evoked the spirit of agitprop art and the revolution it promoted in art and politics—such could be an innocent, artistic reading of the building. But this pub didn't belong to the recent art world of Budapest. It was a pub in a working-class area, in an industrial environment, behind the largest factory in Hungary. The building itself was one of the characterless concrete cubes on the outskirts of a housing project built for the working class. In such an environment, the art-historical *bricolage*, the irony of the red capital letters "WORK-ACT," became dramatic.

The ethos of "work" and "act(ion)" in those years had lost all credibility. Work had no meaning, and there was no social act that could carry any sense. This was a tragic memorial to these two ideological notions, purportedly still cherished in a rotten and decrepit social environment. Not coincidentally, one year later, the local authorities closed the Work-Act Pub.

Bachman's work was an utter provocation, provoking the existing society and the rule of the Communist Party—and this was just what he wanted to achieve. It was the point where he stopped playing, left his slightly narcissistic Romanticism, and entered the realm of social responsibility. The Work-Act Pub is thus strongly linked with the rest of the works that Bachman executed together with László Rajk, such as the Radical Party congress and, as we will see, the funeral ceremony design for Imre Nagy and his comrades.

In the 1990s Bachman became an increasingly international artist.[29]

Attila Kovács: From Universal Postmodernism to Recognition of Local Conditions

Attila Kovács (born in 1951) started his career as a practicing architect who was influenced, on the one hand, by Makovecz and the fashionable organic tradition and, on the other, by the radical eclecticism of contemporary postmodernism. At the same time, he rejected from the outset the rational spirit of modernism. He recreated different myths and made films and photo exhibitions about the Grail.[30] Kovács admired traditions, the different periods of historical past—which we always perceive as a foreign country—and everything that happened before the age of rationalism and socialism. One of his first architectural plans was his own family house near Budapest, which he built strictly as an imitation of a neoclassicist villa. (Nevertheless, he applied one of his characteristic tricks: The indoor style didn't resemble the neoclassical, Palladian villa imitation. The indoor staircase, for example, recalled Romanticism, rather than classicism.)

The recreated myths and the imitation of different past art-historical styles revealed the same attitude—rejection of the present and nostalgia for the past. Kovács—unlike his friend and colleague Bachman—never was a defender of radical biologism, nor was he a dandyist decadent, which was one of the most important social characteristics of Bachman and some other Hungarian artists at the time. He was alone in the collective society, lonely with his nostalgic ideas. However, in addition to its nostalgic character, there is another element in his art—in his stage and architecture designs (he planned the largest Hungarian Jugendstil exhibition) and later in his painting—due to which his works are always unmistakable. He has a very strong sense of space as an architectural expression of social and political meanings, such as freedom and oppression.

During the 1970s and early 1980s, he made film and stage sets. He

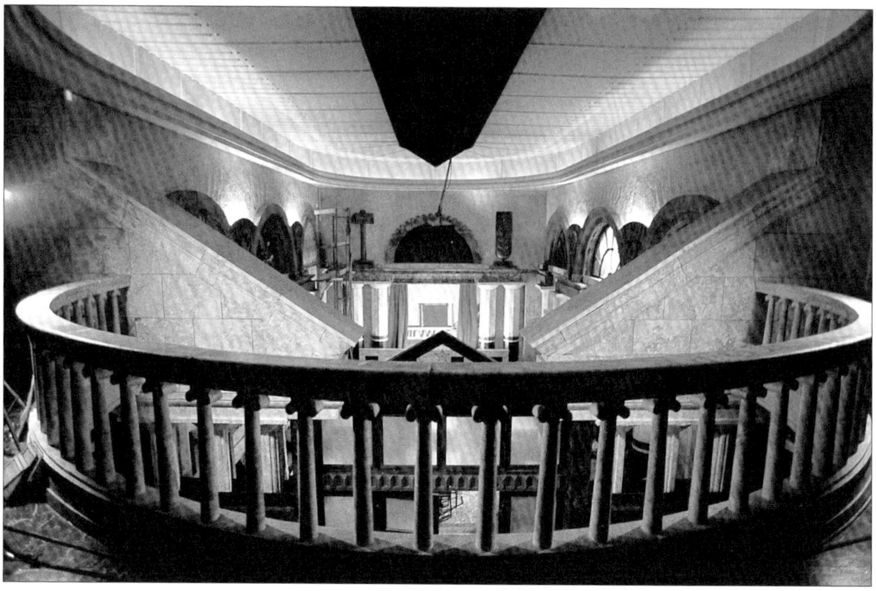

Figure 53 Attila Kovács, Age of Iron, 1981. Set for the film *Daniel Takes a Train* by Sándor Pál.

worked with Bachman on *Narcissus and Psyche*, and in 1981, he constructed two important film sets. The first was for a film by Sándor Pál, *Daniel Takes a Train* (Figure 53), which was about the fate of the young generation in the revolution of 1956. (*Daniel Takes a Train* was probably the first frank and honest film about the revolution.) The film is about a hotel near a border, which carries a strong symbolic meaning. (The border is between the East and the West, between freedom and oppression, between life and death, etc.) Kovács designed the interiors of the hotel, which imitated Socialist Realism but sometimes resembled the design of the Atlantic Wall by Hitler and Albert Speer. The imitation of Socialist Realism, not coincidentally also innocently resembling Nazi design, is the starting point of this design and its interpretation. The scenographic world of Attila Kovács, besides imitating political architectural narratives, always carried some serious metaphysical meaning. He understood and expressed absolute hopelessness and loneliness: empty walls and deep vaults could well represent the fake and meaningless faith offered by socialism. The imitation stadiums, churches, and Party buildings that formed a part of the film set represented a threat to the defenseless citizens. The infinite spaces of the set revealed their unsuitability as habitats for normal humans, not to mention for intimate life. These were the spaces of political control, just as in the films of Leni Riefenstahl.

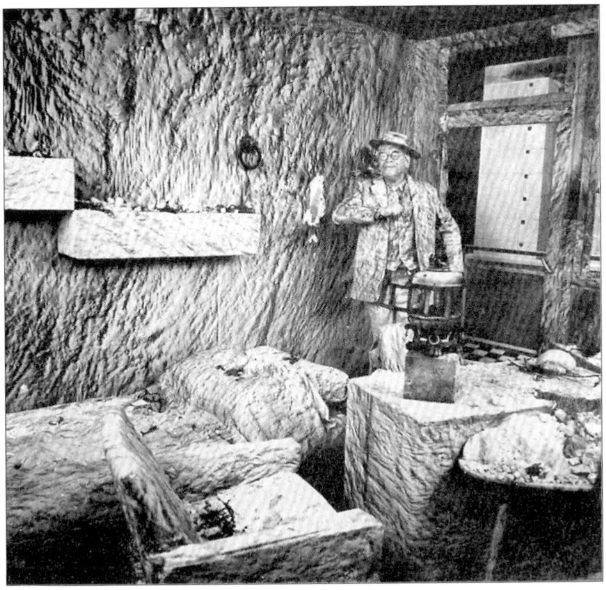

Figure 54 Attila Kovács, Stone Room, 1982. Set for the film *Dream Brigade* by András Jeles.

In the same year, 1981, Kovács planned another film set, this one for *Dream Brigade,* one of the last Hungarian films to be banned. András Jeles's film was perhaps the most sarcastic and ironic critique of late socialism, and also an important piece of postmodern art. It was founded on the fusion of visual and verbal quotations. Kovács designed the Stone Room (Figure 54), which is probably the best architectural symbol of the late period of the Kádár regime. The *Stone Room,* according to this fiction, was a closed and windowless space where everything was made of marble. Marble—imitation, naturally—was the material from which not only the walls, but the bed, table, and all other objects were made. Needless to say, the owner of the Stone Room was made from marble, too. Kovács's representation of the society of this decade in his work was complex and refined. He destroyed the division between the living and dead, between organic and inorganic, between inner and outer space, between human beings and their environment. Everything was made of marble—in this society, everything and everybody was dead.[31] The Stone Room was the first memorial to the Kádár regime, and almost everybody understood the critical intention behind it.

There was another aspect to this criticism—the actor, Robert Rátonyi, a very important element. Rátonyi was a famous musical star during the 1960s and until the late 1970s—he was the Hungarian Gene Kelly, and also the first national TV star. He represented the spirit of Hungarian light opera—operetta—which has always been a part of the Hungarian national identity and the national collective memory. Jeles chose Rátonyi to play the inhabitant of the Stone Room, someone who is unable to speak, who only stutters, without producing any meaning, thus representing the final decline of this cultural tradition and the taste appertaining to it.

In this period, everything died: the low-cultural and mass-cultural heritage, as well as socialism. The division between organic and inorganic became invisible and the necropolis replaced the living city. The world's spirit was Brezhnevism.

During the 1980s, Kovács continued his stage and film designs and became known outside the Hungarian borders. In 1987, he organized one of his most influential and important exhibitions, *The Necropolis*. This exhibition become the turning point not just in his career, but in the history of contemporary Hungarian art. He exhibited large metal sculptures (Figure 55) resembling at the same time models of factories, crematoriums, and various industrial devices. These were geometrical structures or chimneys that recalled the architecture of concentration camps, the Gulags, and at the same time the architecture of ordinary socialist industrialism. They could be read as a critique of Communism or any totalitarianism, of the mindless and meaningless decades, as well as of the unintelligent effort of the masses, the hopeless sacrifice of the working class, but also as a clear and severe criticism of the legacy of modernism itself.

Kovács exhibited the polished and etched surfaces of his pictures made from sheet iron in dark oak frames. The iron pictures represented industrial landscapes, factories, thermoelectric plants, and the heroes of these decades and social environment (Figure 56; see Plate 13).There were male nudes with body-builder muscles—the imagined heroes of the working class who sacrificed their lives without hope of historical salvation. The working-class heroes who lost their pictorial representations, as offered by the official Soviet propaganda, had no access to a technology of creating a collective memory and were suppressed again and again by the silence of the media. Kovács's iron pictures recall the "men of iron" with "steel muscles" who toiled like machines, stretched like springs, and now have been forgotten by art.

The days of the Kádár regime were numbered: the *Necropolis* exhibition became its *Mene Tekel*, the last depiction of a decrepit and cynical system. Kovács started his career with radical eclecticism and at its culmination arrived at the most serious kind of criticism, offering a rare visual representation of the most common heroes of the now-obsolete industrial epoch.

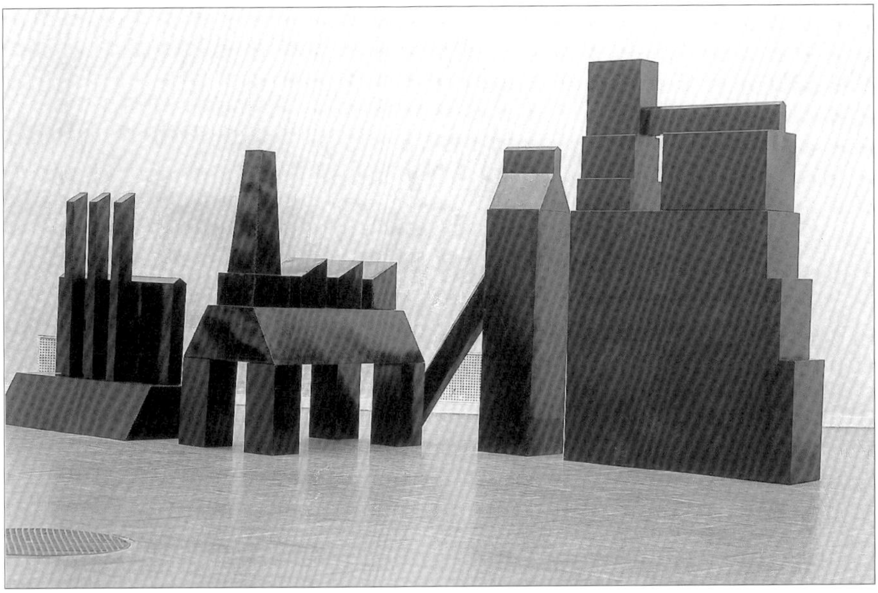

Figure 55 Attila Kovács, *Necropolis Block I–IV*, 1987, tar-painted iron, 3.5 × 12 × 2.5 m.

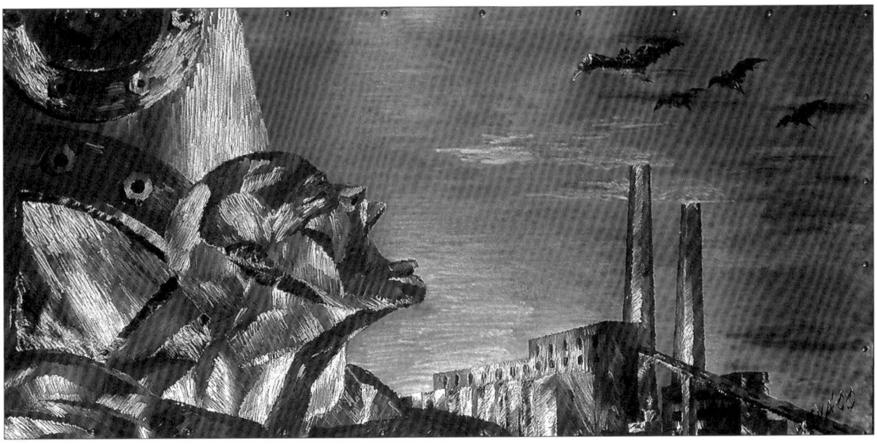

Figure 56 Attila Kovács, *AAA . . . AA*, 1987, polished iron sheet, 100 × 200 cm. Lyon, Musée d'Art Contemporain.

Tibor Szalai, or Abstract Experimental Architecture

Tibor Szalai (1958–1999) started his career a few years later than Kovács. He belongs to the next generation, and his was a different world from that of those who were shaped by the Hungarian postsocialist condition. In spite of being related to the work of his three older colleagues, his work bears witness to the fact that Constructivism in architecture doesn't necessarily entail a political position, as was the case with Bachman and Rajk.

Szalai was an architect, too, but he never touched political or social issues. Instead, he always remained within the abstract realms (Figure 57), avoided political liaisons and struggles, and remained detached from the social context. He never confronted the one-party system. His generation was socialized in different conditions, at a time when politics and social consciousness no longer had the same meaning and position.

Szalai was influenced by body art and actionist traditions. In his early period, he made lyrical self-portraits—photographs in which he played with light and shadow. In the years in which he made these self-portraits—a few of them were nude and resembled the Victorian photography of Julia Margaret Cameron—he founded the Brettschneider group in cooperation with his friends László Vincze, Ferenc Salamin, and István Kotsis. Using the emblem BSCH, they organized concerts and exhibitions and built spatial structures from paper. From the outset, it was clear that Szalai was the leader of this group. The others have become independent architects. Szalai's invention was the reinterpretation of Dadaist and Suprematist spatial constructions, the tradition of Merzbau, and the experimental architecture of Liubov S. Popova. Szalai also has combined pure geometry, contemporary Italian postmodern, post-Constructivist design, and paraphrases of different Merzbaus, the abstract architectural structures of Kurt Schwitters. Szalai learned from Schwitters the ways in which the prophet of the Hannover Dada movement combined ready-made and strictly abstract elements, the political and the metaphysical levels of a work. Szalai's reinvention is not one of homage, but a reinterpretation of the art-historical legacy in the late period of state socialism, the period of sincere cynicism, in which all values and rules of life were being eradicated. Szalai belonged among the postmodernists, but not among the cynical, purely imitative ones. He built abstract spatial structures with no visible and clear constructions and was always balancing on the borderline between the organic and the geometrical. Navigating between different poles, he tried to preserve his independent position. Szalai thus managed to preserve his identity in spite of artistic, political, and other changes

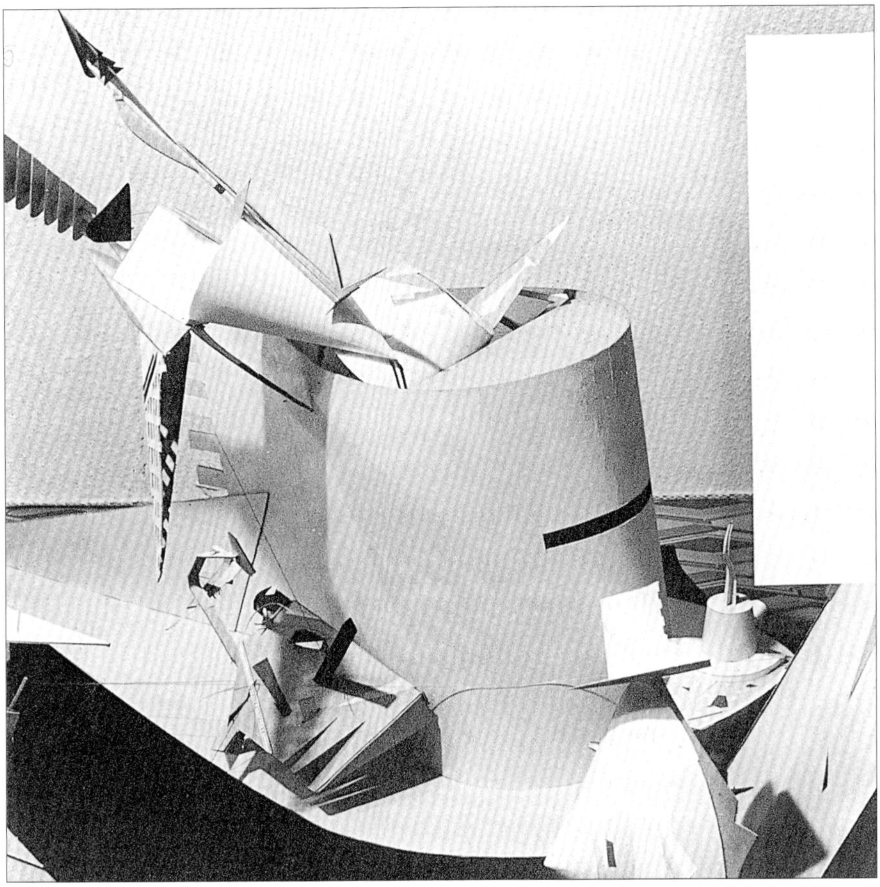

Figure 57 Tibor Szalai and István Kotsis, *BSCH Architecture*, 1984, paper, 120 × 50 × 70 cm. Brettschneider Foundation (photo: László Vincze).

of historic proportions that occurred in Hungary in the last decade and a half of the twentieth century.

The Transition to Democracy: Political Representation (The Imre Nagy Funeral and Memorial)

The transition to democracy in Hungary was connected to the public reinterpretation of the revolution of 1956. The Kádár regime took cruel revenge after the revolution, executing hundreds of people and finally hanging Imre Nagy, a former Communist and the prime minister at the time of the revolu-

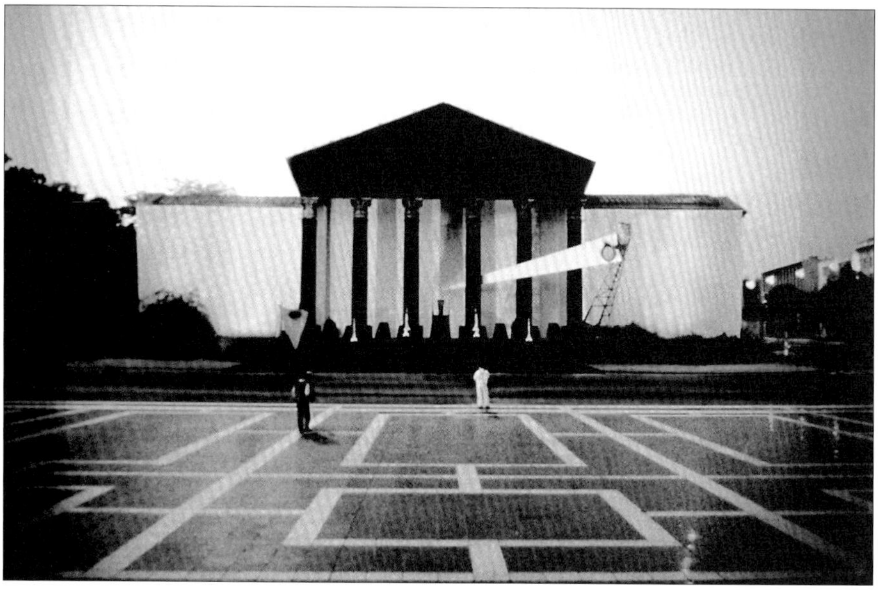

Figure 58 Gábor Bachman and László Rajk, *Project for the Funeral Ceremony of the Martyrs of the 1956 Revolution*, 1989.

tion. They then prohibited official memorials to the revolution and presented an erroneous version of events in school curricula. Nobody knew where the graves of Imre Nagy and the other revolutionaries were. Remembering or forgetting the revolution thus became the key issue of the transition period.

With the collapse of socialism during the late 1980s, the artistic canon and the representational infrastructure gradually collapsed. When in 1989—finally, and after long debates—the last Communist government gave permission to rebury Nagy and the other heroes of the revolution, it was not in a position to control the artistic realization of the memorial to the 1956 event. Consequently—and this was a very exceptional moment in Hungarian artistic and political history—there was an open competition with no political directives. The jury decided to erect a memorial to Imre Nagy and commissioned György Jovanovics. His highly artistic and very elegant memorial is not connected to any historical narrative—there are no heroic sculptures. It is a memorial in the spirit and name of the mixed tradition of antiquity and Suprematism. Later, there were scandals because different political groups didn't understand the meaning of the absence of any narrative representation.[32]

The other official commission was concerned with the setting of the reburial. This project was designed by Rajk and Bachman (Figure 58). On June 17, 1989, hundreds of thousands went to Heroes' Square, where the coffins of Imre Nagy and his comrades were arranged in a line. The catafalque was set in front of the main entrance to the Műcsarnok Municipal Gallery, a typical Budapest neoclassical building. Rajk and Bachman had covered the columns with black-and-white linen. In this way, their environmental design recalled at the same time the works of Christo, Malevich, and Rodchenko. For one very important day, the political dissidents and marginalized artists thus stood at the center of political representation. It was a rare and fantastic occasion. The memorial to Imre Nagy and the representation of the revolution became the symbol of the contemporary Hungarian avant-garde and the turning point for its members.

Conclusion

Hungarian post-utopian art in the late period of the Kádár regime belonged partly to the traditions of the Soviet art world and partly to the contemporary Western art world and was therefore at the same time connected with Eastern (and Soviet) and Western traditions. The economic and social contexts of the artist community and the social role and function of art, of course, were socialist, which naturally influenced its orientation. But in a curious way, in the 1970s and 1980s, the lack of a dominant ideology and of aggressive oppression resulted in an unusual freedom of art. The Hungarian contemporary art discussed in this essay was independent of the gallery system and, in the last years of the regime, free from oppression, as well. Artists did not simply want to imitate contemporary Western art movements. They weren't interested in the fashions of the Western art world. They felt free to criticize the socialist regime in their own ways, by the reinvention and reinterpretation of different high-modernist and Leftist traditions of the 1920s. With their activities, they finally became very deeply involved in the political history of the last period of state socialism. The Hungarian avant-garde community was also deeply interested in the artistic and social representation of the revolution of 1956.

Since the transition in the late 1980s, the cultural and political landscape has changed, and the philosophical problem of a divided world has disappeared. A single art world is again emerging, connected with universal civilization and the market. Conditions vital to the Soviet art world and the world of late socialist art have disappeared. This period became merely another of the historical periods from which we have inherited artistic artifacts. When we interpret them today, we are investigating our common past. In this way, problems concerning art works of late or postsocialism have become issues of our human essence and our personal history.

Notes

1. Frankly, we have some problems with categories. The artistic phenomena that I analyze here also could be partly described using the categories of social position. The Hungarian artists whose work I discuss belonged to what could be called the world of half-official and marginal art. Some of these artists also belonged to the inner circle of political dissidents. There also existed other marginalized artists whose work is ignored here because, in their case, the similarities between them were limited to their social position, not their artistic expression. From the art-historical perspective, some of the art under discussion would be labeled either "postmodernist" (such as that of Sándor Pinczehelyi), Neoconstructivist (some of the work of György Jovanovics), or Deconstructionist (the recent work of Gábor Bachman). Members of the group whose works I partly analyze—László Rajk, Gábor Bachman, Attila Kovács, Tibor Szalai—not only knew each other, but also exhibited together a few times. The common feature of their work is their shared interests, partly stylistic, partly political, and the way in which they articulated them in their art.

2. Boris Groys, *The Total Art of Stalinism: Avant-Garde, Aesthetic Dictatorship, and Beyond,* trans. Charles Rougle (Princeton: Princeton University Press, 1992). Groys explains how the Stalinist state finally destroyed the borders between life and art. The unitary artistic plan and the strict hierarchy of art and Party under state control were profoundly linked.

3. This is the reason that art historians often get confused when they have to describe Soviet art or the heritage of Socialist Realism. Were the artworks of the Soviet art world a part of universal Western high-cultural tradition in the classical meaning of the term? Very often, Central and Eastern European art historians themselves made a very strong distinction between the permanent and classical canon and hierarchy of "art" and the more recent politicized and ideologically founded practices of their own countries. Art-historical appraisals and historico-political judgments about the recent past of these societies are unavoidably linked.

4. See Serge Guilbaut, *How the New York School Stole the Idea of Modern Art: Abstract Expressionism, Freedom, and the Cold War,* trans. Arthur Goldhammer (Chicago: University of Chicago Press, 1983), Diana Crane, *The Transformation of the Avant-Garde: The New York Art World, 1940–1985* (Chicago: University of Chicago Press, 1987), Erica Doss, *Benton, Pollock, and the Politics of Modernism: From Regionalism to Abstract Expressionism* (Chicago: University of Chicago Press, 1991).

5. The expression is Boris Groys's. See Groys, *The Total Art of Stalinism,* p. 75.

6. "We [Russians] are like a Bermuda triangle for all 'isms,' including postmodernism." Arkadii Dragomoschenko, in "Symposium on Russian Postmodernism," *Postmodern Culture* 3, no. 2 (January 1993). //Http://jefferson.village.virginia.edu/pmpc/issue.193/sympos-1.193.

7. The slogan of the "Three Ts" was part of the resolution on the main principles of education and culture passed by the Hungarian Socialist Labor Party on July 25, 1958. According to this policy, an artwork is relevant primarily from the point of view of political power. Aesthetic values were considered to be independent of the power categorization: An artwork could be aesthetically valuable, but at the same time its content or style could be "hostile" or antagonistic toward the regime and, consequently, the Party simply prohibited it. In the same

way, something that was aesthetically awful could be very important for the Party because its content or style "supported" the system. The interpretation of what was antagonistic toward the regime and what was pleasing for the Party changed constantly according to the changes in global political games and in the power games between the Hungarian and the Soviet Party. Having a successful artistic career depended on the ability to recognize the rhythm and the periods of political change, as well as the ever-shifting borders of what was accepted. The best course for an artist was to find a balance in the Three Ts between Support and Tolerance. If somebody followed the current politico-artistic line of Support without any hesitation, unable to understand the rules of this game, he or she wasn't worthy of attention. If somebody always followed the line, it meant that he or she was *already* the Party's "property." If somebody was somewhat independent, the Party found such a person valuable enough to attempt to buy. The whole vicious circle was founded on the cynical appropriation of human independence.

8. See *Pécsi Műhely: 1970–1980*, edited by Péter Kovács (Székesfehérvár: István Király Muzeum, 1980), pp. 44–50.

9. See Fredric Jameson, *Postmodernism, or, The Cultural Logic of Late Capitalism* (London: Verso, 1991), esp. p. 9.

10. See Lóránd Hegyi, *Pinczehelyi Sándor* (Pécs: published by the artist, 1995).

11. The history of the Samizdat Boutique is an important chapter in the history of the Hungarian marginal art world and of the dissident circles. In the late 1970s, Rajk had a little flat in the heart of downtown Budapest, in Galamb Street. Here he started to collect and sell different kinds of *samizdat* publications. Consequently, his flat became one of the most important cultural political meeting places in the city. Those in academic circles and the whole city knew from mouth-to-mouth information that there was a place where they could buy the most recent *samizdats*. The boutique became the place where those who didn't dare to join the dissident circles were able to meet with the dissidents. It was the place of civic consciousness—and the Party and the police did not then feel themselves strong enough to close the place. For the police, this was also a very comfortable and easy way to control the visitors. The Samizdat Boutique, the play with the police and the Party, or, rather, the play *between* the dissidents and the Party, had no equal in other Central European countries under Soviet control. The history of this dissident institution reveals the nature of the "soft" Kádár regime and the techniques of "soft" dictatorship.

12. This wave of international postmodernism was introduced into Hungary mainly by the art historian and curator Lóránd Hegyi. The first postmodern show, *New Sensibility*, took place in December 1981 in the club of the traditional Budapest artists' colony, the Fészek Club. Hegyi organized collective exhibitions in 1983, 1985, and 1987, all of which were very popular and successful. These were the first occasions when a new artistic fashion, not the traditional power games controlled and invented by the Party, divided the Hungarian art world. Nevertheless, for the cynical Party, the New Sensibility was more comfortable than the post-utopian artists discussed here, who always played with the traditions and traditional symbols of state socialism. The painters of New Sensibility didn't want anything to do with political power and weren't interested in local contexts. Since they wanted to be successful financially, they wanted no part in the political game.

13. I am using the term *Gesamtkunstwerkman* because it is commonly used in Hungary and denotes artists who pursue the Romanticist and avant-gardist notion of the universal work of art.

14. Together with the sociologist Iván Szelényi, Konrád wrote *The Intellectuals on the Road to Class Power* (1978). Iván Szelényi had to leave the country in 1975, together with Ágnes Heller, Ferenc Fehér, and György and Mária Márkus.

15. Bachman's new works—such as the three Fuggerhaus Projects from 1993—sometimes make explicit references to Tschumi's Parc de la Villette project. His other works—

such as the NA-NE Gallery (1990) and the *Free Worlds* installation, which was exhibited in Toronto in 1992—resemble the constructions of Georgii A. Stenberg and the exhibitions of OBMOKhU (the Society of Young Artists) in 1921 in Moscow. See Christina Lodder, *The Russian Constructivism* (New Haven: Yale University Press, 1983), pp. 66–70.

The history of the NA-NE Gallery would warrant an essay of its own. The gallery, founded in 1990 and opened by György Konrád, was built in a Neoconstructivist style, a style so typical of Bachman, with a red flag on the sidewalk and black metal structures. It was a private gallery, probably the first one after the free elections. It was also a financial failure and closed in 1991.

16. László Rajk, "The Activities of the United Nations in the Field of Housing, Building and Planning between 1945–1976" (master's thesis, McGill University School of Art, 1976).

17. Among other works, he also made a series of comic strips for the *Bibó Memorial Book*. István Bibó, who later become a symbol and living myth of the revolution, originally started his career as a university professor and then, in 1956, became a minister in the Nagy government. He was influenced by the contemporary liberalism and populism and was never a Communist. After his death in 1979, the Hungarian dissidents made a large *samizdat* memorial book for him. Rajk made a comic strip about the political resistance in which he mixed photographs of the Paris Commune and the American Civil War with his own text and Bibó's. But the cartoons were not well received by his fellow political dissidents. They misunderstood Rajk's intentions, and in the end, they didn't include his work in the volume. A few years later, Rajk made a comic book about the struggle of the Polish freedom movement, Solidarity that—unfortunately, only the original existed—was confiscated by the Communist state police when they closed down the Samizdat Boutique.

18. By "critical regionalism," Frampton meant a condition in which a local architecture consciously evolves in express opposition to the domination of a hegemonic power. While it accepts the potentially liberating role of modernization, it resists being totally absorbed by optimized production and consumption. See Kenneth Frampton, "Place-Form and Cultural Identity," in *Design after Modernity*, edited by John Thackara (London: Thames and Hudson, 1988), p. 277.

19. The translation is difficult. The original Hungarian title—*Szemét* (trash, rubbish heap) *rakás –szemét lakás* (flat) is an untranslatable language game. The title includes another sarcastic and politically ironic element, for it is dedicated to those who didn't receive flats from the state—the mainstream in the socialist system—and who had to build their houses without any government support.

20. This was the *Fővárosi Hulladékhasznosító Mű* project (1983), designed by IPARTERV (Antal Lázár, Márton Dobó, Gyula Gyalay Korpos, László Rajk, and Attila Szabó).

21. Károlyi was the first president of the Hungarian Republic after the collapse of the Austro-Hungarian monarchy. He was both a very rich Hungarian aristocrat and a libertarian democrat. He emigrated for the first time after the Communist revolution in 1919, and then again in 1949, this time to Vence. His widow founded the Károlyi Foundation. After her death in 1990, the foundation ceased to exist and the building designed by Rajk was destroyed.

22. *Bricolage* in this case diverges from the traditional sense of the term that connotes the free use of whatever materials are at hand. In Hungary and elsewhere in Central Europe it signifies the combination of local, soft, primitive technological solutions and developed Western technologies. The reception of Western technology and its adaptation to local, low-tech contexts is the method or process of *bricolage* there. *Bricolage* is well known everywhere on the margins of Western societies. From my point of view, *bricolage*—or in Hungarian, *buherálás*—is the social process of the creative adaptation/domestication and understanding of the often alien international high tech.

23. Cicciolina—originally Ilona Staller—was a Hungarian making her living as a porn star in Italy. In 1989, in a Catholic church in Budapest, she married the American artist

Jeff Koons, whom she later divorced. Together they made an artistic porn project, *Made in Heaven* (1990).

24. The *Letatlin* was Tatlin's project between 1931 and 1933. Tatlin reinvented Leonardo's flying machine and in this way expressed his imagination about the social role of the artist. Rajk's paraphrase—the language game with the name—is a typical tactic of post-utopian art.

25. Gábor Bódy was born in 1946 and killed himself in 1985. He was the first avant-garde artist who succeeded in making independent films in the social environment of the Hungarian state socialist film industry. *Narcissus and Psyche* (1980) was the first really Wagnerian *Gesamtkunstwerk* in the history of Hungarian avant-garde and alternative culture. He worked together with Bachman, Attila Kovács, and almost everybody in the closed circle of the Budapest avant-garde during those years.

26. See *Bódy Gábor, a Presentation of His Work*, edited by László Beke and Miklós Peternák (Budapest: Palace of Exhibitions, Central Board of Hungarian Cinematography, Ministry of Culture, 1987), pp. 190–93.

27. Bódy's death signified an end of a historic period in the life of this generation. His funeral could be compared to the funeral of Malevich. Many of his friends couldn't continue their artistic careers without him.

28. Esterházy, for example, wrote the script for Péter Gothar's film *Idő van* (Time exists), the set for which was made by László Rajk.

29. See *Gábor Bachman: Architectural Paintings and Architectural Projects* (Budapest: Ludwig Muzeum, 1994). In 1996 Bachman represented Hungary at the Architectural Biennial in Venice. He held solo exhibitions in Paris (Jeu de Paume, 1992) and Stuttgart (Solitude Schloss Akademie, 1994).

30. See *Bachman, Kovács, Rajk, Szalai* (Budapest: Dorottya Street Gallery, 1986), *Attila Kovács: Necropolis* (Pécs: Gallery Pécs, 1987), and essays in that catalog by Katalin Néray, László Beke, Péter György, and Lóránd Hegyi.

31. I can't avoid mentioning here the influence of the Polish director Tadeusz Kantor. His famous production *Dead Class* (in 1975 in Wroclaw) was a turning point in the Polish theater. Its message strongly resembles that implied by Kovács's Stone Room.

32. The absence of symbols became a tradition of the revolution. On the first afternoon of the revolution—October 23, 1956—at the demonstration against the Communist government, the "semantic war" began, too. The revolutionaries demonstrated with the red, white, and green Hungarian flag, but they cut out the star, the symbol of the Communist Party. Consequently, in the middle of the flag—instead of the symbol of the Party—there was a hole. This flag with a hole has become the symbol of the revolution. Such a solution was acceptable to different groups of revolutionaries, including social democrats and Rightists. Decades later, Rajk and Bachman brought back this hole with their *Project for the Funeral Ceremony of the Martyrs of the 1956 Revolution* (Figure 58).

The New Cuban Art

Gerardo Mosquera

A question of major importance in Cuban culture is the link between radical political and artistic positions, something that usually occurs in small, poor, subaltern countries where culture carries a marked social edge attuned to the circumstances in which it is produced and where it has been forced to construct a national identity in the face of colonial and neocolonial powers. On the island of Cuba, this trait goes back to the onset of the independence movement—inspired by the French Revolution—at the beginning of the nineteenth century. A large number of the most important intellectuals were also truly outstanding political figures. The paradigm is José Martí, Cuba's national hero, organizer of the war that led to independence from Spain in 1898 and at the same time one of the great writers in the Spanish language. But what is still more telling is that the first possible Cuban Catholic saint to be beatified and now in the process of canonization is Félix Varela, a priest from the early 1800s, professor of philosophy, publicist, political figure active in the courts of Spain, and the first to support the independence of the island, a cause he championed until his death in exile, that is, someone who could be on good terms with both God and the devil.

The weight of a liberal and enlightened tradition in the formation of the Cuban nation, along with the social sense of the intellectual avant-garde as well as the geographical and historical location of the island in the Occidental sphere, established a specific background for the socialist regime in Cuba that was different from the case in Asia or Central and Eastern Europe. On the other hand, these coordinates are to be found in greater or lesser degree in Latin America in general. Moreover, in the early 1980s, when the so-called New Cuban Art movement was consolidated, many intellectuals of the island still harbored a hope for the nationalist and Third World utopia of social justice promised by the Cuban revolution and based on indisputable social gains. In addition, the regime's powerful propaganda apparatus and control of information always worked efficiently in constructing a favorable image, enhanced by the charisma and glamour of Che Guevara and Fidel Castro. Despite the similarity between New Cuban Art and the artistic processes that took place in other socialist countries at similar dates, the historical and sociocultural conditioning of Cuban art and its position in relationship to the regime were often quite different with respect to what occurred in other countries, as presented in other chapters of this book. For this reason it is worthwhile to begin with a very brief introduction concerning events from the first appearance of modern art in Cuba until the emergence of the new art.

From Modernism to Revolution

Cuba is very Hispanic (an anthropologist called it "the whitest of the Antilles"), due to the fact that it was the last colony to gain independence from Spain (1898) and the fact that immigration of Spaniards to Cuba continued at a high level until the middle of the twentieth century. (Castro himself is the son of a wealthy immigrant from Galicia.) The sociocultural ambiance of Cuba always favored the acceptance and integration of the immigrants into the Creole society, instead of the establishment of ghettos. Since the aboriginal population—not very large—had been eliminated in the seventeenth century, slave labor was imported from Africa for centuries. This meant that, together with its "Europeanism," unique in the Caribbean, Cuba also possessed at the same time the most varied traditions of all the African diaspora in America, with four religious-cultural complexes of African origin: Santería (Yoruba), the Palo Monte (Kongo), the Regla Arará (Ewe-Fon), and the secret society Abakuá (cultures of Calabar). The men and women who grow up in these traditions are not particularly different from other Cubans. They feel and behave as Cubans. Nevertheless, African cultural values that are not dissolved in the new mestiza culture evolve actively, as cores of practices, beliefs, customs, and views of reality. They are the cultural nuclei that we might call "Afro-Cuban," to differentiate them from the Cuban culture of synthesis within which the integrated African group also operates. These nuclei constitute not living fossils, but components that evolved in the new medium on the other side of the Atlantic, hybridized, inventive, and influential in the construction of contemporary culture. Moreover, these nuclei were already transracial in the nineteenth century, although blacks and mulattos from the popular levels of the society predominate. Beyond these and other group differences, a unitary national identity exists, deeply rooted historically, which has always been a subject for art.

Modern art began in Cuba in the 1920s, countering an academic practice that went back to the early nineteenth century when the Academia San Alejandro was founded in Havana, directed at first by a French painter and follower of Jacques-Louis David. The avant-garde current formed part of a critical movement in all of Cuban society, a movement of nationalism and social affirmation often clearly in opposition to the neocolonial interference of the United States and linked to political positions of the Left. Some advocates of modernism were even members of the Communist Party, founded in 1925. The modernist intellectuals of the time were looking within the country and its vernacular culture while still keeping an eye on what was happening in Europe. The major concern for Amelia Peláez, Carlos Enríquez, Eduardo Abela, and other artists was to construct a Cuban identity that would go beyond the epigonic expressions of the Paris School. They succeeded in using modernist formal and ideo-aesthetic ruptures as a means of affirming a Cuban visual culture in "cultivated" art. Thus, methods taken from Cubism, Expressionism, and Surrealism were spontaneously coupled with popular imagery, the Baroque tradition, and the visual ambiance and sensuality of the landscape and the people.

In the 1940s, a second generation gathered around the Grupo Orígenes, whose center was José Lezama Lima, the most famous Cuban writer. Painters such as Mariano and René Portocarrero moved away from the "social" focus typical of the first generation and toward an introspective sensibility, although without abandoning the nationalist preoccupation, now directed toward a "Cubaness of essences." At the beginning of the decade, Alfred H. Barr, Jr., spoke of a "School of Havana" characterized by bright color, vivacity, and exuberance in contrast to the Mexican tradition's political inclination.[1] In 1944, Barr organized, at the Museum of Modern Art in New York, with which he had been associated since 1929, the first important exhibition of Cuban art in a U.S. museum, including modernist artists of both generations.

A little earlier Wifredo Lam, back in Cuba because of the war in Europe, had made a historically important shift, in presenting the first vision stemming from the Afro-American presence in the plastic art of the West.[2] He used modernism as a space to construct a mythology of the Caribbean. For introducing meanings of African origin into the art of the European tradition without exceeding its limits, Lam considered himself a Trojan horse.[3] Actually, his work was less an infiltration in the strict sense than a decentering operation, a participation in modernism from another laboratory. Although Lam is one of the paradigmatic figures of Latin American modern art, the significance of the displacement he effected has not been well recognized in its active sense as transformative reinforcement of modernism in general. Lam, the most widely known Cuban painter, established no school on the island but was paradigmatic for some transformations brought about forty years later by the new art.

In contrast to similar movements in Europe and Latin America, the Cuban avant-garde had neither manifestos nor consciously structured schools. And it had no prophets in the manner of an André Breton, a Kazimir Malevich, or a Joaquín Torres-García. Not one artist, no matter how influential he or she may have been, left a programmatic legacy. This absence of proclamations has continued to characterize the art of the island to this day. In this atmosphere, modernism exfoliated in a great variety of manifestations, and its process consisted of successive confrontations of diverse poetics, kept taut by the contradiction between the influence of currents called "international" and the affirmation of those that were our own.

Although some of the important artists achieved their best works then, at the beginning of the 1950s, a certain general exhaustion was apparent. Visual art became stereotyped in derivative tendencies—especially a honeyed Picasso style—and the redundancy extended toward a "Creolist" mannerism. The awareness of this exhaustion prompted an increase of abstraction under the influence of North American Abstract Expressionism. This move helped young artists to break with the tropical sweetness, to rebel against the establishment, and at the same time to attempt a more international discourse. The group called Los Once (The Eleven) formed the advance guard of this orientation, assuming a critical stance toward the "School of Havana." It is interesting that this group, while opposing figuration in art, maintained a political posture against the dictatorship of Fulgencio Batista. Abstraction was for them a critical instrument, culturally nonconformist. Moving beyond the rupture provoked by Los Once and motivated by the international abstract wave of that time, numerous artists slanted their language toward the nonfigurative, above all toward geometric forms. Nevertheless, the abstractionist predominance passed quickly, even among the "Action" painters. In contrast to that in Argentina or Brazil, Cuban visual art has never shown an informal or Constructivist inclination.

The revolution of 1959, despite its radicalism, did not mean a sharp break in the culture. No official guidelines were dictated, as occurred in the Communist regimes of Asia or Eastern Europe, but neither were there any Tatlins or Rodchenkos, caught up in a dream of transforming the culture and, by means of it, the whole of life. In Cuba, as we just saw, modern art formed part of the fabric of a liberal tradition. It was equally well established in the cultural and in the political spheres, given both its nationalist affirmation and frequent social bent. The revolution accepted modern art, which proceeded along its own course, without the alterations that might have been expected. The motto "With the Revolution, everything; outside the Revolution, nothing" established the cultural policies of the Cuban regime in the most general terms. It was proclaimed in 1961 by Fidel Castro in a speech before intellectuals and is still valid today.

This apothegm, and the meeting with intellectuals, resulted from fear on the part of the intellectuals when faced with the first big case of censorship of art, which happened with the banning of the documentary film *PM,* made that year by Sabá Cabrera Infante and Orlando Jiménez Leal, which described Havana nightlife. The film was not shown again in Cuba until very recently, when it could be proved how innocuous it was and how the reaction of that time—headed by the supposedly liberal official Alfredo Guevara—was exaggerated, the consequence of a sort of revolutionary moralism. Although Castro did not nullify the decision regarding the documentary, skirting the affair, his speech was harsh but conciliatory and had the virtue of establishing the rules of the game very clearly: If work never went against "the Revolution," one could do anything at all in art and culture.

The problem was that the entity determining what could affect "the Revolution" was the regime itself, from the cultural institutions to the state security apparatus. The breadth or narrowness of the criteria for this determination varied with different periods, institutions, and officials, but except during the 1970s, no one interfered much with artistic and aesthetic questions per se, only with tendencies toward political protest. The maxim inspired by the postulate "Let a thousand flowers bloom and a thousand schools compete" from the most liberal period in Mao Zedong's China has most of the time been a sword of Damocles in Cuba. This edict, however, proclaimed by the maximum leader in person, has served artists and intellectuals as a means of defense against bureaucrats. Taking advantage of its positive side, we have used it as a motto in favor of creative freedom, confronting concrete aspects having to do with art and culture arising from the system itself. In truth, the Cuban revolution has maintained the least restrictive cultural policies in the history of the socialist camp, in accordance with the tradition of the country. This perspective inspired the aesthetic work of the Spanish-Mexican philosopher Adolfo Sánchez Vázquez, which, among other things, is an attempt to join Marxism and modernism. At the same time, the work functioned in Cuba as a Marxist base for a liberal orientation for culture.[4]

Another important aspect to keep in mind is that Cuba had undertaken and defended a socialist system on its own, very far from the Soviet Union and its tanks, and very close to the United States, both of which exercised a strong influence over the island. The revolution and the change toward socialism had not even been led by the local Communist Party, but by the 26th of July Movement and other anti-Batista groups that did not proclaim a Marxist program in the early days. All of this made it possible for the Cuban regime to maintain relative independence from the Chinese and Soviet orbits in the 1960s, despite its increasingly closer relationships with those countries and the decisive economic, political, and military support offered by the Soviet Union from an early date. It is the opinion of some that Cuba's move toward the Communist nations was stimulated by the aggression, arrogance, and lack of diplomacy typical of the North American political stance toward the Cuban revolution. The case of Cuba did not fit into the existing American view of the world, and the United States mistakenly confronted it in the spirit of the Cold War and the old politics of the big stick.

Castro and Guevara, leaders with strong personalities, had their own liberation projects on a global scale and ran Cuba as an ideological and logistical-military center of a violent internationalist revolution, mainly in Latin America and Africa. The Guevarist motto "to create one, two, three, many Vietnams" aimed at the overthrow of "imperialism" by revolutionary means, but did not fit with the policies of thawing relations and peaceful coexistence launched by Nikita Khrushchev and the rapprochement between the Soviet Union and the United States that got underway then, after the most tense years of the Cold War. The Soviets tried to dissuade the Cubans from their neo-Bolivaresque dreams, but maintained an astute policy of keeping their distance while at the same time using Cuba to offer support to revolutionary movements elsewhere. The missile crisis in 1962, the moment when the Cold War was closest to turning into a nuclear conflagration, clearly showed the differences between the bellicose attitude of the Cubans and the much more responsible and diplomatic stance of the Soviets. In contrast, when the Soviet Union took military action, crushing the Prague Spring and supplying logistical support to North Vietnam, Castro publicly expressed his support—as he did much later during the events of Tiananmen Square—and only asked himself if the Soviets would do the same for Cuba in case of a North American invasion of the island.

The political change of 1959 in Cuba brought notable state support for culture through the creation of spaces, institutions, and events in all areas. The utopian enthusiasm of the 1960s, when it was believed that the country would be transformed into a paradise and—due to the experience of the Cuban revolution—would foster a revolution in the Third World on an international scale, manifested itself with unusual vigor in the culture. Of prime importance was the establishment of a system of free art education, one of the bases for the artistic blossoming of the 1980s that, with limitations, continues today. During the 1960s, some of the most important artists of the avant-garde carried out nontraditional pedagogical activities that were key to the orientation of artistic viewpoints. Something similar occurred in the 1980s, when several practitioners of the new art became professors at the Instituto Superior de Arte (Graduate Institute of Art) immediately after completing their studies, thus making this center the focal point of cultural disquiet. In contrast, the pedagogy of the Soviet professors who were present in Cuba during the 1970s never went beyond technical aspects. The sparseness of the Soviet cultural influence over the Cubans is surprising, not only with regard to art, but also in general, despite the Soviets' heavy presence in all fields and the links and interchanges between the two countries for three decades.

Perhaps the most important and paradoxical cultural effect of the revolution was that it set off a permanent exodus of Cubans, leading to the emergence and consolidation of strong Cuban communities in the United States (two million Cuban-Americans versus eleven and a half million inhabitants of the island), Puerto Rico, Spain, Venezuela, and other countries, to such an extent that today Miami is the city with the second-largest Cuban population. This circumstance diversified the culture, for the first time and permanently, into expressions on the island and in the diaspora. We Cubans were not an emigrant people. On the contrary, we provided the receiving country for immigrants coming from Spain, Eastern and Central Europe, the Middle East, and the Caribbean, and we have not yet been able to grasp our new diasporic condition in all its implications. Political extremism on both sides has contributed nothing productive to what constitutes in reality an enriching situation. The Cuban emigration is at the forefront of a remarkable cultural life, above all in popular music and other forms of vernacular culture, literature, and the visual arts. It includes numerous artists and intellectuals of the first rank, as many exiled as those educated or born in Cuba. In the plastic arts, one should mention José Bedia, Agustín Cárdenas, Luis Cruz Azaceta, Teresita Fernandez, Félix González-Torres, and Ana Mendieta, among many others.

Despite the political violence, the harshness of the process of change, and the exile of eminent artists and intellectuals—among them figures of the greatest importance such as the folklorist Lydia Cabrera, the writers Guillermo Cabrera Infante and Lino Novás Calvo, the "Queen of Salsa," Celia Cruz, the composer Ernesto Lecuona, and the historian Herminio Portell-Vilá—the decade of the 1960s was a period of cultural splendor for the island, a time when numerous tendencies were in play. During those years, Tomás Gutiérrez Alea filmed *Memorias del subdesarrollo* (Memories of underdevelopment), considered the most important Cuban motion picture; Lezama Lima published *Paradiso,* the most widely known Cuban novel; the most impressive complex of modern architecture in Cuba was built, the National Schools of Art;[5] the musical and poetic movement of Nueva Trova emerged; memorable theatrical and dance programs were presented; and poster art reached its peak, among many other events. Pop Art, the new figuration, and the dialogue between them set the tone for the visual arts of that time in curious local reinterpretations and embellishments of the "internationalist" tendencies then in vogue—all in the midst of the revolutionary atmosphere.

Raúl Martínez—a member of the Los Once group—took advantage of an ingenuous Pop Art style to construct an iconography of the revolution that was at one and the same time grandiose, cheerful, and everyday, free of the least hint of an official air, by taking inspiration from popular images tinged by the grotesque. His paintings characterize in exemplary fashion the utopian vision and the reality of those years by commingling them. These works are important also as antecedents of the new art of the 1980s, above all in the free, antirhetorical treatment of patriotic symbols; the "primitivization" of revolutionary icons, which are mixed with the vernacular and the everyday; and the representation of the epic years of the 1960s on the level of life in the street. In his painting *Isla 70* (1970), Martínez presents, in North American Pop Art style, a huge crowd—recalling the large political gatherings of the epoch, but also the jacket of the Beatles album *Sergeant Pepper*—that includes ordinary people, along with Oscar Wilde, one of the Beatles,

Martínez himself, Ho Chi Minh, Camilo Cienfuegos (a hero of the revolution who disappeared in a possible airplane accident in 1959), Fidel Castro, and even a parrot and a monkey.

Martínez based a good part of his work on constructing a pictorial imagery of the revolution. Other important artists of the decade, such as Chago Armada, Antonia Eiriz, and Umberto Peña, however, never bothered with that and developed more reflective and existential discourses. There was an interest in the sexual, and Peña and Servando Cabrera Moreno made the first gay art, without using that term, of course.

Despite what was said above, it is important not to mythify the 1960s in Cuba as the realization of a cultural utopia. In that period, the concentration camps of UMAP (Military Units of Production Support) were created—although for only a brief time. Homosexuals, the religious, and young artists were sent there, among them Pablo Milanés, who later became one of the most outstanding Cuban musicians. We must not forget that the history of culture during the revolutionary period began with an act of censorship that was not rectified, as we have seen. The cases of censorship and the marginalization of intellectuals continued to occur throughout the entire period—it is enough to recall the closure of the excellent cultural weekly magazine *Lunes de Revolución* at the beginning of the decade. It is also important to stress that the Cuban position has never been monolithic and the cultural policies of the regime have been followed in very different ways, according to the persons involved and the contexts.

The failure of the guerrilla movement fostered by Cuba in Latin America and the economic and administrative chaos of the country led the Cuban government to enter the orbit of the Soviet Union after ten years of relative independence within a situation of conflictive intimacy. Until it was overtaken by its own chaos after perestroika, the Soviet Union saved the regime from total chaos with subsidies: They usually advanced two billion dollars per year, in addition to pardoning debts and offering very favorable prices, technical aid, and other concessions. Naturally, they imposed conditions. These included the reorganization of the state and the institutions of the country on the Soviet model, joining COMECOM (Council of Mutual Economic Assistance)—although not the Warsaw Pact—and indirect Soviet control over economic decisions and international policies.

The fundamental result for culture was the closing of the plural, intense, and quite autonomous scene that had prevailed. In 1971, Castro himself established a new cultural policy in a Congress for Education and Culture. In his speech there, he launched a new motto: "Art: A Weapon of the Revolution." It is important to emphasize that in Cuban socialism, the regime has governed largely through speeches and slogans that dictate the guidelines to follow at each moment. Like the texts of the great religious books, these discourses and slogans were often contradictory, although they all lived together in the pantheon. The new mantra did not specifically nullify the motto "With the Revolution, everything; outside the Revolution, nothing." It was not rejected in official rhetoric, but was in fact suspended. The neutrality implicit in it did not accord with a militant function for art.

The government, despite certain hints in favor of Socialist Realism, dictated, not an official style, but a practice of culture as ideological propaganda, along with a stereotyped nationalism. It was required that art participate in the ideology of the revolution and that it express the Cuban and Latin American identity. However, because modern art and the simultaneous pursuit of a variety of artistic tendencies were so rooted in Cuban culture, in contrast to the Soviet Union and other Asiatic and Eastern European cultures, art as a "weapon of the Revolution" retained an inclusive character and a margin of freedom. Thus, art could be politicized within a freedom of styles. Very talented artists of the time, such as Nelson Domínguez and Roberto Fabelo, went from dramatic and existential Neoexpressionism, which they had practiced under the influence of Eiriz, to depicting farmers and soldiers using a sweetened Neoexpressionism. Obviously, radical Expressionism and abstraction were viewed with suspicion as displaying antihumanism, escapism, or decadence. In those years, it was expected that every exhibit or book of poems have at least one "political" piece. Since Soviet financing increased the budgets dedicated to culture, bureaucratic opportunism also grew among artists, who combined the "political" with nationalism by painting waves of cane cutters, heads of blacks, bucolic country girls, and modernist revolutionary heroes in styles ranging from Surrealism to Op Art.

The task of representing Cuban identity allowed artists a less committed space with more direct representations of revolutionary ideology. They could make art with greater freedom and justify it as a work striving to reflect the national identity. However, some also went to ridiculous extremes of opportunistic discipline vis-à-vis the official edict. I remember one painter during those times who, among other things, would put palms in his canvases to signify the Cuban landscape, machetes for life in the countryside, Afro-Cuban signs to include that important ethnocultural aspect, guitars to refer to the Hispanic component, and swishing hips to express

Caribbean sensuality. In those days, a Cuban cow set a world record in milk production and its photograph with Fidel Castro came out on the front page of the leading newspaper. In the heat of the event, an exhibit titled *Art and Cattle Raising* was hastily organized and reviewed in glowing terms by the most widely published critic of the moment. When the animal died, a bronze statue of it was made, but not commented on by the critics. Although other cases may not have gone to such extremes, events propagandized by the regime indeed were usually motivation for art exhibits.

The entrance into the Soviet orbit determined more than an ideological change in cultural policies. The entire surface of the cultural terrain was swept with great vigor. Almost all the cultural officials who had maintained a liberal policy were removed from their posts, particularly the writers and artists. Named as replacements were members from the military, most of them of a low cultural level. The presidency of the Consejo Nacional de Cultura (National Council of Culture), the highest position in this field, was awarded to a captain who, from the pages of a magazine put out by the Ministry of Armed Forces, had upbraided many writers for their "ideological problems" and cultural institutions for their "liberalism." These military personnel established moral and ideological parameters for those occupying positions in the cultural field. Those who did not comply were *parametrados*, that is, they were not allowed to work, exhibit, publish, teach, or occupy posts of technical or political leadership in cultural institutions, even on the lower, community, level.

As a result of this witch hunt, many of the leading intellectuals were marginalized for "political" or "moral" reasons, among them the writers Reinaldo Arenas and Virgilio Piñera, the dramatists Roberto Blanco and Vicente Revuelta, and the painters Cabrera Moreno, Manuel Mendive, and Tomás Sánchez. The most valuable members of the Cuban intellectual community were deprived of their means of work, buried for not being "Marxists" or for being "decadent" or "petit bourgeois," homosexuals, or religious. Eiriz and Peña, in one of the most dramatic gestures ever made against censorship, protested in silence, sacrificing what is most important to an artist: They stopped painting for the rest of their lives. Eiriz returned to it only at the end of her days, after going into exile in Miami. The 1970s were a dark period, supporting an art that was complacent in the face of officialdom and its tide of opportunism and mediocrity. Nevertheless, various meritorious artists went on with their work, often without being able to show it. It was also during this decade that Cuba began its wars in Ethiopia and Angola, which involved hundreds of thousands of Cubans and left no trace in art or in culture.

The New Art

During the second half of the 1970s, some young artists became interested in photorealism. Although this type of realistic painting, based on copying a photo, was often used to make large portraits of revolutionary heroes, the most important painters went in another direction. Very refreshing canvases appeared with no explicit references to Cuban culture, showing young people in the informal activities of daily life. The artists were Flavio Garciandía, Gory, and others who had only recently appeared on the stage. Gory himself also created simple and enigmatic scenes with a certain surreal atmosphere, while Eduardo Rubén painted plain constructive elements. Tomás Sánchez made landscapes from the point of view of a mystical-contemplative vision influenced by Eastern philosophical religions.

The Ideological Confrontation

The sotto voce challenge to a militant and nationalist art extended by these artists did not pass unnoticed by the officialist critics. The photorealists were accused of following a nihilistic, dehumanizing, foreign artistic tendency that denigrated the artist's creative role and social responsibility. This set off a polemic in the cultural press, the first case in which the artists could respond publicly to the opinions of the officialist critics. It is interesting to note that in Cuba, unlike the countries where the canon of Socialist Realism prevailed, the appearance of a hyperrealist current meant a deviation from the official lines.

But the true transformation would come from the hands of various artists who were still younger, born in the revolutionary period or a little before. They were trained entirely in this period, and the revolution was not a Romantic utopia for them. It constituted the hard reality of everyday life and was their only experience. In 1977, they began to try to show their work, but they were unsuccessful until the early 1980s, as were some of the participants in the ephemeral Cuban photorealism group.

In the decade of the 1980s, these young people unleashed a movement that renovated not only the plastic arts, but the entire culture. It was a collective phenomenon that spread throughout the culture, not a program directed by a leader or the result of great individual personalities who drew others along with them. For that reason, this chapter, unlike the others in this book, will focus more on general, collective processes. It will give a broad overview, with no pretense of offering a detailed, or even a halfway exhaustive, account. The new art maintained the Cuban tradition of not being an organized enterprise, nor did it have a program, and, in addition, it embraced diverse artistic poetics. Its proponents sought to make art without restrictions or impositions, to take advantage of the languages and methodologies developed during the 1960s in the West (especially Conceptual Art), and to be open to the world, defending an autonomy—and an ethic—of artistic production. They wanted an art that would defend its own quests and values and not march to the drumbeat of slogans. They also wanted to break with the stereotyped dogma of national identity. They were very critical of the Cuban modernist pantheon, venerated in derivative fashion by the artists of the 1970s. Only Lam and another artist or two were saved, retaining high esteem in their eyes, along with Armada, Eiriz, Martínez, and Peña among their contemporaries.

The new artists, rather than rebel in face of those clichés and impositions, ignored them with an Olympian air. Their resolute stance allowed them to prevail despite the hostility that surrounded them. They were favored by an atmosphere that was slowly admitting more fresh air following the creation of the Ministry of Culture at the end of 1976 as part of the process of the institutionalization of the country. The ministry gave greater status to the cultural sphere in the government, a status that was reinforced by the naming of Armando Hart to the post of minister. Hart was a "historic" leader with great political weight, a member of the Politburo of the Communist Party, and close to Castro from the beginning of the struggle against Batista. He was in addition a civilian. For some ten years, he promoted a policy of reconciliation, unity, and liberalization of cultural activities that later would cost him his membership in the Politburo. This policy no doubt was an attempt to rectify the repressive excesses after the Congress for Education and Culture, given the unease that such excesses produced in the cultural milieu. Many intellectuals who had been marginalized were rehabilitated, and some even became the new official figures. But as always, the regime wished to do everything "from above," under strict control.

The new artists went beyond the expected ways of behaving, acting on their own initiative and with great conviction. They managed to survive only after a sharp ideological-cultural clash that led them to protest publicly in conferences, roundtables, and other gatherings. The artists were the targets of an array of accusations, tarred with labels ranging from counterrevolutionaries and diversionists to deviationists. Some critics, who developed a very useful instrument for their defense, supported them. The instrument consisted in maintaining their ideo-aesthetic positions effectively within a theoretical discourse of the Left. By the middle of the decade, these positions had been consolidated, guaranteeing a proper space for the new art, from which it spread outward. As a result, the renovation of the entire Cuban culture began with the plastic arts. The visual arts gradually assumed a more active, critical, and independent role, spurred by social preoccupations.

The system maintained—and continues to maintain—an ambivalent relationship vis-à-vis the new art, a relationship kept tense between the attempt to manipulate it and the level of tolerance that a military *caudillista* regime is capable of supporting by virtue of its own character. The new artists brought strong pressure to bear on the brand-new Ministry of Culture and its liberalizing proclamations, but had to wait four years before being able to exhibit. They could do so only after opening an exhibit in one of the artists' homes. Unlike the "apartment shows" in the Soviet Union, this was not an event for just a group of fellow artists. They invited the entire cultural community, officials included, and announced the event throughout the city by means of handmade posters. The event terrified the system and led to permission for them to make the historic show *Volumen 1*,[6] inaugurated in a central gallery of the Boulevard de San Rafael in Havana in January 1981. This exhibit, even though it was quite mixed and somewhat ingenuous, was a blast of freedom, fresh air, and youthful energy in the arid ambiance of the Cuban plastic arts of the time, breaking attendance records and having a tremendous effect. The same officialist critics who had attacked photorealism labeled the show "provocation in the boulevard." When those critics encountered the public in the gallery, a very heated debate took place that set off the profusion of conferences, panels, and every sort of forum typical of the ambiance surrounding the plastic arts during the 1980s. At that time, the positions of the new art were imposed, the clichés typical of the 1970s withdrew, and an informed critical evaluation of art began to be practiced that continues to flourish today.

Throughout the decade, some powerful officials supported the new artists. These included Marcia Leiseca, the vice minister of culture, and Beatriz Aulet, the director of plastic arts and design at the Ministry of Culture.

They used the young artists as a way to renew Cuban participation in international biennials, interrupted during the backlash of the 1970s, opened doors for them to exhibit on the island, sent them on trips abroad, and made it easier for them to accept the invitations to other countries they began to receive during the second half of the 1980s. But the state did not offer them any commissions at all, when these commissions were then the only way that allowed artists to live from their work and even to make quite a good income. The Cuban Cultural Goods Fund, which held the monopoly for the commercialization of art, did not promote the work of the new artists. The National Fine Arts Museum did not acquire their pieces, either. In fact, in official circles, there was never any conviction regarding the artistic value of these works despite the fact that from their beginning in 1984, the Havana biennials served as a showcase for the new art, which received the highest praise from critics and curators from abroad. In addition to these international encounters, the biennials allowed the Cubans to have a lively contact with the world of contemporary art.

Volumen 1 has remained the landmark event of the new art, because it released the greatest energy in the history of Cuban plastic art, leading to the art "most alive in Latin America," according to Jürgen Harten and other observers.[7] In a symbolic coincidence, that same year, Ana Mendieta, who had been in close contact with the young artists during her trips to the island, worked for the first and only time in Cuba, making works in Jaruco and Varadero. Mendieta developed a mutually advantageous relationship with the artists, passing information on to them and putting them in contact with the New York scene. They discussed their work together, and the Cubans were very important in Mendieta's "retour au pais natal," since she based her work, precisely, on the return to origins.

From this groundswell, the New Cuban Art emerged,[8] an artistic-cultural movement that continues to the present. Its characteristics surprised everyone. "It was never believed that a socialist republic could appear with a new exuberant art, that takes in kitsch, folklore, popular religions, and postmodernism," said Lucy R. Lippard, "an art that takes on the mestizaje and the syncretism which are also beginning to be major themes in North America," and that opens "a truly 'democratic' impulse that excludes neither the history of art nor the formal advances of the West, nor the populist vitality of the developing nations."[9] These traits have to do with the multiplicity of Cuba itself, a poor island with a brilliant intellectual life since the eighteenth century, an intellectual life disproportionate in comparison to its infrastructure. It is important to point out that we are dealing with a Third World Caribbean country with an influence in the region disproportionate to its small size, a country that at this moment combines socialist fundamentalism with neoliberalism, a country whose clocks show the same hour as those in New York and that is ninety miles from the greatest power of the world, with which it has maintained a love-hate relationship.

Art and Vernacular Culture

The new artists came from different groups of society, and because of the peculiarities of Cuban life—widespread poverty, a shortage of housing and other basics, social mobility, collectivization, pseudo-egalitarianism—they remained immersed in the social milieu from which they came, active bearers of a folkloric tradition and at the same time trained professionals, thanks to the free and generalized system of education. Many of them make "high" art shaped from within by values, sensibilities, and views of the world from those vernacular groups. It is thus no longer a matter of the "primitive" or the vernacular *in* the "cultivated." This displacement of the old divisions of "high" and "low" culture constitutes without any doubt an artistic and cultural transformation of extraordinary importance, paradigmatic of the functional pluralizations that are beginning to restructure contemporary art within the intricate dilemmas of globalization and difference in today's world.

"Bad" Forms in Good Shape

The new art widened the sensibilities, aesthetic tastes, and values of the urban vernacular culture and even of marginal sectors that have tended to become increasingly influential in the habits of daily life. Beginning with Flavio Garciandía, a total aesthetics of "bad forms"[10] was legitimized, elaborated from the point of view of a "scandalous" Baroque type with popular domestic and festive decorations. It was not a critical program against kitsch, but rather the recuperation—not lacking in humor—of stereotyped signs such as the "exoticistic" representation of the coconut palm. It employed abstract ornaments used in spontaneous decorations made by nonprofessionals and other ornaments of worse taste fabricated by professionals for kiosks, fabrics, carnival floats, and so on. These disparaged forms served Garciandía—paradoxically, the possessor of great *métier*—for an ironic reelaboration that at the same time reinforced the aesthetic possibilities of such items for the "cultivated" sensibility, a *gute Forme* of the nullified "bad forms," at least on the phenomenal plane, of Clement Greenberg's old contrast between avant-garde and kitsch.

Garciandía began in the early 1980s with an interest in the contents of decorative urban clichés—particularly evident in his series of popular proverbs—and even in the possibility of commenting by means of such proverbs on events outside the vernacular kitsch. The best example is his installation of 1986, *The Marco Polo Syndrome,* presented at the Second Havana Biennial, in which he tackled the paradoxes of contact between distinct cultures and the local distrust of the outside and the diverse using comic-strip style and an array of chinoiserie. Afterward, he concentrated on painting scenes like still frames from an animated drawing, showing an unusual Eden where diverse cultural stereotypes cohabit. In this imaginary paradise of kitsch, the clichéd symbols are protagonists, but in addition, the methods are taken from the arsenal of "bad taste," whether they are his own inventions or transformations of the styles of "universal" art. He has developed a truly erudite treatment of kitsch that, added to his erudition about "elevated art" and his highly refined professionalism and taste, produces a visual universe filled with tensions and at the same time totally coherent. It resembles a *pittura colta* of kitsch.

Garciandía has said: "I am interested, in general, in the infinite complexity of the syncretic processes and those of transculturation. And in particular, the confrontation in the same scene (the work) of opposing or paradoxical elements."[11] Often the meanings go beyond the cultural problematic toward external questions. His personification of the hammer and sickle in a series of paintings made during the time of perestroika in the Soviet Union is the clearest example. He anthropologizes the symbol of Communism and sets it to making love or marching, or converts it into a phallic symbol (Figures 59 and 60; see Figure 2). His images weave together a discourse of multiple meanings. It is not a matter of poking fun, although his work is based on humor. There is a sense of alluding to perestroika as a fruitful revitalization of socialism that provoked an active rejuvenation of an old, fossilized sign. In Cuba, this sign, by virtue of the personality and historic process of the Cuban revolution, was received more as a representation of the Soviet Union than of Communism in general. It is important to know that with Cuba's turn to socialism, the country's symbols were not changed (flag, national seal and anthem, heroes of the wars of independence, etc.), although

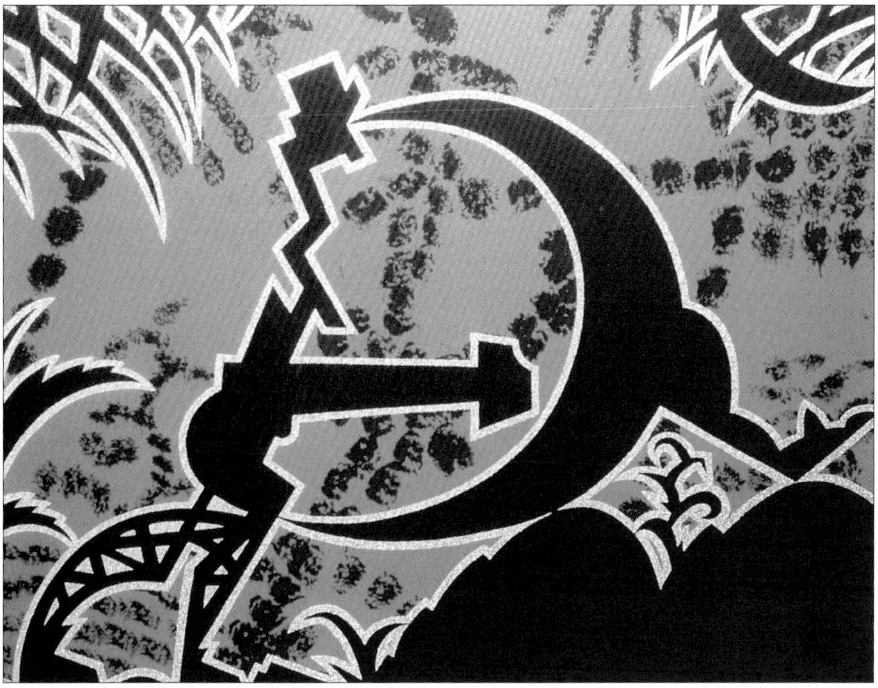

Figure 59 Flavio Garciandía, *Untitled,* 1985, mixed technique on canvas.

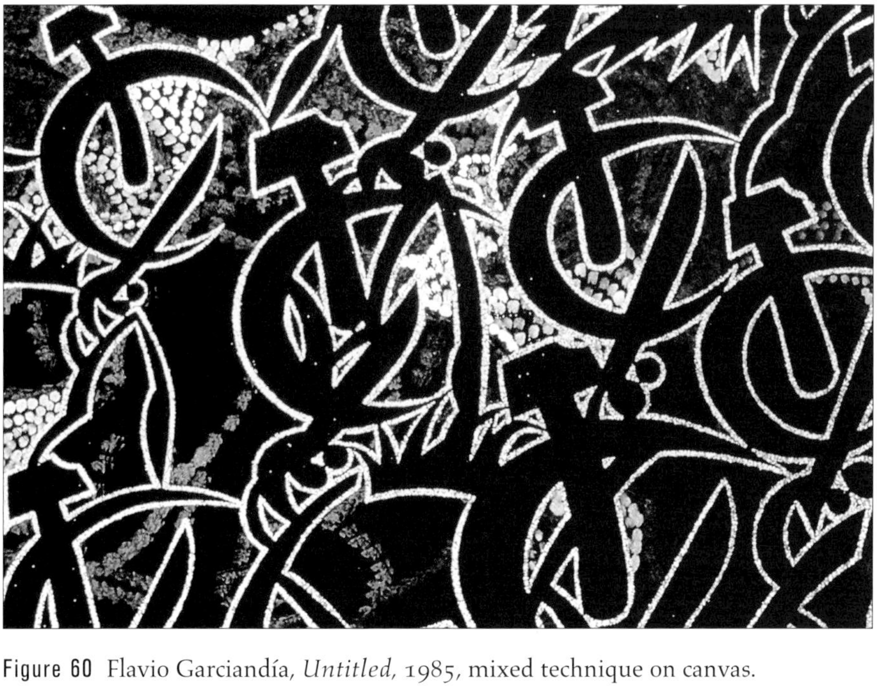

Figure 60 Flavio Garciandía, *Untitled,* 1985, mixed technique on canvas.

new heroes and patriotic dates were added, and Castro proclaimed the revolution as the culmination of the history of Cuba. Garciandía's paintings could be a postmodern allegory of a renovating change in "true socialism." On the island, this would acquire another meaning: It became a critical allusion to the position of the Cuban government, which was kept outside the process and disagreed with the policies promulgated by Mikhail Gorbachev.

In tandem with these approaches is a carnivalization (in the Bakhtinian sense) of the emblem, directed in critical fashion against the grandiloquence and overblown ceremoniousness that the socialist regime has caused to proliferate in its events and official representations in Cuba. This trait, which persists today, contrasts with the populist spontaneity of the beginning days of the revolution, which was transformed completely under Soviet influence during the 1970s. The ritual pomp of the regime clashes with the Cubans' offhand idiosyncrasy and the Caribbean ambiance in general. This series of Garciandía's thus falls within one of the principal orientations of the new art: its will to deconstruct the propagandistic mythologies of power.

There is another aspect of the work described above. The hammer and sickle that referred to the worker-peasant alliance in Soviet Russia became the universal symbol of socialism. It was a Eurocentric universality within the referent itself, given the presence of the wheat-associated sickle, which was replaced by a machete in the flag and seal of Angola. Garciandía carried out a "Third World" appropriation of the emblem of socialism in the sense of resignifying it in an area of hybridizations and syncretisms proper for the culture of the Caribbean. Jorge Luis Borges affirmed the possibility that Latin Americans can treat all the European themes without superstition and with irreverence.[12] Garciandía does so programmatically, but at the same time works with the structure of the particular situation, that is, *with* it, as well as *from* it. In this direction, he also underlines the greater interpenetration between the popular and the "cultivated" in Latin America and in the Third World in general. To carnivalize the hammer and sickle within this system means also to break its orthodoxy in order to make it participate humorously in the multiplicity of the "South." All this fits within and at the same time metaphorizes the orientation of contemporary culture toward pluralism, inclusion, and relativity.

Osvaldo Yero, an artist who emerged in the 1990s, has based his work on the technique and poetics of the plaster figures that proliferate in Cuban shops, given the scarcity of products before the legalization of the dollar in the 1990s and the changes that reoriented Cuba toward a market economy.

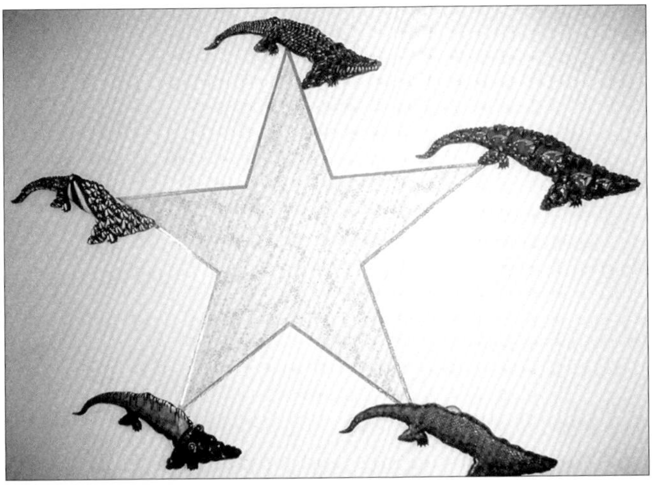

Figure 61
Osvaldo Yero, *Five Cubas and a Star*, 1991, painted clay cast, 400 × 500 cm.

These figures, mostly decorations, but also religious images, were perhaps considered the last gasp of bad taste. They constituted the epitome of "uncultivated" appropriation of icons from the "high" culture as well as from mass culture, done in a poor and artificial material par excellence, worked clumsily in a semi-industrial technique and polychromed with pretentious attempts at elegance. They symbolized the triumph of "vulgarity," the failure of the "aesthetic education of the masses" proposed by socialism.

Yero starts from the poetics of the plaster decorations, in a vision both affectionate and ironic, by assembling large installations on walls. His discourse explores the complex cultural meanings of plaster as means of creating a space of confluence of different aesthetic-symbolic systems (vernacular urban, mass, "high") and kinds of production and functions typical of industry, design, artisanry, art, religion, propaganda, and decoration. He also works with the tensions and at the same time with the communicative ease offered by the overlapping and hybridization of so many discourses, aesthetics, and symbolic codifications. His works resemble Cuban life; they are, a writer said to me, like works by Hieronymus Bosch. Yero uses some of the habitual kitsch representations of the plaster figures, but mostly he brings to plaster Cuban patriotic symbols (Figure 61) and socialist icons, from *The Worker and Collective Farm Girl* (1937) of Vera Mukhina to Fidel Castro himself. Some artists have given priority to an aesthetic reevaluation of "bad forms" or constructed their own discourses from them, but Yero starts from the complex formal scheme and meanings of the plaster to project the political side of conditions prevailing in Cuba. Other artists, such as Tonel and

Adriano Buergo, have in part constructed their poetics by means of "high" elaborations of cultural elements from the marginal sectors. Such decentralizations possess a real cultural base, in contrast to many postmodern pseudodecentralizations, despite the fact that, without doubt, these helped shape the Cuban inclination.

Afro-Cuban World Views and Cultural Identity

The decentralizations turned out to be quite radical in cases of artists initiated in Afro-Cuban religions or formed in environments with a long tradition in them. José Bedia, Ricardo Brey, Juan Francisco Elso, Marta María Pérez, and others probed more deeply into the perspective foreshadowed by Lam, but took a qualitative leap by making "international" art structured from the cosmovisions of African origin alive in those religious-cultural complexes. They did not approach them from outside, as an anthropologist or a Surrealist would do, simply because they did not need to: they were inside. For the same reason, neither was theirs the "informed primitivism" to which Luis Camnitzer has referred in respect to Joseph Beuys and other artists versed in ethnographic knowledge.[13] On the other side, there was no "primitivism" in a state of grace, since, again, they were within the Occidental practice of the avant-garde. They acted from the contents, rather than recreating forms, rites, or myths, as usually happens among contemporary artists of the Caribbean. It could be said that the Cubans are making Occidental culture from non-Occidental bases, and therefore transforming it by diversifying it.

The new artists paid no attention to the obsessive Latin American preoccupation regarding identity and instead confronted the nationalist dogmas. Latin Americans have always had to ask ourselves who we are, simply because it is so difficult to know. We get confused between Western and non-Western, because we have shared in both since the historical beginnings. We have not managed to assume our "inauthenticity," meaning we need to affirm ourselves through ontological stories. Or we proclaim we are as much or more European, Indian, or African than anybody, or have a complex for not being completely so. We believe we belong to a new race of universal vocation, or we feel the victim of a chaos or split between parallel worlds. The new Cuban artists, in not worrying about these obsessions, paradoxically put identity to work. They assumed with ease the pluralities that operate in Cuban culture as dynamic process, situated always at a crossroads of interactions. For the new art, identity was an inner question. As Wole Soyinka said, "The tiger does not proclaim its tigertude: it springs."

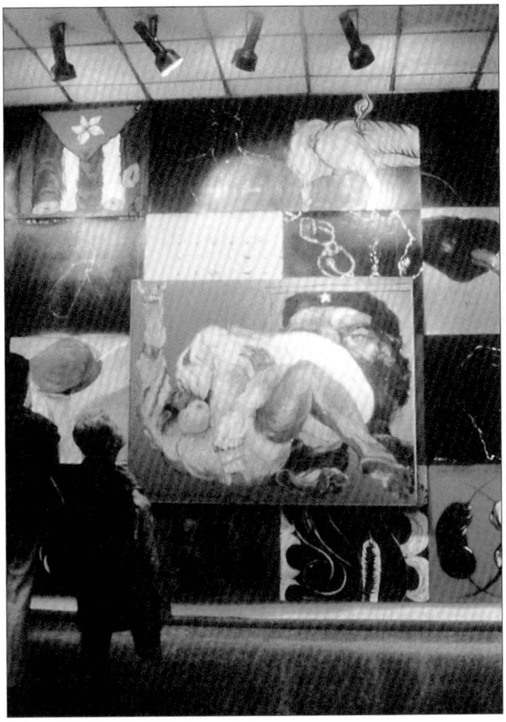

Figure 62 Tomás Esson, *My Homage to Che*, 1987, oil on canvas. The photo was taken during the January 1987 exhibition in Havana, which was closed two days after the opening.

If, in the first half of the 1980s, the predominant focuses were of a conceptual and anthropological nature, in the second, parody and the new allegorical Expressionism prevailed with artists such as Ana Albertina Delgado and Tomás Esson. Although up to a certain point this orientation came from the influence of the Italian Trans-Avantgarde and the "bad" painting of the period, the artists assimilated it in order to develop more radical expressions from popular culture and Cuban contexts. There was a strong presence of the grotesque, the scatological, and sexual impudence typical of the Bakhtinian carnivalesque, an antiaristocratic response of the "low" culture. There was also a marked shift vis-à-vis the rhetorical image of an unsullied country that still today, more and more, is offered by the mass media in Cuba, a resounding clash with hard reality and with Caribbean idiosyncrasy. This orientation sometimes resulted in direct allusions, such as the Cuban flag in the form of sausages and meat painted by Esson and his picture *My Homage to Che* (Figure 62), with two grotesque monsters fornicating before the image of the hero, who is depicted with Negroid features. The exhibition of these pieces at the end of the 1980s provoked a famous episode of censorship. The brazen use of the so-called symbols of the nation in a critical spirit was one of the issues that most upset the bureaucrats and the military.

The Practice of Appropriation

Despite the variety of the new Cuban art, which makes it impossible to isolate stylistic constants, general features exist in its practices. One important trait is the weight given to the conceptual. Even when a work is found at the opposite pole from Conceptualism, it usually possesses discursive, analytical elements or a reflective dimension: It is an art of ideas, giving rise to the frequent use of texts.

Another element often found is humor. Cubans, famous for being lively, have produced an overly serious brand of art and literature. However, since the mid-1980s, a festive character has been introduced in art. This humor is typical of Tonel and the Grupo Puré, which with its first exhibit in 1985 broke with the clean seriousness typical of the first half of the decade. There is also great brashness, with artists appropriating any means whatsoever, no matter where they come from, and putting them into a new context—often "incorrectly"—to respond to their own interests. In fact, what is interesting in every intercultural appropriation is the productivity of the element taken for the ends of the appropriator, not the reproduction of its use in the medium of its origin. This element may be acquired "without comprehension of its place and meaning in the other cultural system, and take on an absolutely distinct significance in the context of the culture that receives it."[14] Such "incorrect" borrowings are usually at the base of the cultural efficacy of the appropriation, like the absolutely ignorant and extraordinarily effective use that European modernism made of African, Oceanic, and Mesoamerican imagery.

The new artists carried that practice of appropriation to extremes of mockery and cynicism. They took excellent advantage of inclusiveness and postmodern plurality, at times with double irony. Thus, Joseph Kosuth, during his visit to Cuba in 1986 to participate in the Second Havana Biennial, regarded the work of Consuelo Castañeda, based on reappropriations of appropriations from the history of art, as a "post-postmodernism." The Grupo Puré, as part of the hyper-Baroque elements in an environment created by them in 1986—in an exhibition at the Instituto Superior de Arte during the Second Havana Biennial—included acknowledgments to all the Italians, Germans, and North Americans they had "copied." Another group of artists (Tanya Angulo, Juan Ballester, José Ángel Toirac, and Ileana Villazón) made rough Xerox copies in black and white of *After Alexander Rodchenko* by Sherrie Levine, taken from magazines (the only way of knowing foreign art in many peripheral countries), and exhibited them under the title *After Sherrie Levine*. The implications of the work pointed as much in the direction of postmodern discourses as to the use of cultural appropriations by peripheral groups.

Even when imposed by a dominant culture on one that is dominated, cultural appropriation is not a passive phenomenon. The appropriators always transform, resignify, and use in accordance with their own visions and interests. An appropriation, especially an "incorrect" one, usually involves a process of originality, understood as a new creation of meaning. The peripheral groups, due to their location on the maps of economic, political, cultural, and symbolic power, have developed a "culture of resignifying"[15] the repertories imposed by the centers. It is a transgressive strategy (or often an unconscious act, almost an instinct) performed from positions of dependency, which are very frequent in Latin America because of its own heterogeneous multiplicity. In addition to confiscating whatever it wishes for its own use, appropriation functions as a questioning of the canons and the authority of the central paradigms. As Nelly Richard points out, the authoritarian and colonizing premises are thus thrown off balance, with the artist re-elaborating meanings and "deforming . . . the original (and at least, questioning the dogma of its perfection), dealing in reproductions and degenerating versions in the parodic trance of the copy."[16] It is not only a matter of dismantling totalizations in the postmodern spirit since, in addition, it brings with it the anti-Eurocentric deconstruction of the self-referential nature of the dominant models and, by extension, the deconstruction of any cultural model.[17]

Social and Political Criticism

Beyond all these artistic-cultural implications, the most important transformation wrought by the New Cuban Art was to direct the culture toward social and political criticism. Although stimulated by the events in the East, this process began before perestroika and glasnost in the Soviet Union, as a result of the evolution of the new art itself within the ideological-social coordinates of that time in Cuba. Since the middle of the 1980s, an unusual fact has occurred. The plastic arts—without stepping beyond their own province—have taken on functions proper to assemblies and the (totally controlled) mass media, becoming a space for expressing the concerns of ordi-

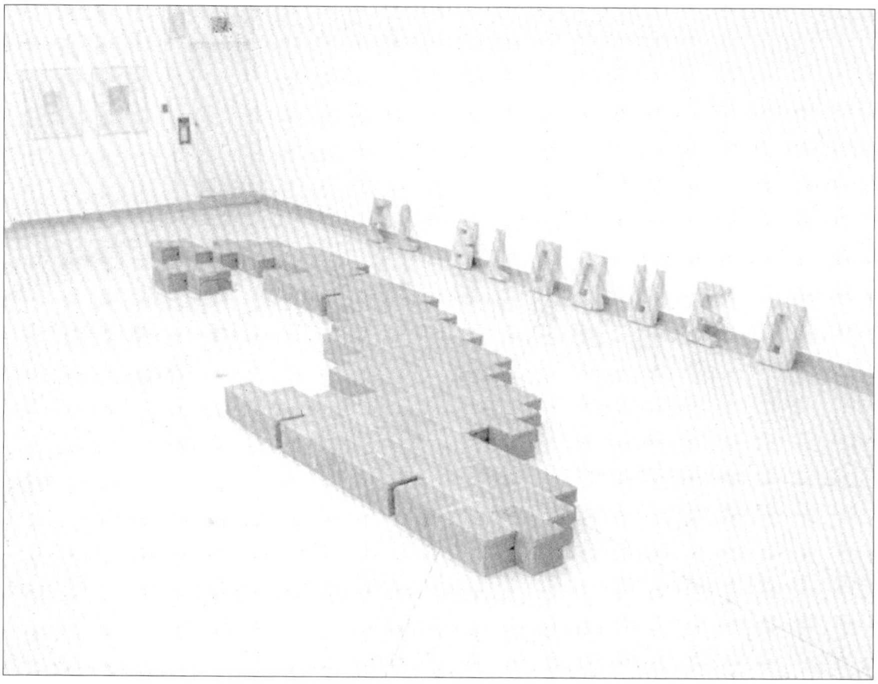

Figure 63 Tonel, *The Blockade,* 1989, construction blocks, 25 × 500 × 900 cm.

nary people. In the beginning, the younger artists reproached their predecessors (who had also been their very young teachers in some cases) for the absence of political edge in their works. In fact, the work of the typical artists of the first five years of the 1980s contained a profound cultural critique. But in the second half of that decade, the plastic arts became the most daring platform, and some street performances of the eighties were true street demonstrations, such as those of the Grupo Arte Calle. Aldito Menéndez, a member of the group, painted the phrase "Reviva la Revolu" (Revive the Revolu[tion]) on a canvas and put a vessel beside it with a sign asking the public for contributions to finish the work. Tonel succeeded in making the most eloquent and complex image-summary of circumstances in Cuba, an installation that, in a certain way, took the place of the social-science analyses of Cuban reality that were never done or published. Titled *The Blockade* (a term used on the island for the absurd commercial embargo by the United States), it reproduced its title in letters of poured concrete next to a map of Cuba nine meters long made on the floor with construction blocks. With great impact, the work referred to the blockade and to the self-blockade, to defense and cloistering, turning its theme of references problematical through a metaphor of synthesis (Figure 63).

Deconstructing Official Rhetoric

One of the most common critical methods has consisted of appropriating the official imagery and rhetoric in order to deconstruct them and point toward a critique of the mechanisms and representations of power, as we saw in the work of Garciandía. The works of Glexis Novoa, Carlos Rodríguez Cárdenas, and Toirac are perhaps the paradigms of the systematic deconstruction of the institutional imagery.

During all the second half of the 1980s and until his exile in the early 1990s, Novoa appropriated the imagery of the official propaganda—imagery that in Cuba fluctuates between realism and sweetened Pop Art, at times mingled—to make paintings and gigantic installations that also included formal references to Russian Constructivism and Futurism. However, these works are dedicated to immortalizing the young artists and critics who have been excluded, of course, from the commemorative pantheon of the revolution. At times, the grandiloquent array of his visual paraphernalia is abstract, remaining like a homage to emptiness. He painted large texts in the manner of propagandistic billboards, simulating Cyrillic letters that no one can read. In this way, he pointed out the devaluation of the sense of the texts, ideas, and orientations that came from the East, the rhetoricizing of its emblems and symbols. He also painted large semiabstract commemorative architecture of a totalitarian aspect. All these elements were combined in large installations such as the *Mausoleum* erected in 1990 for the historic exhibition *Kuba O. K.: New Art of Cuba* in the Kunsthalle of Düsseldorf, where a direct allusion to the logo of the Communist Party of Cuba appeared (Figure 64).

Cárdenas has worked more from the point of view of the grotesque and the scatological in systematically deconstructing the proliferating rhetoric in Cuba, particularly in regard to the mass media and political events. He has done so by means of a linguistic and visual game that would have pleased Ludwig Wittgenstein and might please Jacques Derrida, but is also full of vernacular humor. In his work of the second half of the 1980s, he parodied and carried to the absurd the possible meanings of words and phrases in headlines from the Cuban press, propagandistic billboards, and slogans, dismantling their semantic emptiness and their contrast with reality by set-

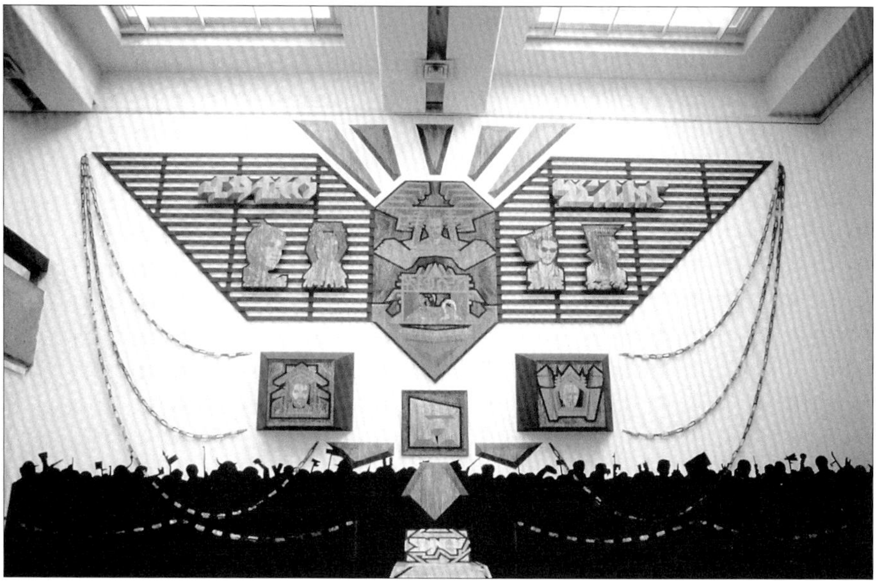

Figure 64 Glexis Novoa, *Untitled (from the Practical Period)*, 1990, installation in Düsseldorf Kunsthalle.

ting the written language against the image he mixed it with. More than using irony in treating the slogans and headlines—which in Cuba have reached the point of a frankly kitschy rhetoric—Cárdenas makes them problematic by using them to analyze the contradictions of socialism. He succeeds by means of the significant tension of his images, seemingly simple, but based on linguistic games. Thus, a work titled *Building the Sky* (1989) (see Figure 5), where the sky appears as a wall of blue bricks, was a powerful reflection on utopia and reality, the end and the means, humans' intervention in nature, and the great efforts of the Third World toward "development." His discourse often invites reading at various levels, which range from direct irony, to a reflection concerning the dilemmas of socialism, to ethical-philosophical questions about human beings and their condition.

Cárdenas's figuration, showing a keen graphic sense, is usually structured by counterpoising soft forms and hard geometrical forms. One of his best-known works is a polyptych done in 1990 in which each panel reproduces a corresponding political slogan in a series of verbs: "Resistir" (To Resist) (Figure 65), "Luchar" (To Fight), "Vencer" (To Overcome). The geometry of the letters of each word in the pictures serves as framework for the development of the actions between "soft" characters that deconstruct each

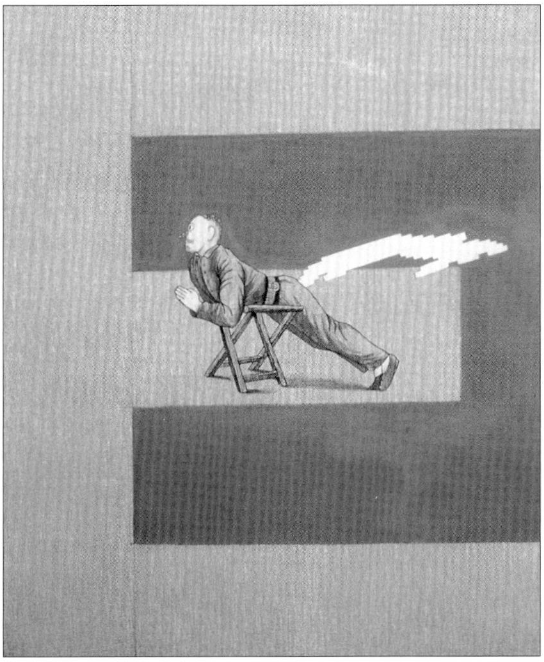

Figure 65 Carlos Rodríguez Cárdenas, *To Resist* (detail), 1990, oil on canvas, 100 × 640 cm.

slogan. For example, in the word "Resist," a character appears who gradually and painfully introduces into his anus a geometrical map of the island of Cuba. As the process continues, the character appears to be made of excrement. The artist thus painted an entire series of works where the figuration seemed to be made with shit. Earlier, Segundo Planes, a very provocative artist, had proclaimed "Everything is shit" as a sort of anti-utopian declaration. In Cárdenas's work, shit acts like an antislogan that grants him new analyses, both "philosophical" and humorous. His grotesque vein is not Rabelaisian, but reflexive, yet without any dulling of its vernacular edge.

Works such as *Resistir, Luchar, Vencer* are a striking rejection of the heroic, military, and *machista* rhetoric of the revolution and of socialism in general, with its call for permanent sacrifice on the altar of a luminous future that never arrives. Moreover, it is a rejection of its Numancian aura, the tragic sense that always speaks of death, as one sees in the highest maxims proclaimed by the regime: "Patria o Muerte" (Homeland or Death), or "Socialismo o Muerte" (Socialism or Death). It is interesting that, like the artists, popular humor has deconstructed such maxims through linguistic means. One popular joke says: "Socialism or Death, same difference." Vernacular humor and that of the artist are of the same type, just as the critical ques-

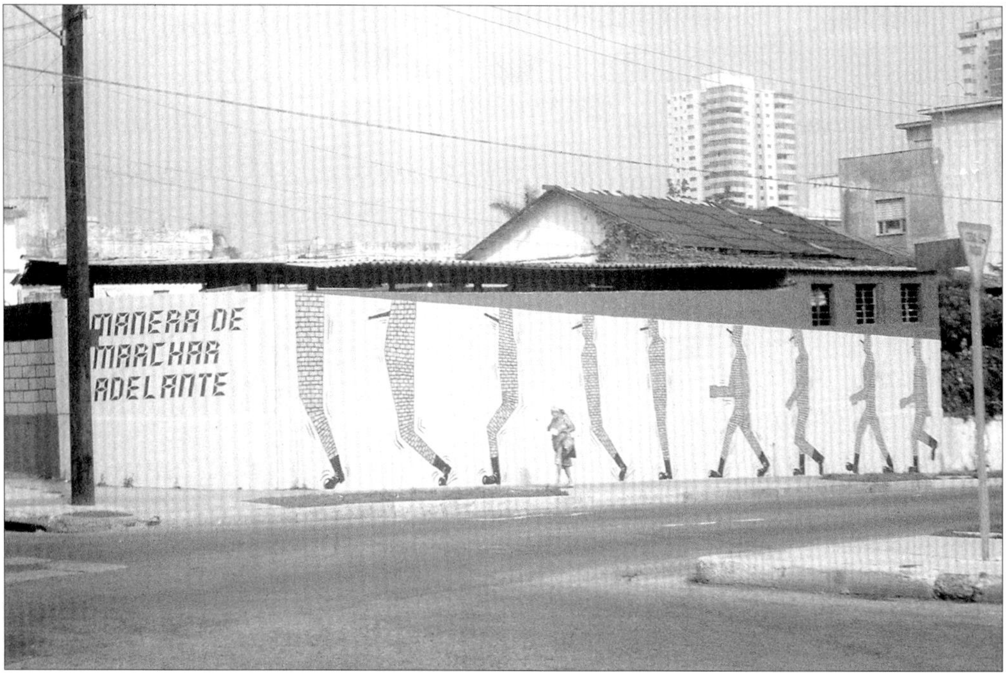

Figure 66 Carlos Rodríguez Cárdenas, *A Way of Marching Ahead,* 1989, acrylic mural, Avenida de los Presidentes, Havana.

tions of art correspond to the complaints of the man or woman in the street. Cárdenas at one time did put art in the streets of Havana with a mural on a permanent wall, commissioned at the end of the 1980s as part of a project of public art organized by the Ministry of Culture. He painted a geometrical character with cap, boots, and the barrel of a gun protruding from his mouth like a cigar. The character (Castro?) was slowly transformed into a construction of blocks as he marched along, until he ended up as a tottering column with boots (Figure 66). The mural was covered years later and the wall repainted with political propaganda.[18]

In this work, as well as in the polyptychs mentioned above, the message is direct, but there are other layers of meaning due to the metaphoric treatment of the image. In the polyptychs, the linguistic element appears in the letters themselves as a structural element of the paintings similar to the decorated capital letters of the ancient tradition of graphic arts. A very subtle, ingenuous, and refined graphic visuality, brimming with meaningful details, is in play along with the caricaturization. It counterpoints the taste for the grotesque and the scatological popular strain—Cárdenas himself comes from the countryside—in a "high" expression from the "low" often found in the New Cuban Art. Again, it is a matter of a carnivalization in the face of the pure aristocratic tone of the rhetoric, which constitutes ivory-tower formalism, a construction aseptically distanced from the way people in the street live. The grotesque and the scatological are a reaction that seeks to "dirty" the rhetoric with the reality. The deconstruction brings with it logic and easy informality, linguistic games, and unabashed, mischievous joking.

Toirac is the artist who has made the greatest systematic effort to criticize the representations of power in Cuba from within. He works mostly with photographs and texts taken from the press. He paints front-page images on canvas, thus transforming their meaning by the simple fact of isolating and enlarging them in the painting. For example, a ridiculous photo of ordinary potatoes that appeared on the front page to report the usual greatly successful harvest became an abstract image when reproduced pictorially. Among other things, the piece alluded to the abstract nature of the numbers and the successes trumpeted by the press, which had little to do with reality. The abundance of potatoes one sees in the newspapers is not seen in the markets: They are abstract potatoes. Toirac has become obsessively occupied with the official representations of Fidel Castro and Che Guevara, showing their religious connotations, transfiguring them in a critical sense, or deconstructing their propagandistic rhetoric in contrast to the capitalist propaganda that recently has appeared in the country (Figure 67; see Plate 14).

Unlike what occurs in other contexts, in Cuba, humor, appropriation, and deconstruction often go hand in hand. The social and political edge with which Lázaro Saavedra and other artists employ humor from the perspective of the man-in-the-street political joke is remarkable. In other circumstances, Saavedra would have been without any doubt a great journalistic humorist in addition to doing artistic drawings and making installations. In Cuba, he has used the space of the plastic arts, less controlled and more permissive because it is a limited and small scene, to carry on a constant humoristic critique of the life of the country.

One memorable work was his buffet table full of paintings, drawings, and objects. The long table presented a true X ray of how things were on the island at the end of the 1980s, where one could choose anything from interpretations of the daily events up to reflections of a philosophical nature. Among other works that created great repercussions, one should mention his *Detector of Ideologies*, a work of art to be applied to works of art. Its nee-

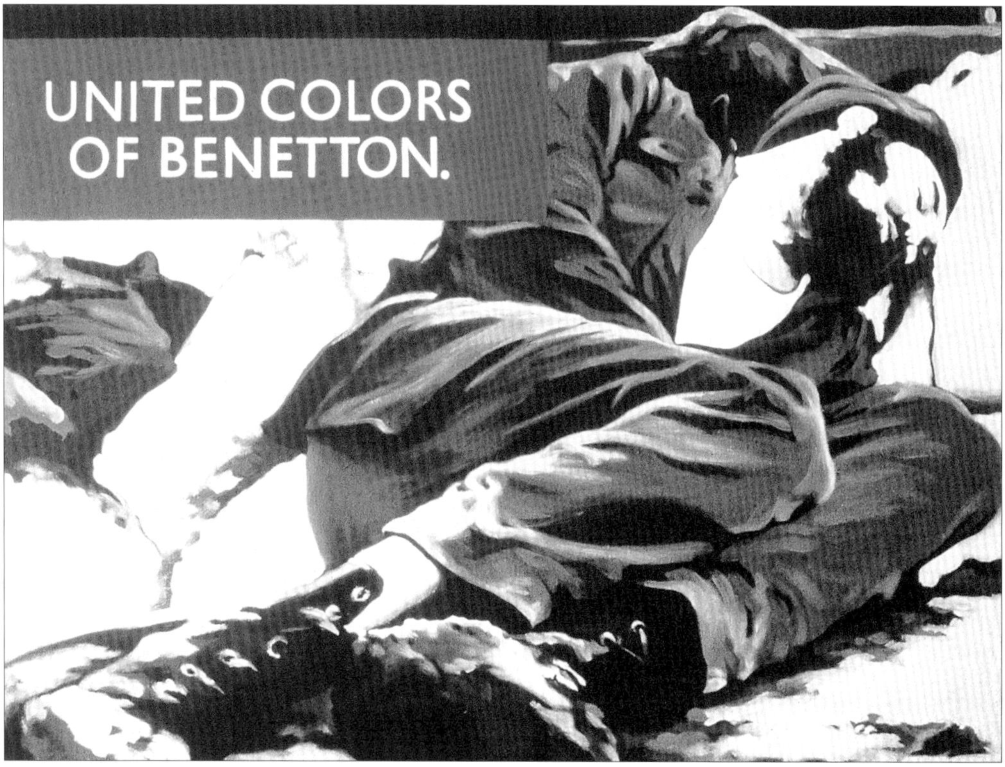

Figure 67 José Toirac, *United Colors of Benetton*, 1994, oil on canvas, 60 × 80 cm.

dle could point from "positive" to "diversionist" or "counterrevolutionary." His *Altar to St. Joseph Beuys* contained the wishes and fears of the Cuban intellectual community in the form of votive candles and petitions presented on the altars of popular Catholicism. In his version of the image of the Sacred Heart of Jesus, very popular in Cuban households, the heart has the colors of the Cuban flag, but, through the bubbles used in comic strips, the image is speaking the sign of the hammer and sickle and is thinking a dollar sign. The work is a picture of the hypocritical morality found in socialism and of the schisms and duplicities typical of Cuba at that time.

The Post-Utopian Situation

It is astounding that the plastic arts took this ideological and social role, because historically they have followed a rather elitist trajectory. Paradoxically, this is exactly what made that role possible, since the authorities did not give much importance to the visual arts. The artists, then, little by little took advantage of the possibilities. This is why the very modest catalogues of the exhibitions (usually only a leaflet or a little pamphlet) have constituted a space of relatively free textuality, much more so than magazines or books, which are controlled by editorial institutions. It is also surprising that the visual arts have carried out this role without detriment to their searching and their artistic experimentation. On the contrary, they take advantage of the symbolic powers of art to carry on a problematic discourse that interweaves the multiple complexities of art and Cuban life. Starting from this focus of freedom, the entire culture reacted. The New Cuban Art has succeeded in imposing a generalized systematic critical voice that can be heard in the theater, in music, dance, literature, and even in the cinema.

The impetus of the visual arts grew like a snowball and at the end of the decade rolled over the limits of what the regime was disposed to tolerate. Efforts at repression ensued. As part of a cycle of shows of young artists in the Castillo de la Fuerza, a space dedicated to avant-garde art, an exhibition of work of two artists working together, Ponjuán and René Francisco (Figure 68), was partly censored after the opening in 1989. Two works in which the image of Castro appeared were withdrawn from the exhibit, and the event caused the fall of Vice Minister Leiseca. The following exhibit in the Castillo, of work by the group made up of Tanya Angulo, Juan Ballester, José Toirac, and Tania Villazón, could not even open on its first night. Titled *Homage to Hans Haacke*, it consisted of works that deconstructed the mechanisms of power in the Cuban cultural camp. The new vice minister could not tolerate a piece that denounced an official painter, the creator of the Cuban Communist Party logo.

Starting with these events a new and this time more subtle cultural closure was imposed. Ángel Delgado, who, as part of a performance, defecated in the middle of the 1990 opening of the show *The Sculptured Object* in the Center for Development of Visual Arts, had to serve six months in prison among common criminals, expiatory victim of a clear warning from those in power to intellectuals. The event was used as an excuse to remove another liberal official, Beatriz Aulet, director of the center. This whole set of circumstances, together with the economic, moral, and social crisis brought about by the cessation of Soviet subsidies, along with international interest in the New Cuban Art, provoked a diaspora of intellectuals that reached its climax at the beginning of the 1990s.

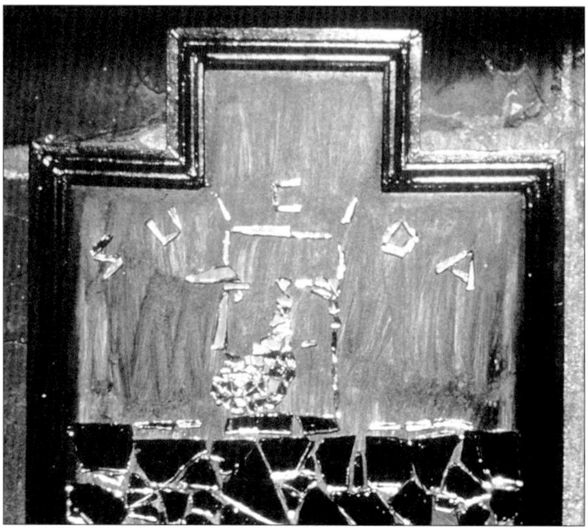

Figure 68 Ponjuán and René Francisco, *Self-Murderer* (detail), 1989, installation.

Despite the heavy loss, the island conserved its cultural energy, thanks to the fact that good artists kept springing up in the midst of enormous difficulties. Art in Cuba is like a machine that has kept on running although the motor has been turned off. This state of affairs is due above all to the existence of a cultural substratum established in the plastic arts similar to what has been formed in music, dance, boxing, and baseball. A level of experience has been established in these areas that prevents them from going lower. In addition, in times of crisis, culture usually grows stronger, acting like a mechanism of social protection. Also, the sustained artistic high point is the result of a new spiritual energy that was strengthened in the 1980s. In another direction, the practice of art results in a source of dollars and in possibilities for travel. Since people in Cuba live at the limits of subsistence, it is actually striking that an even greater commercialization in culture has not taken place.

In contrast, the artists, by virtue of a situation somewhat less restrictive for travel and selling, have been inclined to work and exhibit on the outside while maintaining their residences in Cuba. They are like fishermen: They make their living offshore, but always return to port. The diaspora, the travels, and the resulting interactions now determine the Cuban cultural dynamic and constitute one of its principal themes. A possible taxonomy of the distinct situations in which new Cuban artists find themselves would look like this: those who remain (islanders), those who left (no longer islanders), those who stay but are anxious to leave (involuntary islanders), those who left, pay their taxes, and come back on vacation (low-intensity exiles), and those who go and come ("papinization" types, a term that refers to Los Papines, a group of globe-trotting drummers). Today Cuban art is principally an export product.

The quota of utopianism in Cuban art has gone down as much as the quota of bread. Nevertheless, the social perspective typical of the new art continues, as can be seen in the work of Abel Barroso, Sandra Ramos, Esterio Segura, and others. Even more, in 1997, Tania Bruguera achieved an overwhelming political image, perhaps the most overwhelming ever done by the visual arts of the island. She ate Cuban soil for forty-five minutes, standing facing the busy crowded street of Old Havana where she lives, with a Cuban flag made of human hair behind her. That same year, in the second biennial of Johannesburg, Los Carpinteros presented an installation titled *Cuban Soil for Sale,* a clear reference to present economic policy.

However, connection with the artists' surroundings often turns art more ironic, simulative, and self-referential. The artists react to the contradictions of Cuba today, where Hispanic-American *caudillismo* is joined with "socialist" orthodoxy and, with the opening to foreign capital, the authoritarian system with sexual tourism. The artists now are oriented more within the artistic sphere than toward cultural and social action, although these areas are absorbed as materials of art. The appropriation of images, citations, and parody are frequent recourses (Pedro Álvarez, Carlos Garaicoa, Armando Mariño, René Peña, and others), while the intertextuality between the religious, the political, and the cultural typical of the 1980s is on the increase (Segura and José Ángel Vincench, to name just two).

However, the critical sense, protected "ritually" behind a greater tropological density and a cynical attitude, has expanded. I say "ritually" because, in the final analysis, everybody knows what the works say, but the important thing is that it not be said in explicit terms, giving art a margin of ambiguity, as happened in Spain during the Franco era. Thus, for example, Fernando Rodríguez bases his works on a literary heteronym, Francisco de la Cal, who signs the works with him.

"Francisco de la Cal " is a farmer from the Ciénaga de Zapata, one of the poorest regions of Cuba, which received much attention at the beginning of the revolutionary process. According to the fictitious biography invented by Fernando, the character was a primitive artist but became blind in the mid-1960s. Now he dictates his works to his young colleague, who supposedly reproduces them with great accuracy. The resulting paintings, sculptures, and installations emerge as if from a time machine, since they respond to the utopian dreams of the 1960s. But the effect on the spectator is the opposite, through the sarcastic contrast with present-day reality. The work exaggerates triumphalist expression, turning it in a contrary direction, and at the same time it becomes difficult to censure, since it is in line with official rhetoric. His discourse itself has been structured strategically using a trick designed to avoid repression. In 1991, in the Fourth Havana Biennial, Rodríguez presented a series of works based on a dream of de la Cal: the marriage of Castro to the Virgin de la Caridad del Cobre, the Catholic patron saint of Cuba, sincretized with Oshún, the Afro-Cuban Venus. The series showed all the events of the proceeding, including the couple's visit to the crafts fair in the Plaza de la Catedral (Figure 69), where, among many other things, kitsch images of Che Guevara and other revolutionary heroes are for sale. In the work, Castro is buying his own image, and the Virgin pays for it in dollars.

The painter Aisar Jalil, whose face resembles Castro's, made a personal show of "self-portraits" (Figure 70), in which he presented himself as a decadent emperor surrounded by sheep. Among other scenes, he portrayed himself using his penis as a scale of justice. The exhibit caused a lot of nervousness, but it was very difficult for the authorities to censure it, because if they had, it would have confirmed that the events described in the paintings were linked to Castro, and not to the self-portraits of the artist.

Clever tricks such as these, that play a double game with the forbidden, were one of the critical weapons of art in the 1990s. The inclination to contest power became generalized by diverse routes during the decade. However, along with it, the risk of making art about politics, instead of political art, has arisen, a form of criticism that implies a compromise and no action beyond the offering of a metaphor. What is worse, the opportunism of playing with social and political criticism appears as a fashionable theme and even as a trait of a Cuban style, satisfying clichéd expectations.

Now, however, there are more women who are important artists than ever before. They usually project their life experiences, their intimate feelings, and their own bodies into the discussion of social, political, and cultural problems. In Cuba, a feminist consciousness does not exist, and the female artists usually reject the label, considering that such labeling circumscribes them to a ghetto. Nevertheless, their works contain traits similar to those associated with feminism, although in these works, the problematic situation of the woman usually radiates outward. It becomes a centrifugal feminism. A

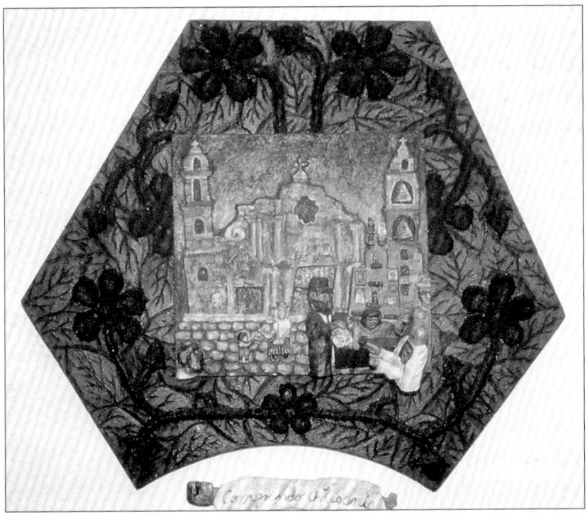

Figure 69 Fernando Rodríguez, *Buying Handicrafts,* 1991, painted wood carving, 95 × 95 × 17 cm.

Figure 70 Aisar Jalil, *I Reflect, but I Don't Doubt,* 1993, acrylic on paper, 50 × 70 cm.

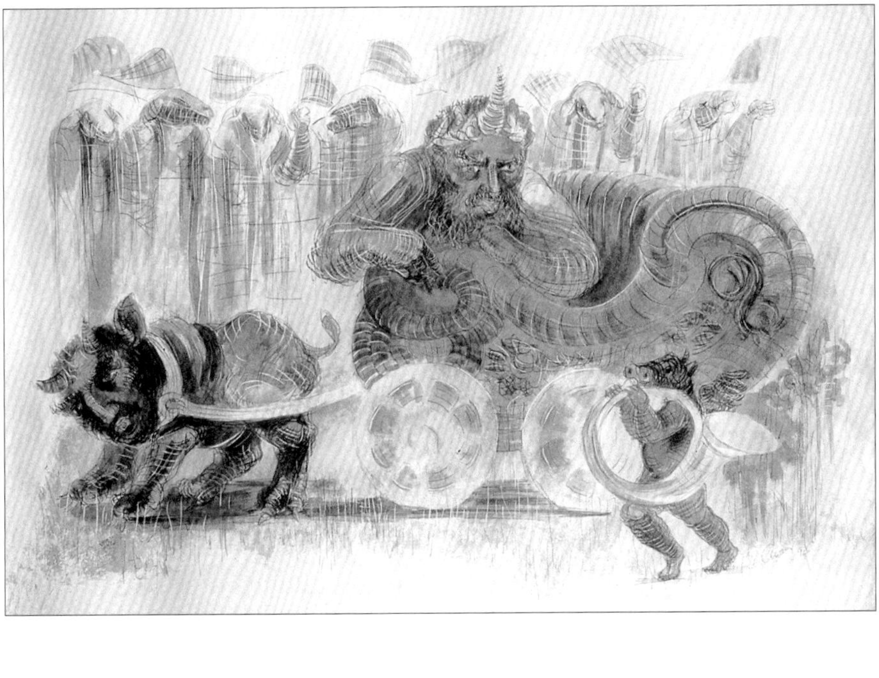

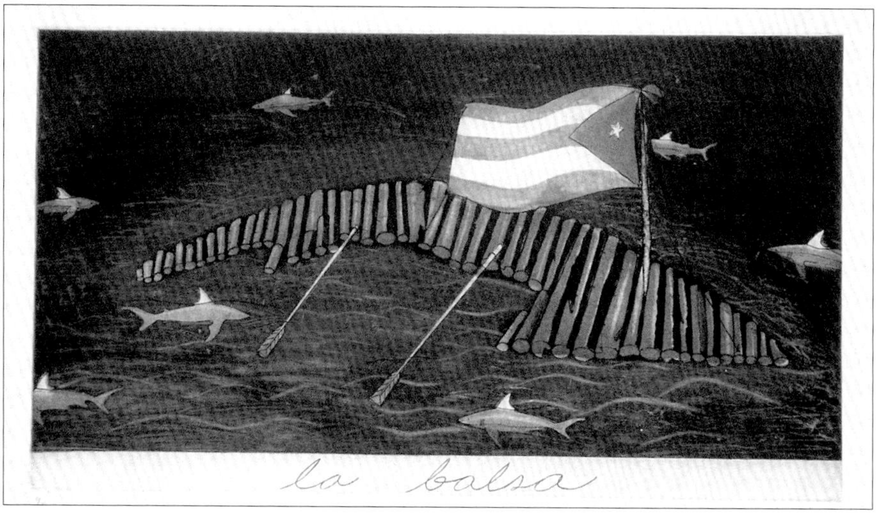

Figure 71 Sandra Ramos, *The Raft,* 1991, silk-screen print, 50 × 90 cm.

frequent trope is the self-portrait of the artist personifying the island or the flag (Ramos, Magalis Reyes), identifying emotionally their personal situation with the suffering of the country. If, according to what we have seen, the artists persist in deconstructing the representations of power, they themselves also integrate the sociocultural fabric where those representations are constructed. Derrida said that "self-deconstruction is the very process of deconstruction." In her painting *The Island That Dreamed,* Ramos herself is the sleeping island.

The theme of the Cuban diaspora, and particularly the drama of the thousands of *balseros* who threw themselves into the sea on precarious rafts, attempting to cross the Florida Straits to reach the United States, was a very common theme in the plastic art of the 1990s (see Plate 15). In 1993, the photographer Manuel Piña produced an image of the exodus: a young man leaping à la Yves Klein toward the sea from a wall of the Malecón in Havana. But Ramos is perhaps the only person who has tackled the event from its different sides. Some time back, Kurt Hollander warned that "the theme of the balsa" could be a style and that in "focusing exclusively on the voyage without mentioning the life before or after, the works would not offer a profound criticism."[19] Ramos, in contrast, took on the diaspora as a social and cultural problem, feeling its diverse implications. She did so from the point of view of a personal testimony that added an emotive quality to the analytical symbolization of the works. The titles of some pieces, such as *It May Be There's Nothing beyond the Water, Fear of Being Far from Home, Solitude,* and *The Dreamed City,* speak of fears, hopes, and experiences that surround the generalized desire to leave, summed up in an overwhelming engraving of the island of Cuba as an enormous raft slowly rowing away (Figure 71).

The artists react to the collapse of a dream, but are at the same time part of it. Here we live in the ruins of past glories, among the rubble of the city and the utopia. They, battered by contradictions, constantly wrestling with power, have maintained in all ways the plastic arts as a site for social discussion in a country where such sites otherwise do not exist. Those in power have had to tolerate it because of the horizontal pressure exercised by the generalized critical weight of Cuban culture today. In addition, it is a matter of limited spaces, where a margin of permissibility is more viable. If, as George Yudice has pointed out, the battle for a civil society in today's world is not being waged in art, Cuba, formerly one of its principal spheres, constitutes an exception.[20] Here, art has concentrated the functions of an almost nonexistent civil society, putting up resistance to authoritarianism. It has put the street into the gallery.

Translated from the Spanish by Cola Franzen

Notes

1. Alfred H. Barr, "Modern Cuban Painters," *MOMA Bulletin* 9, no. 5 (April 1944): 2–14.

2. See Gerardo Mosquera, "Modernism from Afro-America: Wifredo Lam," in *Beyond the Fantastic: Contemporary Art Criticism from Latin America,* edited by Gerardo Mosquera (Cambridge, Mass.: MIT Press, 1995), pp. 121–33. Regarding the displacement of meaning attempted by this artist within modernism, see also Robert Linsley, "Wifredo Lam: Painter of Negritude," in *Art History* 2, no. 4 (December 1988): 527–44, and John Yau, "Please, Wait by the Coatroom: Wifredo Lam in the Museum of Modern Art," *Arts Magazine,* no. 4 (December 1988): 56–59.

3. Max-Pol Fouchet, *Wifredo Lam* (Barcelona: Ediciones Polígrafo, 1976), p. 31.

4. Adolfo Sánchez Vázquez, "Las ideas estéticas en los *Manuscritos económico-filosóficos* de Marx," *Casa de las Américas* (Havana) 2, nos. 13–14 (1962), *Las ideas estéticas de Marx* (Havana: Ediciones Unión, 1964), "El marxismo contemporáneo y el arte," *Casa de las Américas* (Havana) 5, no. 32 (1965), and *Art and Society* (London: Merlin Press, 1973).

5. A recent book dedicated to these buildings presents in addition an interesting description of the cultural atmosphere in the Cuba of the 1960s and of the relationships between culture and ideology: John A. Loomis, *Revolution of Forms: Cuban Forgotten Art Schools* (New York: Princeton Architectural Press, 1998).

6. The exhibitors were José Bedia, Ricardo Brey, Juan Francisco Elso, José Manuel Fors, Flavio Garciandía, Gory, Gustavo Pérez Monzón, Tomás Sánchez, Leandro Soto, and Rubén

Torres Llorca. On the exhibition, see Gerardo Mosquera, "Volumen 1: Cambio en la plástica cubana," *Arte en Colombia* (Bogota), no. 40 (May 1989): 48–51.

7. Jürgen Harten: "Introducción," *Kuba O.K.* (Düsseldorf: Städtische Kunsthalle, 1990), p. 7.

8. A brief bibliography in English about the New Cuban Art includes Luis Camnitzer, *New Art of Cuba* (Austin: University of Texas Press, 1994), Gerardo Mosquera, "New Cuban Art: Identity and Popular Culture," *Art Criticism* 6, no. 1 (1989): 57–65, "The New Art of the Revolution in Cuba," *Art & Text* (Melbourne), no. 39 (May 1991): 22–25, and "Love Is Over: Art in Cuba Today," *Cuba Update* (New York, May 1994), p. 35. See also the catalogues of the following exhibitions: *New Art from Cuba* (New York: Amelie Wallace Gallery, SUNY College at Old Westbury, 1988), *Made in Havana: Contemporary Art from Cuba* (New South Wales: Art Gallery of New South Wales, 1988), *Contemporary Art from Havana* (London: Riverside Studios, 1989), *The Nearest Edge of the World: Art and Cuba Now* (Brookline, Mass.: Polarities, 1990), *Kuba O. K.* (Düsseldorf: Städtische Kunsthalle, 1990), *No Man Is an Island: Young Cuban Art* (Pori, Finland: Pori Art Museum, 1990), and *New Art from Cuba: Utopian Territories* (Vancouver: Morris and Helen Belkin Gallery, British Columbia University and Contemporary Art Gallery, Vancouver, March–April 1997), plus the issues dedicated to Cuba by the journals *Third Text*, no. 20 (autumn 1992), and *Poliester* (Mexico, D.F.), no. 4 (winter 1993).

9. Lucy R. Lippard: "Prólogo" to Gerardo Mosquera: *Contracandela* (Caracas: Monte Ávila Editores, 1995), pp. 11–12.

10. See Gerardo Mosquera, "Bad Taste in Good Form," *Social Text* (autumn 1986): 54–64.

11. Quoted in *Made in Havana: Contemporary Art from Cuba* (New South Wales: Art Gallery of New South Wales, 1988), p. 25.

12. The statement is taken from Borges's well-known essay "El escritor argentino y la tradición," in *Discusión*, 1932. See "The Argentine Writer and Tradition," in *Labyrinths: Selected Stories & Other Writings*, trans. James E. Irby, edited by Donald A. Yates and James E. Irby (New York: New Directions, 1962), pp. 171–79.

13. See Luis Camnitzer: "Arte 'primitivo' en el MOMA," *Arte en Colombia* (Bogota), no. 27 (1984): 21–25.

14. Boris Bernstein, "Algunas consideraciones en relación con el problema 'arte y etnos,'" in *Criterios* (Havana), nos. 5–12 (January 1983–December 1984): 267.

15. Nelly Richard, "Latinoamérica y la postmodernidad: La crisis de los originales y la revancha de la copia," in *La estratificación en los márgenes* (Santiago de Chile: Art and Text Publications, 1989), p. 55.

16. Ibid.

17. Nelly Richard, "Latinoamérica y la postmodernidad," *Revista de Crítica Cultural* (Santiago de Chile), no. 3 (April 1991): 18.

18. I wrote a letter to Surnay Benítez, director of plastic arts and design at the Ministry of Culture, denouncing the event, without ever receiving a reply.

19. Kurt Hollander, "Art, Emigration, and Tourism," *Art in America* 82, no. 10 (October 1994): 45.

20. George Yúdice, Jean Franco, and Juan Flores, "Introduction," *On Edge: The Crisis of Contemporary Latin American Culture*, edited by George Yúdice, Jean Franco, and Juan Flores (Minneapolis: University of Minnesota Press, 1992), pp. 18–19.

Post-Utopian Avant-Garde Art in China

Gao Minglu

There are undoubtedly many common features shared by the former socialist countries, including China, with the notions of postsocialism and postmodernism representing double faces of the predominant political and economic circumstances of these environments. I wish to discuss the significance of these two notions in relation to Chinese contemporary art.

The question may well be posed: How can the notion of postmodernism be used as a broad universal "ism" to generalize the contemporary art of the 1980s in China, a typical Third World country with a long and distinct cultural tradition in which a modernist culture similar to that of the West has never existed? The answer is that the lack of Western modernist tradition is precisely why, in the China of the 1980s, we find a mixture of both modernism and postmodernism, understood according to their original Western definitions. Postmodernism in the 1980s in China did not play a dominant role , nor was postmodernism a period in the sense that it fit into the logic of temporal succession. Rather, it was a superficial consciousness of a new cultural criticism that promotes an iconoclastic attitude and certain pragmatic cultural strategies.

To put it another way: Two absences characterize Chinese modern cultural history. One is the absence of a clear idea of a temporal succession in which modernism is followed by postmodernism, as is the case in the West. For the Chinese, modernism and postmodernism have not involved a consciousness of global historical epochs or of a global philosophy of history, but have been a matter of individual subjectivity within a cultural environment possessing a strong sense of nationalism. For the Chinese, being modern equaled a new notion of the nation, rather than a new epoch,[1] and postmodernity has been just an alternative version of modernity. Postmodernity was perceived as a newer version of modernity proper, instead of as an essential critique of or a break with it. Avant-garde art in China thus became an avant-garde with two heads, one modern and the other postmodern.

The second absence is the lack of a boundary dividing high and low culture, the boundary that is one of the essential differences between modernism and postmodernism. Unlike Russia or some Central and Eastern European countries, where the high-cultural avant-garde movements of the early twentieth century have long been recognized as an indispensable base of the mainstream of Western modern art, in China, the dominant artistic trends in this century have not been academic modernist art schools, but the revolutionary mass art that emerged before the founding of the People's Republic of China in 1949. In the Soviet Union, for instance, the early avant-garde movements supported the October Revolution and worked on the construction of the Bolshevik state, hand in hand with the government. Although the Russian avant-garde and its naive idea of material utopia was gradually replaced by Socialist Realism in the 1930s, artists remained a part of the ideological elite, in accordance with Tatlin's phrase that "artists are the engineers of the human psyche"—which might be an alternative use of Saint-Simon's saying in the early nineteenth century regarding the "avant-garde" in which he referred not only to art, but also to a progressive social role for the artist: "It is artists who will save you as avant-garde . . . what a magnificent destiny for the arts . . . of exercising a positive power over society, a true priestly function, and of marching forcefully in the van of all the intellectual faculties."[2]

In contradistinction to Soviet Socialist Realism, Chinese art during Mao's period was less academic and more akin to the art of low or mass culture. This "low art" was not just a feature of Mao's revolutionary art as it was enforced during the Cultural Revolution, but was characteristic of the whole project of modern Chinese art. This project was initiated by the New Cultural Movement, which emerged in the 1920s. The main goal of this movement was to reevaluate traditional literati culture and to pursue a new, modern system of Chinese literature and art. Although there were many different concerns and experiments directed at this end, the central idea of the movement was *yishu wei rensheng*, "art for people's life." This basic idea transformed traditional self-cultivated and self-entertained elite culture and literati art into popular culture.

The idea of "art for people's life" continued to be used because of the influence of Marxism, the dynamic activity of Left Wing Literature and of the Art Movement in the early 1930s, the outbreak of the Sino-Japanese War in 1937, and, finally, the victory of Mao's revolution in 1949. The idea of "art for people's life" was also embraced, supported, and defined by Mao in his famous phrase that art "serves the people" (*wei renmin fuwu*). The original principle *yishu huadazhong*, "making art to educate the masses," part of the original idea of "art for people's life," also was changed in Mao's dictum into "popularizing art for and by the masses" (*dazhonghua yish*). The fundamental difference between Mao's notion of art for the masses and that of Stalin is that the former emphasizes the change in the position of an artist from a member of the elite (or as an intellectual) into a member of the masses, while the latter still concerns an artistic elite that educates the masses.

The '85 Movement

After the end of the Cultural Revolution in 1976, China opened its doors to the West. Various Western premodern, modern, and postmodern philosophies, cultural theories, and strains of art criticism arrived in China. These theories and the multitemporal phenomena they described were popular among Chinese intellectuals and artists in the 1980s, but they put them to different uses without a clear temporal pattern. These cultural phenomena were complemented by an unprecedented groundswell of avant-garde activities known as the '85 Movement. This movement, which flourished from 1985 to 1989, was very much a reflection of its historical moment, a rebellion against the authority of both state ideology and the institutional apparatus of art as represented by academia, traditionalists, and party bureaucrats. Between 1985 and 1987 more than eighty unofficial art groups expressed their defiance via their art, published manifestos, and organized some one hundred and fifty avant-garde exhibitions and meetings. Over two thousand young artists participated in these activities.

In addition to exposing young artists to Western art movements, the post-Mao period ushered in a wave of political and philosophical discussions on modernity, culture, humanism, and social alienation. The sources of this intense intellectual reappraisal—which touched on human value, dignity, rights, and freedom—were diverse, ranging from Karl Marx's *Economic and Philosophic Manuscripts* of 1844, which were used to indirectly criticize the disregard for the individual in contemporary Chinese society, to translated works of Western philosophy, history, aesthetics, and psychology. At the same time, ancient Chinese philosophy, history, culture, and religion were reevaluated, criticized, or sanctioned according to the newly defined standards of modernity. All of this fed into the burgeoning avant-gardism that finally erupted in the '85 Movement.

When Mao's utopia was suddenly ruined, its majestic dreams and idolatrous enthusiasm were also destroyed. For the generation that was born in the 1960s and that emerged with the '85 Movement in the middle of the 1980s, however, the anti-utopian project of the movement was itself a kind of utopian vision, for it aimed to replace Mao's utopia with that of modernity. The vision of a modernist utopia arose partly from the narratives of the Western avant-garde that had influenced Chinese contemporary art since the late 1970s and partly from the passionate commitment of traditional intellectuals to society. Although considering themselves a transitional generation, most artists of the '85 Movement believed they bore responsibility for the nation's future, a responsibility that included an enthusiasm for social reforms.

Among the artists who embraced this project of Chinese modernity, the Rationalist Painting (*Lixing huihua*) group was the most influential. Representatives of the Rationalists were the North Art Group (*Beifang qunti*), the Pool Society (*Chishe*), and the Red Brigade (*Hongselu*). The North Art Group included artists Wang Guangyi, Shu Qun, Ren Jian, and Liu Yian and was founded in March 1985 in Harbin in Heilongjiang Province, the area formerly known as Manchuria. Its aim was to promote the "civilization of the North." Its members made the rather extreme claim that the culture of the temperate zone was dying and should therefore be replaced by a new culture from northern climates. They pitted masculine strength, believed to be inherent in the northern Chinese culture, against a presumed comparative weakness of both Chinese traditional culture, which they associated with southern China, and modern Western civilization.

Deriving their style from Surrealism, they sought an imagery that would allow them to express the strength and the silent, pure atmosphere of the frigid zone. This pursuit of a quasi-religious purification reflected the desire of these artists to establish a rational social order for China's future on the ruined foundation destroyed by the Cultural Revolution. These artists created their paintings, not for the sake of aesthetics or for individual expression, but for the sake of realizing their utopian goal, a new civilization that would be more progressive than any of the existing ones. As Wang

Guangyi, a major figure in the group and one of the leading painters of Rationalist Painting, said, "Here, both creator and the created are moved by the atmosphere of the sublime and by dignity, rather than by common aesthetic and visual pleasure."[3]

Two distinct tendencies can be observed among the various avant-garde groups of the '85 Movement, one humanist, the other Conceptualist. While the former emphasized utopian notions of art as a blueprint for creating a new society with a strong modernist tone, the latter subscribed to a kind of anti-utopian critique of art as a cultural deconstruction in which various postmodernist strategies were combined with traditional Chan Buddhism.

Humanists saw their art as an instrument for improving a backward society and for reversing its cultural degeneration. Their theoretical foundations lay in traditional Confucianism and partly in modern Western philosophy, including Nietzsche's Existentialism and Bergson's vitalism. Their aesthetic models were Western symbolism, Surrealism, and (mostly German) Expressionism. Two broad styles developed within the humanist camp, Rationalist Painting, which we have already examined, and Current of Life Painting (*Shengmingzhuiliu*), both of which vehemently criticized social and political alienation, albeit from different perspectives. Whereas the objective of the Rationalist painters was to create a new cultural and social order to replace the old, the Current of Life group sought to release suppressed emotions and instincts in order to rescue human nature from alienation. The two groups shared a belief that their art could function on equal terms with science and philosophy. The humanists thus were simultaneously futurists, utopians, and of course modernists in the particular context of contemporary Chinese society. But the anti-Mao utopianism of the humanist avant-garde was, in fact, still based on the pseudo-iconoclastic myth of the artist as creator, prophet, redeemer, martyr, and social engineer.

Like the humanists, Conceptual artists were "revolutionaries." However, they sought not only to go beyond the long-dominant Socialist Realism, but also to break with the new art schools that had emerged after the Cultural Revolution, including the humanists, their colleagues in the '85 Movement. Although Conceptual artists took a strongly antagonistic stance against state ideology, they considered their task to be not to create a new ideology, like their avant-garde counterparts, but rather to completely undermine the methodological foundation of ideological production itself.

Conceptualists recognized that the first step in this program was to demolish the illusion of subjectivity generated by Mao's revolutionary agenda, with its statistical notion of "the people." However, the individualism longed for by avant-garde artists was not that of the "ordinary citizen" or the "little people," but a new kind of revolutionary consciousness, one critical of authority in all its guises. To that end, Conceptualists adopted certain postmodern-type deconstructive strategies such as irony, simulation, and appropriation and created projects that were anti-utopian and that renounced the idea of authorship. As their media and methods they used different cultural and philosophical sources, such as traditional Chinese characters and scripts, Mao's revolutionary language, the imagery and discourse of the Cultural Revolution, Chan Buddhist and Taoist philosophy, and some Western modernist ideas such as Dadaism.

Thus, the approach of postmodernism of these and other artists discussed here, in my view and that of some other Chinese art critics, is not a simple transposition of Western postmodernism: The Chinese artists of the 1980s carried out their project of creating a Chinese modern society as members of the cultural elite whose responsibility it was to enlighten the masses. The project of such artists was therefore fundamentally an iconoclastic rebellion of what would traditionally be considered a characteristically modern bohemia against the previous tradition of Mao's mass art and culture. These Conceptual artists combined Dadaism's fervor for the destruction of any convention and that of traditional philosophy of Chan Buddhism and Taoism for the deconstruction of any doctrine. They were postmodernist, but with a modern revolutionary goal and impulse. From this point of view, in China a Western-type postmodernism thus did not exist as a dominant cultural and artistic trend before the early 1980s, when the global market culture truly reached China.

The initial target of Chinese avant-garde endeavors was not a modernist utopia with its foundation in a revolutionary impulse of the artists' subjectivity, but the economic system, the market, and social institutions. Soon, however, avant-garde art became marginalized and found itself in a suddenly booming consumer society, an alternative socialist society marked by Deng Xiaoping's "socialism with Chinese characteristics." This meant that a Communist government adopted a socialist market economy with a nationalist ideology that started to replace Marxism. Within such a framework, almost no cultural theory and intellectual concern could escape the determination of market forces. Much of the Chinese artistic avant-garde of the eighties, therefore, started to adopt a pragmatic way of serving the masses.

It is this framework of relations that truly formed the basis for Chinese postmodernist practice of the nineties. The pressures from various sources, such as the state, the global market, and the international institutions, forced the Chinese artists of the 1990s to fall into cynicism and abandon any idealism that they may have still had in the 1980s. From this point of view, contemporary Chinese art may perfectly correspond to the emergent postmodern segments of Chinese society.

The Transition of Wang Guangyi: From a Utopian World to Double Kitsch

Among the Conceptual artists, Wang Guangyi, known for his Political Pop art, was a member of the Rationalist Painting group, one of the most influential art groups of the 1980s and a group with an extreme modernist approach. Wang did not become a famous Political Pop artist until 1992, however, when a group of artists started that movement as a part of a broader popular cultural wave called *Mao Re,* or Mao Heat.

Wang Guangyi was born in 1956 in Harbin and was trained at the Zhejiang Academy of Fine Art in Hangzhou from 1980 to 1984. After he returned to his hometown, he and Shu Qun, another Rationalist painter, founded the North Art Group in 1985. Wang intended his 1985 series of paintings entitled *Congealed North Land* to signify "a kind of beauty of sublime reason that contains the constant, harmonious feeling of humanity"[4] (Figure 72). In these paintings, orderly figures face toward the future. His subsequent *Post-Classical Series* employed modified themes of classic Western paintings. In the *Death of Marat* (1987), Wang abstracted the figure of Jacques-Louis David's 1793 monument to the martyred French revolutionary leader Jean-Paul Marat, doubling it in a symmetrically opposed composition painted in a muted palette of grays (Figure 73). This rationalization of sacrifice as an instrument of a more perfect social order employed art like religion to depict a purified Chinese world.

By 1988, a "sociocapitalist" society had begun to develop in China, and intellectuals were becoming disillusioned and fatigued with dreaming of an ideal future. Wang Guangyi, like many of his fellow artist-intellectuals, moved away from grand themes to specific analyses of the social environment. In 1988, he suddenly shifted to a cut-and-paste method. He started to criticize "the modern myth" (*xiandai shenhua*), which may refer to both Mao's revolutionary and the avant-garde iconoclastic utopias. He proclaimed that we must "liquidate the enthusiasm of humanism" (*qingli renwen reqing*)

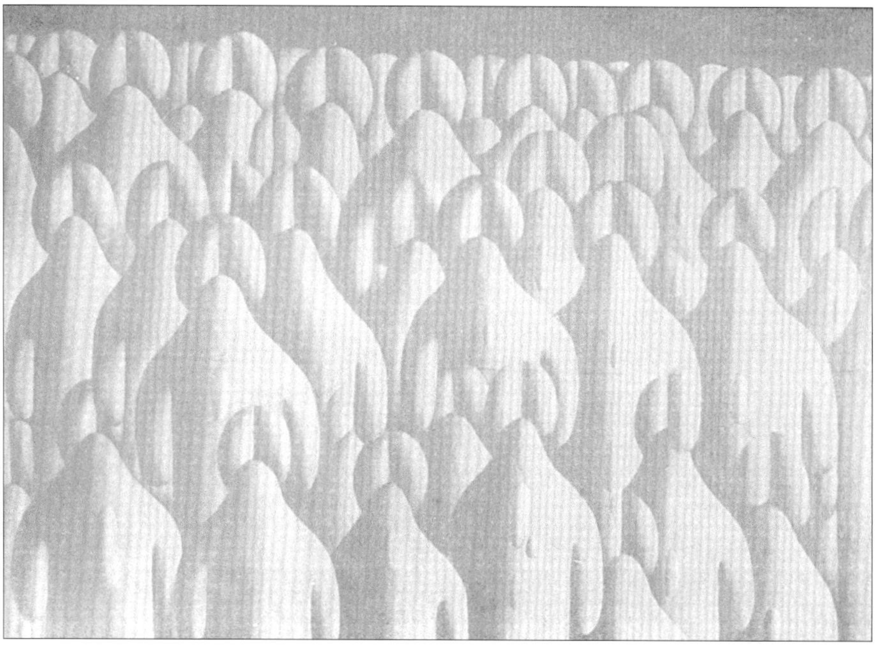

Figure 72 Wang Guangyi, *Congealed North Land No. 28,* 1985, oil on canvas, 125 × 152 cm.

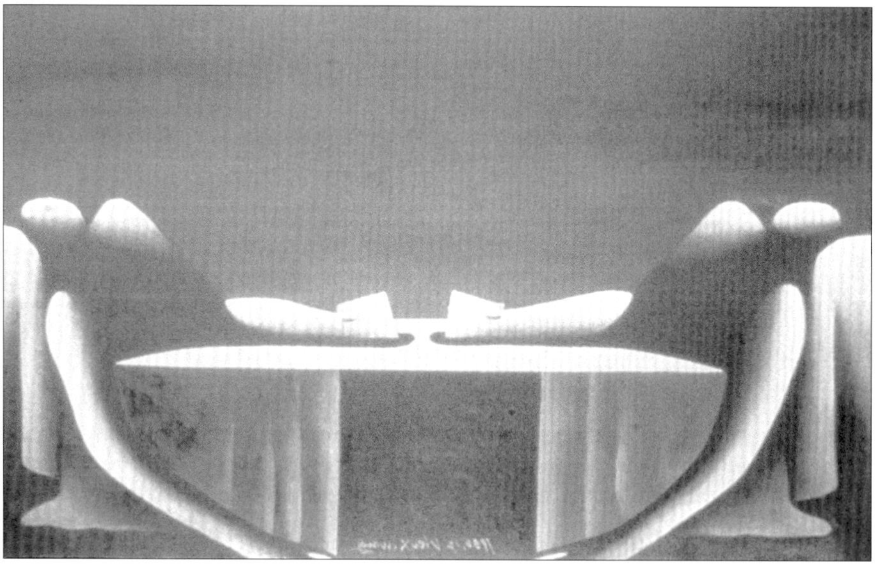

Figure 73 Wang Guangyi, *Post-Classical Series: Death of Marat,* 1987, oil on canvas, 150 × 200 cm. Private collection.

and that art is created only to achieve stardom in media society and the market.[5] He called art just a strategy (*youxi*), and Andy Warhol's Pop Art became his mode.

Wang created a series of portraits of Mao Zedong, and in February 1989, just two months before the student demonstrations began in Tiananmen Square and four months before the Tiananmen incident, he created a sensation by exhibiting *Mao Zedong No. 1* (Figure 74) in the *China / Avant-Garde* exhibition that took place in the National Gallery in Beijing. In *Mao Zedong No. 1*, a grid is superimposed on an official portrait of Mao: The revolutionary leader and the utopia he stood for are imprisoned within the measurable confines of an analytic frame.

This work might have been created with a critical purpose, rather than with an overt commercial goal, for, generally speaking, the avant-gardists of the '85 Movement had not yet become involved in the commercial art market. Since the early 1990s, however, official culture and popular culture have blended in the commercial society encouraged by Deng Xiaoping's economic reforms. This has posed a challenge for the avant-garde artists. Given the weakness of intellectual culture and the effect of the commercial tidal wave, the notion of an avant-garde enlightenment became meaningless. In the face of an inverted social structure, some of the artists shifted from a serious attitude to a trivializing one. Since the old ideological industry had begun producing a kind of "political kitsch," the popular culture started grinding out "commercial kitsch."

"Double kitsch" combines the two mass cultures: socialism and capitalism. To react to this circumstance, Wang Guangyi produced a series of oil paintings entitled *Great Castigation*, in which he juxtaposed political images and commercial signs (Figure 75). They presented heroic figures from the Cultural Revolution alongside company logos such as those of Coca-Cola and Kodak. The paintings were meant to show that although the two systems, the political and the commercial, are not united—are even in conflict—the principal goal of each is to convince the population at large of the authenticity and singularity of its products in modern Chinese society. Thus, swamping the population with Mao's propagandist images, on the one hand, and consumer advertising and entertainment symbols produced by the mass media, on the other, levels the similarity between Mao's mass culture and Hollywood. The utopian avant-gardists reacted against both political and commercial power and started a new project of deconstruction, directly

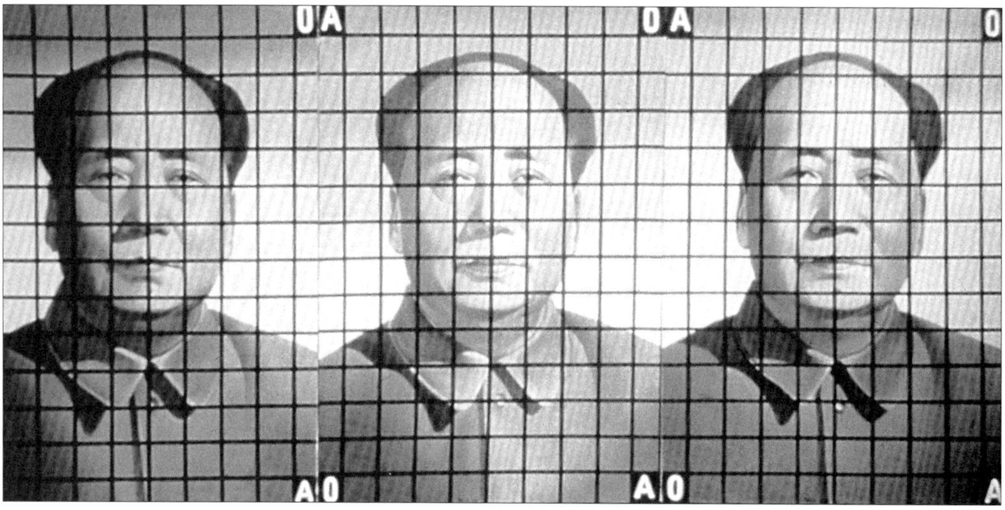

Figure 74 Wang Guangyi, *Mao Zedong No. 1*, 1988, oil on canvas. Three panels: each 150 × 120 cm. Private collection.

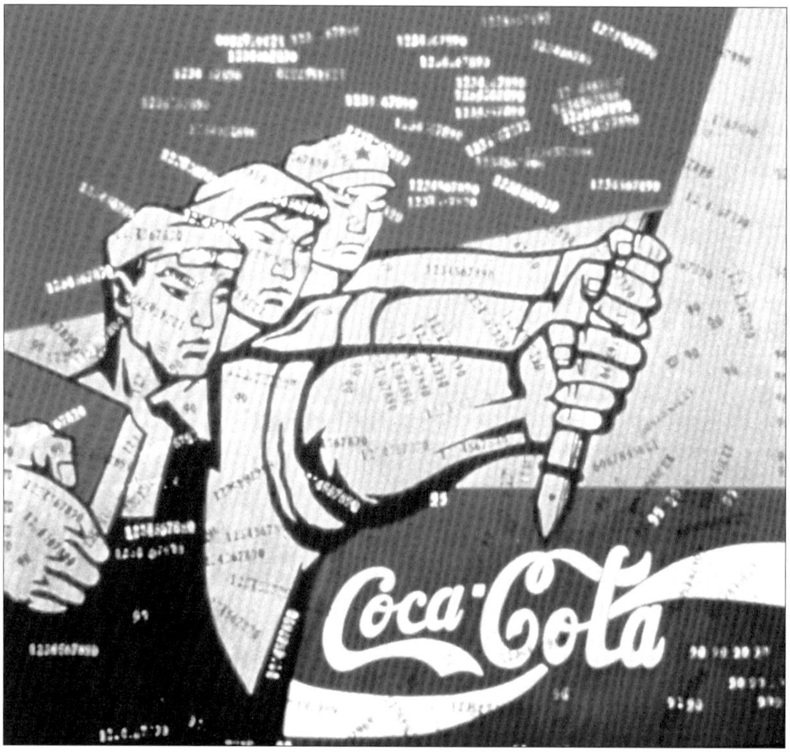

Figure 75 Wang Guangyi, *Great Castigation Series: Coca-Cola*, 1993, oil on canvas, 200 × 200 cm. Collection of the artist.

imitating the discourse of double kitsch. The result, Political Pop, served as a mirror for both sides of double kitsch.

Ironically, Political Pop attracted tremendous attention from overseas art markets and museums and quickly became an international commercial success. In addition to resembling the coexisting discourses of state political propaganda and consumer consumption, double kitsch easily fitted into a transnational art market system in which it was promoted as a new political statement and commodity. A new double kitsch avant-garde evolved from both the internal logic of China's avant-garde and the commercial and ideological fascination of outside observers from abroad. Wang Guangyi's paintings became a kitsch advertisement of an advertisement, and he became a producer of commodities instead of the preacher he was before. Aesthetically speaking, Wang's painting juxtaposes two mass cultural discourses. Sociologically speaking, Wang's practice resembles the new social structure, in which he plays with the market-driven art world and is simultaneously framed by it.

The ideological intention of Political Pop is very similar to that of Sots Art, the Soviet art movement that emerged in Moscow in the early 1970s. This movement, which uses quotation and deliberate eclecticism and delights in the spectacle of antagonistic semiotic and artistic systems destroying each other, emerged two decades earlier than Chinese Political Pop. There had been, however, no connection between the two when the Chinese Political Pop began to emerge in the early 1990s. Rather, Sots Art was unpredictably duplicated by Chinese Political Pop, proving that similar conditions engender similar possibilities.

However, Political Pop has attracted much more international institutional and marketing attention than Sots Art, not only because the emergence of Sots Art occurred in a moment of global political change, the decline of the Communist world and the beginning of the post–Cold War period, but also because China has become one of the major transnational markets, and Political Pop artists have experienced the charm of capitalism much more personally and profoundly than the Sots Art artists. This is why the two otherwise similar unofficial art movements met with a dissimilar fate. The Sots Art artists in many cases emigrated to the United States in the late 1970s and met with commercial success. Very few of the Political Pop artists, however, have left China so far. On the contrary, they quickly became a part of the upper middle class in an economically reconfigured Chinese society. Sots Art, as Boris Groys writes,[6] is not a commercial, impersonal art that responds to and simultaneously strives to manipulate spontaneous consumer demand. In this it is obviously different from Political Pop. It may be proper to say that the nationalism and materialism of Political Pop may share common roots with the government's policy by taking a position of complicity. Thus, its postmodernist artistic production has benefited from the reconfiguration of the postsocialist society of China. On the other hand, its artistic practice has enforced the postsocialist society, as well.

Political / Commercial Mass Language in Recontextualization: Wu Shanzhuan's Red Humor

Another Conceptual artist of the 1980s, Wu Shanzhuan, born in 1960 and trained in Zhejiang Academy of Fine Art, began his postmodernist practice in 1986, at the time of the emergence of the '85 Movement. His *Red Humor* series, which he began in that period, might be seen as an early version of Political Pop, which began later on, in the early 1990s.

Wu Shanzhuan tended to investigate the meaning of authorship by using language. He believed Chinese characters in themselves are a form of visual art and call for no further creative efforts on the part of the artist. Not only are the characters perfect in form, but, more important, they are filled completely with historical and cultural meaning, so they become independent of subjective meaning. Artists can select the meaning of language, but have no ability to give it meaning. With this philosophy in mind, he created signs rather than meaning by juxtaposing randomly selected phrases and characters in quirky or startling ways, giving his work an ironic quality. Wu Shanzhuan made no lofty conceptual claims for his installations and performances or for any of his other art. Yet, as one talks to Wu, reads his writing, and experiences his work, his humorous and seemingly unsystematic comments begin to make sense. Wu's use of simple aphoristic statements and obvious images may be seen as part of an ironic strategy that pushes the viewer to a nonlinear, slightly fragmented, almost intuitive chain of responses that continues well after leaving the gallery. He asks the viewer to experience a series of interlinking meanings, rather than to read any one of them directly. Serious forms from the Cultural Revolution, big-character posters with the red, black, and white colors of traditional China, were diluted by the humorous phrases he used. Wu's Chan Buddhist–like quick wit plunges the viewer into an oddly compelling reality.

There is a pronounced Pop Art flavor that has always been strongly present in Wu's art, beginning with his *Red Humor* installations in Zhejiang in 1986 and 1987. He often uses ready-made objects in his work or simulates the appearance of objects from daily life. Both his 1986 exhibition *70% Red, 25% Black, and 5% White,* a collaborative project installed in an old temple, and his 1987 exhibition *Red Characters: Big-Character Posters* play with text, specifically with fragments of popular language. These are juxtaposed in startling ways in neatly printed phrases and slogans from advertisements, newspapers, classical poetry, Chinese religion, politics, and the discourse of daily life. One painting takes the form of a sign: "Cabbage, three cents a catty." Another says, "Garbage, garbage, garbage," written to resemble a pile on top of which perches the word "Nirvana."

The ratio of colors specified in the title of the *70% Red, 25% Black, and 5% White* exhibition immediately evokes the tensions of Chinese political confrontations, particularly those of the Cultural Revolution, with, in general terms, red representing good Communists, black representing enemies of the people, and white representing the undecided. *Red Characters: Big-Character Posters,* which was installed in the artist's studio, again resembled a chaotic scene from the Cultural Revolution. Wu used the format of wall posters from the Cultural Revolution but drew messages from the surrounding environment to convey the multiple dimensions of contemporary political, social, and economic information. The messages included political slogans such as the Maoist period's "Exercise for strength in the class struggle" as well as price notices, advertisements, newspaper titles, commonly used phrases, classical poems, Buddhist texts, traffic signs, weather forecasts, announcements such as "Mr. Wang, I am back," lines from ancient poetry, and the title of Leonardo da Vinci's *The Last Supper.* On the floor he wrote four Chinese characters "*Wurenshuodo,*" or "nobody can interpret them" (Figure 76).

In his works, Wu represented various discourses in conjunction with their opposing sides: serious and ironic, grand and trivial, religious and secular, revolutionary and capitalist—all devoid of the artist's own voice. In his theoretical writings of the time, Wu expressed a greater interest in the sounds and outward forms of Chinese characters than in their function as language. Yet, because of the rich eclecticism of the popular language he adopted, the viewer of his works naturally associates the images with many aspects of his or her own experience. Each phrase means something different, depending on its social, cultural, or political context. Most installations from his *Red Humor* series create a political atmosphere without stipulating any concrete

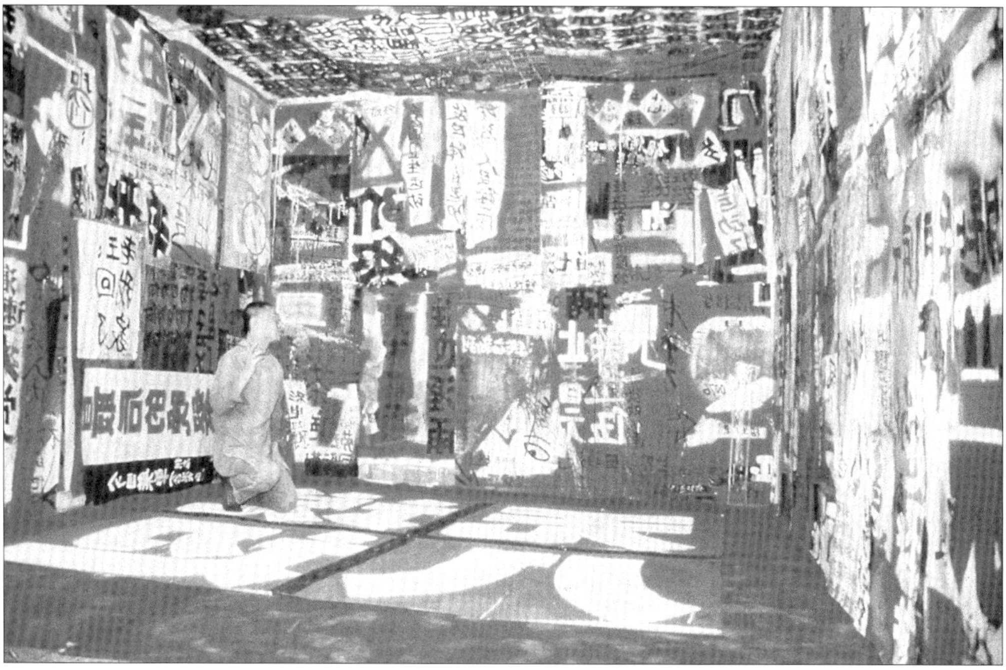

Figure 76 Wu Shanzhuan, *Red Characters: Big-Character Posters*, 1987, mixed media. Collection of the artist.

political content. The result is a mockery of society, of politics, and perhaps even of artists themselves. Going one step further, one could say that Wu's games with the visual language of Chinese politics reduce the deadly phenomenon of the Chinese Communist movement to nothing more than "red humor." On the other hand, Wu himself was also fascinated by the multiple interpretative possibilities of the characters, phrases, and texts created by his random selection, which eliminated the incorporation of his own meaning into his work.

Wu, as the first artist to juxtapose the patterns of Chinese political culture with the forms of Western Pop Art, was a formative figure in the Chinese Political Pop movement. The Conceptual qualities of his art are even stronger, however. Questions about the nature of art have been a constant theme in his work. He describes the relationship of the artist and his or her work in terms of the relationship between the soil and the plant. The earth is necessary to the growth of the plant, but the soil does not determine the species of the plant. Evolution has already made that selection. Similarly, according to Wu, the artist cannot determine the result of his or her work. For

Wu, the artist's intentions or working methods are far less important than the work itself. "In the end," Wu wrote in 1985, "the artwork uses a concrete person (the artist) as a means. The concrete person will die, but the work may continue to exist."[7]

In some of Wu's work, the artist becomes an object, as though he stands outside himself. For instance, in many of his performance/installation works, Wu masqueraded as a new member of the Communist Party taking an oath against a wall on which there were some fake political slogans written with many nonsensical characters, as a chairman of a political meeting giving a speech, or as a "criminal" criticized and punished by the Red Guards (see Plate 16). Wu thus expressed the claim that an artist should not function as the dominant factor in art production. He or she is nothing more than an object, like any art object, a material. Wu's use of the concept of material and object greatly undermined the idealism and subjectivity initiated by the previous utopia-oriented artists. His *Red Humor,* filled with various discourses, is virtually a distracted scene and a hodgepodge made uniform through the use of the color red.

At the 1988 conference on Chinese avant-garde in Tunxi, in Anhui Province, Wu Shanzhuan pointed out that because of the commercialization of the Chinese art world of the late 1980s, artistic activity had become big business. He repeated this view in his "Tourist Information: Alphabetical Aphorisms," an unpublished note on art cowritten in 1992–93 by Wu and his girlfriend, Inga Svala, from Iceland, where he had moved in 1990. There, Wu wrote: "Audience: Wu is surrounded by the audience at his working place. Wu deals with and serves the audience. By this act, the audience is transformed into specified customers" and "Borrow: Wu borrowed the behavior of a shrimp seller for one day, while Wu's performance was on at the National Gallery of P.R. China."[8]

Selling Shrimp, Wu's installation/performance in the *China / Avant-Garde* exhibition in 1989, was his first work to replace political imagery completely with the imagery of daily commerce. Wu personally brought 30 kilograms of fresh shrimp to the exhibition opening from a fishing village in Zhoushan, in Zhejiang Province, where he worked as an art teacher for mass-culture education. He wrote the price of the shrimp on a blackboard and began selling it (Figure 77). After the authorities closed the exhibition down, he marked his shrimp stand "Closed." Wu explained his performance by saying that the National Gallery is not only a place to display artwork, but can also serve as a black market (*heishi*).

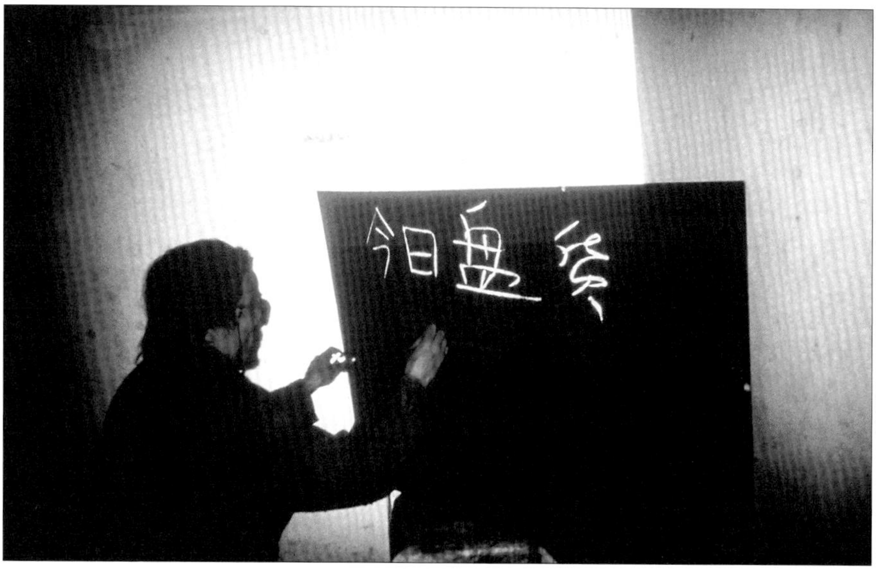

Figure 77 Wu Shanzhuan, *Selling Shrimp, China / Avant-Garde Exhibition,* February 5, 1989 (photo: A-Zhen).

Xu Bing's Art: A Metaphor of Meaninglessness

Well established as a woodcut painter in the early 1980s, another important Conceptual artist of the period, Xu Bing, shifted his attention to installations in 1985. His first major piece of this kind, the *Book from the Sky* (Figure 78), was created from numerous hand scrolls about five hundred feet long with printed texts in what resembled monumental styles. There were also sets of books bound in blue paper covers that perfectly resembled traditional Chinese books. The work was first exhibited in 1988 at the Chinese National Art Gallery in Beijing and subsequently was shown at a number of venues in Asia and the West. What was extraordinary was the fact that the thousands of Chinese characters printed on the books and papers were created by Xu himself. This piece was the product of three years of intensive labor. Xu hand-carved over two thousand pieces of wooden type to print what looked like Chinese characters in the Song dynasty style. Although none of Xu's characters could be recognized and pronounced, since they were invented by the artist and were composed of rearranged elements from real Chinese characters in the Song dynasty style, they were still charming enough to prompt the audience to attempt to read or decipher them. When Xu created the two thousand nonsense characters, he of course knew that

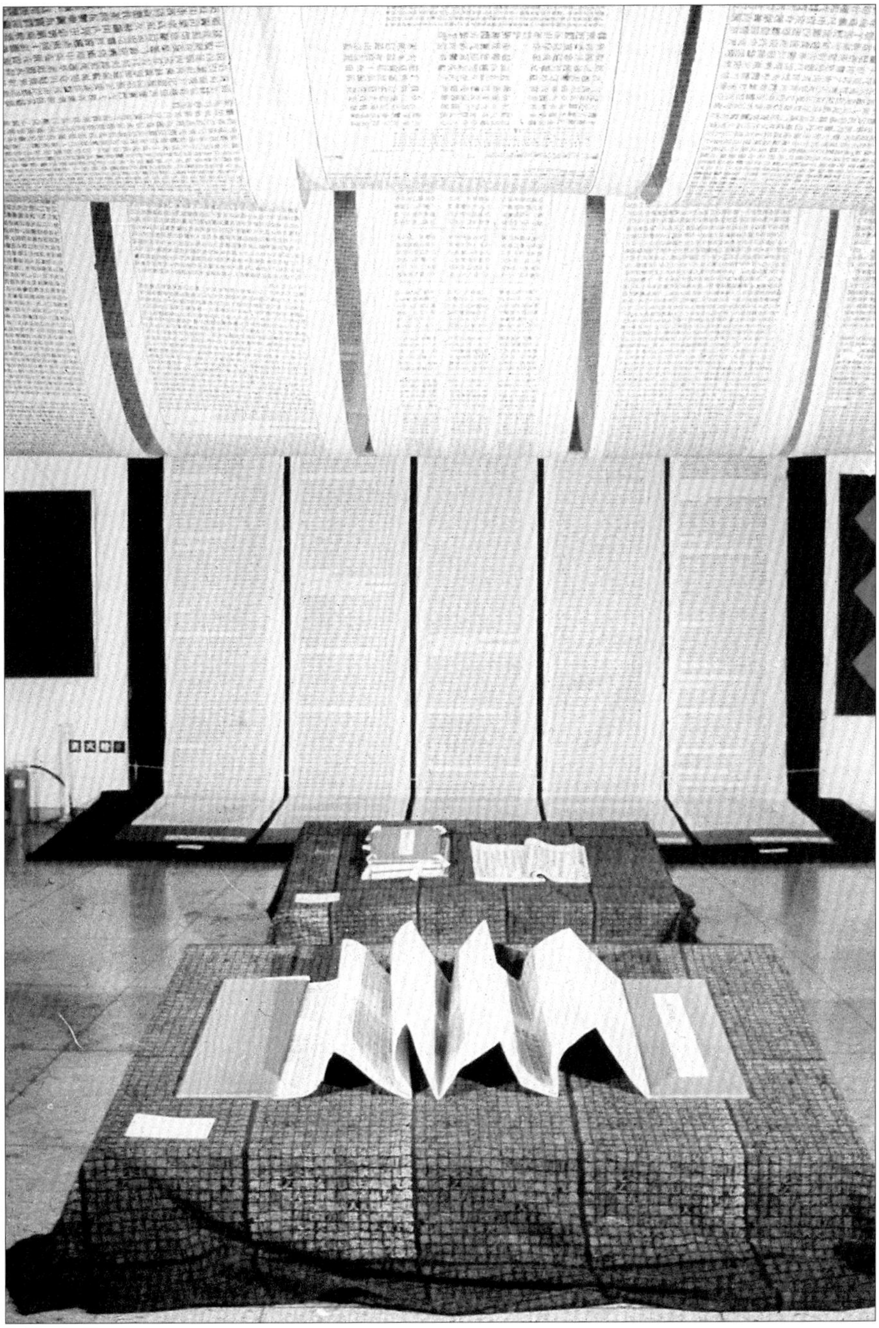

Figure 78 Xu Bing, *Book from the Sky,* 1988. Installation with hanging scrolls and books printed and bound in traditional form; a view of the piece displayed in the *China / Avant-Garde Exhibition,* 1989.

there are another two thousand characters that do make sense. It is this paradox that makes the piece an unpredictable interaction between its superficial textured meaninglessness and the diverse cultural understandings of the readers.

Xu Bing's works might be seen as yet another kind of destruction of traditional culture. The aim of Xu Bing's "destruction," however, was not to erase writing and texts themselves, but to create, in a deconstructive manner, a nonsense text with a monumental, lawful, legitimate, and classical form. On the other hand, by his complete avoidance of legibility in the texts, Xu removed all semantic significance from them. The viewer thus became free to invest the piece with his or her own meaning and to create a new mental space in the space of the installation.

The space created in this particular work of Xu Bing was related to a traditional Chinese philosophical concept, the idea of "emptiness," which is a crucial notion in Chan Buddhism. In Chan thinking, a realization of the concept of "emptiness" is the moment in a person's experience when the mind is open to discover a richer realm of truth—enlightenment. The approach of emptiness comes from the theory of the Sudden School of Chan Buddhism founded by the sixth patriarch, Hui Neng (638–713). The approach of Hui Neng's Buddhist philosophy was completely different from another (coexisting) Chan Buddhist tradition described as Gradual Enlightenment and founded by a Chan master, Shen Hui. Gradual Enlightenment involved a four-part "purification of the mind" that proceeded from concentrating the mind through meditation, physical exercise, and ritual forms over a long period of time. The approach of Hui Neng's Sudden Enlightenment, however, emphasized that when the mind is completely emptied and void, when "all paths of language are destroyed" and "all ways to the mind are cut off," there occurs a spontaneous psychic insight into the absolute nature of the phenomenal world. This new approach completely destroyed the need for all scripture, ritual, and formal meditation techniques and thus won a popular following. The theory of Sudden Enlightenment thus influenced many generations of traditional artists and philosophers alike and has now become a potent weapon for Chinese Conceptual artists such as Xu Bing, Wu Shanzhuan, and Huang Yongping. Almost all of them have proclaimed their allegiance to Chan Buddhism.

Xu Bing's second major installation was *Ghosts Pounding the Wall,* a three-story-high ink rubbing taken from a section of the Great Wall (Figure 79). As displayed in the Elvehiem Museum at the University of Wis-

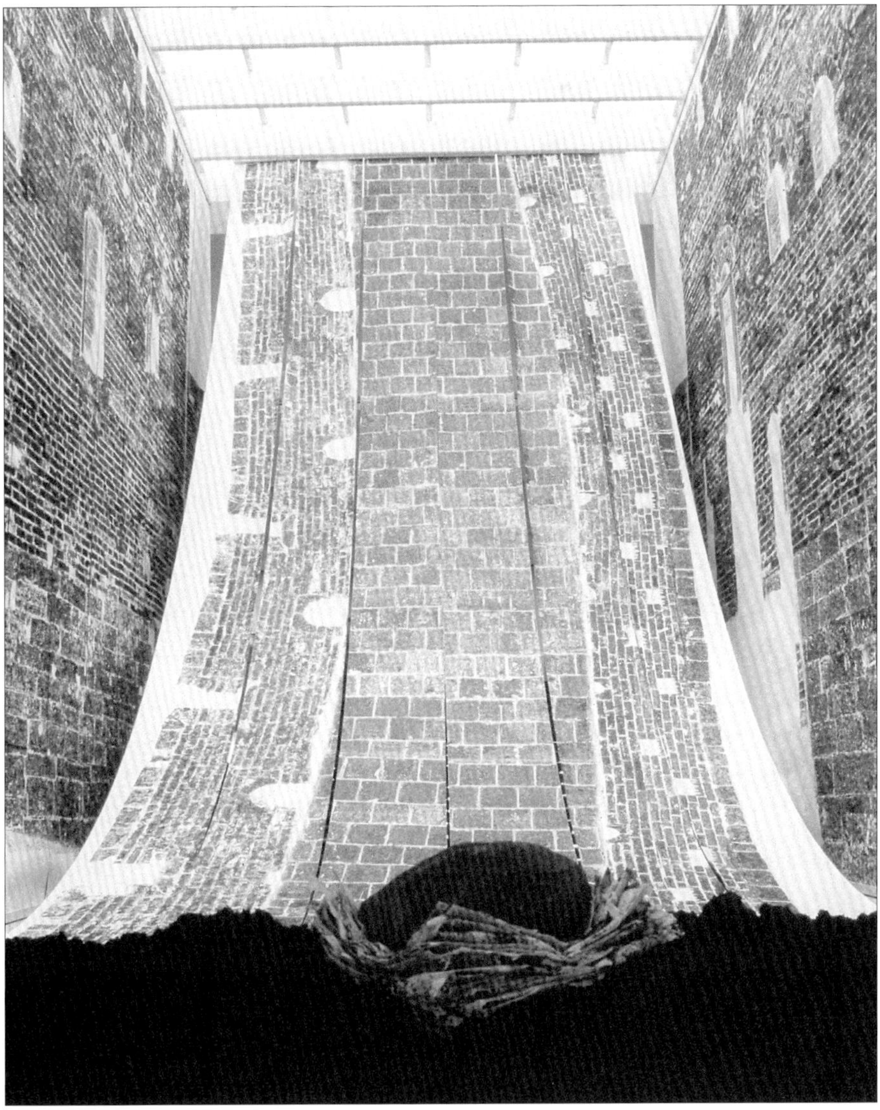

Figure 79 Xu Bing, *Ghosts Pounding the Wall,* 1991, installation.

consin in late 1991, the work involved massive black-and-white scrolls hung from the ceiling to the floor across the building's central court. At the lower end, a mound of dirt that looked like a tomb pinned the scrolls to the floor. Xu Bing and his crew labored in the Badaling mountains in the Beijing rural area for twenty-four days in 1990 to make impressions of the surface of the Great Wall (Figure 80), using a technique traditionally employed for reproducing fine carvings of calligraphy. Over the course of several months,

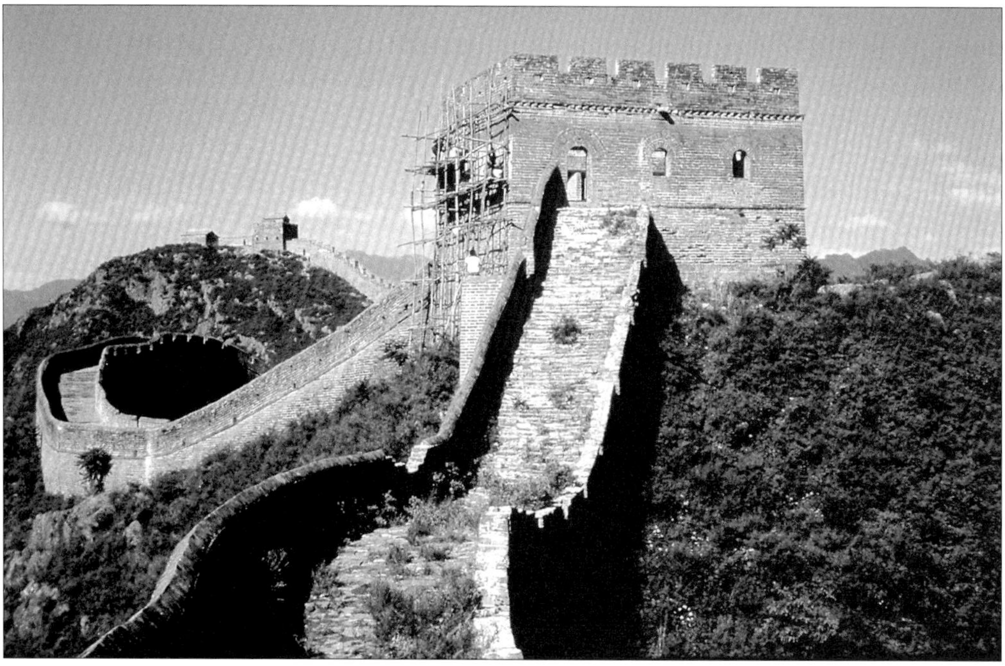

Figure 80 Xu Bing and a group of people are rubbing the Great Wall, 1990.

the ink-smudged sheets of Chinese paper were reassembled and mounted. An extreme effort on the part of Xu was necessary to create an imposing psychological and physical space similar to the space of the Great Wall itself. Yet the piled earth of the tomb at the foot of Xu's paper Great Wall was an obvious symbol of death. The confrontation between the splendid but ghostly paper representation of the Great Wall and the nihilistic physical presence of the earthen burial mound raised doubts about the purpose of human effort, questioning not only the artist's replication of the rough and inelegant surface of the Great Wall, but more generally all human effort, including the construction of the original Great Wall.

The powerful image of the Great Wall, the largest construction in the world and the product of two thousand years of labor, has become a symbol of the greatness of China in the twentieth century. It was a symbol of national salvation and defense against the invasion of the Japanese during the war with Japan. After the founding of the People's Republic of China in 1949, the image of the Great Wall, along with certain industrial landscapes, symbolized a reunified, newborn modern state. Shi Lu's 1959 painting *Changcheng wai* (Beyond the Great Wall), for instance, depicts the happiness of the Mongolian minority people who live within unified modern China and the enjoyment of the modernization symbolized by a railroad that had reached the other side of the Great Wall. The area on the other side of, or "outside," the Great Wall was traditionally a battleground between Han people and the northern nomads. But now the two sides, the Han and the barbarian, are unified.

After the Cultural Revolution, the avant-garde artists of the 1980s appropriated the image of the Great Wall, employing this symbol of nationalism ambivalently in the project of Chinese modernity. The Wall became an ambiguous symbol because, although China was becoming a nation that was developing the strength of a modern state, it was doing so under the control of a conservative state-ideological power. The Wall therefore ceased to be simply an eternal symbol of greatness, and with the success of Western modernization under the control of the totalizing power of the state, it started to represent weakness and doubt.

This skepticism can be found in many performance works and Conceptual artworks dealing with the Great Wall. For instance, in a performance by a group of artists called The Concept of the Twenty-First Century, the artists masqueraded as people wounded and helpless against the powerful Great Wall (Figure 81). Xu Bing's installation sent a very similar message.[9] In his simulation of the Great Wall, Xu Bing embodied the meaninglessness of its construction through his own exhausting activity, pounding the Wall with ink-drenched wads of cloth. Even the title conveys the meaninglessness of human effort, relating as it does to a popular Chinese folk tale in which a traveler, lost in the middle of the night, keeps walking in circles, as if ghosts had built a wall around him to prevent his continuing in his chosen direction.

In spite of its purported meaninglessness, however, Xu's work echoes with meanings related to Chinese politics and reality. The artist appears to mock himself and the futility of his own exertions. Even with extraordinary effort, he is unable to do anything about his own circumstances and environment, just as his ancestors were confined by the barrier of the real wall or the traveler in the folk tale is surrounded by an imaginary one. On the other hand, Xu's work may also be seen as being committed to a strong criticism of the conservatism of authority in contemporary Chinese society. Xu Bing notes that the seventeenth-century historian Gu Yanwu also remarked on the ineffectiveness of the Great Wall in closing China off from the rest of the world.

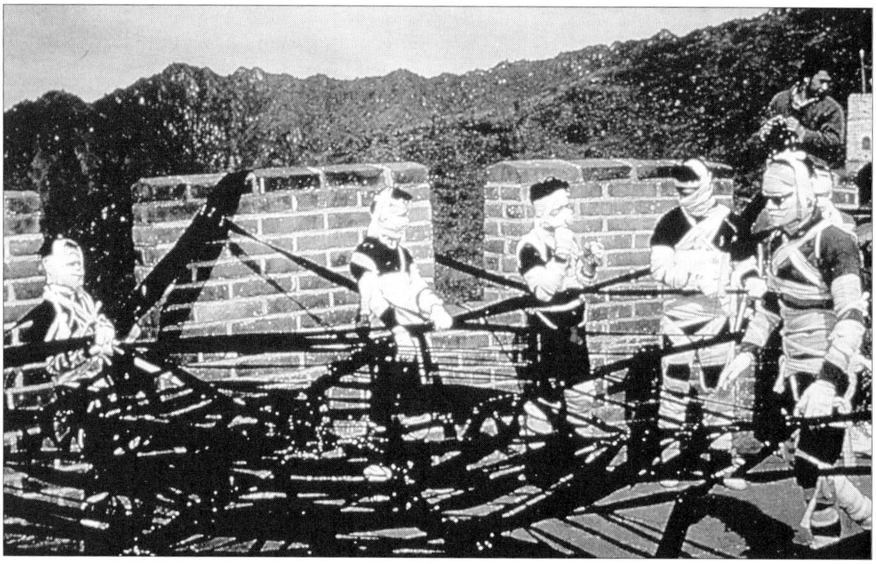

Figure 81 The group The Concept of the Twenty-First Century, *Great Earthquake,* 1988. Performance on the Great Wall.

The meaninglessness of the Great Wall here evokes cultural confrontations of various kinds: between the real creative power of China's ancient people and its simulation by the contemporary artist and between China's heritage of national greatness and its current reality. Xu Bing chooses the written language and traditional monumental image as his medium and the most traditional form of disseminating the language, the hand-printed book, and the Great Wall as the object of his representation. Indeed, his labor-intensive techniques are the most traditional of those to be found in the 1991 exhibition in Wisconsin. His meaningless hand-printed books and rubbings of the Great Wall, however, may be seen not only as questioning the relationships between traditional and contemporary culture, or between East and West, but also as allegories of contemporary representations of reality. Xu Bing's simulated books and the Great Wall challenge our access to reality in a similar way. Indeed, Xu's representations of books that are not really books obscure our apprehension of reality even more obviously than most representations. The meaninglessness of Xu Bing's text, to borrow Brian Wallis's phrase,[10] exposed the "gauze of representation" that inevitably mediates our access to reality. His fake characters reveal the deceptiveness of all representation.

The *China/Avant-Garde* Exhibition: A Great Social Happening

As we have seen while examining the careers of these artists, the *China / Avant-Garde* exhibition was a milestone in the history of the '85 Movement. The exhibition took place in the National Gallery in Beijing from February 5 to February 19, 1989, two months before the beginning of the Tiananmen Square Student Democratic Movement and four months before its suppression by the government on June 4, 1989. The preparations for the exhibition involved many official institutions and governmental departments and raised numerous issues concerning politics, art, and the economy. Therefore, the exhibition was not a pure art show. It reflected the social circumstances of the historical moment as a whole. Various social forces drove it and carried it out amid many dramatic events. Finally, it turned into an artwork itself—a major social happening in contemporary Chinese art history.

The Aborted First Avant-Garde Exhibition

The flourishing of the '85 Movement brought fresh air into the contemporary Chinese art world. Some open-minded middle-aged academic painters organized an official meeting called the National Oil Painting Conference, which took place in Beijing in April 1986. The major academic painters in the nation participated in this conference. More significantly, the organizers also invited some leading artists from various avant-garde groups, including Shu Qun, Zhang Peili, Li Shan, and others, to join the meeting and discuss issues related to art with the academic painters. In the conference, I was invited to give a lecture entitled "The '85 Art Movement" (*Bawu meishu yundong*), in which I offered a general overview of the avant-garde groups and discussed their artistic ideas, activities, and artworks while showing about two hundred slides, which offered an especially convenient and effective means for a thorough overview of the '85 Movement. During the meeting, Shu Qun, Zhang Peili, Li Zhengtian, an artist and critic from Guangzhou, in Guangdong Province, and I discussed the possibility of holding a nationwide slide show in Guangdong. After the conference, Shu Qun and Wang Guangyi, two leading artists of the North Art Group, and I managed to convince the Zhuhai Academy of Painting, which had been just then founded in the Zhuhai Special Economic Zone in Guangdong Province, and the publisher of the journal *Zhongguo Meishubao* (Fine Arts in China) in Beijing to cosponsor the slide show.

In August of 1986, the first large-scale pseudo-official conference of the '85 Art Movement, entitled "Zhuhai Large-Scale Slides Exhibition of the '85 Movement" (*Zhuhai bawu meishu sichao daxing huandengzhan*), was held in Zhuhai, in Guangdong Province. Representatives from avant-garde groups and critics from all over China attended the event. The organizational committee of the exhibition that I led received about twelve hundred slides sent by groups from all over the country. The committee selected and displayed 342 works from 31 groups. The most important outcome of the meeting, however, was a decision to organize a large-scale exhibition of Chinese avant-garde art. Accordingly, I began trying to convince an influential official institution to become a sponsor for such an event.

In China in the 1980s, no exhibition, whether group show or solo exhibit, could be held without an official organization or institution serving as a sponsor. No official institution, however, would agree to take the risk as a sponsor for such an exhibition. Even *Zhongguo Meishubao,* which originally promised sponsorship, finally decided not to get involved due to political pressure. After the failure to find an official sponsor, some young art critics and I were aware that we needed to found our own organization. After some preparational work, in November, the Chinese Modern Art Research Society (*Zhongguo xiandaiyishu yanjiuhui*), a self-organized association of about thirty critics from all over China, was founded in Beijing, in part as a planning committee for the avant-garde exhibition. With the help of the Beijing Young Painters' Society, I found an exhibition space and on January 7, 1987, signed a contract with the National Agriculture Gallery (*Quanguo nongye zhanlanguan*). The opening of the exhibition was planned for July 15 of the same year. The reasons for choosing the National Agriculture Gallery as the place for an avant-garde exhibition were that the Ministry of Culture could not control the agriculture gallery and that an open-minded vice director of the agriculture gallery who had graduated from the Central Graphic Art Academy in Beijing in the 1960s supported the exhibition.

On March 25 and 26, 1987, the first exhibition planning meeting was held in Beijing, and about twenty artists from major avant-garde groups gathered. Just like an underground activity, the meeting site was moved from place to place, the planners even meeting once in the winter in a cluttered courtyard used primarily for storage. These problems were the result of the Anti-Bourgeois Liberalism Campaign, a hard-line political movement being conducted at the time. Student demonstrations were staged in a number of Chinese cities in late 1986. The authorities responded with a campaign against "bourgeois liberalism," targeting all unorthodox political and cultural thought. The campaign continued through mid-1988, significantly hampering the activities of the avant-garde artists. In spite of facing political pressure, the organizers decided the exhibition would nonetheless be opened in the middle of July 1987 in the National Agriculture Gallery under the title *The Nationwide Exhibition of Scholarly Communication of Young Artists* (*Gedi qingnian meishujia xueshu jiaoliuzhan*). The title avoided using some radical terms like "avant-garde," "modern," and so on, which would insult the official political sensibility.

On April 4, 1987, the Propaganda Department of the Central Committee of the Communist Party issued an official document prohibiting professional associations from holding scholarly activities of a national scope. In response, the Chinese Artists' Association, an official organization under the direct influence of the Communist Party, ordered me to cease preparations for the avant-garde exhibition in the National Agriculture Gallery and to dissolve the Chinese Modern Art Research Society. The result was that the first attempt to hold the exhibition was aborted, although most of the preparatory work had already been completed.

Preparations for the *China / Avant-Garde* Exhibition

Although some group shows such as the "Stars" exhibition in 1979 had appeared after the Cultural Revolution, *China / Avant-Garde* was the first nationwide unofficial exhibition in China since 1949. The most controversial point was that it was a show of Western modern and postmodern styles. These art styles and schools have always been considered heretical by the government. Therefore, the exhibition faced the censorship of both the Propaganda Department of the Communist Party and the museums of the Ministry of Culture. The Communist Party organization in the art world is the Chinese Artists' Association, which is directed by the Propaganda Department of the Central Chinese Communist Party. The museums, such as the Imperial Palace Museum and the National Gallery, are directed by the Ministry of Culture. Generally, though, an organization of the Communist Party has more authority than other government departments. Therefore, sometimes an organization of the Communist Party proper will cancel an exhibition although a museum may have already accepted it. Therefore, the only possibility of an avant-garde exhibition being accepted by both the Party and the government is dependent on the occurrence of an opportune moment when the government relaxes its control on art policy, comparatively speaking.

NEGOTIATIONS WITH THE NATIONAL ART GALLERY

In early 1988, the political situation eased, and I recommenced preparations for the avant-garde exhibition. I decided to use the National Gallery as the location for the avant-garde exhibition because of its important role and position. The National Gallery is the only national contemporary art gallery directed by the Ministry of Culture. It was built in 1958, the year before the ten-year celebration of the founding of the People's Republic of China. It is one of the so-called Beijing Ten Great Constructions (*shida jianzhu*) finished at the same time. Each "great construction" is a specific symbol. For example, the Great Hall of the People (*Renmin dahuitang*) is the representative symbol of the people of the whole country. Every important national convention, such as Representative Conventions of the Communist Party and National People's Congresses, have always been held in the Great Hall of the People. Similarly, the Museum of Chinese History (*Zhongguo lishi bowuguan*) is the symbol of Chinese history and has collected important historical materials and displayed ancient and modern revolutionary Chinese history. For the same reason, the National Gallery is a symbol of the highest authority on the national level in the Chinese art world. Therefore, all the important official art exhibitions, such as the National Art Exhibition, which is held by the Chinese Artists' Association and Ministry of Culture every five years, and certain commemorative exhibitions, such as the Exhibition of the Twentieth, Thirtieth, and Fortieth Celebration of the Foundation of the People's Republic of China, have been displayed in the National Gallery. Once an individual artist has a show in the National Gallery it means that his or her art position has already been accepted by the highest national official art authority.

It was precisely for this reason that it was vital for avant-garde art to use and modify the sacred symbolic image of the National Gallery. The Chinese avant-garde could take advantage of putting a heretical show into the sacred art palace it had never been able to touch. For the first time, an unorthodox critical activity would be entering the National Gallery, exemplifying the suppressed, skeptical identity of the avant-garde. This would bear two consequences. It would challenge the authorities in a very aggressive manner and would be a boost to the development of the avant-garde movement because of the anticipated public attention. In order to gain the advantage of having the National Gallery, however, the avant-gardists first had to define a legal identity for themselves, because the National Gallery does not accept shows without sponsorship by an official institution.

Because no such institution wanted to take the risk, the organizers attempted to find sponsors outside the field of art proper. Such a proposal immediately met with support from three major official institutions, led by some of the most influential liberal intellectuals in China—the Publishing Community of Culture: China and the World (*Wenhua: Zhongguo yu shijie*), led by Gan Yang, the Sanlian Publishing House (*Sanlian shudian*), directed by Shen Changwen, and the Chinese Society for Aesthetic Studies (*Zhonghua quanguo meixue xuehui*), chaired by Ru Xin. With a proposal signed by the heads of these three famous institutions in hand, I submitted an application letter, supplementing it with a slide presentation shown to the directors of the National Gallery in April 1988. Soon after, I was informed that the gallery had declined the proposal due to the artistic orientation of the exhibition and its possible political consequences.

In the summer of 1988, the Anti-Bourgeois Liberalism Campaign seemed almost over. Therefore, the organizational work of the exhibition gained support from four additional official institutions, *Meishu* (Fine Arts), *Zhongguo Meishubao, Beijing gongyi meishu zonggongsi* (the Beijing Graphic Art Company), and *Zhongguo Shirongbao* (The Environment in China), which offered to serve as co-organizing sponsors, and from some influential artists of the older generation such as Wu Zhuoren (1908–1995), Liu Kaiqu (1904–1997), Jin Shangyi (1934–), and Zhanjianjun (1931–). Carrying a proposal signed this time by the heads of seven influential official institutions, I applied to the National Gallery again in September 1988. With no solid reason to refuse, the National Gallery accepted the proposal—on the condition that the organizers of the exhibition also procure permission from the Chinese Artists' Association, the most legitimate official institution in the Chinese art world. Therefore, I submitted the same proposal to the Department of the Secretary of the Chinese Artists' Association and gave a presentation to three high-ranking officials. After a three-hour meeting, the Department of the Secretary granted permission for the exhibition on the condition that I agree to accept the demand put forth by the officials that three types of art would not be allowed in the exhibition: those opposing the Communist Party and the Four Fundamental Principles (*Sixiang jiben yuanze*), pornographic images (interpreted as any display of sexuality), and performance or action pieces.

While for the organizers, a performance was just a different kind of art form, it is not difficult to understand why the authorities prohibited performance and action art. Performance art was a totally new art form, representing a complete break with the conventional idea of art. Moreover, in the Chinese avant-garde art movement, performance art was extremely provocative. It allowed for complete individual freedom and often vented long-suppressed intuitive feelings. Finally, since the performances commonly took place unpredictably in a public area as happenings, it was too easy, in the opinion of the authorities, for one of them to transform itself into a political event such as a demonstration.

In order to get the *China / Avant-Garde* exhibition into the National Gallery, I compromised and accepted all three conditions, but insisted on having performance art presented in the form of documentaries. Because of the permission by the Chinese Artists' Association, the National Gallery was forced to accept the exhibition plan, but deliberately chose an unpopular date for the exhibition, the period of Chinese New Year. The opening day would be New Year's Eve, when people are attending family gatherings rather than taking part in a public activity or event. Nonetheless, the organizers had no choice but to accept such terms.

On October 8, 1988, the organizational committee of the *China / Avant-Garde* Exhibition was founded in Beijing. The committee consisted of fourteen members who were active scholars and art critics in the Chinese contemporary cultural world. I was elected the head of the committee and the chief curator. On the same day, the committee released a public announcement that was later published in *Zhongguo Meishubao.* It stated:

> (1) It has been decided that a China Art Show will be held from February 7–20 1989 at the National Gallery in Beijing. (2) The "China / Avant-Garde" exhibition will for the first time exhibit artworks with a modern artistic concept and spirit to artists in China and the world, as well as to the general public. The show will also reflect the artistic trends and experimental explorations in the past few years that are being debated and evaluated by art circles and the value and significance of modern art in the development of Chinese culture. As a high-powered exchange and research event in the field of modern

art, the show will boost the development of artistic pluralism in the Chinese art world.[11]

THE DIFFICULTIES OF RAISING MONEY

It seemed to the organizational committee that the budget problem was even more difficult than the problem of political censorship. The *China / Avant-Garde* exhibition was an unprecedented event in contemporary Chinese art history. It was distinct from the normal exhibitions held in the National Gallery in terms of both its political sensibility and its financing.

It was impossible for the *China / Avant-Garde* exhibition to obtain financial support from the government, and the six sponsors who were struggling with their own survival could provide only moral support. Thus, raising money turned out to be a tough challenge and an unprecedented experience. After the exhibit site was obtained, the organizational committee wrote an open letter to the public seeking support. I now shifted my efforts to raising money, traveling to Shanghai and Nanjing in the south of China, Harbin in the northeast, Wuhan in central China, and Tianjin, my hometown, in the north. At first, one of the largest national corporations, the Panda Electronic Industry Corporation in Nanjing, agreed to donate 200,000 Yuan ($40,000), with the stipulation that the avant-garde exhibition provide the corporation with advertising space in the exhibition venue, in newspapers, and on television and donate to them a number of the exhibited works. Unfortunately, two months after the beginning of the negotiations (and two months before the exhibition was to open), as the president of the company was about to sign the contract, the company changed its mind and withdrew its consent without offering any explanation.

At that time, the committee had received only 2,500 Yuan, which was less than 2 percent of the entire budget of at least 150,000 Yuan ($30,000). The fund-raising of the organizational committee had been unsuccessful, for its requests were refused by almost everyone. The political pressure and lack of financial backing for the exhibition were mainly due to the political sentiments concerning avant-garde art. It also has to be said, though, that because traditional and academic art had always been the dominant art style in China, it was no wonder that, in the public eyes, avant-garde art was a rather incomprehensible art form. Therefore, both its political risks and the miniscule commercial benefits discouraged financial supporters.

Due to these difficulties, the organizational committee was forced to seek other means. They described their situation to friends in the cultural world and to avant-garde artists, asking for their assistance. Then Zhang Kangkang, one of the most famous novelists in China, who was sent to Heilongjiang Province as a student to be reeducated during the Cultural Revolution, published an article expressing her sympathies with the committee and appealed to its readers, especially to Feng Jicai, a popular novelist based in Tianjin, to support the avant-garde exhibition. At that time, Feng Jicai was chairman of the Tianjin Writers' and Artists' Association and strongly supported modern experimental art. He immediately responded and obtained partial funding for the exhibition (20,000 Yuan) from various factories and from the magazine *Free Discussion on Literature* (*Wenxue ziyoutan*) in Tianjin. This money suddenly meant survival for the avant-garde exhibition, although the total amount was still far from adequate. Some artists convinced their friends who ran various businesses or private companies to donate, as well. The upshot was that six factories and companies contributed in total 40,000 Yuan (about $10,000).

Avant-garde artists offered to work as laborers for the contributors, while others donated their works or works from their collections of traditional paintings to them. Moreover, as their contribution to the exhibition, all participating artists voluntarily gave 100 Yuan each, approximately the equivalent of their monthly salary. In all, 186 artists thus contributed 18,600 Yuan (about $2,200).

The most moving story that emerged from the fund-raising efforts was that of a private businessman named Song Wei, who ran The Great Wall Fast Food Company (*Beijing Changcheng quaizan*) and contributed 50,000 Yuan, offering this money without a request for any kind of compensation. He was also ambitious enough to build the first private art museum in China, The Great Wall Art Museum (*Changcheng yishu bowuguan*). After the avant-garde exhibition closed, he collected about fifty major works, thus becoming the first major private collector of Chinese avant-garde art before it received broad attention on the international art market in the early 1990s. Before *China / Avant-Garde* opened, only a few foreigners had bought Chinese avant-garde works. The Tokyo Modern Art Gallery bought six pieces during the *China / Avant-Garde* exhibition and thus initiated the foreign collection of Chinese avant-garde works.

By the time the exhibition opened in February 1989, the organizational committee had collected 118,600 Yuan (about $23,000). Although it was less than sufficient, the exhibition could nonetheless be opened.

Twice Shot Down and a "Small Tiananmen Square"

These political and economic difficulties were not the only obstacles that had to be overcome. Under the censorship law, the committee was required to obtain official approval from the authorities for all of the nearly 300 pieces to be exhibited, which had been executed by 186 artists from provinces all over the country. The exhibition was to be open fourteen days. On February 4, 1989, the day before the opening, the officials of the Propaganda Ministry of the Central Chinese Communist Party, the Ministry of Culture, the Chinese Artists' Association, and the National Gallery came to the gallery to give official approval of the avant-garde exhibition for a public opening. In order to get adequate support, the committee also invited some influential older artists and art historians from the Central Academy of Art to join in the approval meeting. A number of works were criticized for purportedly containing political and sexual meanings. After an intense dispute between the censorship group and the members of the committee and academic experts, these controversial works, with the exception of three pieces, were retained in the exhibition. Among the works criticized by the committee and finally retained, the most controversial was Wang Guangyi's *Mao Zedong No. 1* (see Figure 74), which was accused of putting Mao into a jail.

The *China / Avant-Garde* exhibition finally opened on February 5, 1989, in the National Gallery in Beijing. The works were placed in six gallery halls that occupied three floors. There were 297 pieces in various media, ranging from painting and sculpture to photography, video, and installation art. This day was a mammoth festival for every avant-garde artist in China. They laid out five enormous black banners marked with the title of the exhibition and its logo, "No U-Turn," on the square in front of the National Gallery (Figure 82). The opening ceremony was shrouded in a nervous and solemn atmosphere, as if something was bound to happen. After I said a few introductory words, cheering this important and historic event—the birth of the first avant-garde exhibition in contemporary Chinese art history (Figure 83)—the public entered the gallery. What they were immediately met with were not only the provocative installations and paintings but, more surprisingly, several performances—true happenings.

Wu Shanzhuan began the performance called *Selling Shrimp* in the hall on the first floor. "For the Chinese New Year," he declared, "I have brought first-class, export quality shrimp from my home village to celebrate the holiday and enrich both people's spiritual and material life in our capital. The

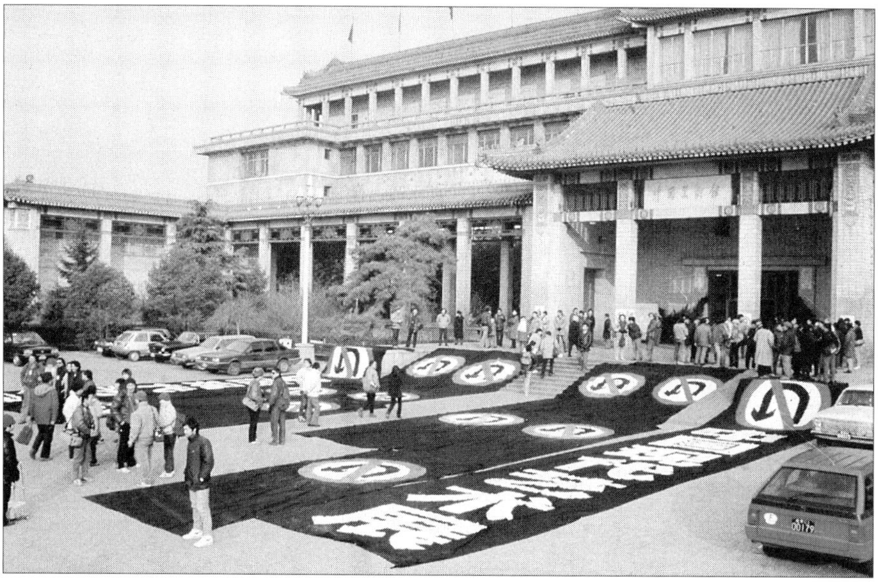

Figure 82 View of the opening of the *China / Avant-Garde Exhibition*, National Gallery, Beijing, February 5, 1989.

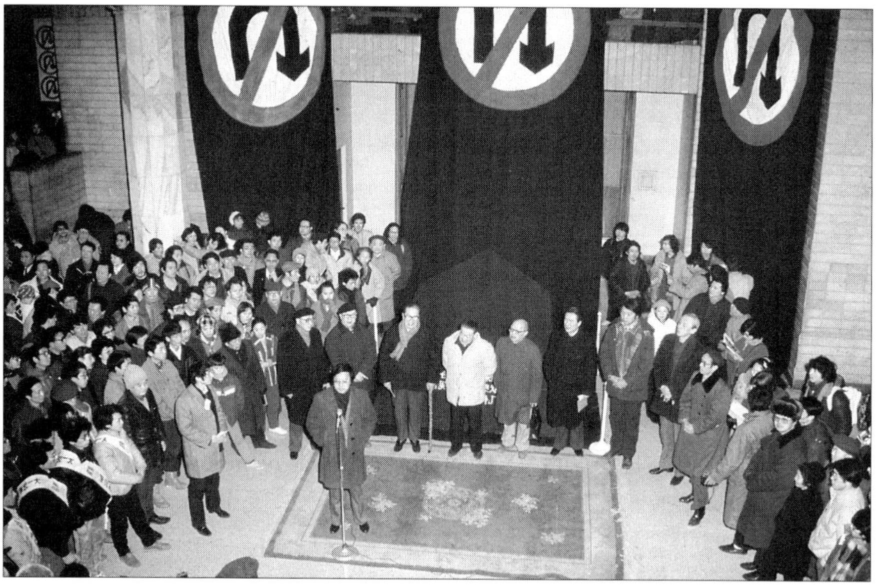

Figure 83 The opening of the *China / Avant-Garde Exhibition*. Gao Minglu is giving a speech to the public.

going price: 9.5 Yuan. Display place: the National Gallery. Great buy."[12] The first buyer was Liu Kaiqu, the honorary director of the National Gallery and one of the most influential sculptors in China. Another performance artist named Zhang Nian, who was not included in the show, sat in a corner of the gallery on the second floor hatching eggs. In his manifesto, which hung across his chest, he wrote: "During the incubation period, I will not discuss theoretical questions with anyone, to avoid harming the younger generation."

The artist Li Shan, one of the most important painters of the Rationalist Painting group, seated himself at his installation and began washing his feet in a basin decorated with numerous portraits of the U.S. president, Ronald Reagan. In the former days, this cynical behavior undoubtedly would have been regarded as blasphemy of the sacred art palace of the National Gallery. An hour after the opening, Wang Deren threw more than seven thousand condoms across all three floors of the gallery. In his statement, he proclaimed that the intent of his performance was to exert hegemony over, to "hegemonize," the works in the exhibition with his personal material marks, namely, condoms.

Then, three hours after the opening of the exhibition, Xiao Lu and Tang Song, two young artists from the Zhejiang Academy of Art, made a performance that literally shocked the National Gallery. Xiao Lu, Tang Song's girlfriend, suddenly pulled out a gun and fired two shots at their installation, *Dialogue,* which consisted of a mirror between two telephone booths in which were placed pictures of a male and a female student talking to each other on the phone. The president of the Beijing Public Security Bureau, who was on the spot, seized Tang Song and ordered me to close the exhibition immediately. The reason given was that they must preserve the scene of the gunshot intact and trace the cause of the incident. Several police cars with armed personnel immediately arrived in the square of the National Gallery. In China, only the police and the army are allowed to own firearms. Therefore, the Beijing Public Security Bureau stated that Xiao Lu and Tang Song had violated the law and should be detained. Later, in the afternoon, encouraged by his uncle, Xiao Lu surrendered to the authorities.

After being detained for two and a half days, both were released, for there was no evidence proving that the two artists had plotted murder or any other crime—except owning a gun, of course. However, because of the shooting and other events, the exhibition was forced to close for three days. The Chinese authorities still thought that this event held political meaning, and most of the foreign news media indeed had reported on it as a political

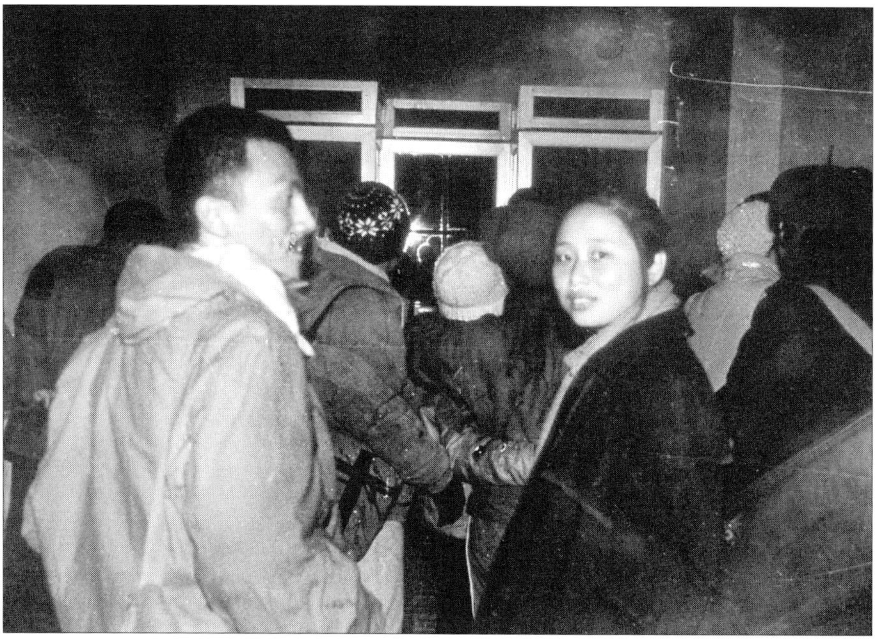

Figure 84 Xiao Lu and Tang Song visiting their installation site after being released by the police.

event. According to the two artists, their shooting was nothing more than an expression of happiness at having finished their installation, no matter how the public interpreted the event (Figure 84).

Because the avant-garde exhibition was the first large-scale completely Westernized exhibition after the opening to the West, the Chinese government probably wanted to use it as a sign of its cultural policy of openness. On the other hand, this situation allowed the avant-garde artists to use this occasion to achieve their own plans and goals. Ann Scott Tyson, a staff writer for the *Christian Science Monitor,* who was at the opening of *China / Avant-Garde,* wrote: "The outrageous stunt revealed how China's avant-garde artists are brashly taking advantage of the opportunity provided by eased state censorship in a bid to spark greater public attention for their highly unorthodox art."[13]

Such performance works, which turned into happenings, reflected and expressed the artists' views on society and art. They provoked a great deal of controversy, especially since they were prepared in complete secrecy. None of the performances had been announced to the gallery or even to the organizational committee before the opening of the exhibition. Consequently, the National Gallery and the authorities accused the organizational committee, rather than the artists, of having run counter to the stipulation that the Chinese Artists' Association had imposed on the exhibition. Hence, the National Gallery decided that the organizational committee of the exhibition should be fined 2,000 Yuan and that the six sponsoring institutions would not be allowed to hold any shows in the National Gallery in the next two years.

After the exhibition had been closed for three days, it opened again, on February 9, 1989. However, the Public Security Bureau forced the committee to hire twenty security guards to enforce the prohibition on performance art. The committee had to accept this and pay salaries to the Public Security Bureau in order to keep the exhibition open.

The remainder of the exhibition was not as peaceful as the National Gallery and the Public Security Bureau had expected. On February 12 the National Gallery, the Beijing Public Security Bureau, and the Beijing city government each received an anonymous letter with the same content, made up of clipped and pasted newspaper characters. It said "You must close the *China / Avant-Garde* exhibition immediately; otherwise, we will set off bombs in three places in the National Gallery." The Beijing Public Security Bureau and the National Gallery nervously discussed the way to deal with this threat. They informed me of the situation, showing me the letters, and demanded that I immediately decide whether the exhibition should remain open or should close. The Public Security Bureau also pointed out that if I decided to keep the exhibition open, I would be held responsible for any explosion that might occur. I declined to take responsibility for the bombs and also refused to close the show. My response instead was, first, the exhibition should remain open, and second, the committee of the exhibition and I would not accept responsibility for an explosion. Third, the Beijing Public Security Bureau, not the committee, was responsible for averting the explosion.

That night, however, the Beijing Public Security Bureau and the National Gallery received an order from the president of the Propaganda Department of the Central Chinese Communist Party and the head of the Ministry of Culture. The order was that the exhibition must close for two days, during which the Beijing Public Security Bureau would search for bombs in the gallery. Armed police units, the latest technical equipment, and search dogs were used to search for bombs in all the corners of the National Gallery for the two days. It was predictable, however, that there were no bombs to be found in the gallery. Was it all a joke? It was, of course, possible that the letter was a real threat, but it was also possible that the letter was part of yet another performance, yet another major social happening like the one provoked by the two gunshots. It was not known who was behind the bomb threat until 1995, when the Zhejiang Public Security Bureau detained an artist named Liu Anping from the Zhejiang Academy of Fine Art and charged him with being the author of the anonymous letters and the performance.

After the exhibition opened again on February 15, the atmosphere became much more tense and sensitive than before. Viewers were required to deposit their bags before they entered the gallery. There were additional guards watching for bombers. The art exhibition seemed to have become a dangerous battlefield in which an unpredictable incident might occur at any time.

Epilogue

The *China / Avant-Garde* exhibition closed on February 19, 1989. Two months after the exhibition, the Beijing student demonstrations broke out. Since the crackdown of the democratic movement by the government on June 4, 1989, the *China / Avant-Garde* exhibition has been repeatedly attacked and cited as one of the most visible manifestations of the evils of bourgeois liberalism. Moreover, the exhibition was referred to in print by some hard-liners as a small Tiananmen Square of the art world, partly because the first gunfire took place in the exhibition.

The *China / Avant-Garde* exhibition, as a historical event, also symbolized the end of the idealism of the '85 Movement, or, to put it differently, it was a mourning of the modernist-type avant-garde movement. It also initiated a shift in the art world of China from the political concerns of the 1980s to the economic concerns of the 1990s, a shift that evidences the process of globalized modernization. The idealist, utopian avant-garde that blossomed in the '85 Movement and that was dedicated to contesting local political and cultural oppression has given way to a pragmatic neo-avant-garde that strives to transcend the local in favor of acceptance in the international arena. This shift is largely a product of post–Cold War external pressures of global materialism.

Thus one might argue that Chinese society is experiencing a historical development similar to that of Western societies a century ago in which two modernist sensibilities operate side by side, one materialist and the other critical and aesthetic, an avant-gardist sensibility challenging materialism as part of a broader social critique. One might, furthermore, argue that when global economic forces drive Third World countries such as China to become deeply involved in a transnational system, any modernist-type utopianism will be undermined and some sort of postmodern cultural reproduction will spread to these Third World countries. It is this situation that may condition what is called "postmodernism" in a global scene.

Notes

1. In the West, according to Jürgen Habermas, the term "modern" in its Latin form *modernus* was first used in the late fifth century to distinguish the present, which had become officially Christian, from the past, which was Roman and pagan. Through various historical circumstances, the term "modern" has described again and again the consciousness of an epoch that distinguishes itself from the past and views itself as a transition from the old to the new. See Jürgen Habermas, "Modernity—an Incomplete Project," in *The Anti-Aesthetic: Essays on Postmodern Culture*, edited by Hal Foster (Seattle: Bay Press, 1983), pp. 3–4. "Modern," for the Chinese in the beginning of their modern history, was used mainly to denote their own reaction to the influence of modern Western powers and culture, rather than to differentiate the present from their own past. Therefore, Chinese modernity is a defensive modernity with a clear nationalistic boundary in mind. It is not a notion of time, but rather a consciousness of space.

2. Quoted in Matei Calinescu, *Five Faces of Modernity* (Durham, N.C.: Duke University Press, 1987), p. 103. Calinescu attributes this saying to a disciple of Saint-Simon's.

3. Wang Guangyi, "Women zhege shidai xuyao shenmo yangde huihua" (What kind of paintings do we need in our age?), *Jiangsu huakan* (Jiangsu painting monthly) (Nanjing), no. 4 (1986): 6.

4. Ibid.

5. Yan Shanchun, "Wang Guangyi hewu tan shehua he youxi" (Wang Guangyi and I talk about myth and strategy), *Xinmeishu* (New art magazine), no. 2 (1988): 25–31. Another version is in *Dangdai Meshuchaoliu zhong de Wang Guangyi* (Wang Guangyi in the trend of contemporary art), edited by Yan Shanchun and Liu Peng (Chengdu: Sichuan Art Press, 1992).

6. See Boris Groys, *The Total Art of Stalinism: Avant-Garde, Aesthetic Dictatorship, and Beyond*, trans. Charles Rougle (Princeton: Princeton University Press, 1992), p. 12.

7. Wu Shanzhuan, "Wuti de meishu pin" (The material work of art), an unpublished essay, 1986.

8. Wu Shanzhuan, "Tourist Information: Alphabetical Aphorisms," a selection of writings distributed by the artist and his Red Humor International, 1992–93.

9. Scholarly research, though, suggests that the wall actually was built over a much shorter period of time and that even in its own day it was strategically useless as a border defense.

10. Brian Wallis, "What's Wrong with This Picture? An Introduction," *Art after Modernism: Rethinking Representation*, edited with an introduction by Brian Wallis (New York: The New Museum of Contemporary Art, 1984), p. xv.

11. See "Zhongguo xiandai yishuzhan chouzhan tonggao, diyihao" (Announcement of the organization of *China / Avant-Garde*), *Zhongguo Meishubao* (Fine art in China), no. 171 (1988): 1.

12. Wu Shanzhuan, "Guanyu Dashengyi" (About big business), a statement published in *Beijing Qingnian Bao* (Beijing youth newspaper), February 8, 1989, p. 2.

13. Ann Scott Tyson, "Avant-garde Bursts onto Chinese Art Scene," *Christian Science Monitor*, February 7, 1989, p. 6.

Contributors

Aleš Erjavec is research director at the Institute of Philosophy of the Scientific Research Center of the Slovenian Academy of Sciences and Arts and professor of aesthetics at the University of Ljubljana. His books include *On Aesthetics, Art, and Ideology* (Ljubljana, 1983), *Aesthetics and Epistemology* (Ljubljana, 1984), *Art and Ideology of Modernism* (Ljubljana, 1988; Sarajevo, 1991), *Ljubljana, Ljubljana: The Eighties in Slovene Art and Culture* (also in English, with Marina Gržinić; Ljubljana, 1991), *Aesthetics and Critical Theory* (Ljubljana, 1995), and *Towards the Image* (Ljubljana, 1996; Jilin, 2003).

Boris Groys was born in East Berlin, studied philosophy and mathematics in St. Petersburg, and worked as a research fellow at various research institutes in Moscow. In 1981, he emigrated to the Federal Republic of Germany. He is currently professor of aesthetics and media theory at the Center for Art and Media Technology in Karlsruhe. His books include *Gesamtkunstwerk Stalin* (Munich, 1988; published in English as *The Total Art of Stalinism*, Princeton, 1992), *Die Kunst des Fliehens* (with Ilya Kabakov; Munich, 1991), *Über das Neue* (Munich, 1992), *Logik der Sammlung* (Munich, 1997), *Unter Verdacht: Eine Phänomenologie der Medien* (Munich, 2000).

Miško Šuvaković is professor of aesthetics and art history in the Faculty of Music of the University of Arts, Belgrade. His books include *Pas Tout: Fragments on Art, Culture, Politics, Poetics, and Art Theory* (Buffalo, 1994), *A Prolegomenon for Analytical Aesthetics* (Novi Sad, 1995), *The Post-Modern* (Belgrade, 1995), *Asymmetrical Other* (Belgrade, 1996), *Neša Paripović: Self-Portraits* (Belgrade, 1996), *Aesthetics of Abstract Painting* (Belgrade, 1998), and *Vocabulary of Modern and Postmodern Visual Art and Theory after 1950* (Belgrade and Novi Sad, 1999). He is the coeditor (with Dubravka Djurić) of *Impossible Histories: Avant-Garde, Neo-Avant-Garde, and Post-Avant-Garde in Yugoslavia, 1918–1991* (Cambridge, Mass., 2003).

Péter György is associate professor in the Department of Aesthetics and Communication, ELTE University, Budapest. He is the author of *The European School* (with Gábor Pataki, Budapest, 1989), *The Sunken Island* (Budapest, 1992), *Art and Society in the Age of Stalin* (also in English and German, Budapest, 1992), *The City of Copies* (Budapest, 1993), *Letter to the*

Master (Budapest, 1994), *The Body and the Eye* (Budapest, 1995), *Digital Eden* (Budapest, 1998), and *The Mute Tradition* (Budapest, 2000).

Gerardo Mosquera is an art critic, historian, and writer based in Havana and a curator at the New Museum of Contemporary Art in New York. He is the author of several books and has contributed to art journals around the world, including *Casa de las Americas, Art Journal, Third Text, Poliester, Kunstforum,* and *Art Nexus.* He has edited *Beyond the Fantastic: Contemporary Art Criticism from Latin America* (Cambridge, Mass. and London, 1996) and is co-editing (with Jean Fisher) *Over Here: International Perspectives on Art and Culture,* (Cambridge, Mass., in association with the New Museum, New York, forthcoming).

Gao Minglu curated the exhibitions *China/Avant-Garde* (Beijing, 1989) and *Inside Out: New Chinese Art* (New York, 1998). He coauthored *The History of Contemporary Chinese Art* (Shanghai, 1991) and *Century's Utopia: The Trends of Chinese Avant-Garde Art* (Taipei, 2001) and has edited *Inside Out: New Chinese Art* (Berkeley, 1998). He is currently an assistant professor in the Department of Art History at the State University of New York, Buffalo.

Index

Designer: Sandy Drooker
Compositor: Integrated Composition Systems
Text: Aldus
Display: Akzidenz Grotesk
Printer and Binder: Friesens Corporation